The American
Immigration Collection

The Old Americans

A Physiological Profile

ALES HRDLICKA

Arno Press and The New York Times

NEW YORK 1970

Reprint Edition 1970 by Arno Press Inc.

Reprinted from a copy in
The Columbia University Library

LC# 75-129402

ISBN 0-405-00555-5

The American Immigration Collection—Series II
ISBN for complete set 0-405-00543-1

Manufactured in the United States of America

THE
OLD AMERICANS

THE CHILDREN OF DR. AND MRS. AUSTIN H. CLARK. OLD AMERICAN ANCESTRY,
BOTH SIDES
(Washington, D. C.)
Austin B. J., age 5; Sarah W., age 3

THE
OLD AMERICANS

BY
ALEŠ HRDLIČKA

BALTIMORE
THE WILLIAMS & WILKINS COMPANY

DEDICATED WITH HIGH RESPECT AND
IN CORDIAL FRIENDSHIP
TO
WILLIAM H. HOLMES

CONTENTS

CHAPTER I

CHAPTER II

CHAPTER III

CHAPTER IV

CHAPTER V

CHAPTER VI

CHAPTER VII

ILLUSTRATIONS

CHAPTER I

INTRODUCTION

I

From early in the seventeenth century, the temperate zone of the North American continent has been receiving successive contingents of the white race, which settled on the available land, multiplied and spread, and receiving ever-growing accessions gradually formed the American nation. These newcomers, while in the main recruited from the people of the British Isles, included also larger or smaller contingents of other Europeans, such as the Spanish, French, Dutch and Swedes, to whom, before the end of the eighteenth century, were added some Germans and individuals of other nationalities. The British colonists were mainly English and later "Scotch-Irish," with the Scotch, Irish and Welsh in smaller proportions. And the aggregate comprised various physical types, from the predominantly light-haired, tall, oblong-headed northerners to the round-headed, brown-eyed and darker-haired Alpines or Gauls, and the still darker elements of the Mediterranean type of white people; for these various types existed not only in geographically different parts of Europe, but due to older wide-spread infiltrations and mixtures they were all found in differing proportions, even as they exist at this day, in all the European countries, including Great Britain, from which emigration to America proceeded.

The earlier comers to this country as well as their successors up to the time when immigration assumed large proportions, may be safely assumed to have been individuals on the whole rather above than below the average in sturdiness and energy, for in those times the coming over meant considerable cost as well as hardship and the weaklings either staid behind or were rapidly eliminated under the strenuous conditions. These facts, supplemented by broad natural and political freedom, abundance of animal food and the healthfulness of most of the new country, with the thousand necessities and incentives resulting from the new environment, could not but act stimulatingly on the pioneer population, which is seen to respond by enterprise, large families and general mental as well as physical robusticity. A thorough accommodation to the new conditions was rapid, and the first generation born here were already thorough Americans, which term, however undefined, meant already something different from the Old World

1

populations to which the pioneers owed their derivation. Then followed gradually contacts of the various nationalistic groups, a great levelling of social distinctions, a growing community of interests and habits, a predominance of one language, to be followed by intermarriages between the various groups of colonists; and the original nationalistic heterogeneity insensibly began to give place to a blend which by the time the Revolutionary period is reached, is found to constitute already a strong new body: the American nation.

How virile and successful in general, this new blend has proven to be, is a matter of history. That in language, behavior and institutions its unification has progressed far, is equally well known; it has in fact progressed so far that since the war of the Revolution the Americans constitute, so far as behavior is concerned, a universally acknowledged, separate and fairly distinctly characterized unit of the white race which is no longer English, Dutch, French or Irish, but American.

In view of all this and the seeming facility with which a "typical" American may be recognized in other lands, a supposition has long existed that there have also been realized already in this new nation changes of physical nature which have produced or tend to produce a separate sub-type of the white people. And the subject has raised other questions. It is known that changed environment and consequent changed habits of life react more or less strongly upon the body and that the latter tends to accomodate itself efficiently, harmoniously and permanently to all enduring influences that affect the individual. Has the American strain been subject long enough to the new influences to establish such an accomodation? And if so, has this accomodation been sufficiently substantial to result in perceptible modifications of the physical type of the people? If such physical changes have taken place or are taking place, are they uniformly in the direction of improvement—or is there also some degeneration? And may not the type have already reached or even passed its zenith, as would seem to be indicated by the lowering birth rate among its latest representatives, a rate now insufficient in many urban communities to keep up the numbers of the Old Americans? And how will the type, if it exists, be affected by the growing mixture with whites of recent immigration? Would it be well to try to keep it pure—have the Old Americans marry only among the Old Americans—or is new blood desirable?

It is well known that such nationalities as the French, English, German and others possess, notwithstanding their mixed and relatively recent origin, distinctive physiognomy and other physical features by which in a large majority of cases it is possible to recognize many of both the men and women

ALL OLD AMERICANS. MRS. WILLIAM T. WILSON AND CHILDREN
Helen, age 9; John, age 6; Margaret, age 4

FOUR GENERATIONS OF OLD AMERICANS
Mrs. E. B. Decker (standing), 27 years; Mother, 50 years; Grandmother, 74 years;
Daughter, 4 years. Original derivation English, Scotch, German.
(Washington, D. C.)

who belong to them; and reasoning from this, analogous development should also apply to the older Americans. Writers and illustrators have made many efforts to define this hypothetical American type, and have even arrived at certain fairly crystallized conceptions, such as "Uncle Sam," the "American girl," and the "American youth," the "American soldier or officer," the "American pioneer," etc. The Southerner in particular, and the Yankee, as well as the westerner, are believed to have distinctive characteristics of their own by which the majority of them can be readily identified; yet at the same time these "types" are supposed to differ from each other so that any one of wider experience can readily tell a Yankee from a Southerner, a westerner from an easterner, etc. The writers who make efforts to define the American physical type, however, do so generally without going into morphological particulars; and the artist either follows certain individual types or creates more or less abstract conceptions or propositions of what he personally conceives as real Americans. Suggestions have even been advanced that the American type is approaching that of the American Indian; the idea being presumably that since American environment produced the Indian—which in reality it has not done or not fully—it would in due time shape other peoples here to similar mold.

As time went on it became more and more desirable to learn the truth in the matter, which could only be done by careful comparative studies on ample series of adults who most properly represented what is generally understood under the term "American." Observations of somatological nature on various contingents of the American people were not wanting. There were many such on the recruits and soldiers of the Civil War, on the children of Boston, Worcester, Oakland, St. Louis etc., on college students, and on the great numbers of applicants to the Insurance Companies (for references and details see writer's "Physical Anthropology," 8°, Wistar Inst., Phila., 919). But these were in a large part unrelated studies, made for other purposes and embracing all the elements of the population, so as to be, for the purpose here defined, of but little direct use; yet they gave valuable indications. To these in 1911 were added the interesting if inconclusive results of the Boas studies on "Changes in Bodily Form of Descendants of Immigrants" (Columbia University Press, 1912), which seemed to show that under the American environment the physical type of Jewish and Italian children changed with remarkable rapidity and with a tendency towards more intermediate forms. Were this true, the formation of a new, more homogenous American type ought to be a question of but a few generations, and the type should be already well advanced toward maturity among the descendants of the oldest American families.

These conditions and uncertainties, together with another important need which will be referred to later, induced the writer to undertake a comprehensive study of the "Old Americans," of which the present work is the result.

II

The studies the results of which are dealt with in this volume were undertaken in 1910 and carried on until 1924. The motives that led to them were, on one hand the desire to learn just what physically, and in some measure also physiologically, the Old American stock represents, what developmental changes, if any, have already been realised in it, and towards what it is tending; and on the other hand a strong need of reliable standards that could be used for comparison in anthropological work in this country.

The essence of anthropological work is comparison. It is its comparative nature which distinguishes anthropology from traditional anatomy, physiology, or pathology. It is the science of human groups rather than of individuals and it can properly describe any given racial or environmental group only by contrasting it with well-known, trustworthy standards. Satisfactory standards of this nature are rare as yet in any countries, and so far as adults are concerned they are practically non-existent in the United States. A considerable amount of scientific work has already been done, as mentioned before, on the American child and adolescent, but almost none outside of the Army and Insurance tests on the American adult.

The want of proper American standards was most forcibly brought home to the writer in connection with his earlier work on the abnormal classes. These researches were carried on under the auspices of the New York State Pathological Institute and eventually with the coöperation of nearly thirty physicians in the various institutions for the insane, feeble-minded, etc., of the State of New York, during the years 1896–98; and after numerous data were gathered on upwards of 11,000 of the abnormals, we were suddenly thwarted by the impossibility of contrasting our records with standard records on normal Americans. It was then that the necessity of establishing such standards was seen to be the foremost necessity of American anthropology, and it was the ever-present consciousness of this want that led, when conditions appreared propitious, to the studies on the "Old Americans."

By "Old Americans" are meant in general those American whites who have been longest in this country. More specifically the writer felt justified in including under this term those Americans whose ancestors on each side of the family were born in the United States for at least two generations—in other words, all those whose parents as well as all four grandparents were born in this country. The third native generation of adults means roughly an ancestry on each side of the family of at least 80 to 150 years American. As a matter of fact the mean "nativity" of those examined was nearer the latter than the former figure and for the whole series it probably surpassed an average of 150 years, for there were many who on one or both sides exceeded the minimum requirement of three generations. In a large majority of cases the American ancestry of the one examined, while only three or four generations on one side, extended to from four to eight generations on the other; and there were fairly numerous instances where the ancestry was pure native on both sides for four generations, while occasionally it was five, six and in a few cases even seven generations.

In the beginning of the studies it seemed desirable to make the limit of four, or still better five generation Americans; but on trial this was found quite impracticable. When the eastern and southern communities where considerable inbreeding has taken place and the subjects from which would obviously not be the most desirable for our purposes were excluded, it was found that those who could qualify to four or five generations of pure American ancestry on both sides were astonishingly scarce, and that also, on the whole, they represented rather too much of social differentiation. Even those of three generations pure native ancestry are far less common than might at first be imagined. Let anyone who may think otherwise make a fair trial, outside of such communities as mentioned above. In undertaking the work and especially after reducing the limit to three generations native-born, the writer anticipated little difficulty in finding all the subjects he needed, particularly in a city so little affected by immigration as Washington. But he soon learned differently. Of good will there was enough, and there were found many three-, four- or more generation Americans on one side; but on the other very often either the birthplace of one or more of the grandparents was uncertain or it was not in this country.

It was not long before requests for help had to be addressed to some of the local patriotic Societies, and in 1915 a special appeal was made to the Daughters of the American Revolution. In the September number of that year the magazine of the D. A. R. with the sanction of Mrs. William Cumming Story, at that time President General of the Society, published a brief article on the subject. One of the encouraging results of these appeals was that volunteers for the examinations appeared from some of the oldest and most prominent families. One of these was no less than ex-President Roosevelt. On March 1, 1915, he wrote to the author: "I am interested in your 'Study of Old Americans.' . . . . If we were in Washington, we would come in to see you and be measured ourselves. Our ancestors were all here prior to the Revolution and some of them have been here three centuries; and we are fairly healthy outfit—ourselves, our children and our grandchildren." And on March 15, in answer to my invitation to come, he responds: "You shall take all the measurements you want."

Unfortunately the promise could never be fulfilled. Ex-President Roosevelt did not come to Washington any more except on one or two flying visits, when his health began to give way. The loss of his record is to be deeply regretted. The data would have been of much historic value and would have, in a way, crowned the whole effort. Accurate records of this nature— as well as faithful life busts—should be preserved of every President, and of every truly great man and woman of this country; and what better place is there to preserve them in than the Smithsonian Institution?

By the end of 1915 the studies here dealt with had so far progressed that it was possible to make a preliminary report on their results before the XIX International Congress of Americanists, which met in Washington in December of that year; and this report, dealing with the first hundred of male and the same number of female Old Americans was published in the Proceedings of that Congress at the beginning of 1917 (pp. 582–601). In this report certain tentative conclusions were reached which since have become fully corroborated, but in most directions the status of the research did not yet permit of definite statements. By 1917 the work in the Laboratory was approaching its set goal, and it was then decided to extend the studies, more particularly the observations on pigmentation, into the field. Trips were made to the Universities of Virginia, Yale and Harvard, for examination of teachers, scholars and some of the local population. At Virginia and Harvard particularly, valuable opportunities for observation were provided by the Summer School for Teachers of each of these Institutions, which attract many hundreds of younger men and women from all parts of the south and east. In 1917 the recruiting and the generous aid of Colonel King of Bristol offered an unprecedented opportunity for the study of the very interesting Old American stock of the Appalachian mountaineers (see Smithsonian Explorations for 1917); and in 1918, through the valuable help of Professor Robert Bennett Bean, of the University of Virginia, a large group of southern "Engineers" were examined on their camp at Charlottesville. Finally, the last five years were devoted to the rounding up of the series; to additional observations, including a visit to a number of the camps during the period of demobilization; and to the preparation of the data for publication. In 1920 a more extended report on the work was presented before the II International Congress of Eugenics at New York City.

The total number of subjects fully examined and measured reached finally well over 900, while the number of those examined specially for pigmentation, etc., was approximately 1000 additional. These numbers are not great, nevertheless they appear sufficient and that they may be so taken is shown by the results of testing the series by fifties; in essentials the data on the separate fifties differ so little that the totals on the whole series may safely be regarded as true representations of the characteristics of the Old American population. Further studies would probably show some geographically localized aberrations in one or another respect from this series; there may also exist some interesting differences from the standards here established in the frontier population of the far west and southwest, which is but sparsely represented in our groups; but for the bulk of the Old Americans the data to be here given are in all probability quite faithful.

A question upon which a few words are called for in this connection, is that of selection. Are our groups representative enough of the part of the population which they concern, or has there been accidentally or otherwise any undue selection of some particular class or classes? In the writer's opinion, the groups as far as they go, are as fairly representative as could probably be made on any subsequent effort. The exclusion of the subadults and the senile, with that of those obviously abnormal in some respect or those in poor health, was clearly indicated, and there was no other selection of any nature. Occupationally the series embraces on the male side clerks, business men, professional men, members of Congress and men of leisure, artisans and farmers. On the female side we have no laborers or servants—there are practically none of these among the Old Americans; they are mainly clerks, women in business or professions, housewives, and women of leisure; but among the clerks, as well as the others, there are women bred in the country as well as under other conditions, for Government clerks, both men and women, are appointed to Washington from all the States and have generally been brought up in other occupations and environment and are therefore no special class of their own, although they do not perform much hard manual labor, and for the most part never have done so. Except therefore, for the absence of actual farmers' wives and others doing hard muscular work, the female group also may be regarded as fairly representative.

There are three classes of Old Americans, however, which are not well represented in the series here dealt with and to which investigations of this nature ought to extend in the course of time. They are the inbred population of the small towns in New England; the old-time middle states farmer; and the western pioneer.

CHAPTER II

BRIEF HISTORICAL DATA ON THE OLD AMERICAN STOCK

The Old American stock to be dealt with in these pages is in general that, of which all the ancestors on both sides of the family were in this land before 1830.   Actually in a large majority of the cases studied, the American ancestry of the subjects on one or both sides dated from before 1800 and in not a few even from before 1700.   Naturally the question to be answered first is, what was the exact racial composition of this ancestry.

To throw full light on this question will not be possible.   The records are not sufficient.   Yet there are records of value.   They include the historic data on the colonies; the State and Federal enumerations of 1765–1790; and the Federal censuses and immigration statistics following.   In addition there are numerous interesting though usually more or less biassed articles and monographs dealing with special nationalistic groups who have contributed their blood to the formation of the older parts of the American people.

DATA ON THE COLONIES

The history of the origins and building up of the colonies cannot be gone into in these connections.   It is recorded more or less adequately in many publications, a partial list of which is given in this section.   The essentials are that, exclusive of the much less consequential Spanish and French elements in Florida, the Southwest, and along the Mississippi, the American colonies were founded by and recruited mainly from the English (and Welsh), with smaller contingents of the Scotch-Irish and Scotch, Dutch, Germans (principally southwestern), French, Swedes and Irish.

But the exact proportions of these groups at any one time are more or less uncertain.   Moreover, these groups were not distinct "races" of man, but mixtures of various older ethnic elements.

As to the proportions of the representatives and descendants of the several nationalities in the American colonial population, the most comprehensive data will be found in the "Century of Population Growth."[1]

In this valuable though much criticised report an estimate of the national-

---

[1] U. S. Census Publ., 4°, Wash., 1909.

istic composition of the American people at the time of the first Federal census in 1790 is based, aside of other data, on the names of the heads of the families enumerated in that census. There is naturally a certain amount of weakness involved in this procedure; yet the errors are possibly not as great as believed to be by some writers. At all events these data represent the closest statistical approximation as to the nationalistic composition of the American people of that period that has so far been arrived at. The principal results for the United States of that time as a whole, and for the separate States follow; supplemented by a map of the United States in 1790 and by a chart showing the distribution of the white population of each nationality in the United States in the same year—both taken from the same volume (table 1).

According to these figures, no less than 89 per cent of the American population in 1790 were derived or descended from the English, Welsh and Scotch; and no less than 91 per cent were derived or descended from the people of Great Britain and Ireland.

TABLE 1

Per cent distribution of the white population of each nationality as indicated by names of heads of families, according to state of residence: 1790

AREA COVERED	ALL NATION-ALITIES 2,810,248 100 per cent	ENGLISH 2,345,844 100 per cent	SCOTCH 188,589 100 per cent	IRISH 44,373 100 per cent	DUTCH 56,673 100 per cent	FRENCH 13,384 100 per cent	GERMAN 156,457 100 per cent	HEBREW 1,243 100 per cent	ALL OTHER 3,835 100 per cent
	per cent	per cent	per cent	per cent	per cent	per cent	per cent	per cent	per cent
State:									
Maine.............	3.4	3.8	2.2	3.0	0.5	0.9	0.3	3.5	6.0
New Hampshire...	5.0	5.7	3.5	3.0	0.3	1.1			2.5
Vermont..........	3.0	3.5	1.4	1.3	0.8	1.1	*		3.9
Massachusetts.....	13.3	15.1	7.1	8.4	0.7	5.6	*	5.4	6.0
Rhode Island......	2.3	2.6	1.0	1.0	*	0.7	*	0.7	0.2
Connecticut.......	8.3	9.5	3.4	3.6	0.5	3.8	*	0.4	0.2
New York.........	11.2	10.5	5.3	5.7	89.4	18.1	0.7	31.0	36.3
Pennsylvania......	15.1	10.6	26.3	19.5	4.6	17.5	70.5	1.7	5.1
Maryland.........	7.4	7.5	7.2	11.3	0.4	10.9	7.9	50.4	5.4
Virginia..........	15.7	16.0	16.6	20.0	1.6	19.8	13.8		23.1
North Carolina....	10.3	10.2	17.2	15.0	1.0	6.5	5.2	0.1	7.5
South Carolina....	5.0	4.9	8.7	8.1	0.4	14.1	1.5	6.8	3.8

* Less than one-tenth of 1 per cent.

TABLE 1—*Continued*

Computed distribution of the white population of each state for which schedules are missing, according to nationality: 1790

NATIONALITY	NEW JERSEY	DELAWARE	GEORGIA	KENTUCKY	TENNESSEE
All nationalities..................	169,954	46,310	52,886	61,133	31,913
	per cent	*per cent*	*per cent*	*per cent*	*per cent*
English...................	58.0	86.3	83.1	83.1	83.1
Scotch....................	7.7	7.5	11.2	11.2	11.2
Irish......................	7.1	3.9	2.3	2.3	2.3
German..................	9.2	0.4	2.8	2.8	2.8
Dutch....................	12.7	1.0	0.2	0.2	0.2
French...................	2.1	0.5	0.3	0.3	0.3
All other*................	3.1	0.4	0.1	0.1	0.1

* Includes Hebrew.

Number and per cent distribution of the white population according to nationality: 1790

NATIONALITY	NUMBER	PER CENT
All nationalities.......................	3,172,444	100.0
English.......................	2,605,699	*82.1*
Scotch.......................	221,562	*7.0*
Irish.........................	61,534	*1.9*
German......................	176,407	*5.6*
Dutch.......................	78,959	*2.5*
French.......................	17,619	*0.6*
All other.....................	10,664	*0.3*

In 1915, in a lecture given at Brown University, a somewhat different estimate has been given by Professor J. F. Jameson, the well-known historian. Thanks to Professor Jameson, a manuscript of this lecture, the title of which was "The American Blood in 1775" and which remains as yet unpublished, was placed at the writer's disposal. Professor Jameson summarizes his conclusions as follows:

If we imagine that 60 per cent of the white American blood of 1775 came from England, 17 ot 18 per cent from Ireland, 11 or 12 per cent from Germany, 7 or 8 per cent from the Netherlands, and a small but indefinite percentage from Scotland, we shall probably be not far wrong. Several of the other national contributions present a story of great interest, but it is not likely that any of them amounted to 1 per cent, though the Swedes and the French may have approached that sum.

INHABITED AREA IN UNITED STATES IN 1790.

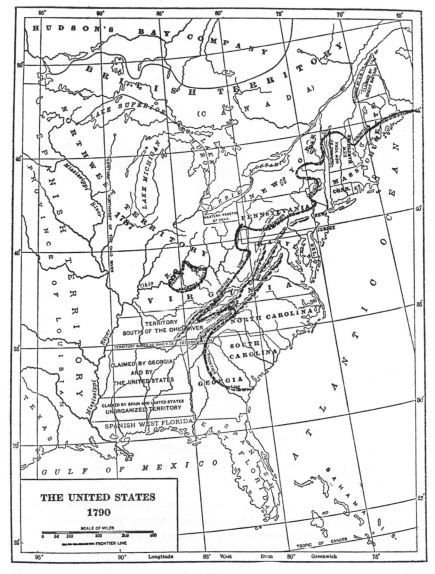

Fig. 1

Under the 17 or 18 per cent from Ireland, however, Professor Jameson includes both the Irish proper and the Scotch-Irish, the latter of whom at that time were doubtless in a large majority.

Whatever may have been the exact proportions of the several nationalities involved in building up the American colonies, it is plain that the English,

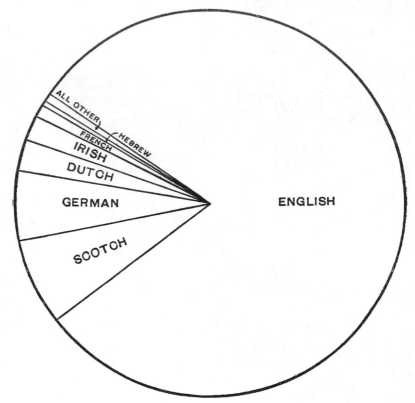

FIG. 2. PROPORTION OF TOTAL POPULATION FORMED BY EACH NATIONALITY, 1790

Welsh, Scotch and Irish, with their descendants, constituted seven-eighths or over of the American stock of 1790 and that a large part of the remainder consisted of or was descended from the Germans, the Dutch, the French and the Southern Irish.

In addition to the preceding many details of value on the separate nationalities will be found in Fiske,[2] Ford, [3] Hanna,[4] MacDougall,[5] Faust,[6] etc.[7]

In addition to the eastern population, in 1804, at the time of the transfer of Louisiana to the American possessions, there were about 3,500 French mixed with some Spanish and much Indian blood in the Mississippi Valley.[8] In 1793, moreover, there were 30,953 Spanish-speaking persons (probably including some Christianized Indians) in New Mexico, and 12,666 of such persons in the Californias.[9]

We thus arrive at a fairly clear concept as to the nationalistic constituents of the American population of 1790. But, as already said, nationalistic composition does not mean racial composition. Nations are not "races," but at best only more or less close approaches to types.

There are generally recognized within the white race three main larger strains, which may be called sub-races or "races" in a more limited sense of the word. These are the Mediterranean, the Alpine and the Nordic. They are according to indications geographic-environmental variations and are nowhere clearly separated, but interdigitate extensively with each other and connect through imperceptible gradations. The people comprised in these three imperfectly limited groups form various "nationalities" and speak different languages. But anthropological data and historical records show that practically all these nationalities are composites of earlier groups and have received even during historic times more or less important accretions from the remaining strains, so much so that no nationality today can be regarded as pure. The nations of today are therefore as a rule composed of former more or less heterogeneous elements; though after centuries of intermarriage and existence as linguistic and political units such groups tend to develop similar habits, similar bearing, similar behavior and gradually

[2] Fiske (John)—The Discovery and Colonization of North America. 12mo., Ginn & Co., Boston, 1905.

[3] Ford (Henry Jones)—The Scotch-Irish in America. Princeton University Press, 1915.

[4] Hanna (Charles A.)—The Scotch-Irish; or, The Scots in North Britain, North Ireland and North America. 2 vols., 8°, New York, 1902.

[5] MacDougall (Donald)—Scots and Scots Descendants in America. Caledonian Publishing Co., New York, 1917. With bibliography.

[6] Faust (A. B.)—The German Element in the United States. 2 vols., 8°, Boston and New York, 1909. With bibliography.

[7] See bibliographies in Fiske, MacDougall, H. H. Bancroft and other historians.

[8] Finley (John)—The French in the Heart of America. Ch. Scribner's Sons, New York, 1915.

[9] Chapman (Charles E.)—The Founding of Spanish California.

even more and more similar physical characteristics especially as to physiognomy, thus coming to constitute fairly readily recognisable types.

Thus, the English type has developed from the Neolithic type of man in Britain, from the broad-headed type that reached the islands during the Bronze period, from the Mediterraneans brought in during the Roman domination, from the Germanic tribes of what is now western Germany and Holland, and from the Normans, French and smaller admixtures. The German type is a result of the admixture of the northwestern Europeans, Slavs and Alpines in perhaps not greatly differing proportions. The French type is the result of the admixture of the Alpines, Mediterraneans, southwestern Germanic tribes and some Normans. The Slavs in turn are old Europeans, modified according to locality by the Finno-Ugrians, Scandinavians, Germans, Alpines, Italians or Turks. The Spanish are a conglomerate of the Iberians, Kelts, Vandals, Suabians, Phoenicians and Moors. The Dutch show at least two native strains besides some admixture with the Spanish and Germans. The Jews carry the blood of every people with whom they lived.[10] And so with others. Upon analysis every larger European group, even the Scandinavians or "Nordics" proper, is found to be a composite of older groups which generally represent all the three main strains of white man, namely the Nordic, Alpine and Mediterranean. And most, if not all, have even traces of the yellow-browns or blacks. Thus, the Scandinavians are not a little admixed with the Lapps; traces of "Mongoloids" are to be found in Germany and even England; the Semites and Mediterraneans bear here and there traces of the Africans, which have also reached some of the French and Spanish, etc.

The types of the English, Welsh, Scotch and Irish people are all intermediate types though there are individuals among them who resemble either the Nordic or the Alpine or the Mediterranean white man. And the same may be said of the Dutch and also of the German, though the physiognomy of the latter has its own prevalent stamp which in turn differs quite perceptibly between the north and the south of Germany. In France there may still be noted a prevalent older type which may perhaps be characterised as the true French; besides which however there is a very strong representation of the Mediterranean type, particularly in southern France, while in Normandy there are still plain traces of the northern invaders.

The racial problem of the Old American stock is therefore far more complex than would be indicated by its nationalistic composition, and all

[10] See Maurice Fishberg: The Jews. 12mo, London and New York, 1911.

that may *a priori* be deduced about it is that from the beginning it was a mixture of most if not all the elements of the white race, though the British and Western European tribes predominated.

Between 1790 and 1820 the immigration from Europe, as shown by the Census and historical records of that time, was relatively small and of such a nature that it in no way altered the composition of the older agglomerate. After 1820 and particularly after 1830 however, the numbers of immigrants began materially to increase and their nationalistic character to change, but this afflux has no longer any influence on that part of the Old American stock which remained unadmixed with the newer elements and descendants of which we shall study in this volume.

THE EXAMINATIONS

With the preceding remarks we may now approach the study itself; and as some explanations have already been given, while others will follow in connection with the related text, all that is needed in this place is to show the exact scope of the work, which will be best done by the following copy of the blanks which, or a modification of which (for twenty-five individuals), were used in the examinations:

SMITHSONIAN INSTITUTION

U. S. NATIONAL MUSEUM

Group............   *Sex*............

No............	FACE:
Name.........	Length to nasion..................
Age...........	Length to crinion..................
Born in..........................	Breadth, bizygom..................
Father............................	Diam. front min..................
Mother...........................	Diam. bigonial....................
P. Gf.............................	*Nose:*
P. Gm............................	Length to nasion..............
M. Gf............................	Breadth......................
M. Gm...........................	
	Mouth:
Measurements	Breadth......................
Deformation of head..................	*Left Ear:*
BODY:	Length......................
Stature......................	Breadth......................
Max. finger reach..................	MISCELLANEOUS:
Height sitting.....................	*Chest:*
HEAD:	Breadth at nipple height.........
Length........................	Depth at nipple height..........
Breadth........................	
Height.........................	

SMITHSONIAN INSTITUTION—*Continued*

MISCELLANEOUS—*Continued:*

Left Hand:

Length..........................

Breadth.........................

Left Foot:

Length..........................

Breadth.........................

Left Leg:

Girth, max......................

Weight of Body.....................
(With shoes, but without outer garments)

OBSERVATIONS

Color of skin........................

Color of eyes........................

Color of hair........................

Nature of hair......................

Moustache...........................

Beard...............................

Forehead............................

Supraorb. ridges....................

Eye-slits...........................

Malars..............................

OBSERVATIONS—*Continued:*

Nasion depress......................

Nose...............................

Nasal septum.......................

Lips...............................

Alveol. progn......................

Chin...............................

Angle of l. jaw....................

Body and limbs.....................

Toes...............................

Breasts............................

PHYSIOLOGICAL:

Pulse (sitting, at rest).............

Respiration (do)....................

Temperature (do, *sub lingua*)..........

Time of day.........................

State of health.....................

Tongue..............................

Strength:

Pressure $\begin{cases} \text{r. hand} \ldots \ldots \ldots \\ \text{l. hand} \ldots \ldots \ldots \end{cases}$

Traction............................

CHAPTER III

Definitions

By pigmentation is generally meant the amount and nature of coloring matter in the skin, eyes and hair; though the condition is also manifest in the mucous membranes, particularly the gums, in the sclerotic, and even in other parts and tissues of the body.

The pigmentation of an individual is not the same throughout his life, and will not appear the same under all conditions. It is much influenced by age, prolonged exposure or confinement (especially the skin and hair) and state of health. In addition the appearance of the skin, eyes, and even hair will be modified by the quantity and oxygenation of the blood (flush paleness or blueness of skin, brightness or dullness of eye, dull dryness of hair), the state of feeling, the presence or removal of the natural sebaceous or oily coating (in the skin and hair), and the presence of minutes air bubbles between the cells of the hair occasionally after great nervous strain, or normally in advancing years, causing or contributing to grayness.

The coloring substance, or substances, the exact nature and differences of which are still a matter of some uncertainty, occurs in the shape of minute granules which, in the skin, are lodged in the deeper layers of the epidermis; in the eye, are deposited in various cells of the iris; and in the hair, where they crowd most of the cells of the hair shaft. The pigment, generically known as melanin is much alike in various organs of the same individual, in different individuals of the same race, and in different races of man; but there are indications that it may represent a complex of related forms differing by slight chemical variations.

The main function of pigmentation is a protection of the skin and of the eyes against those rays of the sun which would be harmful to the organism, in addition to which pigment may possibly serve also as an accessory means for the elimination from the system of certain substances that result from the metabolism in the cells. A complete lack of pigmentation, as abnormally present in full human albinos, is accompanied by weakness of the eyes as well as great delicacy of the skin.

The pigmentation of man is of ancient ancestral origin. According to various indications, early man, up to at least the middle of the Palaeolithic period, was more or less brown in color, with hazel to dark-brown eyes and

17

reddish-brown to black hair.   Before the middle of the glacial period this
early man was well established in western Europe, which according to many
indications was the cradle of his differentiation.   It was primarily from
Europe that he spread into other parts of the world,[1] and it was from western Europe that he eventually followed the final recession of the ice north-
ward, until he peopled what are now Denmark, northern Germany, and the
Scandinavian Peninsula.

These regions concern us particularly in this connection.   Under the
peculiar postglacial climatic and environmental conditions of northwest-
ernmost Europe, combining in all probability considerable cold, damp, and
cloudiness or mists with a diminished amount of light, and the effects of
these conditions on man's clothing, housing, and habits in general, the protective pigmentation of those who lived there became to a large degree
unnecessary, and as organisms will not tolerate for long anything that has
become useless, the pigmentation of the northerners was reduced.   Gradually or by mutations man grew lighter in these lands until he came to constitute a blond "race."   He lost so much pigment that his skin has become
"white," his eyes blue, his hair light, ranging from light brown, yellow, or
golden, to almost colorless.   In the more central parts of Europe the
depigmentation was less effective, and the result is the intermediary
"Alpine" or "Kelto-Slavic" type; while in southern Europe, Asia Minor,
and northern Africa it was still less, leaving the swarthy to brown, dark-
eyed and black-haired Mediterraneans.   It may be noted, however, that,
except in full albinism, even the whitest skin, the lightest blue eye, and the
lightest hair still retain some of the old pigmentation.   The blue eye in
particular is not blue because of a complete loss of pigment or any new form
of coloration, but because the remaining pigment is limited to the
posteriormost cells of the iris, the result of which is that the eye appears
more or less blue on refraction; but viewed from behind in such cases the
iris is not blue.

Effects of mixture

Through long residence in their respective regions and inbreeding, the
three main types of pigmentation, or rather depigmentation, in Europe have
become fairly fixed, so much that even a prolonged residence elsewhere, such
as that of some offshoots of the blond type in parts of the Mediterranean
region and that of the dark Jew or offshoot of the Mediterraneans in northern Europe, has not been potent enough fully to efface either the blondness

---

[1] See writer's The Peopling of Asia.   Proc. Amer. Philos. Soc., 1921, lx, No. 4, 535 et
seq.

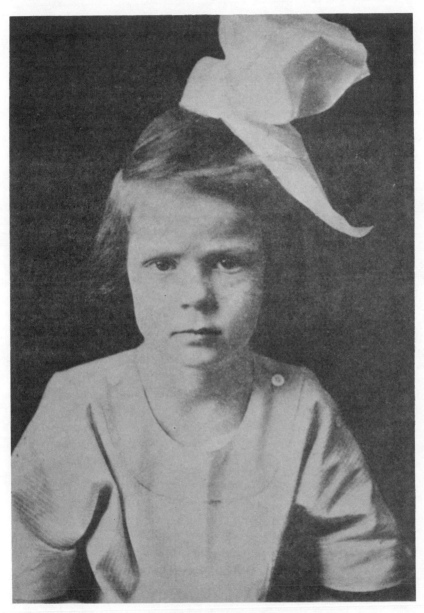

MISS VIRGINIA DEWEY
(Washington)
4 years old; both parents Old Americans

or darkness, though there has not been a complete preservation. There are, however, no sharp lines of demarcation, no breaks of continuity, between the blond and medium, or the latter and the dark type; even where purest they pass on the boundaries imperceptibly into each other.

But due to original individual variation in the grade of the depigmentation, and to the great mixings of the European peoples before and especially within historic times, a large majority of the people of every larger country, and even district, retain some of the old differences in these respects or have lost more or less their one-time purity of type. A great majority of the present population of Europe are mixed bloods—within the limits of the white race—and the mixtures have played havoc with pure strains of pigmentation.

Yet the effect of the mixings in relation to pigmentation has been simple enought, consisting merely of an addition by the darker parent of so much melanin—or more strictly of so much more tendency to form melanin—to the progeny. In the blonds such tendency has been largely lost; in the mediums and darks it is partly to largely preserved; while in the mixtures of darker strains with lighter it becomes more or less restored, and in consequence the progeny will show in varying degrees a darker pigmentation than the light parent. By admixture with a darker line the blond strain returns more or less toward its ancestral pigmented condition. Whether any of the first or second generation of the mixed progeny may, through a Mendelian form of heredity, be born once more pure light, medium, or dark, as were their parents or grandparents, is not yet definitely known, but the plainly evident results of the mixture between different types of pigmentation is a large variety of intermediaries.

The effects of such mixtures are not manifested in the same way in all the involved parts. The skin-hair-eye pigmentation behaves in a large measure as a unit, but in interbreeding not infrequently this complex becomes more or less dissociated and its components enter into differing combinations with the pigmentation factors provided by the other germ cell. The skin, hair, and eyes show somewhat differing tendencies in these directions.

In the skin the usual result of a mixture of two types of color is a uniform "blend," but the shade of this "blend" may vary considerably in different members of the resulting family. There are, however, also cases of irregular "blends." These may be witnessed occasionally in the admixtures of the white with the negro, and, probably more frequently than we are generally aware of, in the mixtures of darks and lights among the white people. The darker strain in these cases manifests itself partly in the form of more or less marked irregular areas or patches, or in larger or smaller "freckles."

Permanent freckles have more significance than they have hitherto received, and even passing freckles may occasionally have a phylogenetic rather than mere ontogenetic, or casual, significance. The characteristic freckled "Scotch skin" is much more probably a record of admixture of a darker with a light type in the past, than a sun effect, or a meaningless individual or tribal peculiarity.

The hair in mixture behaves much like the skin. Generally the result is a "blend," or rather increased pigmentation more or less over that of the lighter parent. But not infrequently in mixed progeny with the lighter shades of hair, particularly in females where due to the length of the hair the conditions may be more easily appreciated, there may be detected strands of darker or lighter hair than the majority. An imperfect blend seems also to exist in some of the "sandy" or "rusty" reds. Individual tufts or locks of black or white hair are anomalies, that may run in families, but have little interest in this connection.

The organs in which the most varied and interesting conditions result in consequence of mixture are, however, the eyes. The original human eye was probably hazel (or medium brown) to dark brown. All the primates, all the colored races of man, and a considerable proportion as yet of the whites have brown eyes. Such eyes in earlier times were doubtless associated with dark hair as well as darker skin. But under the already discussed environmental conditions of northwestern Europe, acting through thousands of years, the protective brown pigment, no longer needed, was eliminated until it almost disappeared from the eyes, disappeared largely from the skin, and was greatly diminished in the hair. The result so far as the visual organ was concerned was the blue eye, which became fixed by heredity. The blue eye, as already noted, is not an eye wholly without pigment—that condition is present only in the eye of the full albino; neither is it an eye with any special pigment. But whatever pigment is present in the blue eye is located only in the posterior columnar epithelium cells of the iris, whereas in gray, brown, and the so-called black eyes pigment is found also in branching connective tissue cells interspersed between the bundles of connective tissue that form the substance or stroma of the iris, and even in the endothelial cells on the front of the iris.

If an unmixed blue-eyed person marries one with brown eyes, the result, as shown in the color of the eyes of the progeny, may be one of several distinct conditions. In a small number of cases of such progeny, taken at large, it will be seen that the brown pigment owed to the darker mate has been distributed uniformly throughout the iris, and, according to its quantity, instead of a blue eye we shall have "grays," possibly some "greens," and light browns, the latter of which in a strong light may show a greenish tinge. But in the large majority of cases the distribution of the brown pigment in the iris will be more or less localized, and we shall have a bluish (never perfectly blue), grayish, or greenish eye with a brown ring or area about the pupil, or brown specks or spots scattered over the iris, with a closer aggregation about the pupil. These cases constitute the large category of "mixed" eyes which are encountered in the central and north European peoples of the present time, and which are very common among Americans. Rarely the brown in an eye may be present in the form of a splotch, or as a clear-cut segment reaching from the pupil to the periphery of the iris.

TABLE 2

Pigmentation

Skin

Light (blond, pale-rosy).	*Medium* (all between light and dark).	*Dark* (swarthy, dusky, light tan).

Hair

Lights proper (blond, yellow and golden, light brown (near blond)).	*Light brown* (not blond)	*Medium* (medium brown, medium dark).	*Dark* (dark brown, dark, near black).	*Black.*	*Red* (sandy, light red, brick, salmon, dark or chestnut red).

Eyes

Pure lights, blue (pure, light, medium, deep); green (pure); gray (pure).	*Intermediates, mixed* (brown spots, splotches, ring, or tinge, in lights; in browns, plain tinge of gray or greenish).	*Pure browns* (light, medium) dark).

Classification

A detailed investigation on pigmentation in a highly complex population, such as that of the United States, offers, due to the conditions enumerated above, not a few difficulties. There are a large number of shades in the color of the skin and hair which pass into each other without any lines of demarcation, and in the case of the eyes there are numerous shades and conditions that are not always easy of characterization. A correct appreciation and recording of the true conditions requires good eyesight in the observer, proper light, distance, and exposure (skin) in examination, a careful effort at distinguishing the true conditions, and the simplest possible thoroughly understood scheme of classification. Fortunately extreme details, except in some special researches, are not necessary, and the many shades met with may be grouped into a few categories that are not only sufficient for ordinary scientific purposes, but are also readily intelligible to the nonscientific man.

The most practical classification for white people of the American type found by the writer, both through considerable experience in examination as well as in the analysis of the obtained records, and one which was therefore used throughout in these studies, is shown in table 2.

In general the pigmentation of a person shows considerable conformity. A light skin will be associated with blond or yellow hair and light to medium blue or greenish eyes; red hair goes generally with a light to pale rosy skin and a light to medium blue or greenish or mixed eye; and a dark brown eye is invariably associated with dark to black hair while the skin will range from medium to darker. As a rule also the unmixed medium and dark types breed true, the lights producing lights and the darks darks, though the range of exact shading in each is fairly extended. But those with medium pigmentation seem less stable and harmonious, and the usually large category of mixtures present frequent smaller or greater disharmonies and irregularities.

COLOR OF SKIN

The special observations on the skin in the present studies, extended to 200 "Old American" males and 250 females without selection. The gross results are shown in table 3.[2]

The figures show that in a little over seven-tenths of the cases in men and in over three-fourths of the women the color of the skin of the Old Americans may be classed as medium; that, particularly in the males, there is in health but a small proportion of lights, but that a very appreciable minority possess skin that, while far from really dark, is perceptibly "swarthier "or darker than the medium.

There is throughout the series a somewhat greater inclination toward pigmentation of the skin among the males than among the females. This to some extent is probably connected with more exposure among the males,

---

[2] It is self-evident that noninstrumental observations such as these, however carefully made, can not claim mathematical precision, and would probably differ slightly not only from observer to observer, but upon repetition even with the same worker; but these differences, with equally instructed students, and the same care, would in all probability not be great enough materially to affect the general results.

TABLE 3

Color of Skin

SKIN	MALES (200)		FEMALES (250)	
	Number of subjects	Per cent	Number of subjects	Per cent
Light (perceptibly lighter than medium).....	1	0.5	13	5.2
Medium...............................	135	67.5	188	75.2
Swarthy or slight tan (perceptibly darker than medium)............................	55	27.5	42	16.8
"Scotch" (freckly), otherwise medium........	9	4.5	7	2.8

TABLE 4

Correlation of color of hair and eyes with the color of the skin in Old Americans

Light skin

NUMBER	SKIN PERCEPTIBLY LIGHTER THAN MEDIUM	HAIR			EYES		
		Blonds	Reds	Light brown	Light blue	Medium blue	Grayish or greenish blue
1	Male...........			1	1		
13	Females........	6	4	3	3	5	5
Total, 14	Per cent......	43.0	28.5	28.5	28.5	35.7	35.7

TABLE 5

Correlation of color of hair and eyes with the color of the skin in Old Americans

Darker skin

NUMBER	SKIN PERCEPTIBLY DARKER THAN MEDIUM	HAIR					EYES			
		Lights		Me-dium	Dark to black	Reds	Lights (blue, gray, green-ish, mixed)	Browns		
		Blond	Light brown					Light brown	Me-dium brown	Dark brown
55	Males...........		(2)	(16)	(37)		(34)*	(7)	(12)	(2)
	Per cent........		3.6	29.1	67.3		61.8	12.7	21.8	3.6
42	Females.........		(1)	(8)	(33)		(21)*	(3)	(13)	(5)
	Per cent........		2.4	19.0	78.6		50.0	7.1	31.0	11.9
Total, 97	Per cent........			3.1	24.7	72.2	56.7	10.3	25.8	7.2

* Mostly "mixed" (blue or greenish or grayish with more or less marked traces of brown).

but it does not seem to be due to this cause alone. The whole showing is noteworthy, for as will be seen presently it is not paralleled in the pigmentation of other features.

A study of the correlation of the skin color with that of the hair and eyes gives results that are uncommonly interesting. There were recorded one "light" skinned male and thirteen females (table 4).

All the subjects with light skin are in hair, it is seen, blonds or near blonds, ·with a few reds. There appears therefore to be a close positive correlation between a lighter than ordinary skin and light hair and eyes. Wherever there is a subpigmentation of the skin, there is also in our subjects a feeble pigmentation of the eyes and hair. But the rule does not work both ways—subjects with light hair and eyes do not always or even very often have also a lighter than medium epidermis.

On the other side of the "medium" we have the more or less swarthy, dusky, or slightly tawny skins, and the correlation of hair and eyes with these discloses some curious conditions.

Table 5 shows that in the darker persons, also, there exists a marked correlation between the color of the skin and that of the hair. There are no "blonds" in the men or women with darker skins, and unexpectedly also no "reds," which points to a rather close relation of these two classes of shades; but there is a very large proportion of darks to black. Also, throughout, there is an evident tendency toward more darkness of hair and eyes in the females than in the males, which, however, as will be shown below, does not apply alone to the cases with darker skin.

As to the eyes, the correlation of their color with that of the skin is plainly less than that of the hair. A good proporton of both men and women with a darker skin and dark hair have blue, greenish, gray, and especially mixed eyes; but there is also a considerable proportion of browns, much above that in the Old Americans at large. The women show again a greater tendency in this direction—they have less "lights" and light browns, but decidedly and progressively more medium and dark browns. Why this should be so is not yet quite clear, but we shall return to the phenomenon, which seems to be generalized among all whites, on another occasion.

The correlations between brunet skin and the color of the hair and eyes may be shown still more clearly by comparing the percental representation of the different classes of shades of the hair and eyes in those with swarthy skins to the whole number of subjects in our series (table 6).

Among those with darker skins there are, in respect to hair, no blonds or reds, only a little over one-fifth as many light browns, and approximately one-half as many medium browns as in the Old Americans taken as a whole, but nearly three times as many darks-to-blacks.   As to eyes, the darker-skinned show one-fourth to one-third less lights but more than twice as many browns, two to three times as many light browns, over twice as many mediums, and over once to twice and a half as many darks than the Old Americans at large.   A greater tendency to eye pigmentation is once more apparent here in the women.

The meaning of these conditions tends to be that a normally darker skin in the American and doubtless other whites is generally an expression of not a localized but a systemic tendency toward "darker" or more abundant pigmentation, and as such is a feature probably of phylogenetic rather than ontogenetic significance; it is, in other words, more probably a survival of a darker ancestry rather than an individual peculiarity.   Just how much more or less of the darker skins there are in the Old Americans than among

TABLE 6

Color of hair and eyes in subjects with skin perceptibly darker than medium compared with that in the series at large

Percental relation to proportion in the whole series

	HAIR					EYES			
	Blonds	Reds	Light brown (not blond)	Medium	Dark to black	Blue, green, gray, mixed	Light brown	Medium brown	Dark brown
Males...............			22	58	279	74	310	225	124
Females.............			24	44	262	65	203	209	243

other whites we shall only be able to tell from similar future studies among these other groups; strictly comparable data so far are wanting.

The "Scotch skin" is a medium white skin with numerous light and rather large and irregular "freckles" on the exposed parts.   On the face these "freckles" extend to the forehead.   It is highly characteristic of a proportion of persons of Scotch derivation and that among the Old as well as recent Americans.   The subject deserves a detailed study of its own.   As already mentioned, there is a strong indication that these "freckles" are merely the remnants of a darker-skinned strain admixed in the dim past into the Scotch people.

COLOR OF HAIR

The records on pigmentation of the hair, being simpler, are much more numerous and comprehensive than those on the skin.   They apply to 1,009 men and 914 women.

The method, based on considerable experience and preliminary work, was to subdivide the large range of colors into as few as possible definite classes, and then to use common sense, with good light, plenty of time, and due care, in determining the shade. In general this method is preferable to that of comparing the hair with given standards, for that takes longer, the standards are mostly not available to the reader, and among such a mixed population as ours we would never have enough standards. It is true that it is not easy in such a visual method to get rid of all personal equation, but the amount of such an equation may be very much reduced and be rendered practically insignificant by due understanding of the subject, with ample practice. The final classification of the shades is not arbitrary. We begin with the safe units of "black," decidedly "blond" or "light," and unmistakably red. This leaves a large category of intermediate grades all of which fall, however, into three subdivisions, namely, light brown (not blond), medium (or "medium brown"), and dark (or "dark brown"). A large majority of cases will readily and unmistakably be placed in one or another of these classes by every properly instructed observer. This will leave as possible sources of error only the transitional shades, for there are between none of the colors any definite lines of separation. These cases, with a careful student, will amount to approximately 10 per cent with the blonds, 20 per cent with the light browns (not blond) mediums darks and reds, and 5 per cent with the blacks. When we add to this that by the law of chance, other things (such as the training of the observers, etc.) being equal, as many of the "uncertains" in each category will be recorded right as wrong, and that those recorded wrong in one class will be counterbalanced by the wrongs of the next, it may be seen that unless there is a lack of due instruction, a negligence, or the development of some special bias on the part of an observer, his records on any large series of individuals will be substantially correct and comparable with those of all other similarly instructed and careful workers. That this is so may be shown in our series in Virginia. In a camp of the United States Corps of Engineers, near Charlottesville, after due initiation the work was left in the hands of Dr. Robert Bennett Bean, of the University of Virginia; and the results, except for a slight difference which developed in recording the eye colors, were practically identical with those of the author as far as the latter applied to the same general territory.

The study of hair color among the Old Americans fully confirms previous observations on the change in the color of the hair with age. Except in those with the darkest shades the hair in general shows from infancy on to adult life and in many cases even through a part of the adult life, a progressive darkening. The lightest hair in an infant may thus eventually become light, medium, or even fairly dark-brown—though not black. Even the red hair darkens or loses its purity. The golden also is unstable. A small series of near-adults found by the writer among the teachers shows, as will be shown later on, a very perceptibly higher grade of lightness than that of the fully adult of the same class. In some persons the darkening of the hair seems to progress until the time when the first traces of graying (in individual hairs) commence. This progressive darkening of the hair has been observed in all white people with hair lighter than dark brown or black. Its

TABLE 7

Old Americans: Color of Hair

	LIGHTS PROPER	LIGHT BROWN (NOT BLOND)	MEDIUM (MEDIUM BROWN)	DARKS (DARK, DARK BROWN, NEAR BLACK)	BLACK	REDS
	per cent	*per cent*	*per cent*	*per cent*	*per cent*	*per cent*
Males (1,009).........	5.3	16.0	50.0	25.0	1.1	2.6
Females (914).........	6.9	14.2	42.9	29.8	1.3	4.9

TABLE 8

Old Americans: Color of hair, details

	LIGHTS PROPER			Light brown (not blond)	MEDIUM	DARK	BLACK	REDS
	Blond	Golden or yellow	Light brown (near blond)					
	per cent	*per cent*	*per cent*	*per cent*	*per cent*	*per cent*	*per cent*	*per cent*
Males.....	1.2	0.6	3.5	16.0	50.0	25.0	1.1	2.6
Females...	0.9	1.6	4.4	14.2	42.9	29.8	1.3	4.9

causes are not yet well understood. It means, of course, a progressively greater production of the hair pigment, but whether this is due to environmental stimuli, metabolic changes, or phylogenetic influence, is not as yet determined. There are decided individual variations in this respect, and possibly also sexual, locality and other differences. The whole subject deserves a separate deep-going investigation.

Our records on the distribution of hair color among the old Americans, as finally tabulated, are shown in table 7.

These figures are striking in more than one respect. Over three-fourths of the adult Old Americans have hair ranging from medium to dark and black, while but one in 14.5 among the females and one in near 16 among the the males is in hair truly blond. The females, as contrasted with the males, show a few more blonds and more reds, but also more darks, while the males give a predominance of the lighter and medium shades of brown.[3] The females show the greater diversity.

An even closer insight into the conditions is, however, possible.   Table 8 gives the more detailed colors.

The golden and yellow among the females are seen to be more than twice, the near-blonds once and a half, as frequent as they are in the males.   The males, as seen before, predominate in the submedium and medium browns. In the darker shades the females have a larger representation than the males, and this domination, as will be noted later on, is of significance.   It may also be stated in this connection that the reds in the females are mostly the more or less golden reds and again the darker reds, while the males appear to monopolize the less attractive shades.

All the above establishes the facts that, (1) the Old Americans are, so far as hair color is concerned, only exceptionally blond, but commonly medium, to brunet; and that, (2) the females show a greater proportion of golden, near-blonds, and reds, but also of dark browns and blacks than the males.   The males are more intermediate, more of a blend, the females apparently more conservative of ancestral differences.

Tested by subdivisions of 100 or more, the above data hold fairly good, so that they may probably be regarded as a true expression of the conditions in these respects among the territorially mixed Old Americans in the eastern half of the United States.   But in localities where some definite group of immigrants has settled, such for example as the Scotch, Pennsylvania "Dutch," the French, etc., the conditions will doubtless differ in harmony with the original pigmentation of the group.   The ancestral influence in pigmentation appears everywhere to be tenacious.

The above results indicate that blondness is not characteristic of the Old Americans.   There are in addition but a modest proportion of reds and exceedingly few true blacks.   Half of the people are medium, three-quarters are medium to dark haired.   The affinity of the Old Americans with the Nordic blonds is seen from this to be rather secondary, unless substantial changes in the direction of greater pigmentation have been realized in the Americans since their sojourn on this continent—which, however, as will be brought out later, is contradicted by facts.

The records on the two sexes show, it was observed, interesting differences,

---

[3] It goes without saying that care was exercised not to include any cases of hair changed artificially.   Fortunately this is not frequent in this class of people, except perhaps among some of the older persons where the object is to mask grayness and simulate the natural shade.

though the total amount of pigmentation in the two sexes is about the same. The women evidently, it may be repeated, preserve better the different ancestral conditions from which the mixture represented now by the Old Americans arose, while the men show more fusion, more blend.   Similar facts, including the preponderance of the darker shades in the females, have been noted elsewhere.   The English observers in particular have shown that the women of Great Britain tend to be darker than the men.   From Beddoe's data Parsons[4] found that among the English the females were, according to regions, darker haired than the men by from 0.6 to 6.5 per cent.   Fleure and James[5] found similar conditions—that is, a greater predominance of darks among the females than among the males—in Wales, and Gray with Tocher[6] in Scotland.   The latter have also shown further by their studies on Scotch children[7] that the greater darkening of the females is a postnatal, or rather postinfantile, phenomenon.

For purposes of sexual as well as group or racial comparison, it would be very convenient if it were possible to reduce the different classes of hair color to approximate numerical values.   It seems well worth while to make an attempt in this direction.   Let us take pigmentless hair as 0, black hair as 100, and medium hair as 50.   It will then be reasonable to assign to the "Light-brown" (not blond) class the mean value of 25 and to the light or blond (with golden, yellow, and light-brown near blond) that of 12.5; while the "Darks" will be 75.   For red hair, the most difficult to gauge, we may perhaps assume the mean value of 35.   These values, which are not as arbitrary as they might seem, will be seen better in a little table:

Assumed values of hair colors

Lights proper (blonds or near)	12.5
Light brown (not blond)	25.0
Medium	50.0
Dark	75.0
Black	100.0
Red	35.0

If now our records on hair pigmentation be presented in these values, we obtain the data in table 9.

The females are on the whole approximately 1.5 per cent darker than the males.   This proportion will naturally differ with region as the actual

[4] J. Anthrop. Inst., 1920, L, 166–167. See also Beddoe, J.—Anthropological History of Europe, 1912 ed., 98.

[5] J. Anthrop. Inst., 1916, XLVI, 49.

[6] J. Anthrop. Inst., 1900, XXX, 109.

[7] *Ibid.*, 115.

TABLE 9

Old Americans: Units of hair pigmentation

(Per 1,000 subjects)

SHADE	MALES	FEMALES
Lights proper.............................	662	862
Light brown (not blond)........................	4,025	3,550
Medium.......................................	25,000	21,450
Dark...	18,750	22,350
Black..	1,100	1,300
Reds...	910	1,715
	50,447	51,227

Males: Females:: 100: 101.5.

TABLE 10

Regional distribution of hair color in the Old Americans

REGION	LIGHTS (LIGHTS PROPER AND LIGHT BROWN)	MEDIUM	DARKS (DARK TO BLACK)	REDS
Males				
New England* (65)......................	26.1	55.4	16.9†	1.5
Middle East and mixed (449)...............	22.4	45.2	29.6	2.7
South (District of Columbia and southward) (369)..................................	22.3	48	27.1	2.7
Appalachians (Tennessee and neighboring) (126).................................	12.7	69.8	15.1	2.4
Females				
New England (41)........................	39.0	34.1	26.8†	
East and mixed (339).....................	21.0	37.2	36.3	5.6
South (534).............................	19.8	47.2	28.1	4.9

	BLONDS AND LIGHT BROWN	MEDIUM	DARK (TO BLACK)	MEDIUM AND DARK	RED
Both sexes					
New England (106)..............	32.6	44.8	21.9	(66.7)	0.7
Middle east and mixed (788).....	21.7	41.3	32.9	(74.2)	4.1
South (903)....................	21.1	47.6	27.6	(75.2)	3.7

* All American ancestors of the subject lived in the regions here given, not merely the individual recorded.

† No blacks.

records may differ, but in all our subdivision the female shows a greater total.

Geographical differences

Attention was given from the start of the studies to possible indications of regional differences in pigmentation, especially between the North and the South; but nothing striking or definite became manifest in this direction. What differences do exist became apparent only after the data were reduced to percentages. The results are shown in table 10.

The regional differences in hair color, it can be seen from the above figures, are not very material; yet there are differences and in a measure, as to between North and South, they partly bear out the common notion. In both sexes among the "Yankees" there is a larger proportion of lights and a somewhat smaller percentage of darks than in the South. The hair among the Old Americans of the South may therefore be said to be less frequently blond and somewhat more frequently dark than that of the same class of the population in the New England region. But the Old Americans of the Middle East and of mixed-State parentage agree very closely with those of farther South, showing, if anything, even a good trace more of darks, though if we take the mediums and darks together the proportions are almost identical. In all the regions it is noticeable that the females present a larger proportion of darks than the males, indicating a deep-rooted tendency in this direction. In the New England States there appear also more female than male blonds and less intermediates. The females show less intermediates throughout the series.

A very interesting locality group is that of the more northern Appalachian highlanders. They show the least lights as well as darks and by far the most intermediates of any of the groups. This is in all probability the result of a more thorough intermixture, due to inbreeding. The mountaineer, as long as he remains in the mountains, marries almost invariably in the mountains. The group affords a good indication of what would very likely eventually take place in the whole body of Old Americans were there no mixture from outside of their own circles.

The conclusions may be summarized in the statement that the ordinary conception of the southern Americans being darker than the "Yankees" or New Englanders is sustained to but a moderate extent; that there is no appreciable difference, as relates to hair color, between the southern and Old Americans at large; but that isolated groups in the South and possibly also in the North may be expected to show more or less exceptional conditions, according to ancestry and grade of intermixture or inbreeding.

Red hair

The subject of red hair, like that of age changes in hair color, is not yet fully understood and needs a thorough reinvestigation. The two prevailing theories are, first, that "it is a variant of fair hair, because it so often accompanies a freckled skin and light eyes;" and second, that "it shows a mixture between a light and a dark race" (Parsons, o. c., 182). The English records "seem to help both theories . . . . Scotland and the north of England are the fairest parts of the kingdom, and it is there that red hair is most marked, but it is also well marked in Wales and in parts of Ireland, especially Kerry, where the nigrescence is very high."

From the English records it would appear that there is no regular sex difference in the proportion of redness. In 66 locality groups (Beddoe's observations), 30 show a larger percentage of reds in the females, 32 in males, and in 4 the proportion was equal. The whole group of Beddoe's males gives a red hair percentage of 4.4, the equally large group of females 4.9. From the same data Persons finds that "red hair is more common in the upper than in the lower classes," to which he adds (o. c., 182) that, according to his own observations, not only is red hair commoner in the upper classes, but that these classes have also an altogether lower index of nigrescence; in other words, are less pigmented than the lower.

In the course of the study on the Old Americans the impression grew that the category of "red hair" is not wholly homogeneous, and that it probably includes more than one related condition. There are "reds" in whom the whole system participates in the phenomenon. The eyes in such individuals are pale light blue or greenish, the skin is akin to the rosy skin of the albino or looks anaemic, the breast areola is devoid of pigment, the mucous membranes are pink red. Also these individuals are generally believed to differ more or less mentally, as well is in their predispositions to various ailments, from the average of the populations. And there are other "reds," generally of the darker and sandy shades, in whom the rest of the system does not participate so much in the condition, is not peculiar, in other words, to any marked extent. It may be that the differences are merely those of degree; we shall not know until the subject is exhaustively investigated by itself. A study of the blood may one day help to clear matters.

Red hair, or at least some of it, also changes with age. Some such hair grows nearer to brown, loses its luster and beauty and loses the golden reflex; while some simply darkens.

A relation of red hair to the brown is very evident. Most brown hair in certain light shows a more or less marked trace of red, and the moustache of brown-haired men is generally more or less "rusty," that is, nearer red.

A relation to the blonds is not apparent, except perhaps through the golden red.   It is a golden red which accompanies all shades of color down to dark brown.   On the whole, red hair seems to imply a partial loss of pigment from the hair, a loss limited possibly to the outer layers of hair cells.   It is most probably a phase of depigmentation, not a variant of blondness; and the red pigment, if it exists as such, appears to be only a form of the ordinary pigment which gives a brown reflection.

The relation of red hair to the color of the eyes will be dealt with later. The relation of red hair frequency to social status, as believed to exist in England, did not become apparent among the Old Americans where, if we leave out the mountaineers, there is little class distinction.   Our highest group socially (on the whole), that of the Laboratory, gave for the men the frequency of 2.2, our lowest 2.0 per cent of red hair; while what could be taken

TABLE 11

Color of eyes in the red-haired

Males

SERIES AND OBSERVER	RED-HAIRED	EYES		
		Light	Inter-mediate	Dark
	per cent of all subjects	*per cent*	*per cent*	*per cent*
Danish recruits, 20 years (2000)*..........	4.7	87.2	11.7	1.1
Swedish recruits (Retzius and Fürst)†.......	2.3	1.6	0.6	0.1
		69.6	*26.1*	*4.3*

* Hansen (Sören), and Paul Topinard, La couleur des yeux et des cheveux en Dane-marck. *Rev. d' Anthrop.*, 1888, III, 39–41.

† Retzius (Gustaf), and Carl M. Fürst, Anthropologia Suecica. Fol., Stockholm, 1902.

as an intermediate group showed 3.0 per cent.   Geographically, the least red hair (men but 1 case, women 0) occurs in our series of the New England States; the most (men 2.7, women 5.6 per cent) in the Middle Eastern States, and in those of mixed parentage from more than one State.

Eye colors in the red-haired.   An interesting inquiry was that into the association of eye colors with red hair.   It is common knowledge that red hair is generally associated with light eyes.

Previous observations on the subject are few in number.   Table 11 shows results of two such series.

Our records will not be strictly comparable with the above, for in the examinations on the Old Americans special attention was given to "mixed" eyes which ordinarily pass for the most part as "light;" nevertheless there will be seen an important correspondence in the low percentage of browns. Our records show the conditions in table 12.

A little over one-third of the red-haired Old Americans have light eyes. A little less than a half of these (46 per cent of the group or 17 per cent of the whole series of reds) are "light eyes—light reds," and to somewhere near that extent only may we assume red hairedness to be directly associated with blondness. In the rest of the cases with pure light eyes the hair was medium-brownish- or chestnut-red.

A large proportion of the eyes in the red haired are mixed. In the whole series studied the proportion of mixed eyes was approximately 48 per cent, in the red haired it is 57 per cent; a plain excess for the latter. This excess, as well as the whole proportion of mixed eyes in the red haired, points to the conclusion that red hairedness is strongly associated with mixture of blonds and brunets; that, in other words, it represents partial depigmentation or repigmentation.

TABLE 12

Eye color in individuals with red hair

Both sexes

BLUE			GREENISH	GRAYISH	MIXED	BROWN		
Light	Medium	Deep				Light	Medium	Dark
per cent	*per cent*	*per cent*	*per cent*	*per cent*	*per cent*	*per cent*	*per cent*	*per cent*
6.2	16.9		7.7	6.2	56.9		6.2	
	23.1							
Lights, 37					Mixed, 57	Browns, 6		

In a small per cent of our cases red hair was associated with eyes that were pure medium brown. The hair ranged in these individuals from light-red and salmon-red to brown-red and chestnut-red. As the brown eye is believed to be dominant over the lights in mixtures, the mixtures of types in these cases may have remained occluded; but a partial depigmentation of the hair from any other cause might possibly have been sufficient. We should scarcely be justified, in other words, without much further inquiry into the subject, in regarding red hair in the progeny of brunet parents as an absolute proof of admixture into the family of either a red or blond haired outsider.

The conclusions concerning red hair may be briefly summarized as follows:

1. Red hair appears to be merely a form of depigmentation (or partial repigmentation).

1

2

3

4

FAIR SAMPLES OF OLD AMERICANS

1. Miss Edith Cherry
(University, Va.)
3. Miss Betsey M. Bull
(Clinton, Conn.)

2. Mrs. Frank J. Hughes
(Omaha, Neb.)
4. Miss May Croskery
(St. Louis, Mo.)

2. In traces and minor degrees it is a far more common condition than generally appreciated.

3. In a large majority of cases it is connected with the mixture of light with darker types of individuals.

4. In a minority of cases it may probably exist without mixture as a variation in the direction of depigmentation (or partial repigmentation).

5. There are red-haired individuals in whom the depigmentation involves markedly the whole system, approaching more or less albinism and an abnormal condition.

6. There is no line of demarkation between red hair and golden on one side and red hair and the different shades of brown on the other.

Anomalies of hair pigmentation

Anomalies of hair pigmentation relate to uniformity in color, occurrence of black or white locks, and premature or delayed grayness. But little in these respects was noticed among the Old Americans, if we disregard slight to moderate irregularities in shading (lighter or darker strands).

Two individuals, however, one male and one female, showed different colored tufts (or locks) of hair. The female had a white lock in dark hair above the forehead; the male a black tuft in otherwise uniform medium brown hair above the fore part of the right temporal region. In one female 45 years of age most of the hair on the right side was medium brown, while the whole left side was (naturally) perceptibly darker.

COLOR OF EYES

To properly gauge the eye color is a fairly simple matter in some groups of the white race, such as the purer Nordics or the Mediterraneans, but it becomes a difficult task in much mixed strains such as that of the English and especially the Americans.

To approach the subject properly we should be clear to start with on the elementary question as to what is eye color. The many shades of eyes to be met with, as with the hair, do not represent so many different pigments but only so many grades and varieties of pigmentation and depigmentation. The eye pigment, like that in the skin and doubtless also in the hair, is there for protection, and though it may not be strictly simple or homogeneous it behaves essentially as one pigment, which is distributed in small granules in the lining and certain interstitial cells of the iris. The color of the iris is a reflection of light according to the quantity, density, and distribution of the pigment granules. If these granules are in considerable numbers and dis-

tributed throughout the endothelial, interstitial, and even epithelial cells of
the iris, the eye is brown to "black," the shade differing with the total
quantity and density of the granules. With the maximum density the
eye is black, as in some negroes; on the other hand, as the quantity of the
pigment decreases we have gradually a lighter and lighter shade of brown
until this passes into light brown, then gray or greenish with brownish tinge,
then bluish or greenish gray, and finally, when no pigment remains in either
the anterior lining or the interstitial cells of the iris with but little in the
endothelium, the eye is blue.

As in the skin and hair, so here again there are no lines of demarcation
between the various shades, and we must make a somewhat arbitrary
classification. In this we may recognize to start with two great groups, the
pure eyes and the mixed. The pure in their turn are capable of three subdivisions, the browns, the blues, and the lights other than blue (gray,
greenish); and the browns and blues are further subdivisible each into the
dark (or deep), medium and light. Intermediary tinges occur appearing
different under varying conditions of light, health, and mental state, and
can be classified only with difficulty.

The "mixed" eye is strictly speaking a misnomer. It does not mean an
eye with a mixture of any two distinct pigments, but an eye resulting from a
mixture of a brown-eyed with a lighter parent, in which the parental conditions so far as eye color is concerned are not well blended. If the eyes of
the parents are on one side brown and on the other light, the eyes of some
the progeny may show a darker or lighter blend of the parental colors; the
eyes of some may show one or the other parental shade dominating with the
other in recession; but the eyes of most of the children will bear traces of
the mixture in an unequal distribution of the pigment derived from the
darker parent.[8] It is these last eyes alone that the observer can designate
as "mixed."

The "mixtures" are of many kinds, but they are all characterized by some
imperfection in the distribution of the brown. This may occur as already
mentioned, as a narrower or broader ring about the pupil; as a greater or lesser dispersion of brown spots, with an aggregation about the pupil; in the
form of brown patches or stains of color over the iris, with lighter regions;

[8] The laws of heredity in this connection are still under investigation. See Davenport
(C. B.)—Heredity of Eye-Color in Man. Science, 1907, XXVI, 589; Hurst (C. C.)—
On the Inheritance of Eye-Color in Man. Proc. R. Soc., 1908, 80: 8; Boas (Helene M.)
—Inheritance of Eye-Color in Man. Am. J. Phys. Anthrop., 1919, II, 15–20; and es-
pecially Bryn (Halfdan)—Researches Into Anthropological Heredity. Hereditas, 1920,
I, 186 et seq.

and rarely in the form of a single brown wedge-shaped segment radiating from the pupil to the periphery of the iris, or a big brown splotch.

From the above it will be seen that the only rational classification of eye color can be about as follows:

Eye colors

(Largely)
Depigmented, pure......Blues....................{Light.
                                                 {Medium.
                                                 {Deep.

                        Gray.
                        Greenish.
                        Grayish-blue.
                        Greenish-blue.

                                                 {Light.
Pigmented.............Brown...................{Medium.
                                                 {Dark.

                        Black, or near black.

Mixed.................Light brown..............} With   rings,   spots,
                      Gray....................} patches, areas, stains,
                      Greenish or blue.........} or segments of brown.

All records on eye color, however carefully made, necessarily bear the following imperfections: A small number of the apparently pure light browns, and other-than-blue lights, will belong to the category of only apparently and unstably, (in relation to progeny) pures; they are mixed in which the mixture is not clearly perceivable. A small proportion of the medium browns will be in the same category. A superficial observation in addition will inevitably result in classing many of the mixeds as pures.[9] The colors which are most free from error are the pure blues and the darker browns, in which it will merely be a question of classification errors along the boundaries.

There have been many former attempts at a satisfactory classification of eye color, and several "standards" have been made by which to record these colors. Being largely empirical, however, none of these, either classifications or standards, are fully satisfactory. In the present studies reliance was placed on the above outlined analysis of the colors, on due regulations of the procedure, on large practice, and on constant intensive care. All eyes were examined in clear light and at the distance of best vision, the "reading distance." The use of artificial standards, after sufficient expertness was acquired, was found unnecessary and hindering rather than facilitating the study.

[9] In old subjects additional difficulties are encountered due to varying senile depigmentation; but seniles do not enter into our series.

With all the above regulations and precautions it is certain that the results on eye color here recorded are still imperfect; though they are probably as near true as they can be made under present conditions.

The number of records on eye color among the Old Americans is the same as that on the hair, namely, 1009 males and 914 females; and the total data give the general results shown in table 13.

More than half of the eyes among the Old Americans are plainly mixed, such an eye, in general, being a light of some sort with specks, ring or other plain traces of brown. Approximately one-third in males and one-fourth in females are as far as can be seen pure lights, and one-sixth in males with one-fifth in females are apparently pure browns. The females have less pure lights and more browns, showing again the tendency towards somewhat greater pigmentation.

The data in table 13 contrast in an interesting way with those on hair (table 14).

There is seen to exist a marked general correspondence of lights with lights, medium hair with mixed eyes, and of darks with darks; but already these gross figures show that there are more light eyes than light hair and more dark hair than dark eyes, indicating that on the whole the hair tends towards a greater pigmentation, or is tardier in depigmentation, than the eyes. It is known that this tendency, while universal, is particularly noticeable in certain districts or among certain racial groups in Europe. The Irish are a good example.

Additional features of interest, so far as the eyes of the Old Americans are concerned, are shown by a more detail classification (table 15).

There are a number of points of special interest. The light-blue eyes are more than twice as common in the males than in the females; the medium blues are about equal in the two sexes; the deep blues are nearly twice as frequent in the females as in the males. There is therefore a tendency in males toward the lighter, in the females toward the darker shades of blue. This is in all probability connected with the general tendency of the females toward a greater eye pigmentation, which is shown very plainly by the browns. The females show also less of both the pure greenish and the grayish eyes, which most likely is equally due to the phenomenon just mentioned.

We may well ask in this place just why this tendency toward greater pigmentation in the female hair and eyes should exist. So far as known to the writer, while this fact has been recorded again and again, no serious attempt has yet been made at showing the reason. Yet there must be reasons, and judging from the generality of the tendency, they are more likely to be of inherited than of individually acquired nature.

The following facts may have a bearing on this question.   In the section
on skin pigmentation it was seen that the skin of the male is more frequently
darker than medium than happens among the females; should this fact be
substantiated elsewhere, we would be justified in assuming that the skin in
the male takes care on the average of a somewhat larger quantity of the pig-

TABLE 13

Old Americans: Color of eyes

	APPARENTLY PURE LIGHTS	MIXED	APPARENTLY PURE BROWNS
	per cent	*per cent*	*per cent*
Males (1,009)............................	31.0	52.5	16.5
Females (914)...........................	24.1	55.9	20.0

TABLE 14

Old Americans: Contrast of hair and eye color

	HAIR			EYES		
	Lights*	Medium	Darks	Pure lights	Mixed	Pure browns
	per cent	*per cent*	*per cent*	*per cent*	*per cent*	*per cent*
Males................	22.2	50.8	27.0	31.0	52.5	16.5
Females..............	22.7	44.6	32.7	24.1	55.9	20.0

* To each category is added one-third of the reds. For details as to eye-colors in the
red-haired see previous section on Red Hair.

TABLE 15

Old Americans: Color of eyes, details

	PURE LIGHTS					MIXED	PURE BROWNS		
	Blues			Other lights					
	Light	Medium	Deep	Greenish-blue and greenish	Grayish-blue and gray		Light	Medium	Dark
	per cent	*per cent*	*per cent*	*per cent*	*per cent*	*per cent*	*per cent*	*per cent*	*per cent*
Males.........	7.9	14.8	1.1	2.2	5.0	52.5	4.5	9.3	2.7
Females......	2.9	15.2	1.9	1.4	2.7	55.9	2.2	13.8	4.0

ment produced in the body, while in the female, should she produce proportionately to her weight as much pigment as man, the surplus would be
likely to go into the eyes and hair.   In addition, the male discharges a
substantial quantum of pigment through his beard, moustache, and greater
body hairiness, as well as through the hair of the head, for due to the fre-

quent cuttings a man produces on the average more hair on his head than a
female.   All this disposes in the male of a considerable amount of the pigment formed in the body, so that if the sexes produced the same or nearly
the same amount per pound of active tissue, there would be a surplus of
pigment in the female which would inevitably, it seems, affect the pigmentation of both the eyes and the hair.   There is no indication that there is any
greater production of pigment in the female, but she evidently differs slightly
in the manner of its disposition and elimination.

The relative pigmentation of eyes in the two sexes may also, as in the case
of hair, be presented in the form of values.   If the subject is carefully
weighed, and taking the completely depigmented eye as 0, with the most
pigmented "black" eye or 100, it will be found that about the following
approximate values may be assigned to the different eye colors here dealt
with:

Assumed values of eye colors

Pure lights:
    Blues—
        Light.. 10
        Medium.. 20
        Deep.. 25
        Greenish... 15
        Gray... 30
    Mixed... 50
Pure browns:
    Light.. 65
    Medium.. 75
    Dark.. 85

Arranging our data on this basis, we obtain the interesting results shown
in table 16.

A few words only are necessary to supplement the above figures.   The
pigmentation of the eye among the females in the Old Americans is to that of
the males as 108.1 to 100; the female eye in other words is approximately 8
per cent darker.   The rest of the differences parallel what has already been
shown by the simple percentages.

It is curious to observe that the differences in the eye pigmentation exceed
those in the hair.   The same phenomenon, as will be seen later, has been
observed in England and is probably true elsewhere.

Geographical differences

As with the hair, so with the eyes the main interest as to regional differences in pigmentation attaches to the question of differences between the
north and south.   Table 17 shows these relations.

The differences in eye color between the South and the North and between either of these and the Middle States, are seen to be only slight, even less

TABLE 16

Units of eye pigmentation

(Per 1,000 subjects)

SHADE	MALE	FEMALE
Purelights:		
Blues—		
Light....................................	790	290
Medium................................	2,960	3,040
Dark.....................................	275	475
	4,025	3,805
Greenish and greenish-blue.....................	330	210
Gray and grayish-blue.........................	1,500	810
	5,855	4,825
Mixed...	26,250	27,900
Pure browns:		
Light.....................................	2,925	1,430
Medium...................................	6,975	10,350
Dark......................................	2,295	3,400
	12,195	15,180
Total..	44,300	47,905

Eyes—Males: Females:: 100: 108.1.
Hair—Males: Females:: 100: 101.5.

TABLE 17

Regional distribution of eye color in the Old American

REGION	BOTH SEXES TOGETHER		
	Pure lights	Mixed	Pure browns
	per cent	*per cent*	*per cent*
New England............................	32.8	48.0	19.2
Middle East and mixed*..................	24.4	55.8	19.8
South...................................	30.8	52.0	17.2
Appalachians (Tennessee and South)........	24.6	62.8	12.6

* Part of forbears from Northern, part from Central, or Southern States.

than with the hair.   There are a few more lights, but also a few more browns among the Yankees than among the Southerners, but the differences are too

small to be given any special significance.   There is, however, as with the
hair, a marked difference from all the other groups shown by the Appalachian mountaineers, among whom there are less pure lights, less pure
browns, and a larger proportion of mixed shades, than in any of the other
Old American series.   It was seen (p. 000) that precisely the same conditions were observed in this special group in relation to hair colors.

Correlation of eye and hair color

In order to make the presentation of the records here dealt with as clear
as possible, it will be necessary to show, besides the separate data on hair
and eyes, also the associations of conditions.   Not every light eye is accompanied with light hair, thereby enabling us to class the subject as blond,
nor every dark hair with a dark eye, giving us a well-marked brunet.   There
are many exceptions in fact to such asociations.   Conditions were found in
brief, as shown in table 18.

TABLE 18

Old Americans: Correlation in eye and hair pigmentation, both sexes

(Percentage in round numbers)

EYES	HAIR			
	Lights	Medium	Dark	Reds
	per cent	*per cent*	*per cent*	*per cent*
Pure lights....................	37.5	48.0	12.0	2.5
Mixed.......................	20.0	50.0	26.0	4.0
Pure browns.................	9.5	43.0	46.0	1.5

Persons among the Old Americans with light eyes that show no trace of
brown, have in nearly two-fifths of their number also light hair, while in
approximately one-half of these cases the hair is medium, and in nearly
one-eighth it is dark.   Red hair occurs in this category, but in slightly
lesser proportion than in the general average.

Those with mixed eyes (lights with more or less marked traces of brown),
have light hair in only one-fifth, medium hair on one-half, and dark hair in
one-fourth of their number.   In respect of both the light and dark hair they
stand, as might be expected, practically midway between the pure light-
eyed and pure brown-eyed series.   But they show more mediums, and
decidedly more reds, than either the pure light-eyed or pure brown-eyed
groups.   The frequency of red hair in this class of subjects indicates the
close association of, perhaps, as many as half of the cases of red hair with
mixture of the lighter and the darker racial elements in the population.

The brown eyed show but a few light haired, and these as a rule of the least blond variety; they have somewhat less frequently than either the light eyed or the mixed eyed, hair of medium shade; but they show in nearly half the instances hair dark to black. Also they show the least reds, and these only in association with the lighter browns of the iris.

Still further insight into these conditions may be obtained if the data are studied with even a little more detail (table 19).

The above figures show conditions quite clearly. The lighter the blue eye, the greater the proportion of light hair and the smaller that of medium and

TABLE 19

*Old Americans: Correlation of eye and hair pigmentation, details, both sexes**
(Percentages in round numbers)

EYES	HAIR		
	Lights	Medium	Darks
	per cent	*per cent*	*per cent*
Pure lights:			
Blues—			
Light..........................	53.0	43.0	2.5
Medium.......................	35.0	48.0	14.0
Deep.	25.0	50.0	20.0
Other lights:			
Greenish and greenish-blue............	31.0	50.0	15.5
Gray and grayish-blue................	34.0	52.5	13.5
Mixed. .'.....................................	19.5	50.5	25.5
Pure browns:			
Light..............................	22.5	50.0	27.5
Medium...........................	9.5	50.0	38.0
Dark..............................	4.0	22.5	73.5

* The Reds need not be considered in this connection.

especially dark hair; the deeper the blue, the less light, the more medium and especially the more dark hair. It is plain that there is a considerable direct correlation between the depth of the blue in the iris and the amount of pigment in the hair. This corroborates the view that the pigment in the blue eye is not different from that in the brown eye, but is merely less in quantity and differently deposited. The greenish and grayish eyes, in relation to hair, are much like the medium blue, though showing somewhat more medium hair. Possibly they hide some mixtures. The brown-eyed show the same type of correlation as the blues—the darker the eye the less light, and even medium, and the more dark the hair. Those with dark-brown eyes have no blonds proper, but a few instances of light-brown—not blond—hair and less than one-fourth of medium, but in nearly three-fourths the hair is dark to black.

The above shows that in general the more pigment there is in the eye the

TABLE 20

AGE	LOCALITY	HAIR	EYES
		Males	
51	Virginia	Dark brown	Mixed; *right* shows more brown than *left*.
43	Virginia	Medium brown	*Right* greenish; *left* fine medium blue.
43	Virginia	Near black	*Right* gray, traces brown; *left*, medium brown, traces gray.
23	Maryland	Medium brown	*Right* medium blue; *left* medium blue, traces brown.
		Females	
18	Virginia	Dark brown	Mixed, *right* shows very perceptibly more brown than *left*.
18	Mixed	Dark brown	Light blue, slight tinge of brown in *left*; more in *right*.
25	Virginia	Light brown	*Right* gray; *left* lighter than right.
30	Mixed	Medium brown	Gray; *right* traces brown, *left* pure.
32	Mixed	Medium brown	*Right* dark brown; *left* greenish-brown.
34	Pennsylvania	Dark brown	*Right* pure grayish-blue; *left* same, but with a nice speck of brown.
45	Virginia	Golden brown	*Right* pure deep blue; *left* same with a brown patch.
		Triangular wedges or segments*—Females†	
24	Virginia	Medium brown	*Right* pure medium blue; *left* same but with large segment of yellow-brown.
24	North Carolina	Medium brown	Light greenish; in *left* a nice wedge of medium brown‡
30	Virginia	Medium brown	Medium gray; *right* shows a clear-cut wedge of medium brown.

* Beginning at a point on the inner and diverging toward the outer border of the iris.

† Since these examinations were terminated a fine example of a stout brown wedge in a grayish-blue iris (the other eye medium grayish-blue with traces of brown) was found in an elderly male of British extraction.

‡ Father has brown, mother light eyes.

more there is also in the hair. There are individual exceptions where the hair is lighter than the eyes, but they are not numerous.

Anomalies of eye pigmentation

Eye pigmentation shows occasionally interesting anomalies. They are limited to the "mixed" eyes, and seem to be more frequent in females. Also, most of them came from the Southern States, which, however, may be an accident. Those observed are shown in table 20.

No case was observed where one eye was brown and the other light though one was learned of.

The most interesting of the anomalies are the wedges or segments of brown in one of the otherwise pure and uniform light eyes. They remind one distantly of the eyes of lizards. The phenomenon is of course a sign of mixture, and possibly also of a peculiar histological condition in the given iris.

Blonds and brunets

The terms "blond" and "brunet" are general terms which have as yet no scientifically fixed meaning. As a result when two persons and even two scientists speak of blonds and brunets their meaning may differ.

"Pure blonds" may be defined as those persons who have flaxen, blond, golden, yellow, or light brown (near-blond) hair, with pure (unmixed) light eyes. More ordinarily, or loosely, all those persons are regarded as "blonds," who have light hair of one or another of the above varieties, with light eyes whether the latter are pure or would on close examination show traces of brown. And in a still more general way there may be classified as "fair" all those who have hair lighter than medium (including all reds except those of the darkest shades), with light eyes, whether the eyes are pure or would show a mixture on closer scrutiny.

As to "true brunets," that class naturally comprises those with dark to black hair and medium to dark brown eyes. "Apparent brunets" would be all those with dark to black hair regardless of the color of the eyes.

Those who do not enter into any one of the above classes are necessarily the "intermediates."

If we arrange our records on this rational though crude basis, we obtain the figures in table 21.

This table shows clearly that over one-half of the Old American males and nearly one-half of the females are neither blonds nor brunets, but intermediates. True and even ordinary blonds are scarce, while true brunets are but little more frequent. Using the most general classification, we see that approximately but one-fifth of the males and one-fourth of the females may be classed as "fair"; and a little over one-fourth of the males with a little over three-tenths of the females as "dark," or apparent brunets. The nature of these results is a good expression of ancestral light and darker types, with the latter probably slightly in predominance.

TABLE 21

Old Americans: Blonds and brunets

(Percentage in round numbers)

	PURE BLONDS	ORDINARY BLONDS*	"FAIR"†	TRUE BRUNETS	APPARENT BRUNETS‡	INTER-MEDIATES
	per cent	*per cent*	*per cent*	*per cent*	*per cent*	*per cent*
Males (1,009).........	3.0	5.0	21.0	6.5	26.0	53.0
Females (914).........	3.5	6.5	24.0	11.0	31.0	46.0

* Includes of course the "pure blonds."
† Includes the pure and ordinary blonds.
‡ Includes true brunets.

TABLE 22

Old Americans: Blonds and brunets according to region, both sexes

(Percentage in round numbers)

	PURE BLONDS	ORDINARY BLONDS*	"FAIR"†	TRUE BRUNETS	APPARENT BRUNETS‡	INTER-MEDIATE
	per cent	*per cent*	*per cent*	*per cent*	*per cent*	*per cent*
New England (106)........	(13) 12.0	(18) 17.0	(32) 30.0	(4) 4.0	(22) 21.0	(52) 49.0
Eastern States and mixed State ancestry (788)......	(29) 4.0	(49) 6.0	(171) 22.0	(83) 10.5	(256) 32.0	(361) 46.0
South (903)...............	(19) 2.0	(38) 4.0	(211) 23.0	(77) 8.5	(250) 28.0	(442) 49.0
Appalachians (126).........	(3) 2.5	(6) 5.0	(16) 13.0	(1) 1.0	(19) 15.0	(91) 72.0

* Includes pure blonds.
† Includes pure and ordinary blonds.
‡ Includes true brunets.

The females, even better than in their separate determinations on the eyes and hair, show plainly somewhat more blonds and "fairs" and again more darks, with less intermediates; thus preserving better than the males the ancestral conditions.

Regional distribution

The regional distribution of the blonds and brunets is shown in the table 22.

It is seen that conditions appear with especial plaineness in this form. New England stands well above the other groups in the proportion of blonds, and is also below all except the Appalachian group in the proportion of darks; but it has as many intermediates as the South, and even a few per cent more than the East and mixed States.

The South shows fewer true blonds than any of the other groups; but the "fairs" in general are fully as common in the Eastern States as in the South, while brunets, both true and apparent, are even more numerous in the Americans of Eastern and mixed State ancestry than in those of the South.

The Appalachian group is, as has already been shown, quite exceptional, showing but few blonds and even "fairs," but few brunets, and a very large proportion of intermediates.

The relative darkness of the Old Americans of the Eastern States and of mixed State ancestry is not easy to explain, but they have, doubtless, more Dutch and German and also Irish ancestry than the American of New England or the South, which may account for the showing.

Comparative

The interest of the results of the observations on pigmentation that form the subject of this paper, would be much enhanced could we contrast them with observations on the Americans at large, and on all related peoples. An ideal condition would be if we could also compare them with similar data on the early representatives in America of the families involved, as the present data may perhaps eventually be compared with those on the Americans of the future; but we have no old records of this nature.

The ancestors of the Old Americans, as apparent from the information given the examiner, were very largely, probably more than four-fifths, immigrants from the Britsish Isles. They were English, Welsh, Scotch, Scotch Irish, with a scattering of Dutch, French (Huguenots), Irish, and German. In the absence of Old American records on pigmentation it would in the second line be most desirable, therefore, to have such data from the seventeenth to nineteenth centuries from Great Britain, but these are also wanting. All that is available are data on the English-speaking people from this and the latter part of the last century, and even these we can use only to a limited extent, the observations having been made and recorded

in a different manner. As to data from Holland, Germany, or other countries, they could hardly be of help in this connection.

As to data on Americans in general, there are only the very imperfect
records of the Civil War, and those equally imperfect obtained during the
demobilization after the end of the World War. In neither case were the
observations made by scientific or properly trained men. Baxter (Statistics, etc., I, 60) says of those in the Civil War: "The instructions given to
surgeons of boards of enrollment were framed with a view to the speediest
achievement of the object of the draft, and not to the acquisition of anthropological facts. Thence arose defects in the data, from a scientific point of
view, which have often been regretted during the preparation of this work."[10]
The "Army Anthropology" volume of the World War[11] charitably says nothing about the *actual* methods of securing the data, though it would have been
better to make a straightforward statement. It may suffice to say that the
actual examinations and recording, though under the general supervision
of good men, had to be made in this case after a brief and insufficient instruction, and often under stress and hurry, by numbers of unselected men from
ranks assigned for the "work' by the officers of the camps; men who had no
heart in the work, who had never done anything similar, were unacquainted
with the metric system, had inaccurate instruments as well as classification,
were often seen by the writer, who hoping against hope, visited several of
the camps to satisfy himself as to the nature of the examinations, to be
grossly careless. Moreover the World War records on the pigmentation
of the American-born were made wholly worthless by an incomprehensible
inclusion into these data of those on the "colored." It would be useless to
try to contrast such data with those that are the subject of this memoir.

As to England, the foremost students of pigmentation in the British Isles
so far were Beddoe,[12] Gray and Tocher,[13] Fleure and James,[14] and Parsons.[15]

---

[10] For originals see Gould (B. A.)—The Military and Anthropological Statistics of the
War of the Rebellion. 8°, New York, 1865; Baxter (J. H.)—Statistics, Medical and
Anthropological, of the Provost-Marshal-General's Bureau, 4°, 1875, I, 60. See also
Statistical Report of Sickness and Mortality in U. S. Army from 1839 to 1855. 4°,
Washington, 1856; and Military Statistics of United States of America, 4°, Berlin, 1863.

[11] Davenport (Charles B.) with A. G. Love—Army Anthropology. 8°, Vol. XV of Sta-
tistic Med. Dept., U. S. Army, Washington, 1921.

[12] Beddoe (John)—Races of Britain, 8°, London, 1885.

[13] Gray (John) and Tocher (J. F.)—The physical characteristics of adults and school
children in east Aberdeenshire. J. Anthrop. Inst., 1900, XXX, 104–124; also Trans.
Buchan Field Club, 1897.

[14] Fleure (H. J.) and James (T. C.)—Geographical Distribution of Anthropological
Types in Wales. J. Anthrop. Inst., 1916, XLVI, 35–153.

[15] Parsons (F. G.)—The Color Index of the British Isles. J. Anthrop. Inst., 1920, L,
159–162.

From their data it appears that the pigmentation of the hair and eyes—the skin has not been considered—differs very materially in the different districts and portions of the isles, due to ancestral differences, to an imperfect fusion of the heterogeneous elements of which the population is composed, and to local survivals or domination of certain types. The classification of the color of the hair used by these observers agrees fairly well with ours, and we shall be enabled to make some general comparisons; but with

TABLE 23

Classification of hair and eye color in England and in Old Americans

		ENGLISH	OLD AMERICANS
Hair....		Fair	Light—Blond, golden and yellow, light brown (near blond).
		Brown	Light brown (not blond), medium.
		Dark brown	Dark.
		Black	Black.
		Red	Red.
Eyes....		Light	Pure lights—Blues (light, medium, deep), greenish, grayish.
		Intermediate or neutral	Mixed.
		Dark	Pure browns—Light, medium, dark.

TABLE 24

Color of hair in England and Scotland, and in the Old Americans

Males

HAIR	OLD AMERICANS (1,000)	PRESENT ENGLAND AND SCOTLAND (14,557)
Lights proper....................................	5.3	16.7
Light brown (not blond).........................	16.0	
Medium...	50.0	38.3
Dark...	25.0	34.8
Black..	1.1	5.8
Red..	2.6	4.4

the English data on eye-color comparison will be very difficult. The English records were recently partly summarized by Parsons.[15]

Following Beddoe, the English observers classify the hair into fair (corresponding to our "light"), red, brown (our "medium"), dark and black; while the eyes are classed as light, dark, and intermediate. The relation of this classification to ours will appear best in the table form (table 23).

In the case of the hair the two methods agree tolerably closely, except as to our "light brown (not blond)" which class is omitted from the English records. In the case of the eyes, however, there is much less agreement. Some of the light browns had probably been recorded by the English among the "intermediates;" many light eyes with a brown ring about the pupil, or brown spots, which in our records are all marked as mixed, were doubtless counted by the English among the "lights"; and the slate blues, with some of the darker mixed, they very likely included with the darks.

An additional difficulty for comparing our results arises from the way in which the English records are published. Neither Beddoe nor his followers have given the general averages for the whole of England and Scotland. They report their observations by counties, cities, and other localities, which is of but little use for our purpose. We have no means of finding out from just what parts of England and Scotland the ancestors of our Old American families were derived, and the best we can do in trying to find what differences if any, there are now between the people of Great Britain and the Old Americans, is to compare the combined records of the latter with similarly combined records on Great Britain, or at least on England and Scotland. In order to make some such comparison possible it was necessary to count up Beddoe's detailed data as given by Parsons.[15] The results, contrasted with ours, are given in table 24.

These figures are rather striking. Even if we allow for some error in assigning the different colors to their proper classes on each side, enough seems to remain to show that the English present a greater heterogeneity in hair pigmentation. The Old Americans have apparently less real blonds and certainly less darks and blacks as well as reds, with more blends or intermediates. While the total amount of pigmentation is not greatly different in the two units, in the Americans it shows fewer extremes, which is just about what could be expected from their great intermixture. To make the two series still more comparable, the proportion of the "light brown (not blond)" hair among the Americans could probably be safely distributed one-half to the "fair" and one-half to the "medium" series, in which case we obtain the relations shown in table 25.

We still have for the Old Americans less blonds and reds, less darks, and decidedly more intermediates.

So much for the men. With the females the conditions are similar (table 26).

On the whole the British and the Old American females seem to agree better as to hair color than the males, but like the males show a considerably larger proportion of dark hair than occurs in the Americans.

The records on eyes show the conditions in the two groups under consideration to be as shown in table 27.

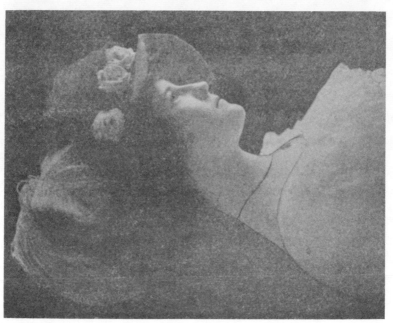

Miss Romar Hening Smith—now Mrs. James Rea Stannard
(New Orleans, La.) (Philadelphia, Pa.)
(Daughter of Mrs. Eleanor Drew)

TABLE 25

Color of hair in England and Scotland, and in the Old Americans

Males

HAIR	OLD AMERICANS	PRESENT ENGLAND AND SCOTLAND
	per cent	*per cent*
Fair...	13.3	16.7
Medium...	58.0	38.3
Dark..	25.0	34.8
Black...	1.1	5.8
Red...	2.6	4.4

TABLE 26

Color of hair in England and Scotland, and in the Old Americans

Females

HAIR	OLD AMERICANS (900)	PRESENT ENGLAND AND SCOTLAND (11,172)
	per cent	*per cent*
Fair (+ one-half light brown not blond in the Old Americans)..................................	14.0	13.1
Medium (+ one-half light brown not blond in the Old Americans)..................................	50.0	38.1
Dark..	29.0	39.3
Black...	1.3	4.8
Red...	4.9	4.7

TABLE 27

Color of eyes in Old Americans contrasted with that in Great Britain

	MALE			FEMALE		
	Light	Inter-mediate or mixed*	Dark (medium and dark brown)	Light	Inter-mediate or mixed*	Dark (medium and dark brown)
	per cent	*per cent*	*per cent*	*per cent*	*per cent*	*per cent*
Old Americans.....................	31.0	57.0	12.0	24.2	58.0	18.0
	88.0			82.2		
England, Wales, and Scotland.......	66.0		34.0	53.3	15.2	31.5
				68.5		

* This group includes also our light browns (in 4.5 of 2.0 per cent), which the English would scarcely have included in their darks.

In view of the manner in which the English records were made, there are no means of separating the pure lights from the mixed lights as in our series, but the English "dark" eyes ought to correspond more closely to our medium plus dark browns class. The results show, however, a very much larger proportion of "dark" eyes in Great Britain than among the Old Americans. The more common occurrence among the English of dark to black hair would lead us to expect also a moderately greater frequency in the same series of dark eyes, but the excess of dark eyes is so great as to justify the suspicion that the Beddoe "dark" eye series includes various eyes besides the medium and dark brown, which makes it uncertain for comparison with our data. After an earnest effort to utilize the English eye records, we are thus left quite helpless. The probability is that the average present eye pigmentation in Great Britain differs only slightly from that of the Old Americans.

Since Beddoe, the English observers have another and convenient, though somewhat artificial, method of expressing their records on pigmentation, and that is through their so-called "index of nigrescence." This index, as modified by Parsons,[16] is obtained by adding the percentage of the dark brown and black hair to that of the dark plus one-half of the intermediary or neutral eyes, and dividing the results by two. Unfortunately, as already seen, their classes of eye colors are very different from ours, which precludes any direct comparison.

However imperfect our efforts at comparison with the English may have been, they leave two impressions of value. The first is that both the Old Americans and the English, if classed by the mean value of their pigmentation, fall not into the "fair" but into the intermediary or medium-pigmented group, which tapers on one side to the fair and on the other to the brunet. We shall come to this point once more later. The second fact is that the English show in their midst less intermixture with consequent blends than do the Old Americans.

The lack of marked difference in pigmentation between the Old Americans and the English does not denote, however, that no changes in this respect have taken place in the Americans since the arrival from Europe of their ancestors. It is quite possible that a gradual progressive darkening may have proceeded in both groups. There are observers in both countries who incline to that opinion. Pigmentation is essentially an environmental and changeable condition, however slow the changes may be. Neither England, nor certainly the United States, are in the sphere of the nordic

[16] J. Anthrop. Inst., 1920, 162.

countries, where blondness was produced and where it is being sustained. And the composition, climate, habits and food of the people in the United States and Great Britain are so similar that the two people might well be assumed, on general considerations, to show a parallel line of changes in a physiological characteristic such as pigmentation.

The whole subject in both countries needs a thorough scientific restudy on a large scale It would be a fallacy to believe that observations, however

TABLE 28

*Color of eyes and hair in the Old Americans and northwestern Europeans**

MALES	EYES			HAIR			
	Light	Inter-mediate	Dark	Blond	Medium	Dark	Red
	per cent	per cent	per cent	per cent	per cent	per cent	per cent
Old Americans (1009)..............	31.0	52.5	16.5	13.3†	58.0	26.1	2.6
England and Scotland (Beddoe's data given by Parsons; 14,557 individuals).....................	66.0		34.0‡	16.7	78.9		4.4
French (Topinard; Department of the Seine, including Paris)........	21.3	48.0	30.7	17.3	45.3	37.4	§
Denmark (Jutland; Sören Hansen; 2000 Recruits).................	76.35	20.4	3.25 -	16.65	63.35	15.3	4.7
Norwegians (Topinard) (data of Arbo and Fay; Recruits).........	80.9	16.8	2.3	52.8	24.4	19.4	3.4
Swedes (G. Retzius; 44,900 Recruits)	66.7	28.8	4.5	75.3	21.6	0.8	2.3

* Data on Scandinavians and Danes rearranged after those in G. Retzius and Carl M. Fürst's Anthropologia Suecica, fol., Stockholm, 1902, 296–7. Those on England are from Beddoe and Parsons.

† Lights (5.3 per cent) together with one-half of light browns, not blond (total of which is 16 per cent).

‡ Doubtless an overstatement due to inclusion of intermediates.

§ Not received.

superficial they might be, if only made on a large enough number of subjects, would ever show true conditions; such data can at best only approximate, but may also more or less mask, if not pervert, the real facts.

Thanks to Topinard, Hansen and Retzius, there are available several additional series of data on western Europeans which show, in rough at least, the general state of pigmentation in these groups and the correlation in hair and eye color. They are given (tables 28 and 29) together with Beddoe's records on the British and the writer's on the Old Americans. They extend to the French, Danes and Scandinavians. Regrettably, however, the data have been gathered by different observers who used different schemes of classification of the color, especially as relates to the eyes. Nevertheless the records are of much interest.

The six series of data divide plainly into two widely separated groups, the first comprising the Americans, British and French: the second the Norwegians and the Swedes. In the first group light eyes occur in less than one-third of the population and blond hair in not over one-sixth; while dark eyes in this group are present in from one-sixth to over one-third and dark hair in from 26 to over 37 per cent of the individuals. In the Scandinavian groups, the light eyes are considerably more than twice, the light hair three to four times as frequent as they are in the British-American-French series; while dark eyes are much scarcer, and dark hair, while present in nearly one-fifth of the cases on Norwegians, is almost absent in the Swedes. The Danes occupy a peculiar position. In regard to eye color they agree

TABLE 29

Relations of color of hair and eyes in recruits, Sweden (G. Retzius)

HAIR	EYES			
	Light	Intermediate	Dark	Totals
	per cent	*per cent*	*per cent*	*per cent*
Blond......................	54.4	19.1	1.8	75.3
Brown....:................	10.5	8.7	2.4	21.6
Black......................	0.2	0.4	0.2	0.8
Red........................	1.6	0.6	0.1	2.3
Totals....................	*66.7*	*28.8*	*4.5*	*100.0*

with the Scandinavians—in regard to hair color they come much closer to the Americans, British and French. These conditions are not readily explained, but it seems plain that the Danes are less advanced in depigmentation, particularly in that of the hair, than are the Scandinavians. The larger proportion of dark hair in the Norwegians than in the Swedes is possibly the result of admixture with the dark-haired predecessors (Finnish or Lappish) of the Norwegians in these regions. The most striking fact, however, shown by these comparisons is that in pigmentation the British and the Americans are very distinct and far apart from the "Nordics," so that even if they have a considerable nordic admixture they cannot properly be classed with that type of the white people.

NATURE OF HAIR

Under this heading are generally comprised the physical characteristics of the hair, which are principally its thickness and shape.

In *thickness* the hair in healthy Old American adults may usually be classified as about medium, with an occasional tendency to moderate fineness. No marked difference was observed in the two sexes. But the exact condition remains to be shown through measurements.

As to *shape* the hair of the head in the Old Americans is generally straight or nearly so. Pronounced natural wave is very exceptional, and naturally curly hair was met with in only one instance, a male.

Observations on the beard are very scarce due to the almost universal habit of shaving both beard and mustache. In the rare cases where the beard is worn it shows mostly a slight to moderate tendency to wave.

GRAY HAIR

In 250 of the examined men and 200 women, special attention was given to the subject of the graying of hair.

The ordinary notions as to grayness are very empirical and superficial, and there is much of interest to be learned in this connection. The condition, however, is not easy to study. Few elderly people remember correctly when they began to notice gray hairs or how the process progressed; and even for the scientific observer it is not easy to estimate correctly the many grades of the change.

The best way to proceed in the study of graying was soon seen to be the statistical, and the only effective way of recording was found to be by estimates in percentages of the quantity of the gray hair in relation to all the hair on the head. Accordingly the incidence of gray hair was recorded as: None; few; some to one-third; approximately one-half (two-fifths to four-sevenths); two-thirds to nearly all; and all. The observations gave the results shown in table 30.

These data only show that grayness long before old age in both sexes is frequent; that there evidently is throughout adult life a slightly less tendency to it among females than among the males; that for some, perhaps not strictly physiological, reason there is an undue frequency of the two-thirds to all grays in both sexes, and that both in appearance and progress of graying there are great individual differences.

Some further light on the condition may be had by arranging the data by age (table 31).

Thirty per cent approximately of the Old American men and 11 per cent of the women have a few to over one-third of gray hair before they pass

TABLE 30

Old Americans: Grayness

	NONE	FEW	SOME TO ABOUT ONE-THIRD	APPROXI-MATELY ONE-HALF	TWO-THIRDS TO NEAR ALL	ALL GRAY (MORE OR LESS COM-PLETELY)
	(107)	(47)	(33)	(11)	(41)	(11)
Males (250).....	42.8%	18.8%	13.2%	4.4%	16.4%	4.4%
Age (general mean 42.6 years)......	22–48 yrs.	24–55 yrs.	25–57 yrs.	37–58 yrs.	39–65 yrs.	48–65 yrs.
	(104)	(30)	(29)	(9)	(21)	(7)
Females (200)...	52%	15%	14.5%	4.5%	10.5%	3.5%
Age (general mean 41.8 years)......	24–48 yrs.	24–55 yrs.	30–58 yrs.	37–59 yrs.	39–60 yrs.	51–60 yrs.

TABLE 31

Old Americans: Grayness of hair in relation to age

AGE AND NUMBER OF SUBJECTS	NONE	FEW	SOME TO ONE-THIRD	ABOUT ONE-HALF (TWO-FIFTHS TO FOUR-SEVENTHS)	TWO-THIRDS TO NEAR ALL	ALL
Males						
24–30 (100)............	74.0	18.0	6.0	1.0	1.0	
31–40 (63)............	44.4	27.0	19.0	3.2	6.4	
41–50 (44).............	9.1	20.4	27.3	11.4	27.3	4.5
51–60 (35)............	2.9	8.6	8.5	8.6	51.4	20.0
61–65 (8).............					75.0	25.0
Total (250).........	42.8	18.8	13.2	4.4	16.4	4.4
Females						
24–30 (80)............	85.0	11.2	3.8			
31–40 (63)............	47.6	25.4	19.0	4.8	3.2	
41–50 (29)............	13.8	17.2	37.9	10.3	13.8	6.9
51–60 (28)............	7.1		10.7	10.7	53.9	17.6
Total (200).........	52.0	15.0	14.5	4.5	10.5	3.5

their thirtieth year. Between 31 and 40 years less than half of the males and a little less than three-fifths of the females are without gray hair, and the proportion of such persons is reduced to a little over 10 per cent during the next decennium. Over 35 per cent of the males between 41 and 50 and 16 per cent of the females between these ages show already grayness that involves from two thirds to all the hair; and for those between 51 and 50 this proportion rises to very nearly three-fourths of the males and seven-tenths of the females.

The females show throughout slightly less tendency to graying than the males. Undue predominance of the two-thirds to nearly all grays is shown again.

Some day, when there shall be equally detailed data on graying in other peoples, the above figures ought to make interesting comparison and lead to some definite deductions of anthropological nature.

Temporary grayness. The phenomenon of sudden or very rapid graying, generally under the stress of great fear, anxiety, or other deeply disturbing nervous effect, is well known, though more so popularly than to science; but the sequences of such a change are only seldom mentioned. A striking case came to the writer's attention in the course of the studies here reported. It concerns General Greely the Arctic explorer. General Greely was born in 1844. His hair when he reached the adult life was "chatain" or rather dark brown and it remained so, with probably the appearance of a few gray hairs, until 1884, or towards the end of his exceedingly difficult trip of Arctic exploration. Then within the period of some months, under the anxieties and privations of his position, his hair turned completely white. But upon a return to civilization the whiteness began gradually to disappear until the hair returned to nearly its former condition, after which graying progressed naturally. The following brief personal statement will make a clear record of the case:

Cosmos Club,
Washington, D. C., March 8, 1922.

Dear Dr. Hrdlička: Referring to our conversation a few days since, I confirm my statement that when rescued at Cape Sabine in 1884 my hair was entirely white, due probably to the continuous condition of semistarvation from which I suffered for over nine months. Within a year my hair darkened very considerably, though it never returned entirely to its original chatain coloring.

Yours,
A. W. Greely, *Major General.*

LOSS OF HAIR

In modern civilized men the hair of the head does not merely tend to grow gray earlier than in more primitive people, but generally also it is more or less shed as ageing advances, showing a reduced vitality. It would be wrong to attribute either of these phenomena to any particular habits of civilized man or to pathological conditions, though both of these may play a part at times; the real causes are already hereditary and thereby of a phylogenetic nature. The hair tends towards an earlier senility and loss

TABLE 32

Old Americans: Loss of hair

LOSS	MALES (250)			FEMALES (200)		
	Cases	Ages		Cases	Ages	
		Average	Extremes		Average	Extremes
	per cent			*per cent*		
None plainly appreciable.....	45.2		24–60	85		23–60
Slight......................	13.6	37	24–60	11	44	29–55
Some to one-third...........	22.4	39	24–57	3		
Approximately one-half.......	7.2	46	29–65	1		
Two-thirds to near all........	11.6	49	35–64			

TABLE 33

Old Americans: Loss of hair in relation to age

AGE AND NUMBER OF SUBJECTS	NONE PERCEPTIBLE	SLIGHT	SOME TO ONE-THIRD	APPROXI- MATELY ONE-HALF (TWO-FIFTHS TO FOUR- SEVENTHS)	TWO-THIRDS TO NEAR ALL
	Males (250)				
	per cent	*per cent*	*per cent*	*per cent*	*per cent*
21–30 (100)................	68.0	11.0	17.0	3.0	1.0
31–40 (63).................	46.0	17.5	22.2	4.8	9.5
41–50 (44).................	29.6	18.2	34.1	6.8	11.3
51–60 (35).................	8.6	8.6	25.7	20.0	37.1
61–65 (8).................		12.5	12.5	25.0	50.0
	Females (200)				
21–30 (80).................	98.8		1.2		
31–40 (63).................	95.5	1.5	1.5	1.5	
41–50 (29).................	85.0	5.0	10.0		
51–60 (28).................	84.3	5.0	7.1	3.6	

because it has become of less organic use to man living under modern conditions than it has been in the past, and nature does not tolerate long what has become useless or weakened. Both early graying and physiological loss of hair are a part of the trend of present evolution in civilized humanity.

Unlike grayness, however, normal loss of hair is largely linked with the male sex. Women lose hair too, and that probably at an increasing rate, but not nearly in the proportion in which the progress goes on in the males.

A special inquiry into this subject among the same 250 male and 200 female Old Americans in whom grayness was observed and taken without any selection, showed the interesting results given in tables 32 and 33. As all the females were examined with their hair undone and freely hanging down to permit the unimpeded taking of head measurements, there can be no question of the observer having been misled.

The figures in tables 32 and 33 show that loss of hair in the Old Americans presents wide individual and even wider sexual variation. There were seen men and women of sixty in whom there was as yet no appreciable loss; but on the other hand plain thinning was seen not merely in some of the youngest male adults of the series but even in some not included subadults down to 18 years of age. The progress of the condition, once it has set in, is generally continuous, though not always regular.

The great difference in the frequency and average grade of the loss of hair between the males and females is difficult to explain. Possibly the weight of the female hair acts as a tonic. The differences between the head covering in the males and females may also have an effect. But in all probability a more or less male-linked predisposition to the condition is already inherited.

In this case, again, we have no similar data on other peoples that could be used for comparison; but as interest in these secondary manifestations will grow, such data will doubtless be forthcoming.

CONCLUSIONS

The above data on the skin, eyes, and hair, permit the formulation of the following conclusions regarding pigmentation in the Old Americans:

Skin

Two-thirds of the old stock males and three-fourths of the females show skin that may be classed as medium.

In only 5 per thousand in males, but in 52 per thousand in the females, is the skin plainly lighter than the medium. All of these cases are associated with pure light eyes and light or red hair.

In a little over one-fourth of the males and in one-sixth of the females the skin is slightly to somewhat darker than medium. Such skin is generally associated with brown eyes and medium to dark hair.

Hair

Only 1 among 16 males and 1 among 14.5 females among the Old Americans has real blond hair.

One-half of the males and over four-tenths of the females show medium dark (or "medium brown") hair.

In one-fourth of the males and three-tenths of the females the hair is dark ("dark brown") to near black.

In approximately 1 per cent in the males and but a little more in the females the hair is fully black.

In 2.6 per hundred of males and 4.9 per hundred of females the hair is red or near red.

The females show a slight to moderate excess of true blonds (especially golden and yellow), but also of darks, blacks, and reds, over the males.

There are some areas in which hair pigmentation among the Old Americans, due to isolation and more thorough mixtures, differs from that of the group as a whole.

Differences between the "Yankees" and the Southerners in this respect are only moderate, the former showing somewhat more lights, less darks, few if any true blacks and less red. But the Southerners show almost identical conditions in regard to hair pigmentation with those of the central states and those of mixed-state ancestry.

Eyes

Approximately one-third of the eyes of the males and one-fourth of the eyes of the females of the Old Americans are pure lights.

One-sixth of the males and one-fifth of the females show eyes the iris of which is pure brown (light, medium, or dark).

Over one-half of the males as well as females have eyes that show plain traces of brown with light.

There are on the whole more light and less dark eyes than there is of light and dark hair.

Regional differences are less marked than with the hair, except in isolated localities.

There is a considerable but not a complete correlation between the pigmentation of the eyes and that of the hair. Light eyes may in some instances be associated with dark (though not black) hair; but medium to dark brown eyes are as a rule accompanied by medium, dark, or black hair.

Blonds or brunets

The classification of the Old Americans on the basis of both the color of the eyes and hair brings out with special clearness a number of the conditions relating to pigmentation.

Over one-half of the males and nearly one-half of the females are "intermediates."

Blonds are scarce, as are also true brunets, but the latter are plainly more frequent, especially in the females.

The females show slightly more blonds, more brunettes and less intermediates than the males.

Character of hair

The hair is generally about medium (for whites) in thickness.

It is generally straight or nearly so, occasionally slightly or moderately wavy.

Curly hair is very rare.

Gray hair

In general, grayness manifests itself early in the Old Americans.

In the males, grayness proceeds apparently faster than in the females.

There is wide individual variation.

Loss of hair

There are great sexual differences in this respect. The males lose hair sooner, more rapidly and much more extensively than the females.

CHAPTER IV

MEASUREMENTS AND MORPHOLOGICAL OBSERVATIONS

The measurements chosen, on the basis of experience, for the study of the Old Americans, have been outlined and discussed in the Preface. Their results will be presented in as simple form as possible so as on the one hand to make them more generally intelligible, and on the other to facilitate comparison with other data. The use of higher mathematics with an unclassifiably mixed anthropological series such as ours, is of doubtful value and the results would only be a higher class of complexities without further elucidation. For those however who may feel the desire for such further treatment, the detailed records will be available.

The visual observations relate in the main to the facial features. The novelty in this connection is that the data were obtained on the basis of a definite preliminary classification of form, grade, etc., and recorded by definite abbreviations or marks, thus approaching as closely as feasible technical data and being capable of similar treatment, which means a considerable simplification of former difficulties, as well as a closer approach to accuracy.

One of the greatest obstacles to presenting the data on the Old Americans with a due perspective, was found to be the scarcity of similar observations on related peoples, more particularly the British. With all that has been done in the past in anthropometry, the fact is that no branch of the white race has as yet been thoroughly studied and with many, the British especially, the defects, particularly as far as the adults are concerned, are still greater than generally appreciated. In part these deficiencies will be met by our records on twelve series of immigrants, but much remains to be desired in this direction.

STATURE

The subject of stature in the United States has received considerable attention in the past, through several channels. The three main agencies in this respect were, first, the Army and Navy, then the Colleges and Gymnasia, and finally the Insurance Companies. The object in all these cases was primarily utilitarian. Scientific work proper, so far as American adults are concerned, is as yet practically non-existent.

The mass of data on stature (and weight) accumulated through the above sources is very great, but its value is more or less limited. As a rule the records make no anthropological distinction outside of the nativity of the persons examined, and some of the most extensive data, such as those of the "Medico-Actuarial Mortality Investigations," fail even in this respect. Generally also the series, particularly those of the Colleges and the Army and Navy, include subadults; and the methods of taking the measurement in some of the cases, such as in recruiting in large numbers, as during the Civil and the late war, but also in the insurance examinations, leave much to be desired.

Notwithstanding these defects the accumulated measurements are useful in more than one direction. They give approximate means for the American people at large, and separately those for several groups of the foreign-born. They give the height and other measurements for the rather selected class of the college students; and, what is of permanent and decided value, they give for both sexes and—if we include the numerous studies on children— for all ages, the correlation of weight with stature.

The data at our disposal from the above sources, on adults and near adults, may briefly and conveniently be shown in table 34.

In stature the American soldier, it may be seen from the above records, averages in general, all nativities mixed, between 171 and 172 cm., or roughly between 5 feet 7⅓ and 5 feet 7 ⅔ inches; while the native-born (leaving out the Navy and the "full statures") range in their averages, according mainly to locality, between 171.35 and about 173.5 cm., or between 5 feet 7½ and 5 feet 8⅛ inches.

Table 35 gives the measurements in the Colleges.

The male college students, though of a lower mean age, are seen to average (leaving out the old records) between 171.2 and 175.2 cm., or from 5 feet 7⅜ to 5 feet 9 inches. They are of a superior stature to the native soldiers, due doubtless to their average better environmental conditions.

The full-grown or nearly full-grown young women of the United States higher schools and colleges, are seen from table 36 to average in stature from approximately 159 cm. or 5 feet 2½ inches to 162.4 cm. or 5 feet 4 inches, without characteristic distinction as to location.

The men and women in the United States at large, or those classes— doubtless the mostly native and better-to-do classes—that apply for insurance, show a mean stature in both sexes that represents about the mean found in higher schools and colleges of the country, though of course the college population is the younger and will finish taller when its "full stature" is completed (see table 37).

Further comment on the preceding data must of necessity be limited. The records are neither uniform nor highly satisfactory as to nativity, ages

TABLE 34

United States Army and Navy

NATIVITY	YEARS	SERIES	REPORTED BY	AGES	NUMBER OF SUBJECTS (MALE)	AVERAGE STATURE	
						Inches	Centimeters
United States...	1840–'56	Native-born soldiers	Coolidge[1]	"Full stature"[2]	1,800	68.8	174.8
	1861–'63	Native-born recruits, U. S. Army	Elliott[3]		25,878	68.2	173.3
	1861–'65	Native-born recruits, U. S. Army	Gould[4]	"Full stature"	160,181	68.5	174.0
	1861–'65	Native-born recruits, U. S. Navy	Gould[4]	"Full stature"	21,321	Approx. 66.8	Approx. 169.7
Native born...	1864–'66	Native-born recruits, U. S. Army (special measurements for the U. S. Sanitary Commission)	Gould[4]	"Full stature"	15,114	Approx. 68.4	Approx. 173.9
	1861–'65	Enlisted men, U. S. Army (of the North) Native-born	Baxter[5]	All ages, (average stature)	315,620	67.67	171.9
	1861–'65	Enlisted men, U. S. Army (of the North) Native-born	Baxter[5]	25 to over 40 years	91,373	68.2	173.3
Native born and others.........	1892	Accepted white recruits U. S. Army (no distinction as to nativity)—(for 1892)	Surgeon-Gen. U. S. A.[6]	20 to 34 years	7,341	67.45	171.35
	1893	Accepted white recruits U. S. Army (no distinction as to nativity)—(for 1893)	Surgeon-Gen. U. S. A.[7]	20 to 50 years	7,687	67.45	171.35
Native-born...	1894	Accepted white recruits U. S. Army (no distinction as to nativity)—(for 1894) Native-born	Surgeon-Gen. U. S. A.[8]	20 to 49 years	4,246	67.52	171.5

	Year	Description	Authority	Age	Number	in.	cm.
Native-born	1895	Accepted white recruits U. S. Army (no distinction as to nativity)—(for 1895) Native-born	Surgeon-Gen. U. S. A.[9]	20 to 49 years	5,605	67.68	171.9
	1896	Accepted white recruits U. S. Army (no distinction as to nativity)—(for 1896) Native-born	Surgeon-Gen. U. S. A.[10]	20 to 39 years	5,479	67.75	172.1
	1906–'15	Accepted recruits U. S. Army (without distinction as to nativity)	Hoffman[11]	21 to 25 years and over[12]	260,060	67.33	171.0
	1918	Soldiers, U. S. Army (without distinction as to nativity)	U. S. A.[13] Medical Museum	"Average age 30.9 years"		67.4	171.2
Native-born and others	1917–'18	Recruits at mobilization of U. S. A. (without distinction as to nativity or color)	Love[14] and Davenport	21 to 30 years	868,445	67.49	171.4
	1919	Soldiers U. S. Army (during demobilization, without distinction as to nativity)	Davenport and Love[15]	All ages (probably 19 to over 30 years)	96,596	67.71	172.0

[1] Coolidge (Richard A.).—Statistical report on the sickness and mortality of the army of the United States (1840–1856); 4to, Wash., 1856.

[2] Under "full stature" Gould understands the highest attained stature of a person. The age at which this is reached differs in different groups. In the native-born whites of the U. S. full stature appears not to be attained generally until well after the 25th year; though this does not seem to be borne out by newer records (see Fisher, in Hoffman,[7] p. 38).

[3] Elliot (E. B.).—On the military statistics of the United States of America. 4to, Berlin, 1863.

[4] Gould (B. A.).—Investigations in the military and anthropological statistics of American soldiers. Mem. U. S. Sanitary Commission, 8°, N. Y. 1869.

[5] Baxter (A. H.).—Statistics, medical and anthropological, of the Provost-Marshal-General's Bureau. 2 vols, 4to, Wash., 1875, 1, 19, 21, 24, 25, 29.

[6] Report, Surg.-General, U. S. A. for 1892.

[7] Report, Surg.-Gen. U. S. A., 8°, Wash., 1893, 226–'7. The total number of recruits accepted was 8,555 between the ages of 16 and over 50, and the average stature of the whole number was 67.42 in. or 171.25 cm.

[8] Do, for 1894, 160–1.

[9] Do, for 1895, 180–1.

[10] Do, for 1896, 234–5.

[11] Hoffman (Frederick L.).—Army anthropometry and medical rejection statistics. 8°, Newark, N. J., 1918, 31 et seq.

[12] The averages were: for 21 years—67.3; 22 years—67.3; 23 years—67.3; 24 years—67.4; 25 years and over—67.3 in.

[13] Chart in the U. S. A. Medical Museum, based doubtless on the records of the War Department.

[14] Love (Albert G.) and Chas. B. Davenport—Physical examination of the first million draft recruits. 8°, Wash., 1919.

[15] Davenport (Chas B.) and Albert G. Love—Army Anthropology. Statistics Med. Dept. U.S. Army in the World War. 8°, Wash., 1921, 34, 117 et al. This series must be regarded as somewhat selected and also affected by their training and service.

TABLE 35

United States College Students

Males

YEAR	NATIVITY	COLLEGE	REPORTED BY	AGES (MEAN OR EXTREMES)	NUMBER OF SUBJECTS	AVERAGE STATURE	
						Inches	Centimeters
1857-8	U. S. (with few exceptions)	3 Southern Medical (S. C., Tenn., La.)	Dickson[1]	21.5–24.5 years	386	(695) / 68.5[2]	(176.5) / 174.0[2]
1858	No distinction (mainly doubtless U. S.)	Jefferson Medical Coll., Phil.	Dickson[1]	22 years	75	(69) / 68.0	(175.3) / 172.8
	No distinction (mainly doubtless U. S.)	Ann Arbor Med. Coll.	Dickson[1]	24.5 years	53	(68.8) / 67.8	(174.75) / 172.25
	Native-born	Milit. Acad., West Point	Dickson[1]	20.1 years	211	(69.0) / 68.0	(175.3) / 172.8
1865	No distinction (mainly U. S.)	Jefferson Med. Coll., Phila.	Dickson[1]	24.5 years	133	(68.25) / 67.25	(173.35) / 170.85
	Native	Ky. Med. Coll.	Dickson[1]	25 years	34	(71.0) / 71.0	(180.3) / 177.8
1865 (or a little later)	No distinction (but mostly native)	Harvard and Yale	Gould[3]	24-27 years and over	42	(68.7) / 67.7	(174.5) / 172.0
1861-9	No distinction (but mostly native)	Amherst	Allen[4]	20.3 to slightly over 23 years	"8 years"	67.8	172.2
1861-88	No distinction (but mostly native)	Amherst	Hitchcock and Seelye[5]	16-26	670	67.9	172.5
1860-90	No distinction (but mostly native)	Amherst	[6]	18-25[7]	1,280	68.2	173.2

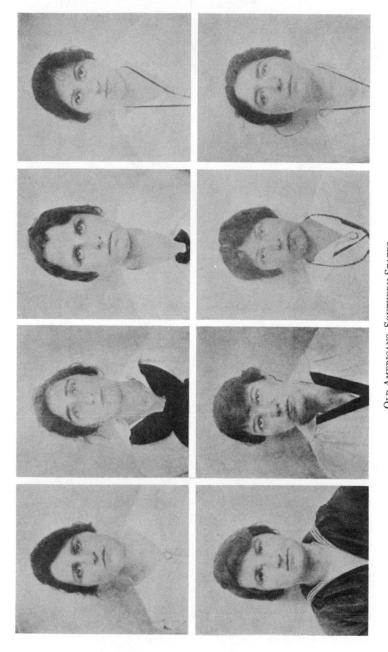

OLD AMERICANS, SOUTHERN STATES
Attending the Summer School at the University of Virginia
(1917)

Date	Native distinction	College	Author	Age	Number		
1884–89	No distinction (but mostly native)	Amherst	Hitchcock[8]	21 years 1 month	2,000	67.99	172.7
Up to 1893	No distinction (but mostly native)	Harvard	Sargent[9]	22–26 years		Mean 68.3	Mean 173.5
1894–6	No distinction (but mostly native)	Columbia	Cattell and Farrand[10]	About 17–24 years	100	About 68.1	About 173.1
Up to 1902	No distinction (but mostly native)	Y. M. C. A. Colleges, etc., Neb, Mass., Conn.	Hastings[11]	20 years (each)	736	67.8	172.2
N.d.	No distinction (but mostly native)	University of Pennsylvania	[12]	19.6 years (16.5-25.7)	2,000	Mean 67.4	Mean 171.2
Before 1909	No distinction (but mostly native)	Yale	Seaver[13]	20	2,700	68.1	173.0

[1] Dickson (S. Henry)—Statistics of height and weight. Am. J. Med. Sc's., Phila., 1866, LII, 373–380. (Earlier data by same A. in Charleston Med. J. and Rev., 1857, 1858. All given in the latest article). Statures have evidently been taken with shoes and clothes on (See Charl. Med. J, 1858, 504).

[2] After allowance of 1 in. or 2.5 cm. for heel.

[3] Gould (B. A.)—Investigations etc., 1869, 130–1 (Stat. with shoes on?)

[4] Allen (Nathan)—Physical culture in Amherst College. 8°, Lowell, Mass., 1869, Append, 41.

[5] Hitchcock (E.)—and H. H. Seelye—Statistics bearing upon the average and typical student in Amherst College. J. Anthrop. Inst., 1888, XVIII, 357–8; also 1889, XVIII, 192–199.

[6] The anthropometric tables of Amherst College. 8°, 1892, 7 pp., 3 charts (no author).

[7] Mean stature remained unchanged from the 18-year group.

[8] Hitchcock (E.)—A comparative study of average measurements. Proc. Am. Ass. Adv. Phys. Educ., 1891, 37–42. (Embraces Amherst data published before.)

[9] Sargent (D. A.)—Anthropometric charts; etc. Fol., Cambridge, 1893 (no text).

[10] Cattell (J. McK.) and Livingston Farrand—Physical and mental measurements of the students of Columbia University. Psychol. Rev., 1896, III, 618–648. (Reported as 175.1; but as measurements were taken with shoes on, only 1.4 cm. substracted for the heel, and in some cases no subtraction was made, it is necessary to make further reduction, which in all probability cannot be substantially less than 2 cm.)

[11] Hastings, (Wm. H.)—A manual for physical measurements. 4to, Springfield, Mass. 1902, 95.

[12] A chart, n.d. (no author).

[13] Seaver (J. W.)—Anthropometry. 8°, 1909, 95.

TABLE 35—*Continued*

YEAR	NATIVITY	COLLEGE	REPORTED BY	AGES (MEAN OR EXTREMES)	NUMBER OF SUBJECTS	AVERAGE STATURE	
						Inches	Centimeters
Up to 1909	No distinction (but mostly. native)	University of Wisconsin	Elsom[14]	No det.	8,000	67.9	172.5
1909–10	No distinction (but mostly native)	University of Wisconsin, "short course"	Elsom[14]	21.7 years	150	67.7	172.0
1909–10	No distinction (but mostly native)	University of Wisconsin (Freshmen)	Elsom[14]	19.7 years		67.8	172.2
Classes 1910–11	"About 50 per cent native-born"	Columbia	Meylan[15]	17–19 years	790	67.45	171.3
1911–13	Mostly native-born	Princeton	Raycroft[16]	18 years 9 months	1,243	68.98	175.2
1915	Mostly native-born	University of Wisconsin	Elsom[17]	19 years 8 months	1,000	68.1	173.0
1915	Mostly native-born	Yale	Elsom[17]	20th year	1,000	68.8	174.75

[14] Elsom (J. C.)—Statistics regarding short course students. Univ. of Wisconsin, 1909–10. Am. Phys. Educ. Rev., 1910, XV, 348–9. (Gives also data on 8,000 students, but no details).

[15] Meylan (G. L.)—Some physical characteristics of college students. Science, May 1, 1908, 711–13.

[16] Personal communication to the author by Dr. Joseph E. Raycroft, Director of the Dept. of Hygiene and Physical Education, Princeton University. The statures were taken with the students stripped, and apply to the freshmen entering the College. No explanation of the high average (which held for every one of the three years) was suggested.

[17] Elsom (J. C.)—Communication to the writer, May 22, 1922.

or classes of the subjects.   They all show plainly, however, that the American people are of tall stature; that this condition has in a large measure become generalized; that it dates from a time before the Civil War, probably long before it; and that the stature does not tend to decrease with time notwithstanding the   influx of shorter Europeans, but rather the reverse.

It is a highly interesting and stimulating record, and one that makes doubly desirable the data on the older contingents of the American population.

Old Americans

The measurements of stature among the Old Americans extend to 727 men and 212 women in good physical condition.[1]   These numbers are not large, but a test of the series by groups of 100 indicates that for the group as a whole they are fairly sufficient.   They even permit some geographic comparisons; but details as to special States or regions must be left for future determination.

The main results of this as well as other measurements will be reported throughout in the form of averages, which after all are the simplest and most generally useful expressions of conditions.   The composition of the series will be seen in the seriation charts and tables.

Stature in the group as a whole

The average stature of the Old Americans is 174.32 cm. (68.63 inches) in the males and 161.83 cm. (63.71 inch) in the females.   The sex difference, 12.49 cm. (M:F::100:92.9), is quite normal and near the general average in white people.

The range between the observed minimum and maximum for the males is approximately 39, for the females 32 cm. or respectively 20.4 and 17.9 per cent of the total range, which for a series of this size is also quite normal. The standard deviation (m. 5.8 cm. f. 5.39 cm.) and the co-efficient of correlation (m. 3.33 per cent, f. 3.33 per cent), are equally normal and rather moderate for white people of mixed parentage.   See the tables of frequencies (tables 38 and 39) and corresponding charts (figs. 3 and 4).

The curves showing the dispersion of stature in the three separate male groups afford some very interesting comparisons.   The three curves are substantially similar.   Their averages are almost identical.   And all three

[1] It is barely necessary to state that the measurement here dealt with is the standard anthropometric stature in stocking feet (see author's Anthropometry, Philadelphia, 1920, Wistar Inst.)

TABLE 36

United States women

YEAR	NATIVITY	LOCATION	REPORTED BY	MEAN AGE (OR LIMITS)	NUMBER OF SUBJECTS	AVERAGE STATURE	
						Inches	Centimeters
(1858)	(Mainly born in U. S.)	(Southern States)	Dickson[1]	Children to adolescents			
1875	Native-born	Boston and vicinity	Bowditch[2]	18-19 years	118	62.1	157.7
1881	Native-born: parents native-born	Milwaukee	Peckham[3]	17.5-19.5 years	57	62.9	159.8
1890	Mainly native-born	Worcester	Boas and Wissler[4]	21-37 years	49	62.8	159.6
To 1890	Mainly native-born	Schools and colleges, Mass.	Bowditch[5]	17 years upward	1,107	62.5	158.8
1892	Mainly native-born	High schools, St. Louis	Porter[6]	20-21 years	122	62.8	159.6
To 1893	Mainly native-born	Harvard	Sargent[7]	18-26 years		63.3	160.8
About 1895	Mainly native-born	High schools, Oakland, Cal.	Boas[8]	18 years and older	82	63.1	160.2
1897	"White girls American parentage"	High schools, Washington, D. C.	McDonald[9]	17.7-20.8	194	63.02	160.1
Up to 1899	Mainly native-born	University of Nebraska	Clapp[10]	16-25 years	1,500	63.0	160.0
(1881-1915 1881-4	Mainly native-born	Wellesley College Wellesley	Data communicated to author	19 years	200	62.8	159.6
1884-9		Holyoke and Wellesley	Hitchcock[11]	Near 19 years	"5 Freshman years in each college"	62.64	159.1
Up to 1893		Wellesley	Wood[12]	20.1 years	1,600	Mean 63.2	Mean 160.5
1915		Wellesley	Data communicated to author		200	63.43	161.1
1886-1915	Mainly native-born	Oberlin College	Communicated to author[13]	19.25 years	3,200	62.45	159.9
1884-1920	Mainly native-born	Vassar College	Newcomer[14]	18.6	7,064	63.94	162.4
1891-1921	Mainly native-born	Stanford University	Mosher[15]	"Freshmen"	"20 classes"	63.5	161.3
1901-1921	Mainly native-born	Smith College	Richards[16]		9,655	63.62	161.6
1921-2	Native-born	Berea College	Hutchins[17]	19.3 years	176	63.24	160.6

[1] Dickson (S. Henry)—(Earliest data on American girls). Charleston Med. J. and Rev., 1857, 1858; Am. J. Med. Sci. 1866.

[2] Bowditch (H. P.)—The Growth of Children. 8th Ann. Rep. St. Bd. Health, Mass., 8°, Bost., 1877, pt. II; s. a. Supplem. Investig., Bost., 1879; and XX Ann. Rep. St. Bd. Health, Mass. (also in Roberts' Anthropometry, 1878, 88–9).

[3] Peckham (Geo. W.)—The Growth of Children. 6th and 7th Ann. Rep. Bd. Health, Wis., Madison, 1882, 1883.

[4] Boas (F.) and Clark, Wissler—Statistics of Growth. Rep. Commissioner of Educ. for 1904, Wash., 1905, 118 et seq.

[5] Bowditch (H. P.)—The physique of Women in Massachusetts. 21st Ann. Rep. St. Bd. Health, Mass., Bost., 1890, 287–304.

[6] Porter (Townsend)—The Relation between the Growth of Children and their Deviation from the Physical Type of their Sex and Age. Trans. Ac. Sc., St. Louis, 1893, VI, No. 10, 248–9.

[7] Sargent (D. A.)—Anthropometric Charts. Fol., Cambridge, 1893 (no text); also "The United States of America," 1894, II, 452–475.

[8] Boas (F.)—The Growth of Toronto Children. Rep. Commissioner Educ. for 1897, Wash., 1898, p. 1570.

[9] McDonald (A.)—Experimental Study of Children. Rep. Commissioner Educ., 1898, Wash., 1899, 1069.

[10] Clapp (Anne L. Barr)—Anthropometric table of Measurements of 1500 College Girls at the University of Nebraska. 1899, 1902. (Also in Siever's "Anthropometry," 1909, 99).

[11] Hitchcock (E.)—A Comparative Study of Average Measurements. Proc. Am. Ass. Adv. Phys. Educ., 1891, 37–42.

[12] Wood (M. Anna)—Anthropometric Table Compiled in Percentile Form from the Measurements of 1600 Wellesley Students. 1893. (Also in Siever's "Anthropometry," 1909, 98.)

[13] Hanna (Delphine)—Anthropometric Table in Percentile Form from the Measurements of 1500 Women of Oberlin College. 1894. (Also in Siever's "Anthropometry," 1909, 97.)

[14] Newcomer (Mabel)—Physical Development of Vassar College Students, 1884–1920. Quart. Publ. Am. Stat. Ass., Dec. 1921, 976–982.

[15] Mosher (Clelia D.)—Concerning the Size of Women. Calif. St. J. Med., Feb., 1921.

[16] Richards (Elizabeth)—N. Y. Herald, May 8, 1921, Sec. VII, p. 4.

[17] Hutchins (Wm. J.)—Transmitted to the author by Professor Hutchins, President of the Berea College. Measurements of the 1921-2 entrance examinations, made by Helen C. Paulison, Director of the Physical Education of Women, Berea Colleges, Ky.

TABLE 37

Insurance companies

YEAR	LOCATION	REPORTED BY	NUMBER OF SUBJECTS	AVERAGE STATURE			
				Men		Women	
				Inches	Centimeters	Inches	Centimeters
1882	Mainly New England	Foster*	1,121	68.0	172.7		
1897	United States and Canada	Shepherd†	74,162				
1900	United States and Canada	Nat. Frat. Cong.‡	133,940	Near. 68.0	Near 172.7		
1912	United States and Canada	Med.-Actuaries§	{ Men 215,183 Women 120,716	67.75	172.1	63.50	161.3

* J. Inst. Actuaries., 1885, XXV, 253.
† Proc. Assoc. Life Ins. Med. Directors, 1897.
‡ Proc. XIV Sess. Nat. Frat. Congr., Buffalo, 1900, 140.
§ Medico-Actuarial Investigation. 3 vols. 4°, N. Y., 1912, I, 21 *et seq.* The whole male series of 221,819 includes 5227 subjects below 20 and 1409 above 59; the female series of 126,000 including 4596 below 20 and 688 above 59 years of age. The subjects were all measured *in their shoes*. The general averages obtained for stature were 5′ 8¾″ for the men and 5′ 4¾″ for the women. Discounting the effects of the inclusion of immature and old subjects on one hand and the measuring with shoes on in the other, (with allowance of 1 inch for shoes in males and 1¼ inch in females) the approximate above figures are obtained.

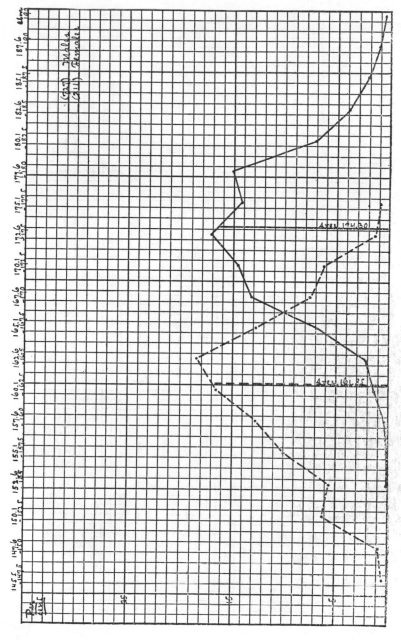

Fig. 3. Old Americans: Stature—Whole Series

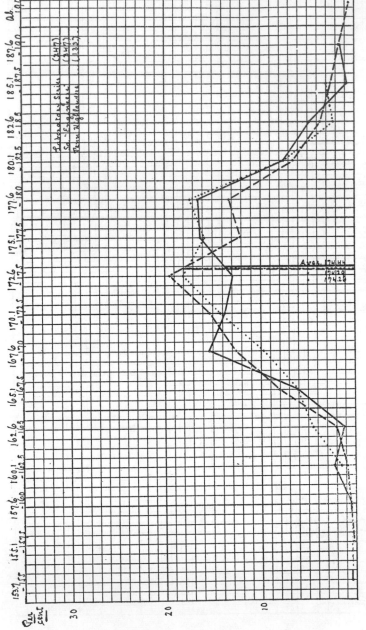

FIG. 4. OLD AMERICANS: STATURE BY GROUPS—MALES

TABLE 38

Old Americans, males: Stature

Number of individuals measured: 727
General average: 174.3 cm. (68.6 in.)

1st series of 100: 173.8 cm.	4th series of 100: 173.9 cm.
2nd series of 100: 175.0 cm.	5th series of 100: 174.6 cm.
3rd series of 100: 174.5 cm.	6th series of 100: 175.4 cm.
	7th series of 100: 173.7 cm.

Minimum: 153.7 cm.   Maximum: 193.0 cm.
Standard deviation 5.80 cm.; Coefficient of variation 3.33 per cent

TABLE OF FREQUENCIES

	152.6-155.0 cm.	155.1-157.5 cm.	157.6-160.0 cm.	160.1-162.5 cm.	162.6-165.0 cm.	165.1-167.5 cm.	167.6-170.0 cm.	170.1-172.5 cm.	172.6-175.0 cm.	175.1-177.5 cm.	177.6-180.0 cm.	180.1-182.5 cm.	182.6-185.0 cm.	185.1-187.5 cm.	187.6-190.0 cm.	190.1-192.5 cm.	192.6-193.0 cm.
Number of cases (727)	1	1	3	10	16	50	96	106	124	103	110	52	28	15	8	3	1
Per cent......	0.1	0.1	0.4	1.4	2.2	6.9	13.2	14.6	17.1	14.2	15.1	7.1	3.9	2.1	1.1	0.4	0.1

TABLE 39

Old Americans, females: Stature

Number of individuals measured: 211
Average: 161.85 cm. (63.71 in.).   (1st 100: 161.3; 2nd 100 : 162.2)
Minimum: 145.5 cm.   Maximum: 177.3 cm.
Standard deviation 5.39 cm.; Coefficient of variation 3.33 per cent.

TABLE OF FREQUENCIES

	145.1-147.5 cm.	147.6-150.0 cm.	150.1-152.5 cm.	152.6-155.0 cm.	155.1-157.5 cm.	157.6-160.0 cm.	160.1-162.5 cm.	162.6-165.0 cm.	165.1-167.5 cm.	167.6-170.0 cm.	170.1-172.5 cm.	172.6-175.0 cm.	175.1-177.5 cm.
Number of cases.....	1	2	13	12	21	27	35	39	27	16	13	3	2
Per cent.............	0.5	0.9	6.2	5.7	10.0	12.8	16.6	18.5	12.8	7.6	6.2	1.4	0.9

Difference between males and females : 12.49 cm.
F : M :: 92.9 : 100

curves are bimodal, though the condition is most marked in the Laboratory group.

The bimodal character of the stature curve in each of the male groups and in the male series as a whole, must have a definite significance, but the nature of this is not clear. One reason that suggests itself is that perhaps the tendency to tall stature is not quite universal, or not equally active, in the Old American families, so that a proportion of these are more and a proportion less conservative of the older conditions. The presence of the peculiarity in all the male groups, which differ considerably in their environment, habits and occupations, would seem to speak against the peculiarity being of a simple functional nature, though this view is rather favored by its presence alone in the males. The point is one of the many encountered in the course of the closer study of our data, that will need further attention.

The averages for groups of 100, and the distribution of the measurements, are well shown in tables 38 and 39 and figures 3 and 4. The form of these, particularly in the females, is that of a heterogeneous but fairly well mixed population. There is no evidence of any tendency towards a persistence of two or more ancestral types, but rather of one towards a fusion into a single new grouping.

The averages exceed, by approximately two-thirds of an inch (or 2 cm.), those of Americans in general, and even those of the "native-born" (see previous tables), a good proportion of whom are second (or) more generation Americans; and as they hold true for every subdivision of the series, we may regard as established the first fact of importance, which is that in general the Old Americans are the tallest among the American people.

Upon further comparison they are also seen to be the tallest, both as to men and women, of all the existing other larger groups of the white race. This will be seen plainly from table 40, which are limited to males, but what is true of males in this respect is true of both sexes.

Stature and age

That age, even after the adult stage of life (full second denture) has been reached, has still an influence upon stature, has long been known and has been discussed by many authors,[2] but the data of various observers and lands show little agreement. What is known in general is that growth in height ceases decidedly sooner in the females than in the males; that in individual

[2] See especially Topinard (P.)—Étude sur la taille. Rev. d'Anthrop., 1876, V, 34 et seq. Also Pagliani (L.)—I fattori della statura umana. Rome, 1877; abstr. in Bull. Soc. d'Anthrop. Paris, 1877, 623–32; Martin (R.)—Lehrbuch der Anthropologie, 1914.

TABLE 40

The stature of the Old American contrasted with that of other white peoples

YEAR	NUMBER OF SUBJECTS	REPORTED BY	AVERAGE STATURE
		Old Americans	
			cm.
1912–21	*727*	*Present report*	*174.3*
		Scotchmen	
1861–65	7,313	Gould[1]	170.8
1861–65	3,478	"Full Stature"[2]	171.65
1861–65	3,476	Baxter[3]	170.4
1861–65	5,731	Baxter[4]	172.5
1869	2,678	Beddoe[5]	172.0
1883	1,304	British[6] Committee	172.97
1919	2,074	Davenport and Love[7]	172.5
		Irish	
1861–65	467	Gould[8]	169.3
1861–65	50,537	Baxter[9]	169.5
1861–65	88,128	Gould[10]	170.0
1861–65	24,149	Gould[11]	170.5
Before 1870		Beddoe[12]	Approx. 169.3
Before 1870	1,517	Beddoe[13]	170.8
1919	6,164	Davenport and Love[14]	171.36

[1] Gould (B. A.)—Investigations in the military and anthropological statistics of American soldiers. 8°, N. Y., 1869, 105.

[2] Stature of full grown men (during years when no more increase nor any diminution are yet observable).

[3] Baxter (J. H.)—Statistics, medical and anthropological of the Civil War. 4to, Wash., 1875, I, 23. Scotch in U. S. Army.

[4] "Army Contractor" fr. the *Edinb, Med. Sure. J.* (quoted by Baxter, I, LXXI).

[5] Beddoe (John)—On the stature and bulk of man in the British Isles. Mem. Anthrop. Soc., Lond., 1869, III, 545; also in sep., 8, Lond., 1870. Believes (p. 164) the average stature for Scotchmen to be "perhaps as high as 5ft. 7½ in. (171.4 cm.)".

[6] Final report of the Anthropometric Committee. *Rep. B. A. A. S.*, 1883, 256. (Due to an error in computation the report gives the height as 174.6 cm. or 68.71 in. As this figure was out of harmony with any of the other larger records on the Scotch, the writer re-counted the data, and they give the average of 68.1 in. or 172.97 cm. The error here mentioned has been widely copied (see Deniker, Martin etc.).

[7] Davenport (Charles B.) & Albert G. Love—Army anthropology, 8°, Wash., 1921, 113 (Soldiers during demobilization).

[8] *o. c.* 284. Soldiers examined for the U. S. Sanitary Commission.

[9] *o. c.* I, 23. Soldiers in U. S. Army.

[10] *o. c.* 105. Enlisted men, U. S. Army.

[11] *o. c.* 125. "Full stature" soldiers, U. S. Army.

[12] *o. c.* 164.

[13] *o. c.* 145. Recruits, 23 years and upwards.

[14] *o. c.* 113. Soldiers U. S. Army during demobilization.

TABLE 40—*Continued*

YEAR	NUMBER OF SUBJECTS	REPORTED BY	AVERAGE STATURE
English			
1860–65	16,196	Baxter [15]	169.1
Before 1870	1,886	Beddoe[16]	Approx. 169.3
1861–65	30,037	Gould[17]	170.1
Before 1870	2,068	Beddoe[18]	170.15
1861–65	8,899	Gould[19]	170.16
1875–83	6,194	A. C.[20]	171.2
Welsh			
1861–65	1,104	Baxter[21]	168.7
1875–83	741	A. C.[22]	169.4
Canadians			
1861–65	520	Gould[23]	169.9
1861–65	31,698	Gould[24]	170.7
1861–65	6,667	Gould[25]	171.6
Norwegians			
1861–65	2,290	Baxter[26]	171.4
Scandinavians			
1865	3,790	Gould[27]	171.35
Norwegians			
1913	16,532	a. Hoffman[28]	171.8
Before 1900	106,446	a. Deniker[29]	172.0

[15] *o. c.* I, 21, 23. Enlisted men in the U. S. Army.

[16] *o. c.* 163. Englishmen at large, all England, all classes.

[17] *o. c.* 105. Soldiers U. S. Army.

[18] *o. c.* 145. English recruits 23 years and upwards.

[19] *o. c.* 125. "Full stature" men enlisted in the U. S. Army.

[20] Final Report of the Anthropometric Committee. Rep. B. A. A. S. for 1883, (Lond. 1884) 256. Males (at large) 23–50 years of age.

[21] *o. c.* I, 23. Enlisted men U. S. Army.

[22] *o. c.* (ref. 25), 256.

[23] *o. c.* 276. Soldiers U. S. Army measured for U. S. Sanitary Commission.

[24] *o. c.* 104. Soldiers U. S. Army.

[25] *o. c.* 125. do "full stature."

[26] *o. c.* I, 23. Norwegians enlisted in the U. S. Army.

[27] *o. c.* 125. "Full stature" of Norwegian soldiers, U. S. A.

[28] Hoffman (Fred. L.)—Army anthropometry and medical rejection statistics. 80°, Newark, N. J., 1918, 31–2. Conscription in Norway.

[29] Deniker (J.)—The races of man. 12 mo, Lond., 1900. Norway soldiers.

TABLE 40—*Continued*

YEAR	NUMBER OF SUBJECTS	REPORTED BY	AVERAGE STATURE
		Swedes	
1861–65	1,190	Baxter[30]	169.9
Before 1900	232,367	a. Deniker[31]	170.5
1914	32,322	a. Hoffman[32]	171.86
		Danes	
Before 1900	3,000	a. Deniker[33]	168.5
1916	18,727	a. Hoffman[34]	169.0
		Danes of Schleswig	
Before 1900	4,964	a. Deniker[35]	169.2
		Danes	
1861–65	383	Baxter[36]	169.3
		Germans	
1861–65	256	Gould[37]	168.8
1861–65	54,944	Baxter[88]	169.0
1861–65	89,021	Gould[39]	169.3
1861–65	32,259	Gould [40]	169.5
		French	
1831–62		Elliott[41]	165.5
1861–65	3,243	Baxter[42]	168.3
1861–65	6,809	Gould [43]	169.0
1919	1,457	Davenport and Love[44]	168.6

[30] *o. c.* I, 23. Swedes in U. S. Army.

[31] The races of man, 1900. Soldiers of Sweden.

[32] *o. c.* 31–32. Swedish conscripts.

[33] *o. c.* Soldiers.

[34] *o. c.* 31–32. Conscripts in Denmark.

[35] *o. c.* Soldiers.

[36] *o. c.* I, 23. Enlisted men in U. S. Army. See also Westergaard (H.)—Investigations on the stature of the male population in Denmark. Med. Danmarks Antrop., 1911, I, 351.

[37] *o. c.* 284. U. S. Army; measured for the U. S. Sanitary Commission.

[38] *o. c.* I, 21, 23. Enlisted in U. S. Army.

[39] *o. c.* 105.

[40] *o.c.* 125. "Full stature" enlisted men U. S. Army.

[41] Elliott (E. B.)—On the military statistics of the United States of America. 4to, Berlin, 1863, 16.

[42] *o. c.* I, 23. Enlisted U. S. Army.

[43] *o. c.* 105. do. (See also p. 179.)

[44] *o. c.* 113. do. (Measured at demobilization.)

males a full stature may be reached even as early as the twentieth year; but that in the majority there is a slight increase even after 24, and that in some men and probably under special circumstances, growth may continue to and rarely even slightly beyond the thirtieth year. It is further known that with the setting in of senility, which again differs considerably in different individuals and in the intensity or evenness of its course in the same individual, the stature begins to diminish. There is further a strong probability that there are racial and environmental, as there are class, occupational and still other differences, in these respects, all of which calls for much further investigation.

TABLE 41

Full Stature in the Old Americans

(Laboratory series)

GENERAL AVERAGE		AVERAGE "FULL STATURE" (IN THOSE OF 30–50 YEARS INCLUSIVE)		AVERAGE STATURE (IN THOSE OF 26 YEARS OR LESS)	
Males	Females	Males	Females	Males	Females
(247)	(211)	(114)	(104)	(50)	(46)
174.44	161.83	174.8	162.1	174.03	162.3

TABLE 42

Old Americans: Stature and age

(Laboratory series)

	YEARS				
	22–29	30–39	40–49	50–59	Above 59
Males (247) . . . . {	(91) 174.14	(63) 174.97	(47) 174.54	(34) 173.98	(12) 174.78
Females (210) . . . . {	(73) 162.57	(71) 161.96	(36) 162.42	(27) 159.18	(3) (166.07)

As to the present series of observations on the Old Americans, we are unable, on account of the relatively small numbers available, to go into any great details, which must be left to special studies. But so far as age is concerned, a few tests show that the general average statures obtained on the whole group are only slightly inferior to the "full statures" in this group. This can best be shown in table 41.

This may be supplemented by table 42, which applies to the Laboratory series comprising adults of all ages within the limits set for these studies. These figures show that the group of those between 50 and 59, in both scxcs, is of lower stature than any of the other subdivisions. This can hardly be the effect as yet of senility; more probability it means that at the time these men and women became adult the mean stature of the stock was slightly lower than it became since. The stature of the few subjects above 59 is elevated, due doubtless to some form of unintentional selection—the stipulations were that none of the more aged would be included except those who were still in good physical condition. Finally, the youngest group of the females gives a true higher stature than those at any other age, a point the probable significance of which will be seen later.

In the group of "Engineers," however, whom Dr. Bean and the writer measured in Virginia and among whom there were a fairly large number of from 20 to 24 years of age, and to some extent even in our female series, matters are less simple due to the presence of another factor. The youngest of these series show higher average statures than the groups as a whole, due to the fact that, in some parts of the country at least, stature among the Old Americans is still on the increase. The average stature of the Engineer group is 174.26, that of the thirty youngest males of this group 175.50 cm.; the mean of our whole female group is 161.84, that of the thirty youngest of this group 163.10 cm. This matter will be dealt with further in another connection.

Influence of type

The influence of type upon the stature in the Old Americans, as in related groups, appears to be quite secondary. The assumed influence of blonds as carriers of a higher stature is not sustained. Imperfect as they are, we have some valuable data on this point from the Civil War (see table 43).

Two consecutive series of "lights" and "darks" among the Old Americans give the harmonizing results in table 44.

The results are in accord with the data of the Civil War. The lights (blonds and near) have average stature very near the same as the darks (brunets). If anything there is a slight excess in favor of the darks. In the first series (Laboratory, all States) both these purer strains are below the average height of the intermediates; in the second, (Virginia and neighboring States) they are just about the average (174.2 cm.) of the series.

Influence of class, occupation, environment

As to probable class, occupational, and city vs country differences, special further studies will be required on much larger numbers. If is well known that in general the well-to-do classes, including probably the prosperous farmer and rancher, and the men engaged since adolescence in healthy outdoor occupations, show a higher stature than the poor, the city workman and those since apprenticeage of confining or unhealthy occupations; and it may probably be safely assumed that the same holds true in these respects for the Old Americans.

TABLE 43

*Stature in light and dark complexioned men**

NATIVITY	LIGHT COMPLEXIONED	DARK COMPLEXIONED	MEAN HEIGHT OF LIGHTS	MEAN HEIGHT OF DARKS
United States	*126,445*	*64,176*	*171.84*	*172.15*
British America..............	9,506	4,859	170.61	170.37
England.....................	6,804	2,845	169.12	169.22
Ireland.....................	20,378	8,617	169.56	169.56
Germany....................	20,559	9,041	168.99	168.98

*Baxter (J. H.)—Statistics etc. I, 24.

TABLE 44

Stature in "lights and darks"† among Old Americans*

	MALES					
	Lights			Darks		
	Average stature	Below 170.0	Above 175.0	Average stature	Below 170.0	Above 175.0
First series.....	(25) 172.8	8	8	(25) 173.1	8	10
Second series....	(25) 174.1	8	8	(25) 174.2	4	10

* Both hair and eyes light.
† Both hair and eyes dark.

TABLE 45

Stature and extremes of head form

	MALES				FEMALES			
		Age	Cephalic index	Stature		Age	Cephalic index	Stature
Most dolichocephalic........	(25)	41.8	73.22	176.1	(15)	34.7	74.01	161.6
Most brachycephalic........	(25)	33.3	84.64	173.4	(20)	31.9	84.70	161.2

Stature and head form

The general impression on this subject is that among Western and Northern Europeans at least the more oblong head is associated with taller, the more rounded head with medium or shorter stature. Among the Old

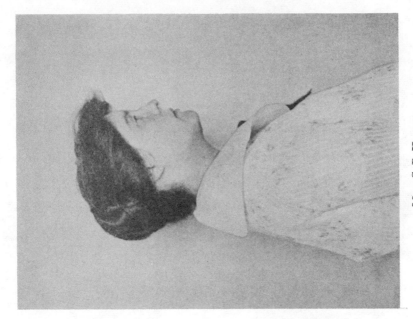

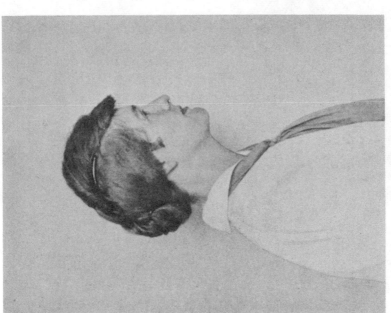

Miss A. Hodges   Miss C. B. Hodges

Sisters, showing quite different types. Extended American ancestry, both sides.

Americans, as will be seen from table 45, this notion is sustained among the males, but among the females the difference in favor of the dolichocephalic is much smaller.

Geographical Differences

Previous data on the native-born and on Americans in general, seem to indicate rather marked regional differences in stature. There is a great array of records on this point from the Civil and the World War, and these records up to certain points show remarkable agreement. The most copious figures are those of Gould (table 46).

At the time of the Civil War, the tallest men were those of Kentucky, with Tennessee and the other southern states following; during the World War the distinction seems to have passed to certain sections of North Carolina, Arkansas and Missouri. The records in the latter case are somewhat less comprehensive in numbers and more extensive as to geographical distribution, nevertheless the showing of Kentucky calls for explanation which probably will necessitate local studies. The relatively poor showing, both during 1861–5 and in 1919, of most of the New England and Middle Atlantic States, is generally and doubtless justly attributed, in the main, to the large proportion of foreign element in their population.

The records on the Old Americans, as far as they go, show no regional differences of importance, as will be seen from the averages in table 47. It is strongly probable that if we had comprehensive series of measurements from many regions there would be some variation in the means; but it is plain that the old stock from State to State or region to region so far as the average stature is concerned is much more uniform than is the general American population. It is apparently not so much the exact locality but what America stands for in general that favorably affects the growth of the body; and the relatively low mean stature for the population at large in the eastern States is evidently wholly due to the presence and admixture with shorter people of more recent American and European parentage.

That the high mean[3] stature of the Old Americans is an American acquisition and not an old hereditary condition, is substantiated on one hand by the fact that no ancestry of such average height is known or indicated by any evidence there is on the subject, and on the other by the change having been actually observed. Thus Gould showed (Investigations etc., 126–7)

[3] The terms "mean" and "average" are for convenience used interchangeably and both denote the average, unless it should be otherwise specified.

TABLE 46

Stature by states and nativity (Gould)*

I. White soldiers, Civil War, regardless of nativity

	NUMBER OF MEN	AVERAGE STATURE	
		Inches	Centi-meters
New England..	943	67.27	170.9
New York, New Jersey, & Pennsylvania................	3,252	67.10	170.4
Western States (east of Mississippi)....................	478	67.73	172.0
Slave States..	2,024	68.22	173.3

* Investigations etc., 125, 251, 284.

II. White soldiers, Civil War (Gould)

	REGARDLESS OF NATIONALITY			NATIVE-BORN		
	Num-ber of men	Average stature		Num-ber of men	Average stature	
		Inches	Centi-meters		Inches	Centi-meters
New England..........................	1,211	67.20	170.7	33,783	68.32	173.5
New York, New Jersey, Pennsylvania.......	3,765	67.14	170.5	61,351	68.11	173.0
Ohio and Indiana.......................	1,662	67.74	172.1	34,206	68.97	175.2
Michigan, Wisconsin, Illinois..............	1,016	67.26	170.8	4,570	68.86	174.9
Slave States (except Kentucky and Tennessee)	367	67.56	171.6	13,409	68.84	174.86
Kentucky, Tennessee....................	267	68.53	174.1	12,862	69.30	176.0

III. White enlisted men, Civil War (Baxter)†

American-born—Average stature

THE TALLEST STATES		THE SHORTEST STATES	
	cm.		*cm.*
Kentucky.........................174.4		Rhode Island.....................170.9	
Kansas...........................174.1		New York.........................170.88	
Minnesota.......................173.7		New Jersey.......................170.2	
Missouri.........................173.6		New Hampshire...................170.0	
California........................173.5		Massachusetts....................169.9	
		Connecticut......................169.1	

† Statistics, etc. I, 29.

TABLE 46—*Continued*

IV. Soldiers, World War, at Demobilization (Davenport and Love)‡

| STATE | NUMBER | FROM SECTION CHARACTERIZED BY | AVERAGE STATURE | |
			Inches	Centi-meters
		Tall to tallest		
North Carolina	2,738	Sparsely populated mountainous area	68.67	174.4
Arkansas	1,559	Large native white population; hill country	68.64	174.3
Missouri.	1,139	Native white, Ozark region	68.63	174.3
Texas	22,372	Sparsely settled, white	68.50	174.0
Minnesota	6,461	Population largely of Scandinavian derivation	68.44	173.8
Tennessee	5,900	Mountainous region	68.43	173.8
Kentucky	4,033	Mountainous area, native white	68.21	173.3
		Short to shortest		
New York	6,544	Urban area	66.95	170.1
Massachusetts	8,587	Urban area	66.94	170.0
New Jersey	12,181	Mountainous area plus Atlantic County; Plains section, rural	66.83	169.7
Pennsylvania	14,218	Rural area, native stock	66.73	169.5
Pennsylvania	16,085	Urban area	66.62	169.2
New York	46,718	Urban area densely populated	66.46	168.8
Rhode Island	3,928	State undivided	66.40	168.7

‡ Army Anthropology, etc. 35. 101–3 *et. seq.*

TABLE 47

Stature in Old Americans, regionally

Males

GENERAL AVERAGE	LABORATORY (ALL STATES)	EASTERN TENNESSEE (MOUNTAINS AND FOOTHILLS)	VIRGINIA (AND NEIGHBORING STATES)
(727)	(247)	(133)	(347)
174.3	174.4	174.3	174.2

that natives of New England and New York enlisting in the "west" (west of the Alleghany Mountains) gave in all the stages (at all ages) a higher stature than those enlisting in their native States. This was especially marked for those from New York. The mean excess for New Englanders was near ¼ inch, or 0.58 cm.; that for New Yonkers being near ½ inch, or 1.24 cm.

In many of the Old American families, moreover, and even in numerous families of a more recent coming, the increase of stature in the younger generation has well been noted by those concerned and their friends.

Causes

What are the causes of this marked and widespread increase in stature in the United States? They could probably be summed up most simply as *a favorable change of environment*, using the term environment in its broadest sense. It is the stimulation by the American conditions as they have existed in the past and to a material extent still exist, of the mind as well as the body, while at the same time the latter is furnished with ample nourishment. It was the pioneer life, it was and is the more wholesome housing, the more largely outdoor life with plentiful food and especially meat (and possibly maize), the absence of stunting child labor, the sports of the youth. It was and is probably nothing peculiar chemically or dynamically in the new land, though something of this nature may have helped in some sections.

A highly interesting problem is whether or not this tendency towards greater height of the body is still present in the Old Americans. There are good indications that it is still active in the new comers. There are also data that the average height of the students for same ages has been increasing in many if not all of the colleges, without a marked change in the character of their students as far as age, nativity or class is concerned. And there are the already given data on our series of females as well as that of the southern engineers (page 100). But there are also data, particularly those of the Army, which would seem to indicate that the optimum of mean stature may, temporarily or permanently, already have been reached and perhaps even passed in many localities. The subject demands a special inquiry with many additional data. The records bearing on the point aside of those of our series, are as follows:

Dr. Seaver, writing in 1909[4] says, "A percentile study of the records of the Yale students who were in their 20th year of life has been made and the result is shown on the chart on p. 95. A noticeable feature of the results is that this tabulation seems to show a decided tendency to increase in height of students in recent years. This has also been noted in the average tables that have been made at Yale from the records of the freshmen." As may be seen from the table of statures of college students, the average height of Yale students up to 1909 was 173 cm., while in 1915 it is reported to have been 174.75 cm.

[4] Seaver (J. W.)—Anthropometry, 8°, New Haven, 1909, 94.

At Princeton,[5] the entrance examinations for 1911–1913—the only records of this nature, regrettably, for the present available—showed the conditions as given in table 48.

There are especially good data of this nature on the women.   Dr. Clelia D. Mosher of the Stanford University, has given[6] us the entrance examination measurements of 4023 young women of that University.   They are shown in table 49.

On the basis of these data Dr. Mosher believes that the modern American girl is an inch or an inch and a tenth taller than her sister of thirty years ago, and this "in spite of the fact that the average age of the women enter-

TABLE 48

Stature of Princeton men

FRESHMEN ENTERING	NUMBER OF INDIVIDUALS	AVERAGE AGE	AVERAGE HEIGHT	AVERAGE WEIGHT
			cm.	*k.*
1911	400	18 years 11 months	174.34	63.36
1912	415	16 years 8 months	175.44	63.17
1913	428	18 years 7 months	175.7	63.2

TABLE 49

Average stature of 4,023 women of the Stanford University, California

	NUMBER	INCHES	CUBIC METERS
1891–2 to 1900–1............................	1,116	63.2	160.53
1901–2 to 1910–1............................	1,200	63.5	161.29
1911–12 to 1920–21........................	1,707	63.8	162.05

ing the University has grown less" (page 54).   And similar data come from the Oberlin, Smith and Vassar Colleges (see table 50).

There are indications that Bryn Mawr, Wellesley, and still other female colleges, show similar conditions.

The evidence, for the women at least, is so general and uniform that it cannot but be accepted as conclusive.   But the college student is, on the whole, about the most favored class of the population.   The native stock workmen class, the native stock farmer class, in general, are probably not or at least not in all parts of the country increasing in stature any more, or some evidence of such an increase would have become apparent from the measurements of the recruits and the enlisted men during the late war.

[5] Information in a letter of June 24, 1922, by Dr. Joseph E. Raycroft, Director of the Department of Hygiene and Physical Education, Princeton University.
[6] Concerning the size of women.   Calif. St. J. Med., February, 1921.

As to how long and how far changes of this nature may proceed, we may only surmise. It is noticeable that few of the college groups exceed, and a good many do not yet reach the general averages of the Old Americans.

TABLE 50

Women of Oberlin College, Ohio*

	NUMBER	MEAN AGE	MEAN STATURE	
			Inches	Centimeters
		years		
1886–1903	1,600	19.3	62.6	159.0
1909–1915	1,600	19.2	63.3	160.8

Women of Smith College, Mass.†

	NUMBER	AVERAGE STATURE	
		Inches	Centimeters
1903–1909	2,322	63.36	160.85
1910–1919‡	4,332	63.48	161.24
1920–1924	3,001	63.98	162.47

Women of Vassar College, N. Y.

Ages and stature of students averaged by five-year groups, 1884–1920§

	NUMBER	MEANS	AVERAGE STATURE
		years	*cm.*
1884–1890	307	18.8	160.5
1891–1895	621	19.0	160.4
1896–1900	992	19.0	161.5
1901–1905	1,172	18.9	162.4
1906–1910	1,272	18.7	162.6
1911–1915	1,482	18.5	163.0
1916–1920	1,236	18.2	163.7

*Information given to the writer by the Director of Physical Education, Oberlin College, May 14, 1922.

† Richards (Elizabeth)—N. Y. Herald, May 8, 1921, Sec. VII, p. 4.

‡ Exc. 1912.

§ Newcomer (Mabel)—Physical Development of Vassar College students. Quart. Publ. Am. Sta. Assn., December, 1921, 976–'82.

It has also been noted, in the course of the work on the Old Americans, that the oldest of these, the people of five to seven generations American born on each side, were not conspicuous for a higher stature than the rest of the group, though some difference might possibly be found if we could get a good sized unselected series of such individuals. It is not improbable therefore that the present standards of stature in the old United States stock represent, or represent nearly, the maximum of mean stature attainable by the American people under present conditions. Should these conditions remain about the same, the average stature might then be expected to become fairly stationary; should they grow worse through over-population and untoward changes in habits, the stature would doubtless begin to fall; but should favorable new stimuli keep on evolving, the stature could well be expected to keep on responding, until such standards were reached beyond which the increase would begin to prove an organic disadvantage.

Suffice it to say, that the Old American stock, both men and women, is the tallest of any larger group of white people; that under the influence of favorable stimuli and good nutrition the younger elements of the population at large are still advancing further in the same direction; and that under the influence of hygiene, of proper physical training, of plentiful highly nourishing food, and of the many outdoor and indoor sports, the advance is particularly noted in the students of our Colleges.

Stature in Tennessee

The stature in Tennessee was obtained in the eastern part of the State on the young men called by the draft in 1917. Part of the men (51) came from the lower highlands and foothills about Bristol; part (82) from the rugged mountain country about Mountain City. In both regions the ages of the young men ranged from 21 to 31 years, the mean for the mountaineers being 26.1, that for the men of the lower lands 24.5 years. The average stature of the mountaineers was 173.96 cm., that of the younger lowlanders 174.8 cm. The average stature of the 26 mountaineers from 21 to 24 years of age was 173.9, that of the 28 lowlanders of same ages 175.03 cm. The families of the lower lands, which in general are of the same derivation as those of the mountains, are on the whole better off and there is less alcohol as well as less hardship.

Virginia and neighboring region

The measurements secured with Professor Bean's great help at the University of Virginia comprised 347 members of a forming regiment of U. S. Engineers. These men ranged from 19 to 37 years of age, the bulk being between 22 and 30. They included essentially various sorts of mechanics. The average stature of the whole group was 174.26 cm., which is practically identical with the general average of 174.32 cm. for all Old Americans. The eighty-six older men of the group, ranging from 27 to 37 years inclusive, gave an average stature of 174 cm., the 261 younger men, 19–26 years old, that of 174.83 cm. The 30 youngest measured in average, as already mentioned before (p. 81) 175.5 cm.

Kentucky and other southern states

The remarkable showing of Kentucky during the Civil War when it stood at the head of all the States of the Union in the mean stature of its men, and

TABLE 51

Stature of women in Kentucky and other Southern States

	NUMBER OF SUBJECTS	AVERAGE AGE	AVERAGE HEIGHT (IN BARE FEET)	
			Inches	Centimeters
		years		
Kentucky................................	123	19.0	63.16	160.4
Other States (Tennessee, Virginia, West Virginia: North and South Carolina, Alabama, Georgia, Florida, Texas)........	53	19.6	63.32	160.8

TABLE 52

Full stature (or near) in women of Kentucky and other Southern States

	NUMBER OF SUBJECTS	AVERAGE AGE	AVERAGE HEIGHT	
			Inches	Centimeters
		years		
Kentucky................................	33	Near 22	63.75	161.9
Other Southern States.....................	26	22	64.68	164.3

the showing of the State during the World War, when it no longer occupies the first place in this respect, though being still among the highest, induced the writer to address the various Colleges in that State for recent data on their students, with the hope that they might possibly throw some light on the actual conditions. The appeal came unfortunately too close to the end of the academic year for immediate response, but it was received favorably; and one of the most important schools, the Berea College, through its President, Professor William J. Hutchins, has sent us the height measurements of 176 young women from Kentucky and other southern States, entering the College during the current year (1922). These measurements, made by Miss Helen C. Paulison, the Director of Physical Education of Women at the College, show the state of affairs given in table 51.

Having received the individual records, it was possible to reduce these series to women over 20 years of age, in whom the stature is doubtless very near the full stature, with the results in table 52.

A large majority of these women are doubtless of the "Old Americans." The average stature of the women of this group is, as recorded in preceding pages, 63.71 in. or 161.83 cm., or practically indentical with that of the above group from Kentucky. The girls from the other southern States (mostly Virginia, West Virginia and Tennessee) are higher. This would seem to agree with the World War data on southern men. But the above groups are too small to be taken as conclusive and we must await further records.

TABLE 53

Average stature of adult male immigants into the United States, 1913–1914

50	Croatians	171.6	50	Greeks	168.3
35	Irish	171.6	25	Armenians	167.4
50	Poles	170.4	50	Magyars	166.5
50	Russians (non-Jews)	169.8	50	Jews (Russian)	164.6
50	Italians (north)	169.6	50	Italians (south)	163.4
50	Roumanians	168.7			

Stature of immigrants to the United States

In connection with preceding data it will be of interest to see about what, in stature, the United States has been recently receiving from Europe. Before the World War a careful series of anthropometric observations were made by the writer and under his direction by two Surgeons of the Public Health Service, on healthy, unselected, fully adult and not senile immigrants of twelve nationalities, at Ellis Island.[7] The series are not large, yet they give probably a fair indication of conditions, the data agreeing closely with those from other sources on the same groups. They are (with the exception of the English who gave 170.2, but where the series was too small for anything approaching definite showing) as seen in table 53.

[7] Credit for the possibility of carrying out this work, is due in the first place to past Surgeon-General Rupert Blue, of the Public Health Service, and in the second place to Asst. Surgeon M. K. Gwyn, who after due instruction took the bulk of the measurements.

Summary

The average stature of the Old Americans is in males (727 subjects) 174.23 cm., in females (210 subjects) 161.84 cm.

The average for the males is practically the same for a general series from all states, for a series from Virginia and neighboring territory, and for the northeastern Tennessee highlanders. The first series comprises essentially clerical and professional people; the second mechanics and engineers; the third farmers and mountaineers; and there are also some differences in the exact ancestry of the three series.

As it is, the Old Americans exceed in stature the American people at large, all other nationalistic groups within the same, and all larger groups of the white race in Europe.

Increase of stature in incoming people or rather their descendants is apparently still going on; and the same seems true in regard to the older American stock, at least in some regions. The college reports in particular show advances in stature.

No specific single cause is evidently instrumental in these phenomena, what underlies them being probably a complex wholesome stimulation, both physical and mental in character.

Variation. The individual variation in the stature of the Old Americans is large, extending over 40 cm. in the males and 32 cm. in the females; but it is not greater than in other larger groups of whites. The dispersion of the measurements is fairly regular in the females; somewhat irregular (tendency to two modes) in the males.

Influence of age. Up to about the fiftieth year of life the influence of age upon adult stature is more or less obscured by the fact that in the youngest generation of adults stature is not stationary but tends still towards an increase in which other factors than age are concerned. In those after 50, both sexes, stature is lower, but the amount of age influence in this is not certain.

Geographic differences. In the Old Americans geographic differences in stature are astonishingly small.

Influence of type. The average stature of the blonds and near blonds is practically the same as that of the darks.

Head form. The dolichocephals, as usual in Western and Northern Europe, show a somewhat higher stature; the difference is fairly marked in the males but is only slight in the females.

WEIGHT

The study of weight in any group of people is one of many difficulties. Weight is more variable than any other dimension and hence calls for a large number of observations; it differs with stature and age, and to some extent also with habits and occupation; it is most readily influenced by abnormal conditions and disease; and except in recruits it can only be taken with clothing, the weight of which differs with seasons as well as in persons. Due to these difficulties but a few satisfactory studies of weight have ever been made, in the United States or elsewhere, on the general population; to which should be added the fact that in this and other English-speaking countries what data there are on the subject are given in pounds (with stature in inches), which for use in anthropometric comparisons necessitates laborious conversions.

The two largest series of observations on weight of the adults in the United States population are those of the Army and Navy, and those of the Life Insurance Companies. Records on the former are scattered in the numerous annual reports of the Surgeons General, and in the special reports on the Civil and World Wars;[8] while the data of the Insurance Companies are embodied into several "standard" tables that are published by the companies. The weights and heights of the Army and Navy are in the nude, and apply essentially to young adults of some selection. Those of the Insurance Companies which, being taken on hundreds of thousands of individuals of all ages and classes of the population, would be of great value to science if properly secured, represent men and women weighed and measured in their full ordinary clothing as well as their shoes. All of which will permit only imperfect comparisons with our data.

The Old Americans were weighed on a Fairbanks scale, in pounds, without hat and coat in the women, and without hat, coat and vest in the men, but otherwise in their ordinary shoes and clothing.[9] The weights thus obtained were found to be on the average about 4 pounds in the males and about 3 pounds in the females above what they would be in the nude, and they could be estimated as roughly 4 pounds in the males and 3 pounds in the females lower than the weights of the Insurance companies. They will be used throughout the article in reduction to nude values.[10]

---

[8] For references see under "Stature" as well as in this section.

[9] The 130 drafted Tennessee Highlanders were weighed nude.

[10] It would obviate many difficulties if by a general agreement all weights, however taken, were given in reduction to nude weight.

The total number of Old Americans weighed was 867, of which 664 were males and 203 females.   The results appear in table 54.

The most apparent fact from these crude figures is that of the marked differences in weight in the three male groups.   This, as will be shown later, is partly connected with differences in mean age, but so far as the Tennessee highlanders are concerned, also with other conditions.

The range of distribution of weight in the male and female Laboratory series, which are the most representative of the Old American adult population at large, appears in tables 55 and 56.

These tables of frequencies show certain peculiarities, which are especially clearly visible in the chart (fig. 5).   It may be observed in the first place that the subdivisions of fifty, while showing more variation than in the case of stature, are nevertheless, with perhaps one exception in each sex, fairly uniform and grouped close about the general average, thus strengthening confidence in the value of the latter.   The minima and maxima are however, as usual with weight, far apart, the range amounting to 72.2 per cent of the average with the males and no less than 94.3 per cent with the females; and this after the elimination of all who could be regarded as obese, *i.e.*, abnormally stout,[11] as well as the unhealthy and other abnormals.   A range of variation of such magnitude is found in no other measurement of the body.   But there is no reason to see in the above results anything peculiar to the Old Americans.   The greater range in our and probably other females is due to a larger proportion in this sex than in the males of light weights.

The curves of distribution of weight are interesting in both sexes through the rapid ascent to the mode; through their protracted descent, with a tendency at the end of it to a slight rise, or obesity; through the unusual distance between the mode (or first mode in males) and the average; and because of the double mode in the males.   The main cause of all these peculiarities is probably the factor of age, both sexes being represented by more young than older adults.   This condition will best be seen on the second chart (fig. 6).

The two conditions that, as well known, most influence weight, are stature and age.   Figure 6 gives the curves of distribution of each of these features in the Old Americans examined in the Laboratory and there will be perceptible some correspondences as well as disagreements.   The influence of stature and age is apparently not equal in the two sexes.   In the men there seems to exist a greater correlation between weight and stature, in the women between weight and age.   The subject of correlation of weight with both stature and age will be dealt with more in detail later on.

[11] Really obese persons appear to be exceedingly rare among the Old Americans.

TABLE 54

Old Americans: Weight, nude, (in pounds)

SERIES	MALES (664)			FEMALES (203)
	Laboratory (232)	Southern "Engineers" (302)	Tennessee Highlanders (130)	Laboratory (203)
Average weight...............	*150.3*	141.4	137.9	*127.3*

Laboratory series—Females:Males::84.7:100.

TABLE 55

Old Americans (Laboratory), males: Weights (nude)

Number of observations: 232

General average: 150.3 pounds

1st series of 50—147.0 pounds	4th series of 39—151.4 pounds
2nd series of 50—153.4 pounds	5th series of 47—150.9 pounds
3rd series of 46—150.1 pounds	

Minimum: 111 pounds.   Maximum: 219.5 pounds

	TABLE OF FREQUENCIES										
	111-119 pounds	120-129 pounds	130-139 pounds	140-149 pounds	150-159 pounds	160-169 pounds	170-179 pounds	180-189 pounds	190-199 pounds	200-209 pounds	210-219.5 pounds
Number of cases...............	11	19	48	43	48	28	13	9	4	4	5
Per cent......................	*4.7*	*8.2*	*20.7*	*18.6*	*20.7*	*12.1*	*5.6*	*3.9*	*1.7*	*1.7*	*2.1*

TABLE 56

Old Americans (Laboratory), females: Weights (nude)

Number of observations: 203

General average: 127.3 pounds

1st series of 50—127.3 pounds	3rd series of 50—131.6 pounds
2nd series of 50—126.2 pounds	4th series of 53—124.7 pounds

Minimum: 86 pounds.   Maximum: 206 pounds

	TABLE OF FREQUENCIES												
	86-89 pounds	90-99 pounds	100-109 pounds	110-119 pounds	120-129 pounds	130-139 pounds	140-149 pounds	150-159 pounds	160-169 pounds	170-179 pounds	180-189 pounds	190-199 pounds	200-206 pounds
Number of cases.....	3	11	31	47	35	23	17	17	10	6	1		2
Per cent............	*1.3*	*5.4*	*15.3*	*23.2*	*17.2*	*11.3*	*8.4*	*8.4*	*4.9*	*3.0*	*0.5*		*1.0*

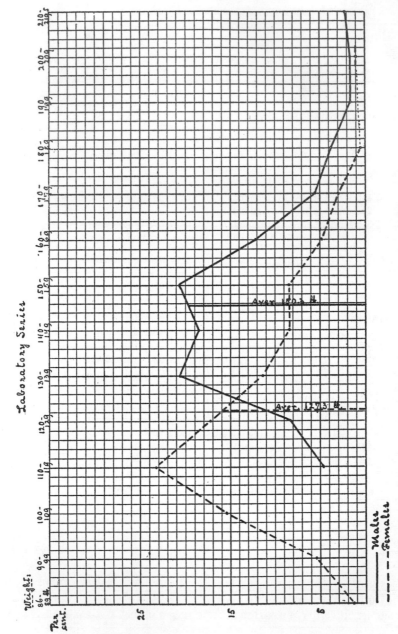

FIG. 5. OLD AMERICANS: WEIGHT (NUDE)—LABORATORY SERIES

With the simple data that precede at hand, the first question that naturally arises is, how do they compare with other like records on American people, and table 57 gives such comparisons as far as suitable data are available.

The comparative data just given are far from what is needed, nevertheless they bring out a number of points that claim some attention.

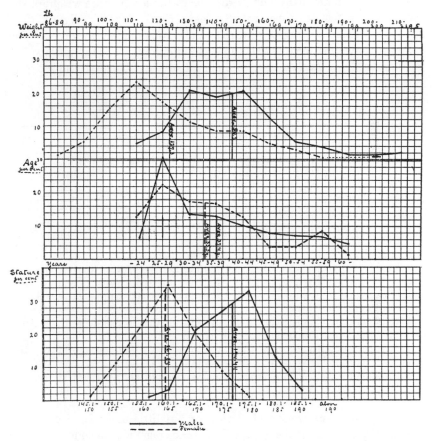

FIG. 6. OLD AMERICANS: DISTRIBUTION OF WEIGHT AND AGE—LABORATORY SERIES

The first is the agreement in weight between the Old Americans and males of the general American population whose stature and age are closest to the Old American average. This however, is comparing our series with a selected group of the general population, a group which, the elevated stature would seem to indicate, may be essentially of the same composition as our series, that is, represent also Old Americans, for there is no other part of the population of the States that shows such a high mean stature. When the Old Americans are compared in weight with the Insurance records at large on only the basis of age, they are in general somewhat lighter, as will be shown presently.

The second noteworthy fact is the somewhat low average weight of the Old American female. She is in the mean nearly 3 pounds lighter than American women at large of stature and age equalling her averages. The males, we have just seen, showed no such difference. The explanation lies most probably in the fact that, while most of the subjects in the series of

TABLE 57

*Weight in Old Americans and other American groups**

OLD AMERICANS		OTHER OLD AMERICANS			AMERICANS IN GENERAL			
Laboratory		Drafted "Engineers," Virginia	Drafted Tennessee Highlanders	U. S. Army Men of Maine†	Accepted Recruits U. S. Army		General U. S. Population (Medico-Actuarial Table) Approximate ¶	
Males	Females				1893–'6‡	1917–'18§	Males	Females
(232) 150.3 lbs.	(203) 127.3 lbs.	(306) 141.4 lbs.	(130) 137.9 lbs.	(1000) 140.9 lbs.	(24,289) 145.0 lbs.	(868,445) 141.5 lbs.	150 lbs.	130 lbs.

* All figures reduced to approximate weight in the nude.

† Baxter (J. H.)—Statistics, Med. and Anthrop. of the Provost Marshal General's Bureau (for the Civil War), 1875, I, 53. Ages 20 to 46; those beween 24 and 44 about equally represented. A large majority of the subjects in this series were undoubtedly Old Americans.

‡ Whites of native parentage. Med. Statistics of the Surgeon-Gen. U. S. Army for 1893–1896. Ages 20 to over 50, but a large majority below 28.

§ Davenport (Charles B.) and Albert G. Love—Army Anthropology, Pub. Med. Dept. U. S. Army in the World War, 8°, Wash., 1921, 119.

¶ These figures apply only to men and women of stature and age closest to the average of the Laboratory series of Old Americans.

Old Americans were women of clerical or but little muscular occupation' a general series such as that of the Insurance companies includes a greater proportion of housewives and muscularly harder-working individuals. In other words, the deficiency in average weight of the Old American women as compared to the women of this country in general, is on the whole most likely connected with less muscular exercise in those classes of the Old Americans that entered into our series, but these classes constitute a large majority of the Old American women of today.

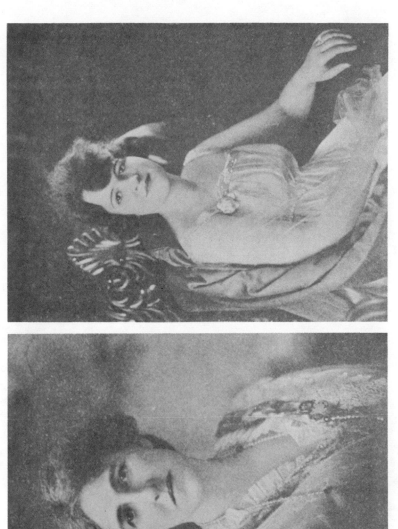

MRS. CARIE WHITE AVERY
(Washington, D. C.)

Past President of the D.C.Ch. of War Mothers and National
Custodian of Records for War Mothers.

More than 3 generations American ancestry, both sides

MARCELITE RAWSON AVERY
(now Mrs. Lockhart)

Daughter of Mrs. Carie White Avery. Old American, both sides.

The frequency of slenderness on the part of the Old American women was repeatedly noted during the examinations.   In adolescence and up to young adult life a marked tendency to lankiness exists in general in both sexes of the older stock, and not seldom the slenderness persists throughout life; but among the women of our series, especially those below forty and again above fifty, spareness was more common and more noticeable than among the men.

TABLE 58

Weight of drafted Old Americans, contrasted with weight of other drafted men

	DRAFTED OLD AMERICANS		OTHER DRAFTED MEN		
	Virginia and neighboring States drafted "Engineers"	Tennessee Highland drafted farmers and mountaineers	Accepted native white recruits (volunteers) 1906–1915*	Accepted recruits world war (white and colored)†	Life insurance data (approximate)
	(306)	(130)	(19,219)	(868,445)	
Average age (years)........	23.15	25.5	20.29	24.9	25.0
Average stature............	174.26	174.30	171.8	171.4	171.5
Average nude weight in pounds.................	141.4	137.9	144.8	141.54	142.0
Average nude weight in grams..................	64,138.0	62,550.0	65,675.0	64,260.0	64,410.0
Grams-per-centimeter ratio..	*368.0*	*358.9*	*382.3*	*374.9*	*375.6*

* Report Surg. Gen. U. S. Army.

† Of the first million examined; Davenport and Love's Army Anthropology.

The southern engineers and the Tennessee highlanders, are also lighter than the Insurance group of males of similar age and stature,[12] but the weight of the engineers agrees closely with that of the United States Army men of Maine (a large majority doubtless Old Americans) and is very nearly identical with that of the recruits of 1917–1918.   Both of these groups, however, were of slightly (by about 2 cm.) lower mean stature, so that the

[12] In these connections again the student of these questions cannot but voice the wish that the records of our great Insurance companies be secured in a scientific manner which would involve but little more time or cost.   With all the future before them it would seem well worth while to commence anew with their measurements of both stature and weight, taking the measurements according to anthropometric standards and separating the results by nationality and class.   It would cost no more, or but little more labor, and the results would not only give greater satisfaction to the companies but would be of much value to science for all time to come.

Old Americans must still be regarded as tending towards a trace greater slenderness.[13]   (See table 58.)

Interesting corroboration of these facts is found in the records of the World War.[14]   Speaking of the demobilization data of this and the Civil War, the authors say (page 164):

It appears that while men 70 inches tall or less were more robust in 1919, those from 71 to 75 inches were less robust in 1919 than in 1865.   This is largely because the later figures contain many Southerners of slender build, who were absent from the earlier Civil War series.

And on page 165:

Of all States and Territories, Alaska stands first in robustness of its drafted men.   This is followed by North Dakota, South Dakota, Montana, Minnesota, Wisconsin, Nevada and Oregon.   The men of the Northwest are tall men, but they are relatively so heavy that there is in those States a high index of build.   In other words, they are large men. However, in the case of Wisconsin the high index of build is partly due to the relatively short stature (although above the average) of its drafted men.   Examining now the bottom of the table, we find that, using the second power of stature as the divisor, the drafted men from Tennessee and Kentucky lie at the very bottom of the list.   Men from these States have practically the same mean weight, but the men from Tennessee are taller.   Accordingly, their index of build is much less than that of men from Kentucky. Indeed, they are less robust than those of any State.   The low rank of these States is due

---

[13] In using the southern "Engineers" series in which a considerable number of individuals were between 20 and 24 years of age, the question arose repeatedly as to whether or not it would be necessary to exclude these subjects; but a comparison with the rest showed them to be so close in all important respects that their discard is hardly necessary. As a matter of fact the younger group, as will be seen below, show already, in harmony with the younger generation of the Old Americans in general, a perceptibly higher stature as well as weight, with correspondingly slightly larger head and face; but their relative proportions remain practically identical with those of their older comrades.

Adults and subadults, Southern "Engineers"

	STATURE	HEIGHT SITTING-STATURE RATIO	WEIGHT	HEAD			CEPHALIC MODULE-STATURE RATIO	FACE			NOSE	
				Length	Breadth	Height		Height to nasion	Height to crinion	Diameter bizygomatic maximum	Length	Breadth
Those of 24 years of age and above..........	173.3	52.3	146.4	19.8	15.3	13.8	94.0	12.3	18.8	13.9	5.4	3.5
Those below 24 years...	175.4	52.3	148.5	19.8	15.4	14.0	93.5	12.5	19.1	14.0	5.4	3.5

---

[14] Davenport and Love's Army Anthropology, 164–6.

especially to mountain sections, although the men of Tennessee seem to be of the tall, slender type throughout the State.

And on page 166:

By any method of calculating built, the Southern States tend to lie toward the bottom of the list. . . . . This low position is due both to the great stature of the men of these States and also to their relatively low mean weight.

In explanation the authors suggest hookworm and malaria as the probable causes of the condition, to which it is safe to add some malnutrition; yet this is not all the explanation. These men are generally Old Americans and a tendency to slenderness, it has been shown here, appears to be characteristic of this type. The Old Americans, in general and normally, tend to be tall and slender. In men the slenderness is relatively unobtrusive and inconsequential; but in a good many of the women when it is marked, it is

TABLE 59

Weight in drafted men, eastern Tennessee

LOWER HIGHLANDS						MOUNTAINEERS					
Number of subjects	Mean age	Mean height	Mean weight	Weight	Grams-per-centimeter	Number of subjects	Mean age	Mean height	Mean weight	Weight	Grams-per-centimeter
		cm.	pounds	grams				cm.	pounds	grams	
26	22.39 (20–24)	173.9	140.9	63,911	367.5	28	22–52 (20–24)	175.03	140.8	63,865	364.9
9	25.4 (25–26)	175.7	142.0	64,410	366.5	15	25.3 (25–26)	173.85	140.2	63,607	365.9

accompanied by subdevelopment of the chest and breasts and constitutes not seldom esthetically as well as physiologically (capacity for nursing, etc.) more or less of a disadvantage.

The Tennessee highlanders show decidedly underweight for both age and stature, and that either as compared to the Insurance records or to our other series of Old Americans. And the underweight was especially noticeable in the mountaineers proper, due doubtless to the disadvantages of their environment. Taking the most comparable age series from the mountains, and from the lower highlands where living conditions are better, we obtain the comparisons given in table 59. To those who know the food and manner of life of the mountaineers, their relatively poor showing in weight will be no surprise; the wonder is how they have reached and preserved their equally tall stature with the rest of the Old Americans, most of whom live under far better conditions.

Weight and age

This subject has already been partly dealt with in the preceding pages. The influence of age upon weight, after eliminating or harmonizing the factor of stature, is shown most conclusively and regularly in the great tables of the Insurance companies. These tables demonstrate that, as a general rule, weight advances in the average person until senility sets in, after which it begins to diminish. In the Old Americans, the only series fit for a more comprehensive test of this point are those of the Laboratory, and they are not sufficiently large to give results as regular as those of the medico-actuarial tables which are based on the records of many hundreds of thousands of subjects; notwithstanding which, the same phenomenon of an increase of weight with age up to approximately middle life is observed,

TABLE 60

Weight and age

Laboratory series

	AGE OF MALES					AGE OF FEMALES				
	24–29	30–39	40–49	50–59	Above 59	22–29	30–39	40–49	50–59	Above 59
Number...............	(83)	(62)	(42)	(32)	(10)	(71)	(70)	(34)	(26)	(3)
Weight.................	146.6	158.6	156.5	159.8	169.6	123.4	127.5	143.9	138.1	142.2
Stature...............	174.4	174.9	174.5	173.3	175.9	162.6	161.9	162.7	158.9	166.1
Gram-centimeter ratio*...	*381.3*	*411.3*	*406.8*	*412.7*	*437.3*	*344.2*	*357.2*	*401.2*	*394.2*	*388.4*

* Grams of weight per centimeter of stature.

after which there is noticed a tendency to decline. The facts are shown with particular clearness by the gram-centimeter ratio. The correlation of weight with age is plainly less regular and important than that of weight and stature. (See table 60).

Weight vs. stature

There are various ways of showing the relation of weight to stature, but the majority are of such a nature that neither the process nor the results give any concrete meaning.

The most generally used forms by which to express the relation are the so-called "ponderal" index of Livi[15] and the "baric index" or "height-weight

---

[15] Livi (R.)—L'indice ponderale etc., Atti Soc. Rom. Antrop., 1897, V, 2 fasc.

index of build" of Rohrer, Giuffrida-Ruggeri and Bardeen.[16]   The ponderal index is the percental relation of stature to the cube-root of weight $\dfrac{(100\sqrt[3]{weight})}{(stature)}$; while the more favored baric index (in German "Index der Körperfülle) is the percental relation to weight of the cube of stature $\dfrac{(weight \times 100)}{(stature^3)}$.

TABLE 61

Weight-height gram-centimeter index

	MALES			FEMALES
	Laboratory (232)	Virginia, etc., "Engineers" (302)	Tennessee Highland drafted men (130)	Laboratory (203)
Stature......................	174.44	174.26	174.30	161.84
Mean age (years)...............	37.2	23.15	25.5	35.8
Weight, nude (pounds)...........	150.3	141.4	137.9	127.3
Weight, nude (grams)...........	68,176	64,138	62,550	57,742
Weight nude, per centimeter of stature (grams)...............	390.8	368.0	358.9	356.8
Approximate nude weight of Americans at large of ages and stature closest to the averages of the Old Americans (M. A. Tables)	150 pounds 68,039 grams 390 grams per centimeter			130 pounds 58,967 grams 362 grams per centimeter

The simple common-sense object in comparing weight with stature, however, is to find what units of mass correspond in a given individual or group to a definite unit of stature.   We wish to know how many pounds and fractions of a pound of weight correspond in a given case to each inch of height, or, in metric form, how many grams of weight there are to each centimeter of stature.   The results are something fairly definite and easy

[16] Rohrer (F.)—Eine neue Formel zur Bestimmung der Körperfülle.   Corr.-Bl. Anthrop. Ges., 1908, XXXIX, 5; Giuffrida-Ruggeri (V.)—L'indice barico etc. Arch. di Fisiol., 1918, XVI, fasc. 1–2; and Riv. di Antrop., 1919, XXIII; see also Martin (R.)—Lehrb. d. Anthrop., 156–7.   The meaning of this index is best explained in Bardeen (C. B.)—The Height-Weight Index of Build etc., Publ. 272, Carnegie Inst. Wash., n.d. (1918 ?), 483–554.   Compare Bardeen, Am. J. Phys. Anthrop., 1923, VI, No. 4.   See also Frassetto (F.)—Height-Weight Index of Build.   Eugenics in Race and State, 1923, II, 34–36; and Davenport (Charles B.)—Body-Build and Its Inheritance.   8°, Carnegie Institute of Washington, December, 1923.

to understand, and the method in the writer's opinion deserves preference in all work of more general interest.

In the Old Americans, after reduction to nude weight and conversion of pounds to grams, the grams-per-centimeter ratios are found to be as shown in table 61.

These data need but little comment for their essentials have already been discussed. They show, it should be borne in mind, weight-stature ratios modified by the potent factor of age. An ideal series, for which at present there are not enough of scientific records, would be one in which the modifying influence of age could be eliminated by having ample groups of subjects of the same ages. As it is, our data outside of points dealt with before,

TABLE 62

Old Americans: Weight and stature

		STATURE OF MALES			STATURE OF FEMALES		
		160.01–170	170.01–180	180.01–190	150.01–160	160.01–170	170.01–180
Laboratory series*...	Number of subjects	(54)	(140)	(33)	(69)	(112)	(20)
	Mean age (years)	38	37	37	36	36	33
	Mean weight	146.3	155.2	166.8	122.4	133.5	144.4
Virginia "Engineers".	Number of subjects	(66)	(182)	(50)			
	Mean age (years	24	23	23			
	Mean weight	139.4	147.0	161.1			
Tennessee High-landers..........	Number of subjects	(28)	(86)	(16)			
	Mean age (years)	26	25	26			
	Mean weight	124.3	139.6	152.9			

* Groups of less than 5 omitted.

indicate only the convenience and possibilities of the gram-centimeter ratio for group comparisons.

A more direct light is thrown on the correlation of weight and stature in the Old Americans by the figures given in table 62. There is, it will be noted, a rather regular and marked increase in weight with increase in stature. In our most representative series, those of the Laboratory, this increase amounts to very nearly 10 pounds for each centimeter in height in the males, and to almost exactly 11 pounds for a similar increase in height in the females. In the Virginia and Tennessee series the progress, while equally marked and of on the whole much the same potentiality, is somewhat less regular.

The best way of showing the weight of a given group is unquestionably that adopted by the statisticians of the Life Insurance companies, as illustrated in the Foster,[17] the Shepherd,[18] the National Fraternal Congress[19] and expecially the Medico-Actuarial Tables.[20]   It consists in giving the mean weight of subjects of similar stature (inch divisions) for each five years of age.   Unfortunately, our group of Old Americans is not large enough for such treatment; moreover, as already mentioned, the Life Insurance tables which if the measurements had been properly taken, would constitute an invaluable basis for anthropological comparisons in this country, represent stature in shoes and weight in full clothing (save only overcoats and hats),[21] so that they can be used only after a double reduction (stature and weight) which can hardly be sufficiently accurate for scientific purposes.   Still as these are the only data of consequence on the general American population, we shall make such use of them as we can.

Reducing both our own and the Medico-Actuarial data to nude weight,[22] we obtain the contrasts given in tables 63 and 64.

Both sexes of the Old Americans are seen to show lighter weight than the American population at large, when compared with the latter in detailed age-stature groups, at most ages.   The actual facts will appear even more strikingly in table 65.

It is seen that, with the males, in 25 of the 32 groups (78.1 per cent) the weight of the Old Americans is less, in but 2 groups (6.2 per cent) it is equal and in only 5 groups (15.6 per cent) it is higher than that of Americans at large as represented in the great Insurance series.   And with the females the condition is even more marked; among 14 groups the Old American females are lighter in 12 (85.7 per cent), equal in 1 (7.1 per cent) and heavier in 1 (7.1 per cent), than the American women of all parentage.

---

[17] J. Inst. Actuaries, London, 1885, XXV, 253 (Charles and Edwin Layton, London, 1886).

[18] Proc. Ass. Life Ins. Med. Directors, 1897 (Medico-Actuarial Investigation I, 19).

[19] Proc. XIV Ann. Session Nat. Frat. Cong., Buffalo, 1900, p. 140.

[20] Medico-Actuarial Mortality Investigation, 3 vols., 4to, New York, 1912, I.

[21] "The measurements of stature are taken with shoes on in all insurance examinations and so far as I know there is no discounting in any way.   The heights are with shoes." Letter May 4, 1922, to the writer from Dr. Louis I. Dublin, Statistician, Metropolitan Life Insurance Company.

[22] *Old Americans:* weight in males reduced 4 pounds in females 3 pounds for part of clothing they wore (see above).

Life Insurance data: weight in males reduced 8 pounds, in females 6 pounds for full clothing and shoes in which they were weighed; also stature reduced in both sexes 1 inch to discount shoes in which they were measured.

TABLE 63

Old Americans: Weight (nude) by age and stature (in stocking feet)

MALES: LABORATORY (232)

AGE		163.8–165.2 cm. (5 feet, 5 inches)	165.3–168.8 cm. (5 feet, 6 inches)	168.9–171.4 cm. (5 feet, 7 inches)	171.5–173.9 cm. (5 feet, 8 inches)	174.0–176.7 cm. (5 feet, 9 inches)	176.8–179.0 cm. (5 feet, 10 inches)	179.1–181.5 cm. (5 feet, 11 inches)	181.6–184.1 cm. (6 feet)	184.2–186.6 cm. (6 feet, 1 inch)	186.7–189.2 cm. (6 feet, 2 inches)	189.3–191.8 cm. (6 feet, 3 inches)
20–29	Life insurance data	132.5	136.0	140.0	144.0	148.0	153.0	159.0	165.0	169.0		
	Old Americans	126.0	133.1	147.7	139.6	141.4	143.2	150.9	148.6	148.0		
	Number of subjects (Old Americans)	(3)	(14)	(11)	(11)	(18)	(10)	(11)	(5)	(3)		
30–39	Life insurance data		142.5	147.5	152.0	157.0	162.0	168.0	174.0	180.5		193.0
	Old Americans		136.7	147.5	150.3	157.8	154.5	158.2	153.6	182.0		183.7
	Number of subjects (Old Americans)		(7)	(12)	(4)	(14)	(11)	(3)	(4)	(3)		(2)
40–49	Life insurance data		147.0	152.0	157.0	162.0	168.0	174.0	180.5			
	Old Americans		149.3	149.4	146.5	157.6	158.2	153.7	174.2			
	Number of subjects (Old Americans)		(4)	(7)	(6)	(5)	(6)	(7)	(4)			
50 and over	Life insurance data		150.0	155.0	160.0	165.0	170.0	176.0	183.0			
	Old Americans		141.5	146.0	157.7	159.3	168.5	183.5	183.0			
	Number of subjects (Old Americans)		(4)	(10)	(6)	(10)	(7)	(2)	(3)			

Note: Wherever but one subject of the Old American series was available for comparison the case was omitted.

TABLE 64

Old Americans: Weight (nude) by age and stature

FEMALES: LABORATORY (203)

AGE		148.8-151.2 cm. (4 feet, 11 inches)	151.3-153.7 cm. (5 feet)	153.8-156.2 cm. (5 feet, 1 inch)	156.3-158.7 cm. (5 feet, 2 inches)	158.8-161.2 cm. (5 feet, 3 inches)	161.3-163.7 cm. (5 feet, 4 inches)	163.8-165.2 cm. (5 feet, 5 inches)	165.3-168.8 cm. (5 feet, 6 inches)	168.9-171.4 cm. (5 feet, 7 inches)	171.5-173.9 cm. (5 feet, 8 inches)
20-29	Life insurance data		112.5	115.0	118.0	121.5	124.5	128.5	132.5	136.5	140.5
	Old Americans		*108.5*	*113.9*	*112.2*	*116.7*	*119.2*	*128.3*	*118.1*	*132.5*	*133.1*
	Number of subjects (Old Americans)		(6)	(5)	(7)	(13)	(4)	(13)	(13)	(7)	(4)
30-39	Life insurance data	116.5	118.5	121.0	124.0	128.0	132.0	136.0	140.0	144.0	156.0
	Old Americans	*98.5*	*110.0*	*104.1*	*117.8*	*120.4*	*129.1*	*153.3*	*126.0*	*140.4*	*139.2*
	Number of subjects (Old Americans)	(4)	(3)	(5)	(4)	(17)	(14)	(3)	(10)	(5)	(3)
40-49	Life insurance data			128.5	131.5	134.5	138.5	143.0	147.0	151.0	
	Old Americans			*112.5*	*131.0*	*135.7*	*126.3*	*137.9*	*161.4*	*150.8*	
	Number of subjects (Old Americans)			(2)	(3)	(9)	(3)	(7)	(4)	(3)	
50 and over	Life insurance data	127.0	130.0	133.0	136.0	139.0	143.0	146.5	151.5	156.5	
	Old Americans	*124.0*	*127.8*	*159.0*	*140.3*	*124.1*	*134.0*	*141.0*	*142.5*	*126.0*	
	Number of subjects (Old Americans)	(2)	(4)	(3)	(3)	(3)	(4)	(4)	(2)	(2)	

The Old Americans vs. other racial groups

As within the United States, so in other countries, while there are many data on the weights of children, students and recruits, there is but little except in Insurance records on the adults of the general population. The best lot of measurements on record, for purposes of comparison with the Old Americans, are those of the British Anthropometric Committee. They

TABLE 65

Weight in age-stature groups of Old Americans and American population at large

AGE GROUPS	MALES			FEMALES		
	Old Americans: Lighter*	Equal	Heavier	Lighter	Equal	Heavier
20–29	8		1	6	1	
30–39	6	1	2	5		
40–49	6		1	1		1
50 and above	5	1	1			

* Than life insurance series of similar ages. Only those groups are included where at least five Old Americans were available for comparison.

TABLE 66

Weight in Old American and the people of Great Britain and Ireland

	MALES				
	Old Americans, Laboratory	English	Scotch	Irish	Welsh
Stature......................	174.44	171.2	172.97	172.6	169.4
Nude weight in pounds..........	150.3	147.0	157.3	146.1	150.3
Nude weight in grams...........	68,176	68,678	71,350	66,269	68,175
Grams per centimeter...........	390.8	389.5	412.5	383.9	402.4

include the older data of Roberts and Beddoe, extent to adults of between 20 and 50 years of age from many parts of the British Isles and are given in a succinct form in the "Final Report" of the Committee.[23] If the weight taken with clothes be reduced to nude weight—deducting 8 pounds in males and 6 pounds in females—the comparisons in table 66 become possible.

These records are of very considerable interest. The English, in their gram-centimeter ratio are exceedingly close to the Old Americans, the Welsh and especially the Scotch being absolutely as well as relatively

[23] Trans. 53rd Meeting B. A. A. S., 8°, London, 1884, 253 *et seq.*

heavier, the Irish absolutely as well as relatively lighter. The bulk of the ancestry of our Laboratory subjects was English.

Beddoe[24] in 1869 estimated the average stature of adult Englishmen to "without doubt lie somewhere between 5 feet 6 inches and 5 feet 7 inches, or 167.6 and 170.2 cm., with naked weight "somewhere about 145 pounds" or 65,771 grams, so that the grams-per-cubic centimeter ratio for adult male Englishmen at large would be *389.1*, which is practically identical with that of the later Anthropometric Committee, and very close once more to that of the taller Old Americans.

TABLE 67

Weight versus height in various Europeans

(All records reduced to nude weight)

	MALES			FEMALES		
	Stature	Weight	Grams-per-centi-meter ratio	Stature	Weight	Grams-per-centi-meter ratio
	cm.	*grams*		*cm.*	*grams*	
Polish Jews (Elkind)....................	161.0	55,000	*341.5*	150.6	50,000	*332.0*
Russian Jews (Weissenberg)..............	165.1	61,300	*371.5*	153.6	53,500	*348.5*
Belgians (Quetelet)*.....................	168.6	66,100	*382.0*	156.4	55,300	*353.5*
Norwegians..........................	170.0	66,000	*388.0*			
Swiss (Schaffhauser).....................	169.4	65,800	*388.5*			
Europeans in general, approximate........	166.0	65,000	*391.0*	154.0	54,000†	*350.5*
Americans at large (life insurance data) approximate...........................	171.5	68,945	*401.0*	160.0	58,967	*368.5*
Old Americans (Laboratory series)........	*174.44*	*68,176*	*390.8*	*161.84*	57,742	*356.8*

* Anthropométrie, 344, 346. Men and women thirty years old.

† Martin's estimate of their weight as 52,000 is too low.

A few other observations on the adult population of Europe, after data gathered by Martin[25] and from other sources, will be of interest (table 67).

From the above, as from all previous comparisons, it is seen that while the general American population is well nourished and somewhat above the European average for similar age and stature, the Old Americans are inclined to greater slenderness. This is plain in the males, who are both absolutely and relatively lighter than any of the groups available for comparison except

[24] Beddoe (John)—On the Stature and Bulk of Man in the British Isles. Mem. Anthrop. Soc., London (1869, III, 384–573; also 8°, London, 1870, 191 pp.)

[25] Lehrb. d. Anthrop., 248.

the Jews, and it is true individually also of many of the females, though the
average of the sex comes close to that of Belgian and other European women
as far as recorded, being notably exceeded only by that of American women
of miscellaneous parentage.

Only a few of the men but more of the women among the Old Americans
tend after 35 to become corpulent; more remain spare, though often rather
wiry, from youth to death.   It is, however, always necessary to bear in mind
that our records (Laboratory) apply mostly to people of clerical and intellectual occupations or those of leisure, and not to farmers or laborers.
Nevertheless the tendency to slenderness is not limited to the classes represented in our Laboratory examinations.   It is equally notable in the drafted
Old Americans who were studied, though they were nearly all workingmen
and farmers.   And it is most apparent in the highlanders from the Appa-
lachians, where it is however not infrequently influenced by subnutrition.
The figures above show the conditions very clearly.

Summary

The average weight of the Old Americans, considering their tall stature,
is moderate, with the usual large range of individual variation.   The dispersion is fairly regular in the females, bimodal in the males.

In both males and females, but especially in the females, the weight of the
Old Americans tends to be less for the same stature and age than it is in the
white American population in general.

No appreciable differences in weight are observed as between the North
and South; but the highlanders and mountaineers of northeastern Tennessee
are notably underweight as compared with any of the other groups of similar age and stature.   The underweight of the Tennessee men is not accompanied by any lowering in stature.

Age.   Weight advances on the average until senility begins to set in after
which it tends to diminish.

Stature.   There is a fairly regular and marked increase in weight with rise
in stature.

Comparative.   The weight of the most comprehensive series (Laboratory)
of Old Americans, stature for stature, is nearly the same as that of the Englishmen in the Beddoe series of measurements; though the English series
probably differed somewhat occupationally.

The tendency to a slightly greater spareness among the Old Americans is
again perceptible when these (males) are compared with the Scotch, Welsh,
and some groups of continental Europeans.

HEIGHT SITTING

The height sitting is one of the most useful measurements in anthropometry, giving on one hand the height of the trunk together with the neck and head, and on the other the length of the lower extremities. The latter is not the absolute length of the lower limbs, the taking of which is impracticable on the living, but the mean length of the two limbs below the ischia, which is both an easy and very desirable determination.

The actual conditions regarding height sitting and its relation to stature in various groups of mankind have recently been amply and ably presented by Bean[26] and Bardeen.[27] As their memoirs show there is a wealth of observations on the subject, and the results are of unusual interest. The relative dimensions of the trunk as compared to stature, are seen to differ considerably during the growth period, sexually, racially, and according to stature, and for Bean these variations have definite genetic significance. Bardeen subjects the data gathered by Bean and others to a more advanced mathematical treatment and obtains some further conclusions of value.

Nevertheless the subject is still full of complexities that have not been fully unravelled. In dealing with the measurement little attention is usually given to the fact that it involves two distinct lines of variation, namely those of the trunk with the upper part of the body, and those of the lower limbs, which may not always be reciprocal or even closely correlated. The trunk and the extremities have each their own phylogeny and their own functional influences, and these demand a separate comprehensive study in each anthropological group, if not in each individual. Without such study it is quite impossible to say that any two relatively long-torso groups or persons present really the same biological condition. The redeeming feature is that when we deal with sufficiently large and as near as possible normal groups, the general biological tendency within such groups preponderates and manifests itself more or less clearly notwithstanding the secondary factors that may also be present. It is in this light that we may employ convenient expressions such as the sitting height-stature index (or the additional indices of Bardeen and Bean) in group comparisons.

In the Old Americans the general conditions so far as the relative trunk length and relative length of the lower limbs are concerned, appear as shown in tables 68 and 69 and figures 7 and 8. The averages are close to the

[26] Relation of the Sitting-Height to Stature. By Bean (R. B.), Am. J. Phys. Anthrop., 1922, V, No. 4.

[27] General Relations of Sitting-Height to Stature and of Sitting-Height to Stature and Weight. By Bardeen (C. R.), *ibid.*, 1923, VI, No. 4.

medium of the white race. The sexual differences are about normal, and the same is true of the range of variation. The range of distribution, however, is somewhat atypical, and that even if we discount the smallness of

TABLE 68

Old Americans: Sitting height-stature ratio

(Laboratory series)

Males (247)   Females (210)
General average *52.94*   General average *53.92*
Minimum—50.2; Maximum—57.4   Minimum—50.7; Maximum—58.6
Female:Male::101.9:100

										DISTRIBUTION							
	50.2–50.5	50.6–51.0	51.1–51.5	51.6–52.0	52.1–52.5	52.6–53.0	53.1–53.5	53.6–54.0	54.1–54.5	54.6–55.0	55.1–55.5	55.6–56.0	56.1–56.5	56.6–57.0	57.1–57.5	57.6–58.0	58.1–58.6
Males.....	(6) 2.4	(10) 4.0	(18) 7.3	(24) 9.7	(31) 12.5	(41) 16.6	(40) 16.2	(38) 15.4	(19) 7.7	(11) 4.4	(5) 2.0	(3) 1.2			(1) 0.4		
Females..		(5) 2.4	(4) 1.9	(10) 4.8	(22) 10.5	(18) 8.6	(22) 10.5	(30) 14.3	(23) 10.9	(21) 10.0	(26) 12.4	(16) 7.6	(8) 3.8	(2) 0.9	(1) 0.5	(1) 0.5	(1) 0.5

TABLE 69

Old Americans: Length of the lower limbs (below the ischia) versus stature

(Laboratory series)

Males (247)   Females (210)
General average *47.06*   General average *46.08*
Minimum—42.6; Maximum—49.8   Minimum—41.4; Maximum—49.3
Females:Males::97.8:100

								DISTRIBUTION								
	41.4–42.0	42.1–42.5	42.6–43.0	43.1–43.5	43.6–44.0	44.1–44.5	44.6–45.0	45.1–45.5	45.6–46.0	46.1–46.5	46.6–47.0	47.1–47.5	47.6–48.0	48.1–48.5	48.6–49.0	49.1–49.5	49.6–49.8
Males.....			(1) 0.4			(4) 1.6	(5) 2.0	(13) 5.3	(21) 8.5	(45) 18.2	(34) 13.8	(42) 17.0	(34) 13.8	(19) 7.7	(17) 6.9	(6) 2.4	(6) 2.4
Females...	(1) 0.5	(1) 0.5	(1) 0.5	(5) 2.4	(7) 3.3	(16) 7.6	(28) 13.3	(18) 8.6	(28) 13.3	(28) 13.3	(23) 10.9	(18) 8.6	(20) 9.5	(7) 3.3	(4) 1.9	(5) 2.4	

the series. This is seen especially well in the chart giving the distribution of the relative length of the lower limbs. Both curves show at least two modes, and in both, but particularly so in the females, the summit is low, broad and dull. Evidently there is an expression here of various agencies

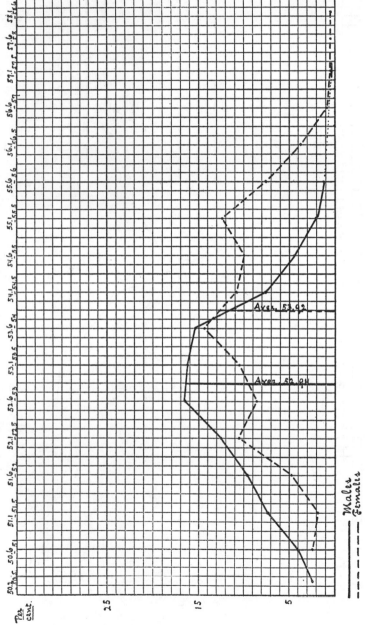

FIG. 7. OLD AMERICANS: SITTING-HEIGHT-STATURE INDEX

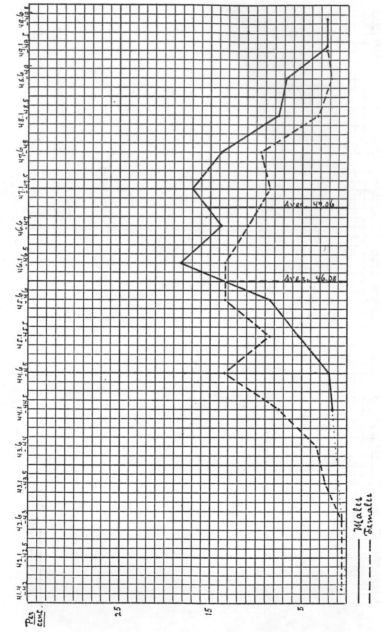

Fig. 8. Old Americans: Length of Lower Limbs (below Ischia) In per cent of Stature

Miss Olive Bachelder
(Dorchester, Mass.)

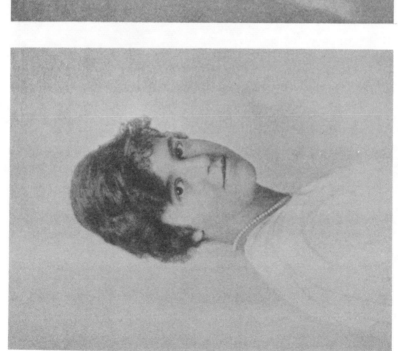

Mrs. Fred. Manville
(Newport News, Va.)

Old American ancestry on both sides, in each

that have acted on the trunk or on the lower limbs, but which it would be difficult to precise or separate.   Should we adopt larger, say double, groupings, the present irregularities would be largely submerged, but such a procedure would hardly be proper; the object of the curve must be to disclose, not to hide, conditions, even though the former aim cannot be perfectly attained with smaller numbers of individuals.

Trunk and lower limbs vs. age, stature, and head form

Length of trunk and length of lower limbs vs. age.   In examining into the length of the arms in the youngest and oldest of our adults it was found, it will be seen, that the arms were relatively longer and that to a very perceptible degree, in the younger generation.   Curiously enough a somewhat similar condition pertains though in less degree to the lower limbs— they also are somewhat longer in the young than in the old.   The explanation here will most likely be a greater exercise of the limbs in the younger Americans.   The amount of exercise in schools, colleges and outdoors has doubtless increased between the time represented by the youth of our younger and our older adults.

Length of trunk and length of lower limbs vs. stature.   The relative length of the lower limbs and of the trunk shows a decided difference in both sexes according to stature.   The short (males and females) have short legs, while in the tall the lower limbs are of a length plainly above the average.   On the whole therefore it is shown that the short-statured have a relatively long trunk and short legs with, as we have seen, long arms in both sexes; while the tall have relatively short trunk, long legs and arms of moderate length.

These conditions are probably very largely if not entirely of ontogenetic significance (nutrition, health, exercise); and in all probability they are not peculiar to the Old Americans.

Length of trunk and length of lower limbs vs. head form.   Our most dolicho- and most brachycephalic groups differ, in both sexes, but little in age and stature; and they differ also but slightly and irregularly in the relative proportions of the trunk and lower limbs.   It may safely be said that as with the arms and many other features, the type of the head has but little if any effect on the absolute or relative proportions of such parts.

Comparative data

The position of the Old Americans, as a group, as to height sitting and its relation to stature in respect to other whites and other races, may in the simplest way be seen from table 72.   While they are the tallest of the

TABLE 70

Old Americans: Sitting height–stature ratio vs. age, stature and head form

(Laboratory series)

Age

	MALES			FEMALES	
	Mean age	Sitting height-stature ratio		Mean age	Sitting height-stature ratio
25 youngest...............	24	52.66	25 youngest	24	53.42
25 oldest.................	59	53.10	25 oldest...............	57	54.31

Stature

	Mean stature	Sitting height-stature ratio		Mean stature	Sitting height-stature ratio
25 shortest...............	164.4	53.60	25 shortest	151.9	54.98
25 tallest	184.4	51.94	25 tallest...............	171.7	53.07

Type of head

	Mean cephalic index	Sitting height-stature ratio		Mean cephalic index	Sitting height-stature ratio
25 most dolichocephalic.....	73.22	52.57	15 most dolichocephalic..	74.01	54.08
25 most brachycephalic.....	84.64	53.04	20 most brachycephalic..	84.71	53.87

TABLE 71

Old Americans: Sitting height by stature

	MALES						FEMALES			
Stature, *cm*............ {	141–150	151–160	161–170	171–180	181–190	above 190	141–150	151–160	161–170	171–180
Sitting height index:										
Old Americans......		(5)	(170)	(445)	(103)	(2)	(3)	(72)	(115)	(20)
		54.9	53.2	52.6	51.9	50.7	55.1	54.4	53.9	52.9
Germans (Pfitzner*)	(34)	(277)	(748)	(295)	(9)		(223)	(612)	(197)	
	53.1	52.6	52.4	52.1	51.8		53.0	52.9	52.6	

* Pfitzner (W.)—Social anthropologische Studien: I. Der Einfluss der Lebenslaters auf die anthropologischen Charactere. Zeitschr. f. Morph. u. Anthrop., 1889, I, 325–377; —Die Proportionen des erwachsenen Menschen. Zeitschr. f. Morph. u. Anthrop., 1902–3, V, 201–314.

TABLE 72

*Sitting height in selected groups**

	MALE				FEMALE			
	Num-ber	Stature	Sitting height	Sitting height index	Num-ber	Stature	Sitting height	Sitting height index
Australians.................	40			45.5	10			47.9
Central Africans............	226			47.4				
Africans...................	3,884			49.9	185			50.3
Melanesians................	200			50.0	10			51.3
Negrito...................	378			50.9	10			49.8
India.....................	598			51.6				
Indians of North America....	1,398			52.0	494			52.1
Malay....................	1,417			52.1	125			52.0
Indians of South America....	2,812			52.4	756			53.2
Asiatics (yellow-browns other than Chinese	158			52.4	46			52.4
Europeans.................	8,499			52.4	1,346			53.1
GENERAL HUMAN MEAN....		165	85.0	52.5		155	80.0	53.5
Old Americans..............	727	174.3	91.8	52.6	211	161.8	87.3	53.9
Aino.....................	90			52.8	71			53.6
Siberians..................	1,417			53.5	72			53.5
Chinese...................	1,429			53.6	25			53.0
Eskimo...................	94			53.7	74			54.6
African Pygmies............	49			53.7	16			52.9

* Body of data after Bean, *loc. cit.*, p. 366.

TABLE 73

Height sitting in various groups of United States whites

GROUP	NUMBER	STATURE	SITTING HEIGHT INDEX
German..................................	7051	172.04	52.52
Scotch..................................	2074	172.54	52.60
Old Americans..........................	711	174.30	52.63
English.................................	4199	172.08	52.67
Hebrew.................................	1684	166.91	52.76
Polish..................................	2404	169.41	52.78
Irish...................................	6137	171.36	52.79
Italian.................................	3506	165.18	53.13
French.................................	1455	168.59	53.07

TABLE 74

Stature, sitting height and sitting height index, in Americans

PLACE	OBSERVER	MALES				FEMALES			
		Number of subjects	Stature	Sitting height	Sitting height index	Number of subjects	Stature	Sitting height	Sitting height index
Soldiers, Camp Lee............	Bean	(610)	172.4	90.6	52.7				
Soldiers, Camp Gordon.........	Bean	(523)	174.8	91.2	52.3				
Soldiers, motor truck camp.....	Bean	(444)	174.1	91.0	52.3				
Students, soldiers and instructors, Virginia....................	Bean	(489)	173.8	90.4	52.0				
General average.............	Bean	(2066)	*174.0*	*90.8*	*52.4*				
Soldiers, white, demobilized.....	Love and Davenport	(96,239)	171.99	90.39	52.56				
University of Wisconsin students entering college (not all mature)...................	Bardeen	(425)	173.35	90.17	52.01	(1,045)	161.57	85.6	52.98
University of Nebraska students (not all mature)............	Clapp,*					?	160.0	85.1	53.19
Old Americans:									
Laboratory................	Hrdlička	(247)	174.4	92.3	*52.94*	(211)	161.84	87.27	*53.92*
Tennessee.................	Hrdlička	(133)	174.3	92.3	*52.97*				
Army camp, Virginia........	Bean and Hrdlička	(347)	174.2	91.2	*52.30*				

*Quoted by Bardeen.

whites (see section on Stature) and give also the tallest mean absolute height of the trunk, the relation of the height sitting to stature is practically identical with that of the European whites and also with the approximate means of humankind as a whole. The arms in the Old Americans are, we shall see, perhaps due to functional causes, relatively somewhat short but the lower limbs, while absolutely longer, just as the thorax with neck and head are longer, retain the same relative value to the rest of the body as they possess in the whites in general. Taking a number of the better represented nationalities in the United States (see table 73)[28] the Old Americans stand naturally between the Scotch and English, whose blood they mostly represent. It is plain again that so far as the relations of lower limbs to the rest of the body is concerned, no noticeable change has taken place in the Americans in from three to five generations.

Taking Old American, or predominantly so, groups from different localities, there is found a remarkable similarity of results, which makes these data of exceptional value for future comparisons. These results are decidedly gratifying, showing the reliability and utility of carefully gathered anthropometric data (table 74).

Summary

The records on the Old Americans are close to the medium of the white race.

The sexual differences are about normal and the same is true of the range of variation.

The dispersion of the observations is somewhat atypical and bi-modal.

Effects of age. The length of the lower limbs—as of the arms—is relatively somewhat greater in the young than in the old.

Effects of stature. The short of both sexes have relatively short legs; the tall relatively long legs.

The short statured have relatively long trunk, short legs and long arms in both sexes; the tall have relatively short trunk, long legs and arms of moderate length.

Effects of head form. As with the arms the type of the head appears to have but little if any effect on either the absolute or relative proportions of the lower limbs of the trunk.

[28] Soldiers at demobilization, published by Davenport & Love; after Bardeen, Am. J. Phys. Anthrop., 1923, VI, No. 4, 362, which work see also for other data on whites.

ARMS

Length of arms

The length of the upper limbs, as compared to the length of the trunk or body, is a character of both phylogenetic and ontogenetic significance. All the living anthropoid apes have relatively long arms, wherefore the assumption seems justified that a similar condition existed more or less in man's Primate ancestors; but the fact is not as yet demonstrable by the few remains of prehuman forms or of early man sufficiently well preserved for the purpose.

The arm length differs considerably among the existing races, the shortest arms being those of the Eskimo and the Japanese, the longest in general those of the African and Oceanian blacks. Some of these differences are doubtless of ancestral, some of acquired nature. The arm length also differs considerably in individuals, where it may be of reversional nature, or a simple inheritance expression (family characteristic), or an individual functional (use or disuse) modification.

The length of arms may be measured and shown in a number of ways. It may be roughly judged of by the reach of the hands on the thighs when a person is standing with arms applied to the body; it may be measured direct on the arms in the living or on the bones of the same in the skeleton; or by the easiest and most common method it may be measured in the living through the maximum arm-expanse ("finger-reach," "la grande envergure"), which is then compared with trunk length (height-sitting) or more commonly with stature. None of these methods are perfect. The best would be the measuremnt of the arm as such in the living, but the proximal landmark of the humerus is often difficult to establish; in the case of the dry bones the hand is lacking; while in that of arm-expanse the measurement includes the breadth of the chest which has its own variations. The last method nevertheless commends itself through the ease with which the measurement is taken; through the fact that notwithstanding individual variation in the breadth of the chest (shoulders), the arm-stretch compare with stature gives remarkable uniform results in groups; and finally for the reason that many measurements of similar nature are already at our disposal for comparison. For these reasons it was this method that was chosen in the study of the Old Americans.

Expressing the greatest arm stretch in relation to stature, it is found that in the Old American males this proportion averages 102.6 (stature = 100), in the females 99.6. Both of these are low values, as will be seen on reference to the table on page 126, which gives the averages of the same measurement in different racial groups. As the Old Americans are not characterized by specially narrow chest or shoulders, their low values for arm expanse can only mean a relative shortness of the arms, which, if long arms may be regarded as primitive, is to be considered as an advanced human character. As such it is probably in part ontogenetic and functional in character. Practically none of the Old Americans comprised in the Laboratory series, which alone are represented in this mesurement, were men or women who ever worked hard manually. Muscular work, however, tends to increase the bones of the arm not only in strength, but to a moderate degree also in length.

TABLE 75

Old Americans, Males: Maximum finger-reach

Number of observations: 245
General average: 179.2 cm.

1st series of 50–177.5 cm.   4th series of 49–177.4 cm.
2nd series of 50–180.1 cm.   5th series of 50–179.1 cm.
3rd series of 46–180.2 cm.
Minimum: 157.0 cm.   Maximum: 200.8 cm.

	TABLE OF FREQUENCIES								
	157.0–160.0 cm.	160.1–165.0 cm.	165.1–170.0 cm.	170.1–175.0 cm.	175.1–180.0 cm.	180.1–185.0 cm.	185.1–190.0 cm.	190.1–195.0 cm.	195.1–200.8 cm.
Number of cases.....	2	5	20	43	55	66	40	11	3
Per cent............	*0.08*	*2.0*	*8.2*	*17.5*	*22.4*	*26.9*	*16.3*	*4.5*	*1.2*

The distribution of the actual measurements in the two sexes is shown in tables 75 and 76, and in figure 9. The dispersion is remarkably regular in both sexes, more so than was the case with stature, weight or the measurements of the lower extremities (*q.v.*); and the curves are remarkably steep, showing at the same time a large aggregation of cases about the average or median. It is thus seen that the necessary inclusion into the measurement of the breadth of the shoulders did not prove as disturbing as might have been anticipated.

Arm length and age

There is no apparent reason why arm spread and arm length respectively should differ with age alone, within the limits of our adult series (24 to 60 years); and should differences appear there would be a rather strong inclination to regard them as accidental or incidental to other submerged factors. Taking the 25 youngest and 25 oldest male and female individuals of our laboratory series, the facts obtained are as shown in table 77. There is a difference, and that by no means a negligible one. The youngest males show a decidedly larger arm spread than the oldest, and though the difference is not so marked, the same condition appears in the females. The differences are plainly not connected with, or at least not fully accountable by differences in stature. They are also not connected with the breadth of the chest or shoulders respectively. The chest is broader in fact in the old of both sexes who have a shorter arm expanse, than it is in the young whose arm expanse is very perceptibly longer.

TABLE 76

Old Americans, females: Maximum finger-reach

Number of observations: 209
General average: 161.2 cm.

1st series of 50–162.2 cm.   3rd series of 50–162.1 cm.
2nd series of 49–159.7 cm.   4th series of 60–160.9 cm.
Minimum: 143.4 cm.   Maximum: 181.6 cm.

TABLE OF FREQUENCIES

	143.4–145.0 cm.	145.1–150.0 cm.	150.1–155.0 cm.	155.1–160.0 cm.	160.1–165.0 cm.	165.1–170.0 cm.	170.1–175.0 cm.	175.1–180.0 cm.	180.1–181.6 cm.
Number of cases.....	3	5	29	56	61	38	12	3	2
Per cent.............	1.4	2.4	13.9	26.8	29.2	18.2	5.7	1.4	1.0

But two reasons suggest themselves in explanation of the above unexpected showing. One is a probably greater exercise of the arms in the younger generation, particularly in games such as baseball; the second being that possibly in the older adults there is somewhat less suppleness of muscles and tendons than in the younger; in other words that the young are able to stretch somewhat more than the old. The author is inclined to give greater weight however, to the first cause.

Arm length and stature

Taking the 25 shortest and 25 tallest individuals, male and female, of our laboratory series, groups which show fairly similar age, it appears that the arm spread is a trace greater in both sexes in the shortest individuals. The difference is somewhat more marked in thefemales than in the males.

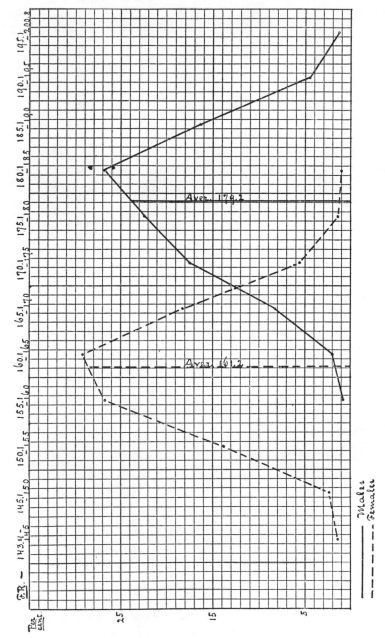

FIG. 9. OLD AMERICANS: MAXIMUM FINGER REACH

TABLE 77

Old Americans: Arm length vs. age, stature and head form

Laboratory series

MALES

	Age	Stature	Cephalic index	Breadth of chest	Arm spread	Difference between arm spread and stature
Arm-spread and age						
25 youngest............	24	173.8		29.0	179.8	+6.0
25 oldest..............	59	174.6		29.9	175.8	+1.2
Arm-spread and stature						
25 shortest............	33	164.4		28.9	169.2	+4.8
25 tallest.............	37	184.4		30.1	188.5	+4.1
Arm-spread and type of head						
25 most dolichocephalic...	35	176.1	73.2	29.6	180.9	+4.8
25 most brachycephalic...	33	173.4	84.6	29.4	178.1	+4.7

FEMALES

	Age	Stature	Cephalic index	Breadth of chest	Arm spread	Difference between arm spread and stature
Arm-spread and age						
25 youngest............	24	163.0		26.2	162.3	−0.7
25 oldest..............	57	160.5		27.0	158.2	−2.3
Arm-spread and stature						
25 shortest............	38	151.9		25.6	151.7	−0.2
25 tallest.............	34	171.7		27.9	170.4	−1.3
Arm-spread and type of head						
15 most dolichocephalic.	35	161.6	74.0	26.6	160.5	−1.1
20 most brachycephalic.	32	161.3	84.7	26.7	161.1	−0.2

Here once more the difference in arm spread is not connected with differences in the breadth of the shoulders or chest respectively; for the latter, and hence undoubtedly the former also, are greater in the tall who have the relatively shorter arm expanse, than they are in the short.

These conditions, too, are difficult to explain. There is no reason to believe that the short have been more active with their arms than the tall; and so the only cause of the difference that suggests itself is that in the short the stature on the average may have been influenced by ontogenic conditions which did not equally affect the length of the arms. In other words, the short, had conditions been favorable, would probably have developed a taller stature, in connection with which their arm length would not have been exceptional.

Arm length vs. type of head

In selecting the 20 most dolichocephalic and 20 most brachycephalic males, with respectively 15 and 20 individuals of the same type in the females, we obtain groups that differ but slightly in age or stature. The differences in arm spread are not large and they do not agree in the two sexes. In the males the arms are slightly longer on the average in the dolichocephals—in the females, in the brachycephals. The figures establish, therefore, nothing definite. The breadth of the chest and shoulders also in these two groups is almost identical.

Comparative data

Little additional needs to be said about the relative arm length except to show its racial distribution. Utilizing the more reliable data[29] we find its distribution as given in table 78 which includes also a number of groups measured by the writer. These data are quite interesting. The lowest relative arm length on the whole is present in the yellow-brown peoples, and the American Indians as well as the Eskimo show once more their close affinity to the yellow-browns of Asia in this respect. The longest arms predominate among the blacks with the exception of the Bushmen and possibly a few other groups. The whites stand intermediate. In all three main stocks however, there is a considerable range of group variation.

Among the whites the relatively shortest arms are found in the Semites

[29] Some of the older data are, for some reason plainly erroneous. This applies especially to the American Civil War records on the Iroquois, whose relative arm length is given as 108.5, a figure which, together with others concerning this group, is certainly incorrect and should not be used.

TABLE 78

Percental relation of greatest armstretch to stature (stature = 100) in various groups of mankind*

	MALES	FEMALES
Whites		
Arabs...	101.3	
Kabyles...	101.5	
Albanians...	101.6	
Old Americans..................................	*102.6*	*99.6*
Polish Jews.......................................	103.2	101.0
Russian Jews......................................	103.3	100.0
Jews...	103.3	
Great Russians....................................	103.6	103.4
Germans, Baden...................................		103.4
Norwegians.......................................	103.7	
South Russian Jews...............................	103.8	102.9
Swedes...	104.0	
American soldiers, Civil War......................	104.3	
Parisians...	104.3	
French...	104.4	
Livonians...	104.5	
Gipsies (European)................................	104.6	
Letts...	104.7	104.6
Belgians..	104.8	101.6
French (Godin)....................................	106.1	
Lithuanians.......................................	106.6	
Esthonians..	107.4	
Esthonians..	108.0	
Yellow-brown		
Asiatic:		
Japanese..	99.2	
Japanese..	102.6	100.5
Chinese, Northern.................................	102.1	101.5
Chinese, Northern.................................	102.1	
Chinese Southern..................................	102.9	
Malays, Perak.....................................	102.8	
Formosans..	103.7	
Koreans..	104.0	
Daiak..	104.5	
Galibis...	104.6	
Tibetans..	104.7	
Buriats...	104.8	
Malays, Menangkaban..............................	104.9	
Tatars..	105.0	103.0
Tatars of Kasimoff................................	105.5	
Aino...	105.9	104.6

TABLE 78—*Continued*

	MALES	FEMALES
Yellow-brown—Continued		
American:		
Eskimo...	99.3	97.9
Eskimo...	99.5	
Eskimo (St. Lawrence Island)........................	*99.7*	*99.4*
Eskimo Koukpagmiut...............................	102.5	100.3
Eskimo Numatagmiut..............................	103.1	102.4
Apache..	*100.6*	*100.6*
Indians of Colorado...............................	100.7	
Tarahumare..	*100.9*	*100.3*
Huichol...	*101.0*	*99.6*
Fuegians...	101.4	
Tarasco...	*101.7*	*102.5*
Aztecs (Tlahuiltec)...............................	*102.1*	*101.3*
Papago...	*102.3*	*100.6*
Otomi..	*102.4*	*101.7*
Sioux (Yankton)..................................	*102.7*	
Pueblos...	*102.7*	*102.5*
Mohave...	*103.0*	*101.8*
Pima...	*103.0*	*102.3*
Athapascan (Tahlta)...............................	103.5	101.0
Maricopa...	*103.7*	*103.1*
Yuma...	*103.8*	*100.3*
Shoshoni...	104.3	
Indians of Brazil..................................	104.5	103.2
Bororo...	104.7	
Yaqui..	*105.0*	
Blacks		
African:		
Bushmen...	102.1	100.8
Masai..	105.0	
Fan..	105.0	105.0
Mawambi Pygmies.................................	105.2	107.3
American Negro (full-bloods).......................	*105.6*	
Lobi...	105.9	104.5
Duala..	108.0	
Dschagga..	108.6	106.4
Oceanian:		
Australians..	104.9	
Negrito, Phillipine Islands..........................	*105.1*	*104.2*
Merauke...	106.5	104.8
Jakumul, New Guinea..............................	106.9	
Toricelli, New Guinea..............................	107.4	
Areep, New Guinea................................	108.8	

* Data after Topinard and Martin; those in italics originals by Hrdlička.

and Old Americans with the addition possibly of a few similar groups; while the relatively longest arms are reported in the Lithuanians and Esthonians; the latter data however, seem to need corroboration.

Among the yellow-browns, the shortest arms relatively are those of the Japanese and Eskimo. In not a few of the Japanese, and as a rule in the Eskimo the chest and shoulders are well developed so that the shortness of the arm spread is not due to any lack in this direction.

Among the blacks, among whom in the wild state the development of the chest and shoulders is not extraordinary, the arms, and as we know from studies on the skeleton especially the forearms, are really long.

In comparing the two sexes it will be observed that wherever the women work a good deal, as among the less civilized whites, practically all the Indians, and most blacks, the relative arm length in the females is close to that in the males and may be quite equal or even a little greater. In the Old Americans the sex difference in this respect is well marked, due probably to both a relatively greater shortness of the arms as well as a relatively slighter development of the chest and shoulders.

Summary

The length of arms in the Old Americans of the non-laboring classes in relation to stature gives low values in both sexes (arm stretch-stature ratio: 102.6 in males, 99.6 in females).

The range of variation is moderate; the dispersion remarkably regular.

Effects of age. The arms are relatively longer in the youngest than in the oldest of the series, particularly so in the males.

The cause is probably a greater exercise of the arms in the younger generation.

Effects of stature. The arm-spread is relatively slightly greater in both sexes in the short than in the tall individuals.

The difference is not due to differing breadth of the chest.

Form of head. The results establish no definite correlation between the form of the head and the length of the arms.

Comparative. The relative length of the arms in the Old Americans, both sexes, is well below the medium of white people in general; but differences in class should receive due consideration.

THE HEAD

Since the beginnings of anthropometry special weight has always been attached to the measurements of the head. The main underlying reason of this is that the head is the seat of the brain and in a large measure an index of its size. In addition, from the very beginnings of craniology a great deal of significance has been attributed to the shape of the skull and the development of its frontal region. Under these conditions, as could be expected, a great deal of attention has been paid to the devising of measurements and other means by which both the size and shape of the skull or head could best be represented. The results of this were on the one hand the invention of a whole special instrumentarium for the measurements and graphic representations of the cranium or head, and on the other the use of numerous measurements as well as methods introduced or favored by individual workers. Some of the instruments and numerous measurements in the course of time became obsolete; but others were standardized and, especially as regards the measurements and methods were eventually fixed by international agreements which are essentially followed today.

The measurements on the cranial vault, or head proper, have been reduced to three, which are the greatest glabello-occipital length, the greatest breadth, and the height. In connection with the last-named measurement however, some discrepancies in methods and instruments still exist, more particularly in the living, where the measurement has been regarded as one of particular difficulty. In the writer's studies these difficulties have been overcome by certain modifications of the *compas d'épaisseur* which is used for the rest of the head measurements, and by a special but relatively simple technique which gives satisfactory results.[30]

The three principal diameters of the head, namely, its greatest length, greatest breadth and its height, together with the module, or the mean of these three diameters, give most useful information as to the size of the skull and brain; while the percental relations of these measurements, namely, the cephalic and height "indices," show clearly the skull shape, and at the same time constitute simple numerical expressions which are of much value for anthropological comparison.

Individual measurements of the head

An analysis of the three principal individual measurements of the head, namely its length, breadth and height, would show many points of interest had we to deal with an unmixed group of population. This in the present instance is not the case. The Old Americans are descendants of all the branches of the white race whose members have reached this country up to

---

[30] See author's Anthropometry, 8°, 1920 (Wistar Institute, Philadelphia).

the beginning of the nineteenth century, and these newcomers have brought with them differing hereditary physical characteristics some of which are known to be very persistent. Where a mixture of this nature has taken place so recently there must be expected a variability of head measurements that has a different and lesser significance than that which would be obtained in an unmixed group. These facts should be borne in mind in connection with the data that will follow. The head height, nevertheless, together with the cephalic module and the relation of the module to stature, will deserve close attention.

Head length

The principal facts shown by the Old Americans through this measurement are given in tables 79 and 80, and figure 10. The results on the Laboratory series of males and those on the Virginia or southern "engineers" were so very close that they have been combined, but the Tennessee highlanders show sufficient difference to necessitate their presentation apart. The range and hence also the curve of frequencies, as could be anticipated, is in all the three resulting groups prolonged and more or less irregular. These are not ranges and curves showing simply the normal oscillation of a character about its mean, but rather those of conglomerate groups in which fusion is as yet imperfect. This is further indicated by the somewhat marked differences in the averages of the male test-series of 100 as shown in table 79.

In the Tennessee highlanders the head length is appreciably smaller than it is in the other Old Americans. This, it will be shown later on, is due simply to a smaller head in this group.

Head length and age. A positive relation of a measurement with advancing age means growth; while an adverse relation, unless incidental to numbers, could only mean that different and more favorable conditions have affected the younger group. As to head growth after adult life has been reached and particularly growth in the different dimensions, we know as yet but little definite. With the separate measurements the subject is greatly complicated through their intercorrelations and their correlation with stature. Notwithstanding these difficulties it may be possible to throw some light on the question so far as the Old Americans are concerned, by our Laboratory records (table 81).

These records indicate that in the Old Americans at least, of both sexes, there is a slight absolute as well as relative (*vs.* stature) augmentation in the length of the head through the larger part of the adult period. The results are too uniform to be accidental.

Mrs. Amanda E. Cooley Holbrook
(Minneapolis, Minn.)
Long American ancestry, both sides

Mrs. Lennoe Drew
(New Orleans, La.)
Long American ancestry, both sides

TABLE 79

Old Americans, males. Head: Diameter antero-posterior

Number of individuals measured: Laboratory and Virginia—594
Highlands of Eastern Tennessee—133
Total 727
General average: Laboratory and Virginia—19.76
Eastern Tennessee—19.50
Laboratory and Virginia
1st series of 150—19.72   4th series of 100—19.82
2nd series of 100—19.88   5th series of 147—19.65
3rd series of 100—19.84
Tennessee series of 133—19.50
Minimum: 18.0 cm.   Maximum: 21.6 cm.

TABLE OF FREQUENCIES

	18.0–18.1 cm.	18.2–18.3 cm.	18.4–18.5 cm.	18.6–18.7 cm.	18.8–18.9 cm.	19.0–19.1 cm.	19.2–19.3 cm.	19.4–19.5 cm.	19.6–19.7 cm.	19.8–19.9 cm.	20.0–20.1 cm.	20.2–20.3 cm.	20.4–20.5 cm.	20.6–20.7 cm.	20.8–20.9 cm.	21.0–21.1 cm.	21.2–21.3 cm.	21.4–21.5 cm.	21.6 cm.
Laboratory and Virginia: Number of cases.......	1	5	8	12	22	28	66	68	85	70	66	65	38	30	15	6	7	1	1
Per cent......	0.2	0.8	1.3	2.0	3.7	4.7	11.1	11.4	14.3	11.8	11.1	10.9	6.4	5.1	2.5	1.0	1.2	0.2	0.2
Tennessee Highlands: Number of cases.......	1	1	3	10	9	11	23	24	9	14	8	7	2	6	2	3			
Per cent......	0.8	0.8	2.3	7.5	6.8	8.3	17.3	18.0	6.8	10.5	6.0	5.3	1.5	4.5	1.5	2.3			

TABLE 80

Old Americans, females. Head: diameter antero-posterior

Number of individuals measured: 210
Average: 18.62 cm. (1st 50, 18.6; 2nd 50, 18.7; 3rd 50, 18.6; 4th 60, 18.55 cm.)
Minimum: 17.3 cm.   Maximum: 20.1 cm.

TABLE OF FREQUENCIES

	17.3	17.4–17.5	17.6–17.7	17.8–17.9	18.0–18.1	18.2–18.3	18.4–18.5	18.6–18.7	18.8–18.9	19.0–19.1	19.2–19.3	19.4–19.5	19.6–19.7	19.8–19.9	20.0–20.1
Number of cases.......	1	1	10	11	18	20	43	17	26	22	14	18	5	2	2
Per cent.............	0.5	0.5	4.8	5.2	8.6	9.5	20.5	8.1	12.4	10.5	6.5	8.6	2.4	1.0	1.0

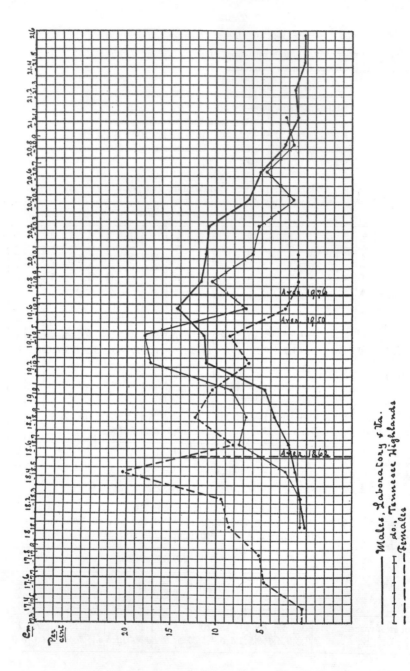

FIG. 10. OLD AMERICANS: CURVES OF FREQUENCY OF DISTRIBUTION OF HEAD LENGTH

Head length and stature.   That a direct positive correlation exists between the head dimensions and stature, is well known to anthropology, but the detailed facts in adults need much further elucidation, to which the present studies on the Old Americans may, it is hoped, contribute.

The data as to the correlation of head-length with stature in the Americans are very plain.   They show throughout the series this correlation to be marked and regular.   They further show some facts of importance regarding the several constituents of the group itself.   The Laboratory and the Southern "Engineers" series give results that are practically identical, while the Tennessee highlanders at every stage lag behind very perceptibly.

TABLE 81

Old Americans: Length of head vs. age

Laboratory series

	YEARS				
	22–29	30–39	40–49	50–59	Above 59
Males (247):					
Number..........................	(91)	(63)	(47)	(34)	(12)
Mean stature.....................	174.14	174.97	174.54	173.98	174.78
Head length.....................	19.71	19.79	19.86	19.87	19.76
Head length-stature ratio..........	11.32	11.31	11.38	11.42	11.31
Females (210):					
Number..........................	(73)	(71)	(36)	(27)	(3)
Mean stature.....................	162.57	161.96	162.42	159.18	(166.07)
Head length.....................	18.55	18.66	18.72	18.59	(18.73)
Head length-stature ratio..........	11.41	11.52	11.53	11.68	(11.28)

Head length and head form.   In general the dolichocephalic head or skull is conceived as long and narrow, and the brachycephalic one as broad and short; but just how the two diameters behave on the road from one form to the other is still somewhat uncertain.   In the Old Americans the head length is modified as shown in table 83.

It will be noted that the greater the dolichocephaly the greater is the length of the head and *vice versa*, and that both absolutely as well as relatively to stature.   Granting brachycephaly to be a later form than mesocephaly or moderate dolichocephaly, it is plain that brachycephaly was reached in part by shortening of the skull.   The important participation in the process of the other two main diameters will be shown later.

Summary.   Head length shows a large range of variation. with rather irregular curves of distribution.

TABLE 82

Old Americans: Head length and stature

	STATURE					
	145.0–150.0	150.01–160.0	160.01–170.0	170.01–180.0	180.01–190.0	Above 190.0
Males:						
Laboratory (247)....... {		(2) (19.20)	(61) 19.54	(147) 19.83	(37) 20.04	
Southern "Engineers" (347)............. {		(3) (18.83)	(82) 19.54	(209) 19.78	(51) 20.0	(2) (20.0)
Tennessee Highlanders (133)............. {			(29) 19.24	(87) 19.56	(17) 19.65	
Females:						
Laboratory (210)....... {	(3) (18.07)	(73) (18.52)	(114) 18.69	(20) 18.72		

TABLE 83

Old Americans: Head length and head form

	MALES						FEMALES	
	Most dolichocephalic			Most brachycephalic				
	Laboratory	Southern "Engineers"	Tennessee Highlanders	Laboratory	Southern "Engineers"	Tennessee Highlanders	Most dolichocephalic	Most brachycephalic
Number of subjects........	(25)	(25)	(24)	(25)	(25)	(22)	(15)	(20)
Mean:								
Cephalic index..........	73.2	72.1	73.6	84.6	84.3	81.8	74.0	84.7
Length of head.........	20.40	20.41	20.02	18.97	19.15	19.04	19.12	18.21
Difference in brachycephals .				−1.43	−1.26	−0.98		−0.91
Stature................	176.1	175.1	173.7	173.4	174.4	172.9	161.6	161.2
Length of head-stature ratio................	11.58	11.66	11.53	10.94	10.98	11.01	11.83	11.30
Difference in ratio in brachycephals........				−0.64	−0.68	−0.52		−0.53

It is much alike in the two main groups of males (with females in normal relation); but smaller both absolutely and relatively to stature in the Tennessee highlanders.

Relation to age: There is observable in both sexes a slight absolute as well as relative (*vs.* stature) augmentation of head length up to about the middle of the adult period.

Relation to stature: There is a marked and regular positive correlation—the higher the stature the greater the head length, in both sexes and all groups.

TABLE 84

Old Americans: Head length vs. head form

GROUPS	CEPHALIC INDEX						
	72.5	72.6–75.0	75.1–77.5	77.6–80.0	80.1–82.5	82.6–85.0	Above 85.0
Males:							
Laboratory and Southern { "Engineers" (594)..... {	(18)	(77)	(162)	(201)	(86)	(37)	(13)
	20.58	20.22	19.96	19.66	19.48	19.19	18.69
Stature.................	175.32	175.19	175.38	173.60	173.23	174.64	171.94
Head length-stature ratio..	*11.74*	*11.54*	*11.38*	*11.32*	*11.25*	*10.99*	*10.87*
Tennessee Highlanders { (133)................ {	(4)	(22)	(44)	(42)	(18)	(2)	(1)
	20.40	19.90	19.56	19.37	19.09	(18.75)	(18.70)
Stature.................	175.92	173.73	174.54	174.68	173.26	(169.30)	(181.30)
Head length-stature ratio..	*11.60*	*11.45*	*11.21*	*11.09*	*10.96*	*(11.07)*	*(10.31)*
Females:							
Laboratory (210)....... {		(19)	(32)	(73)	(52)	(26)	(8)
		19.18	19.02	18.74	18.48	18.15	18.15
Stature.................		161.67	162.19	162.49	161.17	161.91	161.21
Head length-stature ratio..		*11.86*	*11.73*	*11.53*	*11.47*	*11.21*	*11.26*

Relation to cephalic index: As we proceed from dolicho- to brachycephaly, head length plainly and steadily decreases.

Head breadth

The greatest breadth of the skull and head is a measurement which shows a considerable degree of variation even in the purest anthropological groups. In the Old Americans the range extends, in the males, from 13.8 to 17 cm., or 20.7 ($\mp$10.35) per cent of the average, which is a large diffusion indicating not merely a mixed group but a group in which the mixtures have not yet become assimilated. In the females the range is smaller (16.1, or ∓ 8.05 per cent), the reason for which is not quite clear, though probably connected largely if not entirely with the greater variability in the males of the glabella and inion regions. But it is also smaller in the Tennessee highlanders, who through greater intermarriage are more nearly

TABLE 85

Old Americans, males: Head diameter lateral maximum

Number of individuals measured: Laboratory and Virginia—594
Eastern Tennessee—133
Total; 727

General average: Laboratory and Virginia—15.45
Eastern Tennessee—15.10

Laboratory and Virginia

1st series of 100—15.35	4th series of 100—15.42
2nd series of 100—15.45	5th series of 100—15.41
3rd series of 100—15.48	6th series of 94—15.36

Eastern Tennessee: series of 133—15.10
Minimum: 13.8 cm.   Maximum: 17.0 cm.

TABLE OF FREQUENCIES

	13.8-13.9 cm.	14.0-14.1 cm.	14.2-14.3 cm.	14.4-14.5 cm.	14.6-14.7 cm.	14.8-14.9 cm.	15.0-15.1 cm.	15.2-15.3 cm.	15.4-15.5 cm.	15.6-15.7 cm.	15.8-15.9 cm.	16.0-16.1 cm.	16.2-16.3 cm.	16.4-16.5 cm.	16.6-16.7 cm.	16.8-16.9 cm.	17.0 cm.
Laboratory and Virginia: Number of cases.	1	2	3	16	28	43	76	96	92	87	66	30	30	13	6	4	1
Per cent...	0.2	0.3	0.5	2.7	4.7	7.2	12.8	16.2	15.5	14.6	11.1	5.0	5.0	2.2	1.0	0.7	0.2
Eastern Tennessee: Number of cases..		5	3	8	16	17	29	18	14	8	7	4	3	1			
Per cent...		3.7	2.2	6.0	12.0	12.8	21.8	13.5	10.5	6.0	5.3	3.0	2.2	0.7			

a new fused whole than are the males of the other groups. The general data on head breadth, with their seriation and curves of frequency, are given in tables 85 and 86, and fig. 11. The curve of the main body of the males and that of the females are bulky, though less irregular than the corresponding curves of head length. That of the Tennessee highlanders is of much interest. It is much nearer the type of a curve of a homogeneous series, showing the greater fusion and uniformity of this group; and it shows throughout lesser values, which is partly due to the fact that the head of the highlanders is smaller as a whole than that of the males of the other groups, and partly to its being relatively a trace narrower.

TABLE 86

Old Americans, females, head: Diameter lateral maximum

Number of individuals measured: 210

Average; 14.80 cm. (1st 50, 14.8; 2nd 50, 14.7; 3rd 50, 14.8; 4th 60, 14.7 cm.)

Minimum: 13.7 cm.   Maximum: 16.1 cm.

	TABLE OF FREQUENCIES												
	13.6–13.7 cm.	13.8–13.9 cm.	14.0–14.1 cm.	14.2–14.3 cm.	14.4–14.5 cm.	14.6–14.7 cm.	14.8–14.9 cm.	15.0–15.1 cm.	15.2–15.3 cm.	15.4–15.5 cm.	15.6–15.7 cm.	15.8–15.9 cm.	16.0–16.1 cm.
Number of cases.....	2	5	12	11	32	32	35	33	25	12	7	3	1
Per cent...........	*1.0*	*2.4*	*5.7*	*5.2*	*15.2*	*15.2*	*16.7*	*15.7*	*11.9*	*5.7*	*3.3*	*1.4*	*0.5*

TABLE 87

Old Americans: Breadth of head vs. age

Laboratory series

	YEARS				
	22–29	30–39	40–49	50–59	Above 59
Males (247):					
Number...................	(91)	(63)	(49)	(34)	(12)
Mean stature..............	174.14	174.97	174.54	173.98	174.78
Head breadth..............	15.44	15.55	15.47	15.50	15.36
Head breadth—stature ratio..	*8.87*	*8.89*	*8.86*	*8.91*	*8.79*
Females (210):					
Number...................	(73)	(71)	(36)	(27)	(3)
Mean stature..............	162.57	161.96	162.42	159.18	(166.07)
Head breadth..............	14.77	14.82	14.89	14.94	(14.63)
Head breadth—stature ratio..	*9.09*	*9.15*	*9.17*	*8.88*	*(8.81)*

Breadth of head and age.   In the case of head length it was seen that, even though the changes were not great, the dimension in the Old Americans of both sexes increased with age up to the sixth decade.   With breadth, as will be observed in table 87, a similar very slight increase absolutely as well as relatively to stature, is noticeable in both sexes, though in the males

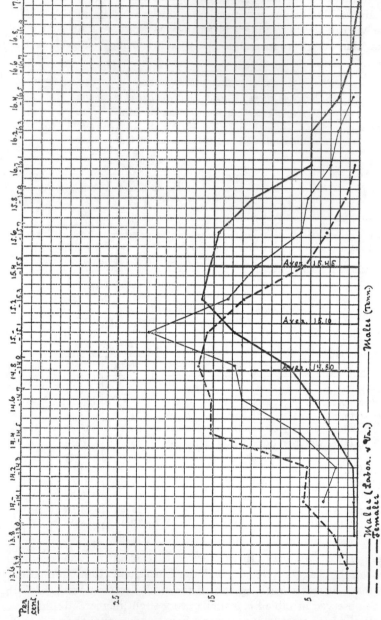

Fig. 11. Old Americans: Head Breadth (Diam. lateral max.)

it is somewhat irregular, while in the females it appears to stop with the fifth decade. The older men and women of both the main series (Laboratory) show, as with length, a trace smaller dimensions than the rest of the adults.

Breadth of head and stature. With head length, the correlation and increase with stature were seen to be definite and quite marked. With head breadth similar but somewhat slighter absolute increase is apparent as the stature rises, except perhaps in the Tennessee highlanders, but relatively the augmentation in head breadth lags considerably behind that in the height of the body.

TABLE 88

Old Americans: Head breadth vs. stature

	STATURE					
	145.0–150.0	150.01–160.0	160.01–170.0	170.01–180.0	180.01–190.0	Above 190.0
Males:						
Laboratory (247)........		(2) (15.50)	(61) 15.45	(147) 15.48	(37) 15.52	
Southern "Engineers" (347)...............		(3) (15.50)	(82) 15.35	(209) 15.35	(51) 15.62	(2) (15.90)
Tennessee Highlanders (133)...............			(29) 14.94	(87) 15.10	(17) 15.40	
Females:						
Laboratory (210)........	(3) (14.40)	(73) 14.76	(114) 14.84	(20) 14.82		

Head breadth and head form. Head breadth differs markedly in heads of different form. Just how large these differences are may be seen from table 89. The simple figures show that the head is decidedly broader in brachy- than in meso- or dolichocephaly. The point of prime interest, however, is how does the participation of the breadth in the transition from dolicho- to brachycephaly compare with that of the length of the head; in other words, are the brachycephals essentially ''broadheads'' or ''shortheads'' or both? This question may perhaps be settled by the comparisons in table 90.

The actual values differ somewhat in the three most distinctive series.

The females differ from the males and the Tennessee highlanders differ
somewhat from the rest of the male subjects. The two main and closely
related series of men, namely those of the Laboratory and the Southern
"Engineers," show by the valuable ratio of the head length and head

TABLE 89

Old Americans: Head breadth and head form

| | MALES | | | | | | FEMALES | |
| | Most dolichocephalic | | | Most brachycephalic | | | | |
	Laboratory	Southern "Engineers"	Tennessee Highlanders	Laboratory	Southern "Engineers"	Tennessee Highlanders	Most dolichocephalic	Most brachycephalic
Number of subjects.........	(25)	(25)	(24)	(25)	(25)	(22)	(15)	(20)
Mean:								
Cephalic index.........	73.2	72.1	73.6	84.6	84.3	81.8	74.0	84.7
Breadth of head........	14.94	14.77	14.74	16.05	16.15	15.57	14.15	15.42
Difference in brachy-cephals.............				+1.11	+1.38	+0.83		+1.27
Stature...............	176.1	175.1	173.7	173.4	174.4	172.9	161.6	161.2
Breadth of head—stature ratio............	8.48	8.44	8.49	9.26	9.26	9.01	8.76	9.56
Difference in ratio in brachycephals........				+0.78	+0.82	+0.52		+0.80

TABLE 90

Old Americans: Differences in head length and breadth in extremes of head form

| | MALES | | FEMALES |
	Laboratory and Southern "Engineers"	Tennessee Highlanders	Laboratory
Most marked brachy—*vs.* most marked dolichocehpals			
Ratio to Stature { Length.........................	−0.66	−0.52	−0.53
Ratio to Stature { Breadth.........................	+0.80	+0.52	+0.80
Length *vs.* breadth ratio (BR = 100)....................	82.5	100.0	66.3

breadth to stature that the breadth in the two extreme forms of head shape
differs more than the length. The same condition but even more marked
exists in the females, where the difference in the breadth-stature ratio
between the dolicho- and brachycephals is one-third (in the males a little

and one-sixth) larger than that in the length-stature proportion. In the bulk of the Old Americans therefore the changes in the breadth of the head are seen to be more influential in the advance towards brachycephaly than are those of the length.[31]

But in the Tennessee highlanders the participation of the two diameters is exactly equal. This cannot be regarded as accidental, the difference is too great. But, if not accidental, then what may be the cause of the peculiar showing? In searching for the cause we must search for the differences between the highlanders and the rest of the Old Americans.

TABLE 91

Old Americans: Head breadth vs. head form

GROUPS	CEPHALIC INDEX						
	−72.5	72.6–75.0	75.1–77.5	77.6–80.0	80.1–82.5	82.6–85.0	Above 85.0
Males							
Laboratory and Southern	(18)	(77)	(162)	(201)	(86)	(37)	(13)
"Engineers" (594)......	14.73	14.97	15.26	15.48	15.73	16.05	16.19
Stature..................	175.32	175.19	175.38	173.60	173.23	174.64	171.94
Breadth-stature ratio......	8.40	8.54	8.70	8.92	9.08	9.19	9.42
Tennessee Highlanders	(4)	(22)	(44)	(42)	(18)	(2)	(1)
(133)................	14.65	14.74	14.94	15.26	15.52	15.90	(16.30)
Stature.................	175.92	173.73	174.54	174.68	173.26	(169.30)	(181.30)
Breadth-stature ratio......	8.33	8.48	8.56	8.74	8.96	(9.39)	(8.99)
Females:							
Laboratory (210).........		(19)	(32)	₍73)	(52)	(26)	(8)
		14.22	14.57	14.76	14.91	15.18	15.56
Stature................		161.67	162.19	162.49	161.17	161.91	161.21
Breadth-stature ratio......		8.80	8.98	9.08	9.25	9.38	9.65

Of these differences there are mainly two that may possibly have an effect in this line; the first is the greater fusion and hence uniformity of these people, apparent throughout the results of their study; the second being their backwardness in that part of their brain and head development which is due to modern education and stresses. Possibly this latter cause is the more potent in this case, for there are some indications that mental

[31] See in this connection "The brachycephalic skull," by F. G. Parsons, J. Anthrop. Inst., 1924, LIV, 166; and "The morphologic types of the skull," etc.; by V. Bunak, Russ. Anthrop. Journ., 1922, XII, 6.

work slightly favors the development of the head in breadth; but here we are treading upon a field which, while tempting, is not as yet sufficiently elucidated.

Summary.   Head breadth shows a large range of variation in the males, somewhat less in the females.   The curves of distribution are more regular than those of length.   The range is less and the curve more regular in the Tennessee highlanders than in the other male groups.

It is much alike in the two main groups of males (with females in normal relation); but smaller both absolutely and relatively to stature in the Tennessee highlanders.

Relation to age: There is a similar increase of head breadth with age as with length up to the fifth or sixth decade of life in the Old Americans, but it is slighter and less regular.

Relation to stature: There is an increase of head breadth with stature similar to, but decidedly lesser than that of head length.

Relation to cephalic index: Increase in cephalic index is accompanied by a steady, marked increase in head breadth.   This increase in the bulk of the Old Americans is even more influential than the concomitant decrease in head length; in the Tennessee highlanders, however, the changes in the two diameters are about equal.

Head height

The height of the head is a character of apparently fully as much importance as the other two main head diameters, and it is only due to the former difficulties of securing the measurement satisfactorily that it has not been made more use of.   The three dimensions of the vault, namely its length, breadth and height, manifest compensatory interrelations, and no study of the head can be regarded as satisfactory without all three being given due attention.

In the writer's work the height of the head has been as obligatory as is the height on the skull, and the measurement is that from the line of the floor of the outer thirds of the two auditory meatus to bregma.[32]   The landmarks for this measurement, while not perfect, prove nevertheless more satisfactory than others that have been proposed in the past, and with due practice and the appropriate instruments, repeated measurements on the same subject give results that do not vary over 2 mm.

The compensatory nature of the height ·(with length and breadth) of

[32] For method and instruments see author's Anthropometry, 8°, Philadelphia, 1920 (Wistar Institute).

the head while evident, is decidedly less marked than is that between the
other two diameters. In general head height shows more independence
than length or breadth, for there are rounded as well as oblong skulls or
heads that are high,[33] and there are brachycephalic as well as dolicho- or
mesocephalic heads that are low.

The principal results of the measurement of head height in the Old
Americans are presented in tables 92 and 93 and figure 12. The general
distribution of the measurement and its range of variation are closely
related to those of the breadth and the curves of both measurements
differ perceptibly from those of the length.

As with breadth, so also with height, the range of dispersion is plainly
smaller in the females than in the males, and is smaller in the Tennessee
highlanders than in the rest of the Old Americans.

The Tennessee highlanders contrast rather poorly in respect to head
height with the rest of the male Americans; while their head shows smaller
in all the diameters, the difference is less in the length than in the breadth
and less in breadth than in height. With a relatively narrower head, if
things were equal, their head height ought to have been greater through
compensation; as it is, however, they are plainly defective in this respect.
The cause is probably the same as that of their relatively small head—
their backwardness in education and in development of their higher mental
faculties.

The sexes both as to height and the other two main diameters of the head,
contrast with each other in a normal way, viz:

$$\text{Females : Males}[34] :: \begin{cases} \text{Length of head,} & 94.2 \\ \text{Breadth of head,} & 95.6 \\ \text{Height of head,} & 95.5 \end{cases} : 100$$

The development of the head in the two sexes follows in the Old Americans,
it is plain, practically the same laws, except for the somewhat greater
volume in the males of the frontal sinuses and occipital ridges which increase the antero-posterior diameter of the skull.

The effect on the head height of stature, age, and dolicho- with brachycephaly, appear as follows:

Head height and age. We have seen that, with length, there was a slight
absolute as well as relative (*vs.* stature) growth with age, through the larger
part of the adult period comprised in our records; and it was noted that a
similar though even slighter and somewhat less regular augmentation up

[33] See writer's Anthropology of Florida, 8°, Florida St. Hist. Soc., Publ. I, 1922.
[34] Exclusive of those from Tennessee.

TABLE 92

Old Americans, males: Head height

Number of individuals measured: Laboratory and Virginia—594
Highlands of Eastern Tennessee—133
Total—727

General average: Laboratory and Virginia—13.95
Eastern Tennessee—13.61
1st series of 150, Laboratory—13.90 cm.
2nd series of 100, Laboratory—13.97 cm.
3rd series of 100, Drafted "Engineers," Virginia—13.95
4th series of 100, Drafted "Engineers," Virginia—13.82
5th series of 127, Drafted "Engineers," Virginia—13.96
Tennessee, series of 133—13.61
Minimum: 12.4 cm. Maximum 15.5 cm.

TABLE OF FREQUENCIES

	12.4–12.5 cm.	12.6–12.7 cm.	12.8–12.9 cm.	13.0–13.1 cm.	13.2–13.3 cm.	13.4–13.5 cm.	13.6–13.7 cm.	13.8–13.9 cm.	14.0–14.1 cm.	14.2–14.3 cm.	14.4–14.5 cm.	14.6–14.7 cm.	14.8–14.9 cm.	15.0–15.1 cm.	15.2–15.5 cm.
Laboratory and Virginia:															
Number of cases (594)..	3	3	9	22	34	74	76	76	104	78	62	21	18	11	3
Per cent......	0.5	0.5	1.5	3.7	5.7	12.5	12.8	12.8	17.5	13.1	10.4	3.5	3.0	1.9	0.5
Tennessee Highlands:															
Number of of cases (133).			4	6	14	15	19	28	20	9	8	6	3	1	
Per cent.......			3.0	4.5	10.5	11.3	14.3	21.0	15.0	6.8	6.0	4.5	2.3	0.8	

TABLE 93

Old Americans, females: Head height

Number of individuals measured: 210

Average: 13.33 cm. (1st 50—13.25; 2nd 50—13.25; 3rd 50—13.35; 4th 50—13.42 cm.
Minimum: 11.9 cm. Maximum: 14.3 cm.

TABLE OF FREQUENCIES

	11.8–11.9 cm.	12.0–12.1 cm.	12.2–12.3 cm.	12.4–12.5 cm.	12.6–12.7 cm.	12.8–12.9 cm.	13.0–13.1 cm.	13.2–13.3 cm.	13.4–13.5 cm.	13.6–13.7 cm.	13.8–13.9 cm.	14.0–14.1 cm.	14.2–14.3 cm.
Number of cases.............	2	2	0	4	14	19	35	32	37	24	19	16	6
Per cent....................	0.9	0.9		1.9	6.7	9.0	16.7	15.2	17.6	11.4	9.0	7.6	2.9

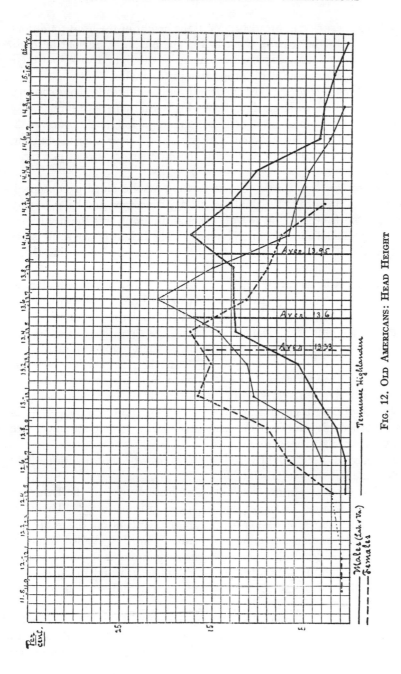

FIG. 12. OLD AMERICANS: HEAD HEIGHT

to middle age occurred in breadth. With the height of the head conditions
are different. In the females there is a slight but fairly regular absolute
as well as relative increase in head height up to the sixth decade; but there
is no appreciable growth in this proportion in the males.

Head height and stature. The head length and head breadth have shown a
marked correlation with stature, increasing with remarkable regularity
as stature increases; and head height is found to follow the same path.
The increase of the measurement with stature is clear cut, though not
exactly the same in detailed values, in the different groups of our series
(table 95).

Head height and head form. So far as the cephalic index is concerned,
the length and breadth of the skull are directly concerned and have, as may
be recalled, both been found to vary, though inversely, as the head form
progressed from dolicho- to brachycephaly. The height of the skull is not
directly involved in this change and it will be especially interesting therefore to note its behavior.

The data in table 96 reveal a number of facts with sufficient definiteness.
The main is that in a progress from dolicho- to brachycephaly there are
changes in skull height, and that they are in one direction, namely towards
augmentation. But these changes are much less than those of either the
length or breadth, so much so that in one of the groups (southern "engineers") they are barely perceptible. Head height therefore may be
regarded as the most stable of the three main head diameters, at least in
the Old Americans. It correlates decidedly with stature and possibly to
some extent also with cultural brain development (note the poor showing
of the retarded highlanders), but only secondarily or not strongly with
the two other main head diameters.

The changes in head height with head form may be shown with perhaps
even more definiteness in tabular form (table 97).

Comparative data. Racial distribution of head height in the living, in
whatever way secured, is as yet known but very imperfectly. There are
however, many series of basion-bregma measurements on the skull and
they show that whole large groups of mankind are low-skulled, while in
others the skull is decidedly high. The differences are doubtless of importance even though, as with variations of skull length and breadth, they
are not yet fully understood. Some data on the subject will be given
later (page 156.)

Summary. Head height: The range and curves of dispersion resemble
more those of head breadth than those of length. The range, as with
breadth, is also larger in the males than in the females. The curves are

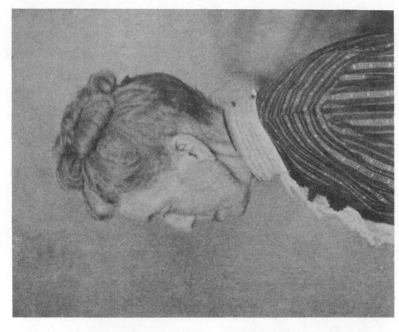

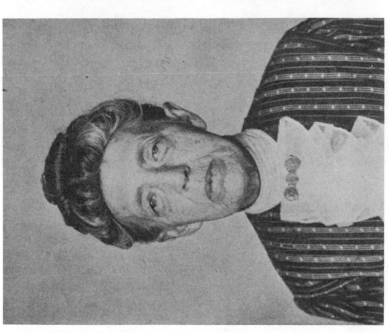

SARAH HALL JOHNSTON (MRS. SANDERS JOHNSTON)
(Washington, D. C.)
For many years Editor of Lineage Book, D.A.R. Long American ancestry, both sides

TABLE 94

Old Americans: Head height vs. age

Laboratory series

	YEARS				
	22–29	30–39	40–49	50–59	Above 59
Males (247):					
Number......................	(91)	(63)	(49)	(34)	(12)
Mean stature..................	174.14	174.97	174.54	173.98	174.78
Head height..................	13.94	13.93	13.97	13.91	13.72
Head-height—stature ratio........	8.0	7.96	8.0	8.0	7.85
Females (210):					
Number......................	(73)	(71)	(36)	(27)	(3)
Mean stature..................	162.57	161.96	162.42	159.18	(166.07)
Head height..................	13.29	13.30	13.46	13.31	(13.23)
Head-height—stature ratio........	8.18	8.21	8.29	8.36	(7.97)

TABLE 95

*Old Americans: Head height vs. stature**

	STATURE			
	150.01–160.0	160.01–170.0	170.01–180.0	180.01–190.0
Males:				
Laboratory (247)......................		(61)	(147)	(37)
Head height......................		13.78	13.96	14.10
Difference from preceding stature group .			0.18	0.14
Southern "Engineers" (347)..............		(82)	(209)	(51)
Head height......................		13.70	13.95	14.13
Difference from preceding stature group .			0.25	0.18
Tennessee Highlanders (133)..............		(29)	(87)	(17)
Head height......................		13.28	13.67	13.70
Difference from preceding stature group .			0.39	0.03
Females:				
Laboratory (210)......................	(73)	(114)	(20)	
Head height......................	13.17	13.38	13.55	
Difference from preceding stature group .		0.21	0.17	

* Groups of less than five individuals omitted.

TABLE 96

Old Americans: Head height and head form

| | MALES | | | | | | FEMALES | |
| | Most dolichocephalic | | | Most brachycephalic | | | | |
	Laboratory	Southern "Engineers"	Tennessee Highlanders	Laboratory	Southern "Engineers"	Tennessee Highlanders	Most dolichocephalic	Most brachycephalic
Number of subjects........	(25)	(25)	(24)	(25)	(25)	(22)	(15)	(20)
Mean:								
Cephalic index..........	73.2	72.1	73.6	84.6	84.3	81.8	74.0	84.7
Height of head........	13.95	13.92	13.52	14.03	13.88	13.54	13.30	13.46
Difference in brachycephals............				+0.8	−0.4	+0.2		+0.16
Stature................	176.1	175.1	173.7	173.4	174.4	172.9	161.6	161.2
Height of head—stature ratio................	7.92	7.95	7.78	8.09	7.96	7.83	8.23	8.35
Difference in ratio in brachycephals.......				+0.17	+0.01	+0.05		+0.12

TABLE 97

Old Americans: Head height vs. head form

| GROUPS | CEPHALIC INDEX | | | | | | |
	−72.5	72.6–75.0	75.1–77.5	77.6–80.0	80.1–82.5	82.6–85.0	Above 85.0
Males:							
Laboratory and Southern "Engineers" (594)......	(18)	(77)	(162)	(201)	(86)	(37)	(13)
	13.92	13.94	13.94	13.89	13.96	13.99	13.86
Stature.................	175.32	175.19	175.38	173.60	173.23	174.64	171.94
Head height-stature ratio..	7.94	7.96	7.95	8.0	8.06	8.01	8.06
Tennessee Highlanders (133)................	(4)	(22)	(44)	(42)	(18)	(2)	(1)
	13.60	13.54	13.63	13.64	13.57	(13.55)	(13.35)
Stature.................	175.92	173.73	174.54	174.68	173.26	(169.30)	(181.30)
Head height-stature ratio..	7.73	7.79	7.81	7.81	7.83	(8.0)	(7.36)
Females:							
Laboratory (210)........		(19)	(32)	(73)	(52)	(26)	(8)
		13.28	13.25	13.33	13.31	13.42	13.50
Stature.................		161.67	162.19	162.49	161.17	161.91	161.21
Head height-stature ratio..		8.21	8.17	8.20	8.26	8.29	8.37

somewhat irregular.   In the Tennesseeans the range is less, the curve more regular, than those of the other males.

It is much alike in the two main groups of males (with females in normal relation); but smaller both absolutely and relatively to stature in the Tennessee highlanders.

Relation to age: In the females there appears a slight but fairly regular absolute as well as relative growth in head height up to the sixth decade; but there is no appreciable change in the dimension in the males.

Relation to stature: There is a clear-cut increase of the measurement with stature as the latter advances, though differing somewhat in the different groups.

Relation to cephalic index: The height of the head is not directly involved in change of head form from dolicho- to brachycephaly; nevertheless in a progress from former to latter condition it shows a progressive slight augmentation.

The height of the head correlates therefore decidedly with stature, and possibly with advanced brain development, but only weakly with the two other head diameters.

The three head diameters

At the risk possibly of some repetition it seems desirable to review together the main conditions shown by the separate head diameters.

It was seen that each one of the diameters showed more or less correlation with age, stature, and head form (*i.e.*, the cephalic index), and these correlations will be found even more instructive when dealt with collectively.

The very interesting behavior of the three main diameters of the head with *age,* in the complete series of the Old Americans, may be brought out with advantage in table 98.

These figures indicate in brief that:

1. The male heads among the Old Americans, excepting those of the northern Appalachian highlands, grow absolutely as well as relatively to stature during the adult stage, up to at least the fiftieth year of life, slightly in length, less so in breadth, and not at all in height.

2. The female head keeps on growing slightly up into the sixth decade in length, into the fifth decade in breadth and into the sixth decade also in height.

3. The southern "engineers" behave as far as the series goes much like the Old Americans in general (the Laboratory series); the somewhat greater differences in these two groups than in those of the Laboratory are doubtless

due to the fact that their 20–29 year group includes a proportion of subjects below 24 which is not the case with the Laboratory series.

4. In the Tennessee highlanders the younger group shows to an advantage over the older one indicating a moderate improvement in the younger generation and holding a promise for the future in the same direction.

The odd difference between the behavior of the three diameters in the two sexes can evidently not be accidental and must therefore have a definite reason. What this is, is not plain. Possibly the men accomplish the growth of their head in height earlier than the females who have not had such intensive education and struggles in the earlier part of their mature life.

TABLE 98

Old Americans, all: Head dimensions and age*

Head length, breadth and height expressed in their relation to stature

AGE	MALES									FEMALES		
	Laboratory (247)			Southern "Engineers" (347)			Tennessee Highlanders (133)			Laboratory (210)		
	Length	Breadth	Height	Length	Breadth	Height	Length	Breadth	Height	Length	Breadth	Height
years												
20–29	11.32	8.87	8.0	11.33	8.83	7.93	11.20	8.66	7.80	11.41	9.09	8.18
30–39	11.31	8.89	7.96	11.44	8.88	8.03	11.11	8.68	7.76	11.52	9.15	8.21
40–49	11.38	8.86	8.0							11.53	9.17	8.29
50–59	11.42	8.91	8.0							11.88	8.88	8.36
Above 59	11.31	8.79	7.85									

* Groups of less than five subjects omitted.

The generally poorer showing of the oldest of our series may possibly be due in part to some thinning of the scalp as senility sets in, but may also be connected, as has already been suggested, with the fact that the oldest generation were not brought up under equal demands on the brain as those following.

The correlation of the three diameters with *stature* is shown most simply in tables 99 and 100, and figures 13 and 14. Without going into details which have been dealt with before, it is seen that:

1. In general the three dimensions augment with stature.

2. The augmentation is on the whole slightly more marked in the males than in the females.

TABLE 99

Old Americans: The three main diameters of the head, and stature

Laboratory series
Absolute proportions

	STATURE	HEAD		
		Length	Breadth	Height
Males (247)				
25 shortest..................................	164.38	19.43	15.29	13.57
25 tallest....................................	184.40	19.92	15.52	14.11
Simple differences in favor of tallest.............	20.02	0.49	0.23	0.54
Percental differences..........................	*10.36*	*2.43*	*1.47*	*3.81*
Proportions relative to stature of each group (S = 100):				
In shortest.............................		11.88	9.30	8.26
In tallest..............................		10.80	8.42	7.65
Percental difference in relative proportions in favor of shortest (shortest = 100).....		*9.09*	*9.46*	*7.39*
Females (210)				
20 shortest..................................	151.32	18.25	14.70	13.08
20 tallest....................................	172.20	18.72	14.82	13.55
Simple differences in favor of tallest.............	20.92	0.47	0.12	0.47
Percental differences........................:..	*12.14*	*2.48*	*0.78*	*3.47*
Proportions relative to stature of each group (S = 100):				
In shortest.............................		12.06	9.71	8.64
In tallest..............................		10.87	8.60	7.87
Percental difference in relative proportions in favor of shortest (shortest = 100).....		*9.86*	*11.43*	*8.91*
Whole series: Males (727)				
25 shortest..................................	162.0	19.37	15.29	13.47
25 tallest....................................	187.66	20.08	15.45	14.07
Simple differences in favor of tallest.............	25.66	0.71	0.16	0.60
Proportions relative to stature of above group:				
In shortest.............................		11.96	9.44	8.31
In tallest..............................		10.70	8.25	7.50
Percental difference in relative proportions in favor of shortest (shortest = 100).....		*9.70*	*12.82*	*9.75*

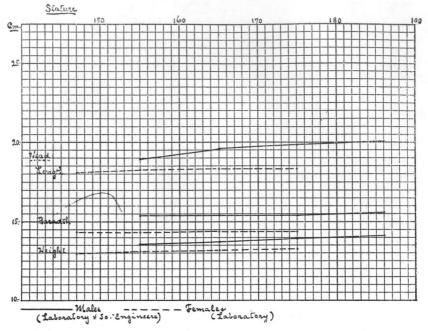

FIG. 13. OLD AMERICANS: PROGRESSION OF THE THREE HEAD DIAMETERS WITH
STATURE

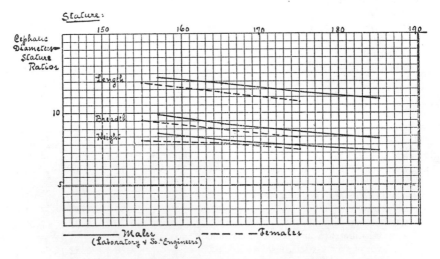

FIG. 14. OLD AMERICANS: MAIN HEAD DIAMETERS-STATURE RATIOS

3. The increase is not the same with the three dimensions. It is most noticeable, particularly in the males, in the length, nearly as much so in the height, but decidedly less so in the breadth.

The three main head diameters and head form. The behavior of the three dimensions, as the head progresses in form from dolicho- to brachycephaly, differs radically:

1. The length steadily decreases;

2. The breadth steadily increases; while

3. The height remains almost the same in the males, rising slightly in the females.

If we reduce the simple measurements of the three head diameters to ratios of stature, thus eliminating to a large extent the disturbing factor

TABLE 100

Old Americans: The three main head diameters and stature

STATURE	MALES (594)				FEMALES (210)			
	Number of subjects	Laboratory and Southern "Engineers"			Number of subjects	Length	Breadth	Height
		Length	Breadth	Height				
150.01–160	(5)	18.98	15.40	13.54	(73)	18.52	14.76	13.17
160.01–170	(143)	+0.56	+	+0.19	(114)	+0.17	+0.08	+0.21
170.01–180	(356)	+0.26	+	+0.22	(20)	+0.03	−0.02	+0.17
180.01–190	(88)	+0.22	+0.18	+0.17				

of stature, the facts remain still substantially the same, though the length and breadth changes appear less pronounced:

1. The head length-stature ratio, though somewhat irregular, shows nevertheless a gradual decrease as the cephalic index grows higher;

2. The head breadth-stature ratio tends towards an increase as the cephalic index increases; while

3. The head height-stature ratio remains near constant for all cephalic indices.

All these phenomena have a bearing on the morphological significance of the differences in head form as expressed by the cephalic index, the variation in which can eventually be fathomed only by an intensive study of such facts.

The data bearing on the above points will be found in tables 101 and 102, and figure 15.

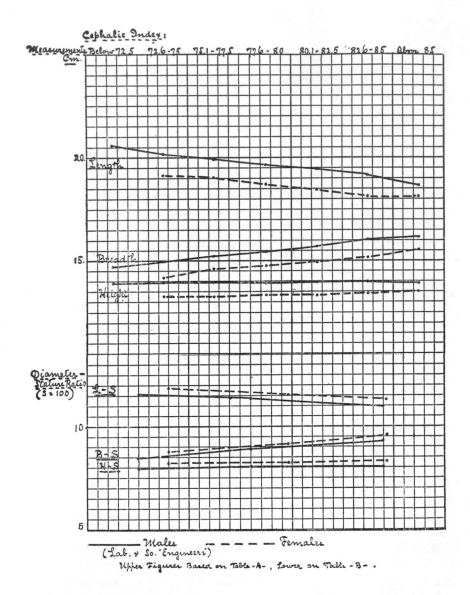

FIG. 15. OLD AMERICANS: THE THREE HEAD DIAMETERS AND HEAD FORM

TABLE 101

Head measurements in dolichocephaly and brachycephaly

SERIES	STATURE	LENGTH	BREADTH	HEIGHT
Males				
Laboratory:				
25 most dolichocephalic (cephalic index 73.2)...............................	176.1	20.40	14.94	13.95
Diameter-stature ratio................		*11.58*	*8.48*	*7.92*
25 most brachycephalic (cephalic index 84.6)...............................	173.4	18.97	16.05	14.03
Diameter-stature ratio................		*10.94*	*9.26*	*8.09*
Southern "Engineers":				
25 most dolichocephalic (cephalic index 72.1)...............................	175.1	20.41	14.77	13.92
Diameter-stature ratio................		*11.60*	*8.44*	*7.95*
25 most brachycephalic (cephalic index 84.3)...............................	174.4	19.15	16.15	13.88
Diameter-stature ratio................		*10.98*	*9.26*	*7.96*
Tennessee Highlanders:				
24 most dolichocephalic (cephalic index 73.6)...............................	173.7	20.02	14.74	13.52
Diameter-stature ratio................		*11.52*	*8.49*	*7.78*
22 most brachycephalic (cephalic index 81.8)...............................	172.9	19.04	15.57	13.54
Diameter-stature ratio................		*11.01*	*9.01*	*7.83*
Females				
Laboratory:				
15 most dolichocephalic (cephalic index 74.0)...............................	161.6	19.12	14.15	13.30
Diameter-stature ratio................		*11.84*	*8.76*	*8.23*
20 most brachycephalic (cephalic index 84.7)...............................	161.2	18.21	15.42	13.46
Diameter-stature ratio................		*11.30*	*9.56*	*8.35*

Comparative data on the three main head diameters

Some racial, or, more properly, intraracial comparisons will be afforded by the data secured by the writer or under his direction on recent normal adult immigrants within the same age limits (24 to 60) as the Old Americans (table 103).

TABLE 102

Old Americans: The three main head diameters, and head form

CEPHALIC INDEX	MALES (594)				FEMALES (210)			
	Number of subjects	Laboratory and Southern "Engineers"			Number of subjects	Length	Breadth	Height
		Length	Breadth	Height				
Below 72.5	(18)	20.58	14.73	13.92				
72.6–75.0	(77)	−0.36	+0.24	+0.02	(19)	19.18	14.22	13.28
75.1–77.5	(162)	−0.26	+0.29	±	(32)	−0.16	+0.35	−0.03
77.6–80.0	(201)	−0.30	+0.22	−0.05	(73)	−0.28	+0.19	+0.08
80.1–82.5	(86)	−0.18	+0.25	+0.07	(52)	−0.26	+0.15	−0.02
82.6–85.0	(37)	−0.29	+0.32	+0.03	(26)	−0.33	+0.27	+0.11
Above 85	(13)	−0.50	+0.14	−0.13	(8)	±	+0.38	+0.09

TABLE 103

The three main diameters of the head in the Old Americans and recent immigrants to the United States

Males

GROUP	NUMBER OF SUBJECTS	CEPHALIC INDEX	HEAD			HEAD vs. STATURE		
			Length	Breadth	Height	Length	Breadth	Height
Old Americans..............	(594)*	78.2	19.76	15.45	13.95	113.4	88.7	80.0
Old Americans..............	(133)†	77.5	19.50	15.10	13.61	111.9	86.6	78.1
Irish.......................	(35)	78.0	19.65	15.30	13.60	114.5	89.2	79.3
Southern Italians...........	(50)	78.8	19.10	15.10	13.60	116.9	92.4	83.2
English....................	(20)	78.99	19.25	15.20	13.70	113.1	89.3	80.5
Greeks.....................	(50)	80.85	18.70	15.10	13.80	111.1	89.7	82.0
Russian Jews................	(50)	82.2	18.80	15.50	13.40	114.2	94.2	81.4
Russians...................	(50)	83.5	18.60	15.50	13.70	109.5	91.3	81.3
Poles......................	(50)	84.3	18.60	15.70	13.70	109.2	92.1	80.4
Northern Italians...........	(50)	84.3	18.65	15.70	13.75	110.0	92.6	81.1
Croatians..................	(50)	85.2	18.40	15.70	13.80	107.2	91.5	80.4
Armenians.................	(25)	85.35	18.10	15.50	13.70	108.1	92.6	81.8
Hungarians................	(50)	85.5	18.20	15.60	13.60	109.3	93.7	81.7
Rumanians.................	(50)	85.9	18.30	15.70	13.80	108.5	93.1	81.8
Mean deviation....................		2.85	4.45	2.0	0.95	2.3	1.7	0.9

* Laboratory and Virginia.
† Tennessee Highlanders.

It is regrettable that the same measurements, particularly as to head height, are not available on all the more important subdivisions of the human family or at least on all of those of the white race, for evidently here is still much to be learned.

The figures given in table 103, and the rough correlation of each of the measurements with the stature of its group, show a number of noteworthy facts. As the cephalic index in the racial groups increases, the mean length of the head decreases, the breadth, though somewhat less markedly and less regularly, augments, while the height remains but little affected. But these, in substance, are the same changes that were manifested within the one racial group which we are studying more particularly.

Between the various subdivisions of the white race, therefore, or at least as far as represented in these records, the head, as the cephalic index changes, differs most in its length, less in breadth and least in height. The wide difference in the cephalic index of these groups is, hence, essentially a matter of skull length, which is especially nicely shown by the mean deviations of the three diameters. In the Old Americans conditions in these respects are fundamentally alike, but the length participates less, the breadth more, in the progression of head form from dolicho- to brachycephaly.

An explanation of the basic unity as well as of the differences in behavior of the head length and breadth as we proceed from dolicho- to brachycephaly in racial groups, and within one such group, can barely as yet be attempted. We are doubtless however confronted here with phenomena of importance which may constitute a valuable lead in studies of skull variation.

Head shape

The shape of the head can no more be regarded, as formerly, as the paramount anthropological character. It is now known to be as changeable a feature as any other, though its changes may on the whole be slow, occasionally even very slow.

The shape of the head or skull is no criterion of either the amount or the kind of intellect; nor can it any more be used as it used to be as a sort of fetish by which to secure a definite racial identification of a given head or skull; but within due limitations it is a character of much weight and usefulness, particularly for comparison of groups within a large race.

The shape of the head can best be expressed by the combination of the cephalic index $\left(\dfrac{\text{Breadth maximum} \times 100}{\text{Length maximum}}\right)$ and the mean height index

$$\left(\frac{\text{Height} \times 100}{\text{Mean of Breadth and Length}} \right).$$ The older height-breadth and height-length indices (of which the first-named is the more valuable) are but partly expressive and tend to become obsolete.

Earlier American data. Earlier records on the cephalic index of adult Americans are wanting. There are, as has been seen in previous chapters, many records on the stature and weight and there are data on other characteristics of the body, but head measurements which require special instruments have been taken neither in the Army nor Navy, nor in the Colleges or by the Insurance companies. In a few studies only have they been taken on children and adolescents.

In 1891-92, several thousands of school children and students of secondary schools were measured by West, Chamberlain, Russell and others at Worcester, Mass., under Dr. Boas' direction. According to West who in 1893 reported on the bulk of the series, this included subjects 66 per cent of whom were of American, 20 per cent Irish, 7 per cent English and 6 per cent other white parentage. The results showed the conditions given in table 104.

In 1897-98 the writer measured the head in 1000 inmates of the New York Juvenile Asylum.[35] Among these 134 boys and 27 girls were American-born white children, the average cephalic index of which was approximately 78.5 and 80.5.

About the same time MacDonald studied the cephalic index in 1074 white school children and adolescents, mostly of American parentage, in Washington, D.C., and similar measurements were taken under his direction by Miss S. G. Chester on 151 children and adolescents among the North Carolina mountaineers.[36] The results, which were not given with sufficient particulars, are shown in table 105.

Whatever the value of the above data may be, they all indicate that the mean breadth-length index of the head of the American children and adolescents towards the close of the last century was mesocephalic, exceeding slightly 78 in the males and ranging about one point higher in the female subjects. This is very close to our results on the adults, as will be seen in what follows.

Cephalic index in Old Americans. The average breadth-length head index of the Old Americans is mesocephalic; as a matter of fact, however,

---

[35] Anthropological Investigations on One Thousand White and Colored Children of the New York Juvenile Asylum. 8°, New York, 1899, p. 54.

[36] MacDonald (Arthur)—Experimental Study of Children. Rep. U. S. Bur. Educ. for 1897–1898, Washington, 1899, p. 997.

TABLE 104

*Cephalic index in children, adolescents and some adults of Worcester, Mass.**

	MALES			FEMALES	
Age	Number of subjects	Mean cephalic index	Age	Number of subjects	Mean cephalic index
6	112	78.9	6	77	79.7
7	145	79.1	7	101	79.6
8	121	79.7	8	106	80.0
9	158	79.5	9	117	79.5
10	153	79.5	10	159	79.9
11	148	78.8	11	150	79.7
12	175	79.4	12	165	79.5
13	168	79.3	13	141	79.2
14	169	78.5	14	115	78.9
15	153	78.2	15	109	78.8
16	96	78.02	16	91	78.7
17	49		17	69	78.6
18†	48	78.08	18	49	79.2
19†	47	78.33	19–35	135	79.1
20–21†	86	78.7			

* Calculated from detailed data in Boas and Wissler's Statistics of Growth, U. S. Bur. Educ. Rep. for 1904.

† After G. Montgomery West (who used a large part of the same data), Anthropometrische Untersuchungen über die Schulkinder in Worcester, Mass., Arch. f. Anthrop., 1893, '4, xxii, 13 et seq.

TABLE 105

North Carolina mountaineers

Measurements by Miss S. G. Chester, settlement worker, under MacDonald (p. 1012)

	AVERAGE AGE		DOLICHO-CEPHALIC*	MESO-CEPHALIC	BRACHY-CEPHALIC
	Years	Months			
Boys (34)...........................	11	8	25	58	17
Of whom 20 bright ones...........	12	5	15	55	30
Girls (117).........................	12	3	18	51	31
Of whom 55 bright...............	11	5	14	41	45
Washington, D. C., school children					
Boys (526)........................	12	9	11	45	44
Of whom 237 bright..............	12	4	8	51	41
Girls (548)........................	13	1	27	52	21
Of whom 269 bright..............	12	10	12	51	37

* MacDonald's subdivisions of the cephalic index are very nearly the same as those used in the present work, namely: Dolichocephaly up to 75; mesocephaly over 75 and below 80; brachycephaly 80 and above.

the head shape in the group shows a great range of variation, such as would naturally be anticipated in a mixed people.

The whole number of individuals on whom the cephalic index was determined amounted to 727 males and 210 females, and the principal results were as follows:

Males:
    Arithmetical mean C. I..................................... 77.95
    Standard deviation.. 3.12
    Coefficient of variation.................................. 4.00 per cent
Females:
    Arithmetical mean C. I..................................... 79.40
    Standard deviation.. 2.89
    Coefficient of variation.................................. 3.64 per cent

Using the simplest classification of head forms, namely, dolichocephalic, index to 75, mesocephalic, 75.1 to 80, and brachycephalic, above 80, the Old Americans taken as a whole show, in rough, the distribution given in table 106.

TABLE 106

	MALES		FEMALES	
	Number of cases	Per cent	Number of cases	Per cent
Dolichocephals...............	121	*16.6*	17	*8.1*
Mesocephals..................	448	*61.7*	105	*50.0*
Brachycephals...............	158	*21.7*	88	*41.9*

In slightly over three-fifths of the males and one-half of the females the head is seen to be mesocephalic or intermediary. Only one-sixth of the males and one-twelfth of the females are moderately dolichocephalic, but one single individual, a male, showing an index a trace below 70. Over one-fifth of the males on the other hand, and a little over two-fifths of the females have an index over 80, and in 31 (4.3 per cent) of the males and 11 (5.2 per cent) of the females this index is over 84 or decidedly brachycephalic. There is plainly in the make-up of the Old Americans more of the element of, or more tending towards, brachy- than dolichocephaly, which is a rather unexpected condition. Its meaning will be seen later.

The sexual differences are of the usual nature, the female skull and head tending more to brachycephaly. This, as well known, is on account of the lesser development in the female of the supraorbital ridges, frontal sinuses and occipital ridges, which in the male add to the length of the skull and in that way decrease its index.

A more detailed range of distribution of the cephalic index is given in tables 107 and 108. The figures need no special discussion, though it is interesting to note how closely allied notwithstanding the very mixed nature of the group, are the averages of the separate subdivisions of 100.

TABLE 107

Old Americans, males: cephalic index

Number of individuals: 727

General average: 77.95

1st series of 100—78.29   4th series of 100—77.76
2nd series of 100—78.29   5th series of 100—77.78
3rd series of 100—77.90   6th series of 100—77.87
                             7th series of 127—77.97

Minimum: 69.70.   Maximum: 90.9

	TABLE OF FREQUENCIES										
	69.1–70.0	70.1–71.0	71.1–72.0	72.1–73.0	73.1–74.0	74.1–75.0	75.1–76.0	76.1–77.0	77.1–78.0	78.1–79.0	79.1–80.0
Number of cases..............	1	4	14	20	30	52	70	97	96	104	81
Per cent......................	0.1	0.55	1.9	2.8	4.1	7.15	9.6	13.3	13.2	14.3	11.2

	80.1–81.0	81.1–82.0	82.1–83.0	83.1–84.0	84.1–85.0	85.1–86.0	86.1–87.0	87.1–88.0	88.1–89.0	89.1–90.0	90.1–91.0
Number of cases..............	51	42	23	11	16	6	4	4	0	0	1
Per cent......................	7.0	5.8	3.2	1.5	2.2	0.8	0.55	0.55			0.1

TABLE 108

Old Americans, females: Cephalic index

Number of observations: 210

Average: 79.40 (1st 100—79.23; 2nd 110—79.55)

Minimum: 72.63.   Maximum: 86.36

	TABLE OF FREQUENCIES														
	72.1–73.0	73.1–74.0	74.1–75.0	75.1–76.0	76.1–77.0	77.1–78.0	78.1–79.0	79.1–80.0	80.1–81.0	81.1–82.0	82.1–83.0	83.1–84.0	84.1–85.0	85.1–86.0	86.1–87.0
Number of cases (210)..	3	3	11	9	14	20	33	29	26	21	13	17	3	6	2
Per cent...............	1.4	1.4	5.2	4.3	6.7	9.5	15.7	13.8	12.4	10.0	6.2	8.1	1.4	2.9	1.0

Another point which may attract attention is the same position in the two sexes of the median, but the mass of the cases precede the ill defined median in the males while they follow it in the females. In an instance like this the median is clearly not of much value.

The significance of the cephalic index showing in the Old Americans may now be approached more closely.

The range of the distribution of the index is such as to oppose the idea of any great amount of fusion of the types from which the group has been built up, and favor that of considerable hereditary persistence. The more marked dolichocephals in the series proceed surely from parents and grandparents whose head was of this type and the same is true of the pronounced brachycephals. In some cases these facts could more or less be verified. As to the intermediate forms, they may either be derived from similar ancestral forms or be the result of intermixture in America. That even they are ancestral in a large measure is indicated by the well known fact that the majority of the incomers to what is now the territory of the United States were already mixed, for all European nations are of a heterogeneous composition and in all there has been within historic times an ever-increasing intermarriage of the component racial elements. Under these conditions the showing of the Old Americans of today, as to head shape, is in the main what might have been expected. The only important questions are whether the grade and distribution of the index was the same here as in the old countries, and whether it has remained constant here or is changing. A good deal of light may be thrown on this by the English records, which will be dealt with later.

A study of the cephalic index in the Old Americans according to territory is of especial interest. There are here to contrast not merely the northerners and the southerners, but also the Appalachian mountaineers. When the averages alone of these three groups are contemplated they stand close enough together to suggest closely alike conditions, though it is noted that the cephalic index in the south is slightly lower than that of the more northern states, while that of the Tennessee highlanders is the lowest of the three groups. The real conditions show clearly however in the distributions of the index (table 109). The figures are so instructive as to need hardly any comment.

The percentage of dolichocephals is the smallest in the northeastern and mixed states, larger in the southern states and largest in Tennessee; while the percentage of brachycephals is largest in the north, smaller in the south and least in Tennessee. There are also the most intermediary forms in Tennessee, which is in harmony with the observations on the eye and hair color of these people. It may therefore be said that the Tennessee highlanders are the most thoroughly mixed of the three groups and that they include a higher percentage of narrow heads and a smaller proportion of broad heads than either of the other groups of the Old Ameri-

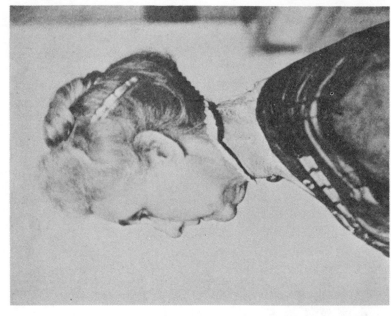

Mrs. Ruth M. Griswold Tealer

(Washington, D. C.)

For many years Genealogist N.S.D.A.R. Extended American ancestry, both sides.

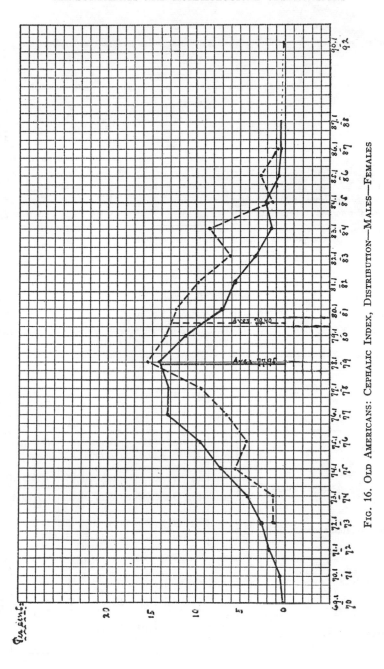

FIG. 16. OLD AMERICANS: CEPHALIC INDEX, DISTRIBUTION—MALES—FEMALES

TABLE 109

Old Americans: Distribution of cephalic index according to territory

Males

	NUMBER OF SUBJECTS	AVERAGE CEPHALIC INDEX	DISTRIBUTION			
			69.70–75.0	75.01–80.0	80.01–84.0	84.01 and over
			per cent	*per cent*	*per cent*	*per cent*
Northeastern, Eastern and Mixed* States............................	338	78.25	14.2	60.6	19.8	5.4
Southern States (mostly southeastern)..	256	77.8	17.2	61.6	17.1	4.0
Eastern Tennessee....................	133	77.5	19.6	64.7	13.6	2.3

* Subjects whose parents came from different regions.

TABLE 110

Old Americans: cephalic index

(By subdivisions of 2.5 points)

Averages. Males: Laboratory—78.28; Southern "Engineers"—77.90; Tennessee Highlanders—77.46. Females: 79.40

	MALES									
	Up to 70	70.1–72.5	72.6–75.0	75.1–77.5	77.6–80.0	80.1–82.5	82.6–85.0	85.1–87.5	87.6–90.0	Above 90.0
Laboratory (247)...............		(6)	(28)	(73)	(78)	(34)	(21)	(5)	(0)	(2)
		2.4	11.3	29.6	31.6	13.8	8.5	2.0		0.8
Southern "Engineers" (347)......	(1)	(11)	(47)	(91)	(121)	(52)	(17)	(6)	(1)	
	0.3	3.2	13.5	26.2	34.8	15.0	4.9	1.7	0.3	
Tennessee Highlanders (133).....		(4)	(22)	(44)	(42)	(18)	(2)	(1)		
		3.0	16.5	33.1	31.6	13.5	1.5	0.8		

	FEMALES						
	70.1–72.5	72.6–75.0	75.1–77.5	77.6–80.0	80.1–82.5	82.6–85.0	85.1–87.5	87.6–90.0
Laboratory (210).........................	(19)	(32)	(73)	(52)	(26)	(8)	
	9.0	15.2	34.7	24.8	12.4	3.8	

cans. The northeasterners and those whose parentage proceeds from
several states show opposite conditions in every one of these respects,
while the southerners make a showing that is throughout between these
two. The cause of this very interesting state of affairs needs further
inquiry; but what is plain is that those of the more northern group stand
on the whole highest in culture, that the southerners, but again as a whole,
come next, while the Appalachian highlanders stand the lowest. It is
further also possible that both the last named and the southerners as a

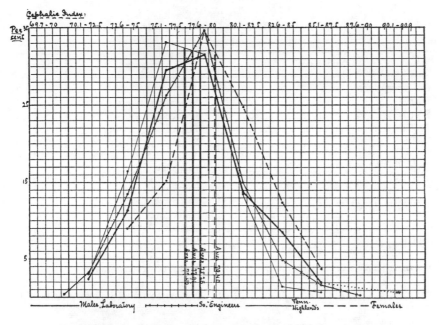

FIG. 17. OLD AMERICANS: CEPHALIC INDEX IN THE FOUR GROUPS

whole carry more Scotch blood (or "Scotch Irish") than the northerners
and this may partly if not wholly account for the above differences.

A further light on the distribution of the cephalic index in the several
groups of the Old Americans will be afforded by table 110 and figure 17,
in which the index is given by the somewhat large but expressive subdivisions of 2.5 points. With these larger subdivisions the irregularities
of dispersion are largely covered and the curves become steep; but the
groups differences are shown very plainly.

Comparative. The bulk of the ancestors of the Old Americans came from
the British Isles. The population of these isles is built up from the neo-

lithic dolichocephals, the bronze age brachycephals, the Kelts, the Romans (Mediterranean), the earlier west European coast tribes and the Normans, with a good addition of French blood. After many hundreds of years of mixture these various elements have more or less blended gradually into what are known today as the English, Welsh, Scotch and Irish peoples, all of whom are well represented in the Old Americans. The head shapes of these mixed groups and of others that are of interest in this connection have been abundantly studied and show the conditions in table 111.

TABLE 111

Cephalic index: Comparative data

Males

NATIONALITY	AUTHORITY	INDEX
Old Americans............................		77 95
Irish...................................	Beddoe and Venn	77.9
Scotch.................................	Beddoe and Venn	77.8
English................................	Beddoe	77.6
Welsh.................................	Beddoe and Venn	78.7
Norwegians............................	Arbo	78.0
	Deniker	78.5
Swedes................................	Hultkranz	77.3
	Retzius and Fürst	77.8
	Hultkranz	78.6
Danes..................................	Hansen	80.7
Dutch.................................	Bolk	80.3
Germans...............................	Means of various groups	77.5 to 85.0
French................................	Means of various groups	79.0–89.0

The index of the Old Americans and that of the English, Scotch and Irish, not to mention other groups, is practically the same. Its distribution also is much the same. The Americans have therefore not changed in head form since on the new continent—unless perhaps the ancestral groups in their old home have changed in the same way and to the same degree within the same period. That some such change may have taken place in the British Isles and is possibly still going on, but that on the whole there has been a remarkable conservation, is shown by table 112, for the gathering of which from many sources we thank F. G. Parsons.[37]

Dr. Parsons' conclusion is that since at least the medieval period, the

[37] The Cephalic Index of the British Isles. Man, 1922, XXII, No. 14.

cephalic index in the British Isles has been, from causes not yet fully determined, slowly rising; and the same slight rise has apparently also gone on in America.   It is possible in fact that notwithstanding the identity of the mean index in the two countries at the present time the change in the direction of relatively broader head has progressed among the Americans even a little faster than among the British.   In the Old Americans the actual range of distribution of the cephalic index extends, in the 727 males, from 69.7 to 90.0, in the 210 females from 72.6 to 86.4; according to Fleure's summary[38] the index "in most samples of adult men in Britain . . . . works out at figures between 69 and 86 with very occasional individuals

TABLE 112

Cephalic index

(On the head)*

	MEANS OF VARIOUS GROUPS
Neolithic: Long Barrows...	72.5–75.7
Round Barrows..	76.7
Bronze Age: Beaker Folk......................................	83.0–85.5
Iron Age..	74.2
Saxon...	75.9
14th–15th century..	77.3–79.2
14th–15th century, Hythe.....................................	81.2
17th century (2 localities).....................................	75.5–76.6
18th century Scotch soldiers (a small number)......................	73.7
18th century Irish soldiers......................................	75.4
18th century English soldiers....................................	76.4
19th and 20th centuries (53 groups)............................	74.9–81.9
General mean approximately......................................	78.0

* Where only skulls were available the cranial index was approximated to the cephalic.

beyond these limits; very few women have this index under 70 and among them the index ranges up to 90 or beyond."   As there are in the Americans practically no indices below 70, the upper limit of the range reaches over 90, and in fully one-fifth of the males and two-fifths of the females it is over 80, it would seem that the tendency towards relatively broader head is here even more substantial than in Great Britain.   Similar changes in the direction of brachycephaly have been manifested in various parts of Europe, particularly among the Slavs and Germans, though elsewhere conditions seem to be more stationary.   Two main factors are generally suggested as the possible cause of these changes.   One is addition of brachy-

[38] Fleure (H. J.)—The Races of England and Wales.   12mo, 1923, 11.

cephalic elements through immigration; the other is civilization and education, in other words refinement. Probably both play a part; on physiological grounds (diminution through refinement of muscles of mastication with the effect this has on the skull) the intrinsic change seems quite as likely as that by immigration.

The data on normal, healthy, adult immigrants to the United States arriving shortly before the war will also be of some interest in this connection, though northwestern Europe is but poorly represented (table 113).

Form of head and age. Between adolescence and the earlier part of adult life the form of the head changes appreciably, at least so in the males, where as already mentioned the length of the head increases more than

TABLE 113

Average cephalic index in recent European immigrants to the United States

Males

NUMBER OF SUBJECTS	NATIONALITY	INDEX
(35)	Irish.	78.0
(50)	Southern Italians.	78.8
(20)	English.	79.0
(50)	Greek.	80.8
(50)	Russian Jews.	82.2
(50)	Russians.	83.5
(50)	Poles.	84.3
(50)	North Italians.	84.3
(50)	Croatians.	85.2
(25)	Armenians.	85.4
(50)	Hungarians.	85.5
(50)	Roumanians.	85.9

other dimensions of the vault and more than it does in the females, due to the development of the frontal sinuses, glabella with supraorbital ridges and often also the occipital protruberance or crest. Influence of age on skull or head form after full development has been reached is not known and scarcely to be anticipated. Actually as will be seen from table 114, none is manifest in the Old Americans.

Head form and stature. It may be assumed that in general the taller the stature in a group the more marked is the development of the bony parts, which ought somewhat to influence the form of the head. But it should also be borne in mind that in a mixed group, such as the Americans, the involved different types may carry tall or short stature as one of their characteristics and that the showing of the resultant group will depend upon just what has entered into it. If we took a group consisting of an admixture of the short Mediterranean dolichocephals with the tall brachycephalic southern Slavs, the relations of the head form to stature in the resultant group would differ from those obtained on a group resulting from the admixture of tall dolicho- and short brachycephals. According to all indications the constituents of the Old Americans were in the main the tall

TABLE 114

Cephalic index and age

	MALES					FEMALES				
	20–29	30–39	40–49	50–59	Above 59	20–29	30–39	40–49	50–59	Above 59
Laboratory.....................	(91)	(63)	(47)	(34)	(12)	(72)	(71)	(36)	(27)	(3)
	78.4	78.6	77.9	78.0	77.9	79.7	79.5	79.6	79.3	78.2
Southern "Engineers"...........	(318)	(29)								
	77.9	77.6								
Tennessee Highlanders...........	(118)	(15)								
	77.4	78.3								

TABLE 115

Old Americans: Cephalic index and stature

	MALES					FEMALES			
	Above 190.0	190.0–180.1	180.0–170.1	170.0–160.1	Below 160.0	180.0–170.1	170.0–160.1	160.0–150.1	Below 150.0
Laboratory and Southern "Engineers".........................	(2)	(88)	(356)	(143)	(5)	(20)	(114)	(72)	(3)
		77.8	77.8	78.8	79.9	79.2	79.4	79.7	
Tennessee Highlanders..............		(17)	(87)	(29)					
		78.4	77.2	77.7					

northern dolichocephals with the not much shorter brachycephalic elements that have reached the British Isles during and after the Bronze time. The actual showing in the relations among the Old Americans of head form and stature, though doubtless a complex phenomenon, harmonizes well with what might be expected on the basis of their probable composition. (See table 115.)

Summary. On the average the cephalic index of the Old Americans shows higher mesocephaly.

In one-sixth of the males and one-twelfth of the females the head is markedly dolichocephalic; in over one-fifth of the males and over two-fifths of the females the head is subbrachy- to brachycephalic.

The sexual differences are normal.

The dispersion and curves of the index are somewhat irregular.

The southern Old Americans, and especially the Tennessee highlanders give a slightly lower cephalic index than the rest of the stock.

The cephalic index of the Old Americans is close to that of the present people of the British Isles.

Influence of age upon the cephalic index after the adult period has been reached appears to be negligible.

Effect of stature: In general tall stature among the Old Americans goes with a lower cephalic index, but the differences are not large.

The mean height index

As already noted, the height of the head contrasted with the mean of its length and breadth gives the "mean height index," which together with the cephalic index facilitates greatly the study of racial relations and skull changes.

The reason for adopting this ratio rather than using the old height-length and height-breadth indices, should be obvious enough after what has been seen concerning the behavior of head length and breadth with changing cephalic index. As this index rises the length of the head decreases and the breadth increases in a closely compensatory manner, while the height remains but little affected. As a result we obtain a low or high height-length or height-breadth index not as an indication of the relative height of the head, which is the point to be ascertained, but as a measure of the changing head length or breadth. The height-length and height-breadth indices of the head or skull are therefore unsuited for the purpose for which they were intended. But their mean is free from this disadvantage; it is a constant that is not affected or not affected materially by the changing breadth-length relations; and contrasting the height with this constant gives a true index of the relative height of the skull or head.

The mean height index averages in the Old Americans, taken as a whole, 79.13 in the males and 79.71 in the females. It is evidently slightly higher in the females only because of the relatively somewhat greater value of the head length in the males due to their larger frontal sinuses and supra-orbital as well as occipital ridges; were it not for this factor the index in the two sexes would be very nearly the same, showing once more that the female skull and brain are built in the same way as those of the male.

In showing the distribution of this index, the writer, as on other occasions, will not attempt any specific nomenclature and subdivision, which in time tend to assume unnatural and more or less fetichistic value. The criteria by which any index or measurement must be judged primarily and above all, are its average, and its curve of distribution; and these for the index under consideration will be given in tables 116, 117 and 118, and figs. 18 and 19.

TABLE 116

Old Americans, males: Mean height index of head

Total number of observations: 727

General average: 79.02.

Laboratory (247), Average: 79.0. Virginia etc. "Engineers" (347), Average: 79.5.

Eastern Tennessee (133), Average: 78.7

1st series of 100—78.77	4th series of 100—79.10
2nd series of 100—78.91	5th series of 100—79.48
3rd series of 100—79.46	6th series of 100—78.96

7th series of 127—78.58

Minimum: 71.9. Maximum: 88.1

	TABLE OF FREQUENCIES							
	71.9–73.0	73.1–74.0	74.1–75.0	75.1–76.0	76.1–77.0	77.1–78.0	78.1–79.0	79.1–80.0
Number of cases............	4	12	17	59	79	97	94	106
Per cent....................	*0.55*	*1.65*	*2.34*	*8.11*	*10.87*	*13.34*	*12.93*	*14.58*

	80.1–81.0	81.1–82.0	82.1–83.0	83.1–84.0	84.1–85.0	85.1–86.0	86.1–87.0	87.1–88.0
Number of cases............	109	73	46	11	10	5	2	3
Per cent....................	*14.99*	*10.04*	*6.33*	*1.51*	*1.37*	*0.69*	*0.27*	*0.41*

From these it will be seen that the range of the index is rather closely comparable to, though less extended and more regular than, that of the cephalic index. Moreover as in the latter, and for the same reason (greater head length, due to greater development of frontal sinuses and frontal as well as occipital ridges in the males), the index in the females is somewhat higher than that in the males.

The second figure shows the mean height index in the several groups of the series and charted by 2.5 points. The curves are steep and remarkably concordant, with the sexual differences shown even more clearly than in the curves of the whole series.

TABLE 117

Old Americans, females: Mean height index of head

Number of observations: 209

General average: 79.72

(Laboratory, All States)

1st series of 50—79.34   3rd series of 50—79.95

2nd series of 50—78.91   4th series of 59—80.51

Minimum: 70.2.   Maximum: 87.1

	TABLE OF FREQUENCIES								
	70.2–71.0	71.1–72.0	72.1–73.0	73.1–74.0	74.1–75.0	75.1–76.0	76.1–77.0	77.1–78.0	78.1–79.0
Number of cases..............	1		2	2	1	9	11	20	32
Per cent.......................	*0.5*		*0.9*	*0.9*	*0.5*	*4.3*	*5.3*	*9.6*	*15.3*

	79.1–80.0	80.1–81.0	81.1–82.0	82.1–83.0	83.1–84.0	84.1–85.0	85.1–86.0	86.1–87.1
Number of cases....................	38	37	26	11	9	6	2	2
Per cent...........................	*18.2*	*17.7*	*12.4*	*5.3*	*4.3*	*2.9*	*0.9*	*0.9*

TABLE 118

Old Americans: Mean height index

(By Subdivisions of 2.5 points)

	MALES							
	70.1–72.5	72.6–75.0	75.1–77.5	77.6–80.0	80.1–82.5	82.6–85.0	85.1–87.5	87.6–90.0
Laboratory (247)......... {		(11) *4.5*	(60) *24.3*	(91) *36.8*	(69) *27.9*	(15) *6.1*	(1) *0.4*	
Southern "Engineers" (347) {	(3) *0.9*	(11) *3.2*	(84) *24.2*	(117) *33.7*	(103) *29.7*	(21) *6.0*	(5) *1.4*	(3) *0.9*
Tennessee Highlanders { (133)................. {		(8) *6.0*	(39) *29.3*	(44) *33.1*	(35) *26.3*	(6) *4.5*	(1) *0.7*	

	FEMALES						
	70.1–72.5	72.6–75.0	75.1–77.5	77.6–80.0	80.1–82.5	82.6–85.0	85.1–87.5
Laboratory (210)............... {	(1) *0.5*	(5) *2.4*	(29) *13.8*	(82) *39.1*	(69) *32.8*	(20) *9.5*	(4) *1.9*

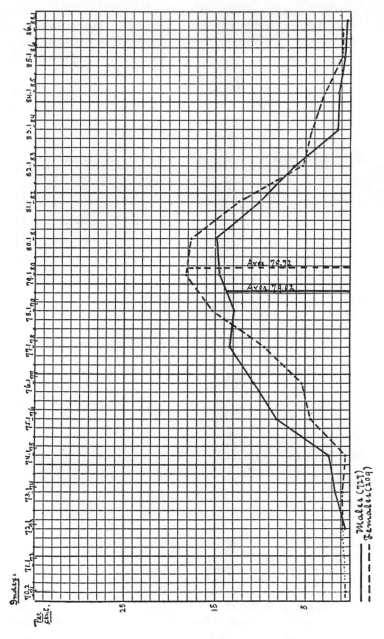

FIG. 18. OLD AMERICANS: MEAN HEIGHT INDEX OF HEAD—WHOLE SERIES

In the several subdivisions of the male Old Americans the index differs but little, yet it is lowest in the Tennessee highlanders, indicating that in these the head is not only absolutely but slightly also relatively lower than in the other groups; and this relative lowness is even more noticeable when the measurement is contrasted with stature (table 119).

The slight difference in the index between the Laboratory group of males and the southern "Engineers," in favor of the latter, is due as will be shown

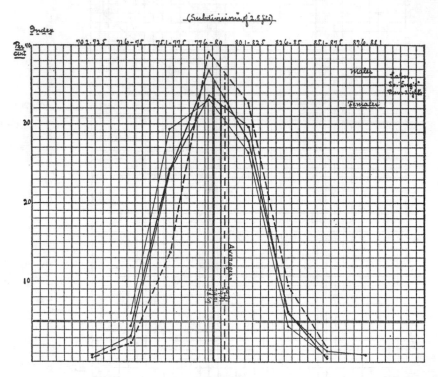

FIG. 19. OLD AMERICANS: MEAN HEIGHT INDEX OF HEAD BY GROUPS—SUBDIVISIONS OF 2.5 PTS.

later on, to the age factor, the latter group including only younger men in whom the index is slightly higher than in the older ones.

The index and age. Comparing the mean height index of the head in the youngest and the oldest adults in our series, it appears that the young of both sexes show a higher index, in other words, a relatively higher head (table 120). The condition is somewhat more marked in the males than in the females. The cause of it is in all probability a difference in stature.

The young adults of both sexes are of taller stature than the old, and in the taller as will be shown a little further on the mean height index of the head is higher.

Additional evidence as to the relation of the mean height index of the head and age is given in table 121. They show also that the index is slightly higher in the young than in the old adults, but in addition there appears also a tendency towards a second maximum during the fifth decade of life. When however we compare the changes in the index with that in stature we see that the two are quite parallel and harmonious. It may be assumed

TABLE 119

Height of head, and height of head-stature index in the main groups studied

GROUP	MALES					FEMALES				
	Number of subjects	Stature	Height of head	Height of head-stature ratio	Mean height index	Number of subjects	Stature	Height of head	Height of head-stature ratio	Mean height index
Laboratory all states....	247	174.44	13.93	79.9	79.01	211	161.84	13.32	82.30	79.72
Southern "Engineers"...	347	174.26	13.97	80.2	79.51					
Tennessee Highlanders..	133	174.29	13.61	78.1	78.67					

TABLE 120

Old Americans: Mean height index and age

Laboratory groups

MALES			FEMALES		
	Stature	Mean height index		Stature	Mean height index
30 youngest.......	175.5	80.1	20 youngest.......	164.5	80.3
30 oldest.........	174.1	78.7	30 oldest.........	159.5	79.6

therefore that it is stature rather than age that has an influence on the index, and that the rôle of age is immaterial.

Relative head height and stature. In studying the three main head diameters we saw that they all increased with stature, the increment being in the males most marked in the length, slightly less in the height and much less in the breadth; while in the females it was the same in length and height and much less in breadth. If the length and breadth, however, are taken together, their mean is found to increase less than the height of the head, so that the ratio of height to the mean of the two other diameters, or the *mean height index,* grows as stature advances. This fact which had already been apparent in dealing with the relation of the index to age, is well demonstrated in tables 122 and 123.

Relation of mean height index of head and cephalic index. Taking the most dolicho- and the most brachycephalic sets of individuals among the Old Americans, it appears that the mean height index shows a tendency to be a trace higher among the brachycephals, though in the southern

TABLE 121

Old Americans: Mean height index of head vs. age

	MALE				
	20–29 years	30–39 years	40–49 years	50–59 years	Above 59 years
All (727).................................. {	(527) 79.1	(107) 78.8	(47) 79.1	(34) 78.7	(12) 78.1
Stature..	174.33	174.22	174.54	173.98	174.78
By series:					
Laboratory (227)......................... {	(91) 79.3	(63) 78.8	(47) 79.1	(34) 78.7	(12) 78.1
Southern "Engineers" (347)............... {	(318) 79.2	(29) 79.0			
Tennessee Highlanders (133)............... {	(118) 78.6	(15) 78.5			

	FEMALE				
	20–29 years	30–39 years	40–49 years	50–59 years	Above 59 years
All (209)..................................... {	(72) 79.7	(71) 79.5	(36) 80.1	(27) 79.8	(3) 79.3
Stature..	162.57	161.96	162.42	159.18	

males and in the females the index in the two head forms is so close as to be almost identical.

The inclination towards a higher mean height index in the brachycephals is not due to stature. As seen in the preceding section the index increases with stature, so that in the absence of other factors it should be higher in the above dolichoes whose stature in every group is above that of the brachys, whereas the opposite is the case—the index is higher in the brachys

TABLE 122

Old Americans: Mean height index and stature

GROUP		MALES			FEMALES	
		Mean stature	Mean height index		Mean stature	Mean height index
Laboratory............	25 shortest	162.0	77.73	20 shortest	151.3	79.39
	25 tallest	187.5	79.20	20 tallest	172.2	80.92
Southern "Engineers" ..	25 shortest	163.8	78.43			
	25 tallest	186.5	79.29			

TABLE 123

Old Americans: Mean height index of head vs. stature

General average: Male—*79.02:* Female—*79.72*

	STATURE			
	150.01–160.0	160.01–170.0	170.01–180.0	180.01–190.0
Sex groups as a whole				
Males* (727)............................	(5) 77.6	(172) 78.5	(443) 79.2	(105) 79.2
Females (209)............................	(72) 79.1	(114) 79.8	(20) 80.8	
Separate male series				
Laboratory (247)...........................		(61) 78.8	(147) 79.1	(37) 79.3
Southern "Engineers" (347).................		(82) 78.6	(209) 79.4	(51) 79.4
Tennessee Highlanders (133)...............		(29) 77.7	(87) 78.9	(17) 78.3

* Subdivisions represented by less than 5 subjects omitted.

notwithstanding their lower stature. The cause lies in the fact, already observed when we dealt with the head diameter, that as the cephalic index increases the head height rises slightly, in partial compensation for the diminishing length. As the head grows shorter it grows broader, but not exactly proportionately and the defect is made good by a slight increase also in head height which is the brachycephals accounts for the trace higher mean height index.

Comparative. The data available for comparison, so far as the white race is concerned, are those on the immigrants measured under the author's direction (table 125).

In their mean head height index the Old Americans stand just about the middle of the twelve available groups of whites. It is not our object to discuss the index in other than the Americans, nor can the figures here be taken as fully representative of the groups concerned, yet it may be remarked how much more limited is the variation in this as compared with

TABLE 124

Old Americans: Mean height index and cephalic index

	MALES			FEMALES
	Laboratory	Virginia and neighborhood	Northeastern Tennessee Highlands	Laboratory
	(25)	(25)	(22)	(15)
	C.I. M.H.I.	C.I. M.H.I.	C.I. M.H.I.	C.I. M.H.I.
Most dolichocephalic.....	73.2 79.0	72.15 79.0	73.6 77.8	74.0 79.95
Stature...............	176.1	175.1	173.7	161.6
	(25)	(25)	(24)	(20)
Most brachycephalic.....	84.6 80.1	84.3 79.2	81.8 78.5	84.7 80.0
Stature...............	173.4	174.4	172.9	161.2

the cephalic index, and also that with a few exceptions the two indices are rather closely related, so that the lower cephalic is accompanied by a low height index and *vice versa*. With more extensive reliable data the mean head height index should prove of much interest.

Summary. The mean height index is shown to be much more significant, and hence preferable, to the older height-length and height-breadth indices.

The values of the index in the Old Americans are close to those of the cephalic index and show much the same differences between the sexes and between the groups: the index is somewhat higher in the females than in the males, and it is lower in the Tennessee highlanders than in the rest of the male Old Americans.

The dispersion of the index is less extensive and more regular than that of the cephalic index.

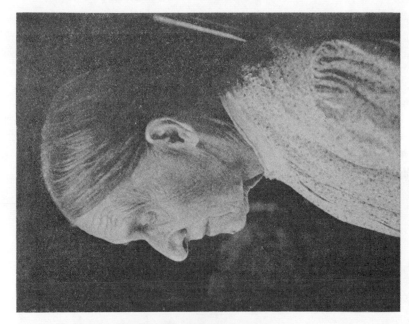

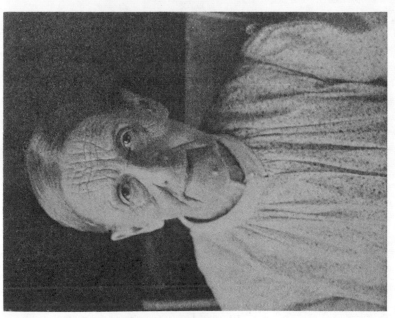

Mrs. Margaret Sipler Roberts
(Bucks County, Pennsylvania)
Born 1820 (photo at 93).   Old American

The index is but little influenced within the adult period by age.

In relation to stature the mean height index of the head grows as stature advances.

The index tends to be slightly higher in brachycephals than in dolicho-cephals, outside of the influence of stature.

In comparison with other groups of whites the Old Americans in the mean height index of the head occupy about a median position.

TABLE 125

Mean height index: Comparative data

Males

GROUP	NUMBER OF SUBJECTS	CEPHALIC INDEX	MEAN HEIGHT INDEX
Old Americans (except Tennessee)............	594	78.2	*79.2*
Old Americans, Tennessee Highlands.........	133	77.5	*78.6*
Immigrants:			
Irish................................	35	78.0	77.95
Russian Jews........................	50	82.2	78.25
Southern Italians....................	50	78.8	79.4
Poles...............................	50	84.3	79.75
English.............................	20	78.99	79.85
North Italians......................	50	84.3	80.0
Hungarians.........................	50	85.5	80.2
Russians............................	50	83.5	80.3
Rumanians..........................	50	85.9	80.9
Croatians...........................	50	85.2	81.0
Greeks..............................	50	80.85	81.4
(Armenians)*.......................	(25)	(85.35)	(81.7)
Mean deviation.......................................		*2.85*	*0.89*

* Possibly due to some undetected posterior flattening of the head, the result of which would be increase in height as well as breadth of the head.

Size of the head

The determination of the size of the head in a given ethnic group is always a matter of importance. The size of the head in man represents approximately the size of the brain, and consciously or not this factor is recognized to be of considerable weight. The feature above all by which man differs from other living beings is mentality, of which the brain is the organ; and it may be safely said that, in general, good mentality is associated with a good brain development and *vice versa*. That this notion is well founded is shown by common observation, by studies on mentally different races,

groups and individuals, by observations on the differences in growth of the
head in college students and in young men without more intensive education,
and by comparing the mentally most efficient with other classes in the
population.[39] Now and then, it is true, a relatively small brain may be
of such a high grade, of such differentiation, that it will enable its possessor
to take his place with the ablest in his line of activities. A brain of a
great artist, such as Rafael, of a remarkable orator, such as Gambetta,

[39] Arloing (Dr.)—De l'influence de l'éducation sur le développement du crâne du chien.
Bull. Soc. Anthrop. Lyon, 1881, I, 44.

Beddoe, (J.)—Evaluation et signification de la capacité cranienne.   L'Anthropologie,
1903, XIV, 267.

Broca (P.)—De l'influence de l'éducation sur le volume et la forme de la tête.   Bull.
Soc. Anthrop., Paris, 1872, VII, 879.

Buschan (G.)—Kultur und Gehirn.   Arch. Rassenbiol., 1904, I, 689; Corr.-Bl.
Anthrop. Ges., XXXV, 127; also Weisbaden, 1906.

Constantin (André)—Contribution à l'étude des correlations physiques et psycho-
sociologiques de la circonférence céphalique.   L'Anthrop., 1919, XXIX, Nos. 3–4, 265–
288.

Costa-Ferreira (A. A.)—La capacité du crâne et la profession chez les Portugais.   Bull.
Soc. Anthrop., Paris, 1903, IV, 417.

Debière (C.)—L'influence du travail cérébral sur le volume du crane.   Bull. Soc.
Anthrop., Lyon, 1885, IV, 29.

Galton (F.)—Head growth in students at the University of Cambridge.   Nature,
1888, XXXVIII, 14; J. Anthrop. Inst., London, XVIII, 155; Nature, 1890, XLI, 450.

Gladstone (R. J.)—A preliminary communication on some cephalometric data bearing
upon the relation of the size and shape of the head to mental ability.   J. Anat. and
Physiol., 1903, XXXVII, 333.

Kohlbrugge (J. H. F.)—Kultur und Gehirn.   Biol. Zentr.-Bl., 1911, XXXI, 248.

Matiegka (H.)—Ueber das Hirngewicht, die Schädelkapazität und die Kopfform sowie
deren Beziehungen zur physischen Tätigkeit des Menschen.   Sitz.-Ber. Böhm. Ges.
Wiss. Math.-Nat., 1903, Cl. 1902, No. 20.

Matiegka (H.)—Ueber die Beziehungen des Hirngewichtes zum Beruf.   Polit. Anthrop.
Rev., 1904–05, III, 7.

Montesori (M.)—Sui caratteri antropometrici.   Arch. p. l'antrop. et etnol., 1904.

Pearl (R.)—On the correlation between intelligence and the size of the head.   J. Comp.
Neurol. and Psychol., 1906, XVI, 189.

Pearson (K.)—On the relationship of intelligence to size and shape of head and to
the physical and mental characters.   Biometrika, 1906, V, 105.   (For additional contributions to the subject by this author see Reid and Mulligan.)

Spitzka (E. A.)—A study of the brains of six eminent scientists and scholars.   Trans.
Am. Philos. Soc. Phila., 1907, XXI, 171.

Weigner (K.)—Ein Beitrag zur Bedeutung des Gehirnwichtes beim Menschen.   Anat.
Hefte, 1904, XXIII, H. 71, p. 67.

For further references see bibliographies in these publications.   Also Relation of Cranial Capacity to Intelligence, by Reid (R. W.) and J. H. Mulligan, J. Anthrop. Inst., 1923,
LIII, 322–331.

of a genius in any one limited direction, may be small, particularly if the possessor is of small stature and delicate build. On the other hand there may be large brains that will produce but very little.

But these are exceptions and in the case of dull, large heads and brains, generally pathological conditions. Normally a good absolute as well as relative (to stature) size of the head is a favorable character.

Measurement. On the living there are only two practicable ways of obtaining the size of the head, the one by taking its maximum circumference above the supraorbital ridges, the other by taking the mean of the length, breadth and height of the vault, its three principal diameters. This second method, which is free from interference by hair, is preferable.

The mean of the three head measurements gives a mean head diameter or *cephalic module*. This mean measurement is not merely expressive in itself but may also be used for contrasting the head size with stature, the module of the face or chest, and other dimensions. Individually the module, similarly as the circumference, is not a perfect representative of the size of the brain, for it is affected by the thickness of the scalp and thickness as well as internal and above all sex-linked peculiarities of the skull. But in group studies these disturbing factors save that of sex, are largely submerged, particularly if we deal with people of the same race and culture. In such cases the value of the module expressed in four figures (to second decimal) is in fact, as tested on series where observations on both the living and the skeletal parts are available, rather close to the cranial capacity in cubic centimeters in males, and within a certain distance of the same in the females.

A disadvantage to the head module up to now has been a paucity of data for comparison. The reason is that it includes the height of the head, for the securing of which there were till recently no satisfactory instruments. It is only since the shaping of special calipers for this purpose[40] that measurements of this height (floor of the auditory meatus line—bregma) have become easier and more reliable. Since then data have been accumulated not only on the American Indian and other colored races, but also on a number of series of white immigrants to the United States, records which ought to be particularly valuable in this connection.

The cephalic module in the Old Americans shows the conditions given in table 126, and figure 20.

The main value of these data will be for future comparisons. They show on one hand a considerable though wholly normal variability, and on the

[40] Figure 10, p. 56, writer's Anthropometry, 8°, Wistar Institute, Philadelphia, 1920.

TABLE 126

Old Americans: Cephalic module $\left(\dfrac{L+B+H}{3}\right)$

General averages (with minima and maxima):
  Males: Laboratory (247)—16.39 (15.03–17.57)
    Southern "Engineers" (347)—16.35 (15.20–17.70)
    Tennessee Highlanders (133)—16.06 (15.20–17.10)
  Females: Laboratory (210)—15.57 (14.60–16.63)

Test series

MALES			FEMALES
Laboratory	Southern "Engineers"	Tennessee Highlanders	
1st 50—16.28	1st 100—16.38	1st 50—16.03	1st 50—15.58
2nd 50—16.33	2nd 100—16.31	2nd 50—16.06	2nd 50—15.59
3rd 50—16.51	3rd 100—16.37	3rd 33—16.09	3rd 50—15.59
4th 47—16.43	4th 47—16.29		4th 60—15.60
5th 50—16.43			

Dispersion

	MALES										
	15.03–15.25	15.26–15.5	15.51–15.75	15.76–16.0	16.01–16.25	16.26–16.5	16.51–16.75	16.76–17.0	17.01–17.25	17.26–17.50	17.51–17.57
Laboratory	(1)	(3)	(11)	(25)	(43)	(76)	(43)	(31)	(11)	(2)	(1)
	0.4	1.2	4.5	10.1	17.4	30.8	17.4	12.6	4.5	0.8	0.4
Southern "Engineers"	(1)	(6)	(17)	(44)	(78)	(85)	(60)	(36)	(16)	(4)	
	0.3	1.7	4.9	12.7	22.5	24.5	17.3	10.4	4.6	1.2	
Tennessee Highlanders	(2)	(10)	(19)	(31)	(31)	(18)	(12)	(8)	(2)		
	1.5	7.5	14.3	23.3	23.3	13.5	9.0	6.0	1.5		

	FEMALES								
	14.60–14.75	14.76–15.0	15.01–15.25	15.26–15.50	15.51–15.75	15.76–16.0	16.01–16.25	16.26–16.5	16.51–16.63
Laboratory	(1)	(10)	(31)	(47)	(54)	(41)	(20)	(3)	(3)
	0.5	4.8	14.8	22.4	25.7	19.5	9.5	1.4	1.4

other a well-marked difference between the two sexes. The average absolute size of the head in the female is very perceptibly smaller than that of the male, but as will be shown later the females make a better showing

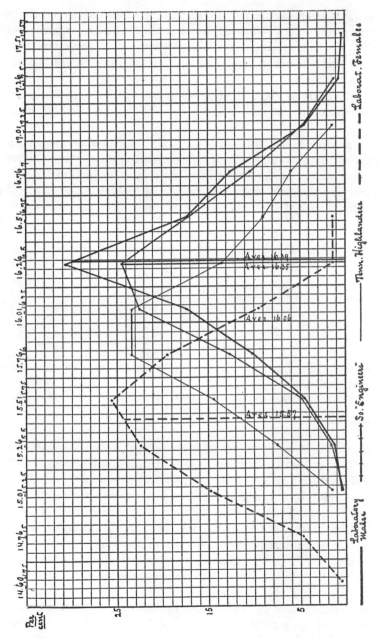

FIG. 20. OLD AMERICANS: CEPHALIC MODULE

than this in relation of the module to stature. Noteworthy conditions
which have already been indicated in our dealing with the separate head
diameters but which are capable of being brought out even more simply
and fully in this connection, are presented by the three groups of males,
as shown in table 127.

The mean stature of these three series is practically identical, but the
size of the head differs; at least it differs between the first two and the last
group.

The first group includes Old Americans of all classes, but as a rule people
of average or above average education. There are some artisans, housewives, a good many clerks and other Government employees, teachers,
professional and business men, and men and women of leisure. The
second group is that of drafted "engineers" which comprises average and

TABLE 127

Old Americans: Measurements relating to size of head according to group

Males

| | STAT-URE | HEAD | | | HEIGHT AURICULAR MEATUS LINE-BREGMA | CEPHALIC MODULE* $\left(\dfrac{L+B+H}{3}\right)$ | CEPHALIC MODULE-STATURE INDEX (S = 1.000) |
		Length maximum	Breadth maximum				
Laboratory series (247)................	174.44	19.78	15.48		13.93	16.39	*94.02*
Virginia, Drafted "Engineers" (347).......	174.26	19.75	15.39		13.97	16.37	*93.94*
Tennessee mountaineers (133)............	174.29	19.50	15.10		13.61	16.07	*92.20*

*Obtained from totals.

higher class artisans, many of whom doubtless had some higher education
and were of mental activity on the average at least equal to that of clerks.
The size of head in these two groups is practically the same.

The third group is that of the Tennessee mountaineers with some of the
lower land people. The latter are in the main farmers; the former are
partly farmers, partly hunters, partly laborers. The educational facilities
of these people were limited and none of them probably have passed through
a High School, nor is their work such as would call for any great mental
activity. The head in this group shows a decidedly lower average in size
than that of either of the other groups.

The test series of 50 or 100 are remarkably uniform, with one interesting
exception. This concerns the third series of 50 in the Laboratory group.
Upon turning back the records in search of an explanation of the exception,

it was found that the majority of these 50 belonged to the staff of one of our Universities.

The dispersion of the mean head diameter is in all the groups remarkably regular, much more so than that of any of the separate head measurements. This indicates a high grade of uniformity in each of the separate groups so far as the development of the head and brain are concerned. The curves of distribution show this regularity to a special advantage; that of the Laboratory males approaches closely an ideal curve of a distribution of a character. All of which has much meaning. The neglected brain remains small, the brain that is used responds by further development, and this under fairly equal demands and opportunities progresses in general similarly within a group, regardless of its physical variations in the form of the head or size of the body.

Size of head and sex. The mean diameter of the head in the male Old Americans of the Laboratory series is 16.39 cm., in the females 15.57 cm. The females in this respect are to the males as 95 to 100, which is seemingly a favorable proportion, the relation of the two sexes in stature being only as 92.8 to 100. Relatively to stature, therefore, the head of the Old American female appears to show more favorably than that of the male.

This showing, however, is somewhat deceptive. It is modified, as will be shown later on, by the peculiarities of the relations between head size and stature as the latter falls or rises. But above this it is modified substantially by an important fact which appeared with especial clearness in the writer's recent preparation of another contribution.[41] This fact is that the external dimensions of the head or skull in the two sexes have not the same relation to the skull capacity or size of the brain.

The mean skull diameter corresponding to the mean head diameter in the living, expressed in four figures, in males is close to the cranial capacity expressed in cubic centimeters. The actual relation of the figures in the males of different ethnic groups so far tested range from 98.5–101 to 100; in other words in males the skull capacity equals 98.5 to 101 per cent of the mean skull diameter in four figures (two decimals). But in the females the capacity equals only between 90 and 94.5 per cent of the figures of the mean skull diameter. This means that relatively to the mean skull or head diameter the female brain is in average about 7 per cent smaller than that of the male. In a male with mean skull diameter of 15.50 cm. the cranial capacity is close to 1550 cc., in a female with mean skull diameter of 14.80 cm. the capacity will be approximately 1360 cc. and may be lower.

[41] Catalogue of Human Crania in the U. S. N. M. Collection. Part I publ. by the U. S. N. M. in 1924, rest in process of publication or preparation.

The female brain is less fully developed than that of the male in the basal and other parts which are not shown in the three main skull dimensions from which the mean diameter is derived, but have an effect on the capacity.

Even though therefore, relatively to stature, the size of the female head among the Old Americans would compare favorably with that of the males, her brain is certainly both absolutely and relatively somewhat smaller, though there are indications that the difference between the female and male brain applies mainly if not entirely to the white matter.

Size of head and age. Already in dealing with the individual head diameters it was seen that, with one exception, they showed a slight, gradual, absolute as well as relative (to stature) increase with age up to the fifth to sixth decades of adult life. The conditions, it may be recalled, differed in the two sexes in the behavior of head height, which did not change perceptibly with advancing age in the males, but kept on augmenting slightly throughout the adult period represented in our series (22–60 years.) in the females. The wholly unexpected gradual increase in head size throughout the first half of the adult period in the Old Americans is shown quite plainly, especially in the females, also by the mean diameter of the head and the relation of same at the different age periods to stature. Up to the sixth decade of life the head, on the average, both absolutely and relatively to stature, gradually increases in size. This is a new fact. The cause in the particular group under study can be scarcely other than a growth of brain. There are only two other agencies which could be instrumental, namely, an outwardly manifested thickening of the skull, or a thickening of the scalp, both of which are very improbable. But if the cause is the prolonged growth of the brain then we are confronted with a newly discovered physiological and physical phenomenon of no small importance. (See table 128.)

Head size and stature. The correlation of head size with stature is, since the works of Parchappe, Bischoff, Broca and others,[42] a well known phenomenon, though one frequently forgotten. As shown in connection with the separate diameters, the head follows the stature by enlargement in all dimensions, though the increase may not be strictly harmonious. The increase is due, in all probability, to the need with greater length and somatic mass of the body of more white brain substance, especially nerve fibers, and is a purely morphological condition, without relation to any ability, inferiority or superiority. The exact ratio of brain size to stature along the extended range of the latter and uninfluenced by other factors, is still a matter of some uncertainty.

[42] See Topinard, Eléments d'Anthropologie générale, 532 *et seq.*, 560.

Taking a fair number of the shortest and tallest Old Americans of each sex of our Laboratory series, with a number who are closest on each side to the average of the group, and taking next the stature-cephalic module relations by regular stature subdivisions, we obtain the figures in table 129.

TABLE 128

Size of head: Cephalic module vs. age

	MALES				
	20–29	30–39	40–49	50–59	Above 59
Laboratory.................................. {	(91) 16.35	(63) 16.40	(47) 16.43	(34) 16.43	(12) 16.27
Southern "Engineers"...................... {	(318) 16.34	(29) 16.39			
Tennessee Highlanders..................... {	(118) 16.09	(15) 15.84			
Laboratory: Stature.........................	174.14	174.97	174.54	173.98	174.78
Relation of cephalic module to stature (S = 100).................................	9.39	9.37	9.41	9.44	9.31
Southern "Engineers" stature.................	174.33	173.54			
Relation of cephalic module to stature.........	9.37	9.44			
Tennessee Highlanders stature.................	174.51	172.60			
Relation of cephalic module to stature.........	9.22	9.18			
	FEMALES				
	20–29	30–39	40–49	50–59	Above 59
Laboratory.............................. {	(72) 15.53	(71) 15.59	(36) 15.67	(27) 15.54	(3) (15.53)
Laboratory: stature.........................	162.57	161.96	162.42	159.18	(166.07)
Relation of cephalic module to stature (S = 100).................................	9.55	9.63	9.65	9.76	(9.35)

The data show much of interest. In the first place, as we proceed from the short to the medium and from the medium to tall statures, the cephalic module, *i.e.*, the size of the head, shows a concomitant and substantial increase. This is true of both sexes and the rate of advance in each sex appears to be fairly even. This is a good demonstration of the positive and important correlation of head and brain size, respectively, with stature alone.   The taller the man or woman the larger on the average their brain and head, regardless of other influences.

However, the *relative* value of the size of the head to stature decreases gradually as stature advances.   The head stands in a direct and important correlation with stature and increases steadily as this increases, but at a diminishing rate.   If we should represent stature and the cephalic module— stature ratio in the Old Americans, and doubtless in any other ethnic group, as two straight ascending lines, these lines would not run parallel but that of the ratio would throughout its course upward converge gradually to that of stature.   The reality is that as we progress from shorter to taller persons the head grows absolutely larger, but its ratio to stature is progressively smaller.

TABLE 129

Old Americans: Measurements relating to size of head according to stature

Laboratory series

	MALES				
	Mean stature	Mean cephalic module	Progression	Cephalic module-statue index	Differences from medium
25 shortest...............	164.38	16.10		*9.79*	*+0.42*
16 medium...............	174.30	16.33	+0.23	*9.37*	—
25 tallest.................	184.40	16.51	+0.18	*9.10*	*−0.27*

	FEMALES				
20 shortest...............	151.32	15.35		*10.14*	*+0.55*
13 medium...............	161.60	15.50	+0.15	*9.59*	
20 tallest.................	172.20	15.70	+0.20	*9.12*	*−0.47*

Thus, a brain and a head which in a short person might be normal or even above the average for that stature, and indicate entirely proper conditions or possibly even a superiority, would in a tall person be below the average of what he or she should have, and would indicate a probable inferiority.   The cephalic module-stature ratio or index should in view of this prove of material and really indispensable aid in qualitative examinations of persons.   It moreover opens a way towards a very promising line of further research.

Theoretically, the uncomplicated line of increment in the size of the head with stature should be uniform and be the expression of a somatic law which should be capable of a mathematical reduction.   Should this prove to be the case we could then establish in anthropometry a most useful scale of normal head increase per unit of stature, as Bischoff attempted with the brain.   But matters evidently are not so simple.   Further light on the problem is thrown by table 130 which extends to the whole series

TABLE 130

Size of head: Mean head diameter vs. stature

	MALES				
	150.01–160.0	160.01–170.0	170.01–180.0	180.01–190.0	Above 190
Laboratory and Southern "Engineers" (594)................................	(5)	(143)	(366)	(88)	(2)
Cephalic module.................	16.12	16.21	16.37	16.55	(16.67)
Progression in module.............		0.09	0.16	0.18	
Approximate relation of module to stature*........................	10.40	9.82	9.35	8.95	
Progression in module-stature index		−0.58	−0.47	−0.40	
Tennessee Highlanders (133)...........		(29)	(87)	(17)	
Cephalic module.................		15.82	16.10	16.26	
Progression in module.............			0.28	0.16	
Approximate relation of module to stature........................		9.59	9.20	8.79	
Progression in module-stature index			−0.39	−0.41	

	FEMALES			
	145.0–150.0	150.01–160.0	160.01–170.0	170.01–180.0
Laboratory (210)............................	(3)	(73)	(114)	(20)
Cephalic module.........................	15.23	15.48	15.63	15.69
Progression in module.....................		0.25	0.15	0.06
Approximate relation of module to stature*..		9.97	9.47	8.97
Progression in module-stature index.........			0.50	0.50

* $\dfrac{\text{Module} \times 100}{\text{Mean stature of the group}}$.   The mean stature was taken midway between the limits of the group, e.g., mean of group 160.01–170 = 165).

of the Old Americans and where the absolute as well as the relative size of the head is given by stature groups of 10 cm. difference.   The results are not uniform.   They differ in the sexes, and they differ even in groups

of one sex. In the Tennessee highlanders and in the females the progression
in the module-stature ratio is, as far as these groups go, very regular; but
in the bulk of the males the rate of change in the ratio diminishes as stature
rises throughout the available subdivisions. The causes of these sex and
group differences are for the present not sufficiently clear and the subject
calls for a separate inquiry; it is plain however that matters are more
involved than anticipated and that no simple generally applicable scale
of head size-stature ratios can as yet be established. Studies on primitive
peoples, where the factors of civilization and mental activities are of much
less potency, should be helpful in this direction.

One of the points which deserves attention once more at this juncture
is the showing in head size, both absolutely and in relation to stature, of the
females as compared to the males. In a foregoing section this subject was
discussed in a more general way; it may now be approached more
analytically.

If we compare males and females of the same stature, we find that the
size of the head in the latter is really smaller, and that this holds good for
all stature groups as far as comparison is possible. The male scalp, however,
is on the average slightly thicker than that of the female, in addition to
which the length of the head in the males is enlarged slightly more than it is
in the females by a greater development of the supraorbital and occipital
ridges and frontal sinuses. If we discount these factors, then the actual
size of the head for a given stature in the two sexes becomes more nearly
equal; yet a slight superiority in the external dimensions of the head remains, as has already been shown by Topinard,[43] for the male. The seemingly favorable showing of the female head size discussed under "Size of the
Head and Sex," is therefore of a somewhat deceptive nature.

The subject may be summarized thus: The head of the female is absolutely smaller than that of the male; strictly speaking it is also slightly
smaller in relation to stature; and relatively the disproportion in favor of the
males is still more marked with the brain. All of which, however, are but
gross morphological facts and no index of the higher qualities of the brain
in the two sexes.

A very interesting line of inquiry in these connections would be to see how
far the *individual* large or small heads, both in those of short and those of
tall stature, correspond to brain force and ability. Some recent observations in this direction[44] would seem to indicate that here again matters

[43] Elém. d'Anthrop. gén., 532, 560.
[44] Reid (R. W.) and Mulligan (J. H.)—Relation of Cranial Capacity to Intelligence.
J. Anthrop. Inst., 1923, LIII, 324; with reference to contributions to the subject by Karl
Pearson and his collaboraters.

are not as simple as might be expected and that individually it might be very difficult if not impossible to establish any direct relation between the size of the head and intelligence as shown by the marks, for instance, in a medical college; but the research on the subject is still far from adequate. It may very well be that what becomes clearly enough apparent when we deal with whole groups will often be obscured in individuals; the main difficulty in dealing with individuals in this important respect being that there is no safe gage as yet of the actual value of a given brain, and school or college marks are not always sufficient in this respect.

TABLE 131

Old Americans, size of head: Cephalic module vs. head form

	MALES			
	Cephalic index	Stature	Cephalic module	Cephalic module vs. stature*
Laboratory:				
25 most dolichocephalic............	73.2	176.1	16.42	93.24
25 most brachycephalic............	84.6	173.4	16.34	94.23 = + 0.99
Southern "Engineers":				
25 most dolichocephalic............	72.1	175.1	16.37	93.49
25 most brachycephalic............	84.3	174.4	16.38	93.92 = + 0.43
Tennessee Highlanders:				
24 most dolichocephalic............	73.6	173.7	16.09	92.63
22 most brachycephalic............	81.8	172.9	16.04	92.77 = + 0.14
	FEMALES			
Laboratory:				
15 most dolichocephalic............	74.0	161.6	15.51	95.98
20 most brachycephalic............	84.7	161.2	15.67	97.21 = + 1.23

*For convenience stature in this case taken as 1,000.

Size of head and head form. One of the oldest and still undecided questions in anthropology, is that of the relative values of the brain in dolicho- and brachycephaly. Claims of superiority backed by some plausible evidence have been made for both, but strictly scientific data bearing on the problem are scarce.

Taking the size of the brain and head as corresponding in general to the value of the former, which when dealing with groups we probably are justified in doing, it becomes of interest to see how the dolicho- and brachycephals behave in this respect in such a comprehensive series as that of the Old Americans. The data are given in tables 131 and 132.

These results are quite instructive. They show that differences in head size in the two extremes of head form are very small; but what difference there is slightly favors brachycephaly. This is most apparent in table 131, where we compare extreme groups of head forms, and it is most marked in the females and the Laboratory group of males, somewhat less so in the

TABLE 132

Old Americans: Head size (cephalic module) and head form

	MALES						
	Cephalic index Up to 72.5	72.6–75.0	75.1–77.5	77.6–80.0	80.1–82.5	82.6–85.0	Above 85.0
Laboratory and Southern "Engineers" (564):	(18)	(77)	(162)	(201)	(86)	(37)	(13)
Cephalic module..........	16.38	16.42	16.41	16.39	16.37	16.36	16.29
Stature..................	175.32	175.19	175.38	173.60	173.23	174.64	171.94
Module-stature ratio.......	9.34	9.37	9.36	9.44	9.45	9.37	9.47
Progressive difference......		+0.03	−0.01	+0.08	+0.01	−0.08	+0.10
Tennessee Highlanders (133):	(4)	(22)	(44)	(42)	(18)	(2)	(1)
Cephalic module..........	16.22	16.06	16.04	16.09	16.06	(16.07)	(16.12)
Stature..................	175.92	173.73	174.54	174.68	173.26	(169.30)	(181.30)
Module-stature ratio.......	9.22	9.24	9.19	9.21	9.27		
Progressive difference......		+0.02	−0.05	+0.02	+0.06		

	FEMALES					
	72.6–75.0	75.1–77.5	77.6–80.0	80.1–82.5	82.6–85.0	Above 85.0
Laboratory (210):	(19)	(32)	(73)	(52)	(26)	(8)
Cephalic module.....................	15.56	15.61	15.61	15.57	15.58	15.74
Stature............................	161.67	162.19	162.49	161.17	161.91	161.21
Module stature ratio.................	9.62	9.62	9.61	9.65	9.62	9.76
Progressive difference................		±	−0.01	+0.04	−0.03	+0.14

"Engineers," and least in the Tennesseeans; yet all the groups tend in the same direction. No definite conclusions should however as yet be drawn from this showing, for we cannot be certain without much additional observation both on the living and on skull capacity, that the results here obtained mean really that the brachycephals possess a slightly larger cerebrum.

Table 132 is less plain, partly in all probability due to the insufficiency of numbers. There is, nevertheless, observable a slight tendency towards a larger head as we progress from dolicho- to brachycephaly. The lower brachycephals (80.1–85) are however practically identical in head size with the preceding mesocephals. The points involved are plainly in need of much further investigation.

Comparative data on head size. Due to the fact that in measurements on the living head, height has been largely neglected, there are no data in literature on the mean head diameter such as dealt with in these studies. Fortunately however we have the identical measurements, taken by the author or under his direction, on recent immigrants to this country. And these immigrants, even though their numbers are not always, or are barely, adequate show nevertheless some highly interesting conditions as to size of the head, which are shown in table 133, and figure 21.

In table 133 A, we see that so far as dimensions alone are concerned, the head in the Old Americans is very perceptibly larger than that of any of the other groups. However, we know that the size of the head to a large extent is correlated with stature and that the Americans are taller than any of the European nationalities. If on the basis of this, as in the second column of our table, we reduce the mean head diameter to its ratio with stature or the cephalic module-stature index, it then becomes apparent that this ratio or index is higher in most of the immigrants than it is in the old native stock. This showing could readily be misleading. The module-stature index of the immigrants is higher than that of the Old Americans for the same reason that the female index among the latter (9.63) is higher than that of the males (9.40), namely, the relatively larger size of the head that goes with lower stature. The only correct way of comparing the head of the immigrants with that of the Old Americans is to compare it in those of equal stature. Such a comparison is given as closely as possible in figure 21 and the results are very striking. The Americans in head size are superior to all the immigrants, the nearest approach for some reason being that of the Irish. The cause of the difference is doubtless the higher educational and cultural development of the Old Americans. The Tennessee highlanders, Old Americans, but culturally retarded and but poorly educated, stand in head and brain size on about the same level as the average immigrant. There is little if any probability that the older American stock have already an inherently larger head and brain, or any of the white immigrants an inherently smaller cranium than others. What differences there are, according to all indications, are matters of greater or lesser functional development of the brain. Here is a factor of great scientific as well as practical importance.

TABLE 133

Head size in the Old Americans and European immigrants

Males

A

PEOPLE	CEPHALIC MODULE	CEPHALIC MODULE-STATURE RATIO
Old Americans (Laboratory and Southern "Engineers")	16.37	9.40
Irish	16.18	9.44
English	16.07	9.44
Northern Italians	16.05	9.46
Poles	16.03	9.40
Croatians	15.98	9.31
Rumanians	15.93	9.43
Russians	15.93	9.36
Southern Italians	15.93	9.73
Russian Jews	15.90	9.66
Greeks	15.87	9.45
Hungarians	15.80	9.49
Armenians	15.77	9.44

B

Immigrants

PEOPLE	STATURE	CEPHALIC MODULE	CEPHALIC MODULE-STATURE RATIO
Old Americans (Laboratory and Southern "Engineers")	160.0	16.14	10.11
	165.0	16.21	9.82
	(160.1–170)		
	170.0	16.29	9.58
	175.0	16.37	9.35
	(170.1–180)		
Southern Italians	163.4	15.93	9.73
Russian Jews	164.6	15.90	9.66
Hungarians	166.5	15.80	9.49
Armenians	167.4	15.77	9.44
English	170.2	16.07	9.44
Poles	170.4	16.03	9.40
Greeks	168.3	15.87	9.45
Rumanians	168.7	15.93	9.43
Northern Italians	169.6	16.05	9.46
Russians	169.8	15.93	9.36
Croatians	171.6	15.98	9.31
Irish	171.6	16.18	9.44

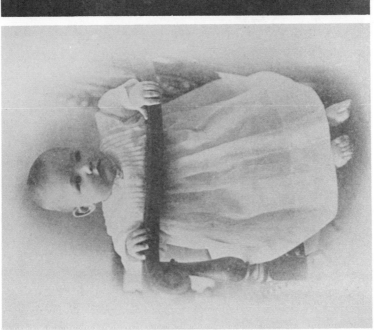

Master John Robinson Smith (9 months) Egmont (2¼ years) and Alden (5 months) Schermerhorn Smith

EXAMPLES OF THE YOUNGEST OLD AMERICANS

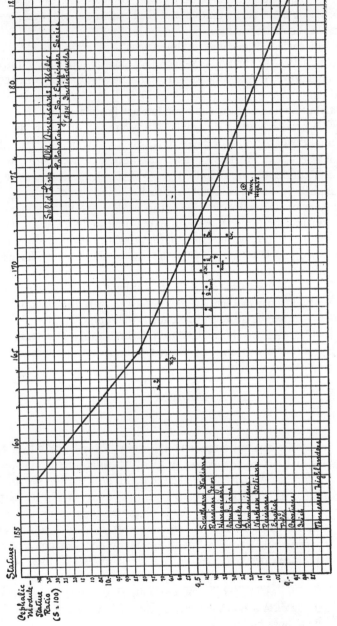

Fig. 21. Cephalic-Module-Stature Index in Old Americans and Recent Immigrants

Summary. The most useful measurement to represent the size of the head in the living is the mean diameter of the head (mean of length, breadth and height), or cephalic module.

The module shows interesting sex differences.

Among the males the module is perceptibly smaller, both absolutely and relatively to stature, in the highlanders of Tennessee than it is in the rest of the Old Americans.

The distribution and curves of the module are fairly regular.

The female head is absolutely small. In groups of similar body height it is also smaller than the male head relatively to stature, but the difference is much less than in the case of the absolute measurement.

Up to the sixth decade of life in both sexes of the Old Americans the head increases slightly in size both absolutely and relatively to stature.

The influence of stature on the size of the head is direct and marked: the higher the stature the larger in general is the head and *vice versa;* the progression, however, is not symmetrical but proceeds at a diminishing rate as stature advances, so that the ratio of the size of the head to stature decreases plainly as stature rises.

Differences in head size between dolichocephals and brachycephals are small, but what differences there are favor very slightly the brachycephals.

Compared with twelve groups of recent white immigrants, the size of the head of the Old Americans, both absolutely and relatively to stature, shows a superiority over every group; the Tennessee highlanders, however, stand on a level with the immigrants.

THE FACE

Descriptive features

Next in interest if not importance to the study of the head is that of the characteristics of the face. But in the living these studies are somewhat more difficult, due to which and to the focussing of attention on the head that contains the all-important organ brain, research on the facial parts has been more or less neglected. This is particularly true among the whites, so that there are no data of this nature as yet on the adult Americans, old or recent, and there is but little on the people from whom the Americans have been derived. Actually more is known in these respects on the American Indian and some savage tribes than on the people of the British Isles. Studies on the facial parts in skulls are of course more numerous, but the data are not directly comparable with and can not fully take the place of those on the living.

The face of the Old Americans while presenting, as in other groups of whites, almost endless physiognomic differences of individual, family and even subracial nature, has nevertheless certain general characteristics by which it may be described.   On the whole, as natural, it is nearest the face of the British, yet in the majority of cases a fresh British face may readily be told in America as can a more typical fresh American face in many instances be told in any part of the British Isles.   But such differences, without our being fully conscious of it, depend much on color (the face of the English shows generally more color), in males the fashion in beard, and on mannerisms, language, and that prevailing habitual mental attitude which, reflected in the face, often gives it, regardless of other things, something of a national character.   Were we to compare the faces of the dead instead of those of the living, our task would be simpler.

After studying closely the American face in over 1500 individuals, and more casually in a larger number, the impression remains with the writer that the female face shows more often or in a clearer way, the various ancestral features.   There appear to be more women than men who show in a typical form the face of the Normans, or French or Scotch or Irish. Among men such occurrences seem much scarcer.   The subject, however, is full of difficulties and a definite judgment is hardly as yet possible.

Due to want of malar and zygomatic protrusion and a rather long nose, the face of the Old Americans in general appears rather long.   In both men and women two facial forms predominate, the one the relatively full face and the other the meagre.   The "full" face does not mean either a rounded or a fat face, nor does the term "meagre" imply angularity, which in fact, especially in the higher classes, is generally subdued or absent.

The most typical Old-American face can again be seen most commonly in the females.   It is a face the outline of which is a fairly long oval, due to good filling almost equally as broad below as above and with the sides almost flat and parallel.   Frequently, however, the lower part of the face will show a slight or more marked tapering towards the chin; but the forehead is normally never disproportionate, either very narrow or very broad.   In such a face are normal white woman's eyes, the malar prominences are hardly visible or only very moderately so, and there is no protrusion at the angles of the lower jaw.   In profile such a face shows a good forehead, faint to sub-medium supra-orbital ridges, a well, but not excessively developed, convex, concavo-convex, straight or mildly concave nose, moderate jaws without any or but slight alveolar prognathism, rather sub-medium lips, and medium chin, with the cheeks evenly filled out to a harmonious, pleasing whole.   In a more masculine form this type of face is frequently met with also among younger males.

In the meagre face, male or female, the eyes appear to be deeper set and the filling of the tissues is more or less wanting so that the bony outlines of the temples and facial parts including the sub-orbital hollows, are more perceptible, even without being more strongly developed.   Such a face—the typical face of Uncle Sam or Lincoln—has more "character" and is most frequent as well as best developed in elderly men.   With a full white beard such a face is not seldom one of distinction.

The more typical Old-American face, whether well filled or meagre, may be characterized as frank, healthy, intelligent.   It is not seldom handsome, though perhaps not more frequently than among other white stocks exceptionally beautiful.

The Old-American face is not marked by especial hairiness.   The quantity of beard in the male, when allowed to grow which is now rare, may be described as good without being excessive; and one practically never meets in the females with a marked down on the upper lip such as is fairly common in the mediterraneans.

Detailed observations on the separate parts of the face will be given in connection with the measurements of these different features.

Detailed observations and measurements: The face as a whole

In the skull the face ends at the naso-frontal articulation (nasion), but in the living it in effect includes also the forehead up to the hair line (crinion). That part up to the nasion is the anatomical or morphological face, that to the crinion is the physiognomy.   In measuring the face of the living we take therefore both its anatomic and its physiognomic height, from lowest point of chin in the median line to respectively the nasion and crinion, and its maximum breadth, which is the breadth between the most distant points of the zygomae.   The percental relation of the anatomic height to the breadth of the face is the "anatomic or morphologic index;" that between the breadth of the face and its total height, is the "physiognomic index." A high morphologic (and low physiognomic) index means that the face is relatively high or narrow, while the reverse, a low morphologic and high physiognomic index, shows that the face is relatively short or broad; just which of these it is being indicated by the respective value of the two measurements concerned.[45]

The face (both anatomic and physiognomic) may be high or low (long or short), broad or narrow.   The possible combinations are given in table 134.

The facial indices, useful as they are, are incapable by themselves of show-

[45] For methods, etc., see author's Anthropometry.

ing just which of these forms is represented, and it therefore is necessary in all facial studies to take into consideration and show also the actual measurements.

The meaning of the various forms of the face, as well as that of its size, is partly functional and evolutionary, partly that of correlations.

The ancestral human face was broader, higher—at least so in its subnasal portion, and in general heavier than it is today. It diminished in all or nearly all dimensions as well as in strength as the requirements (chewing) on the teeth and jaws diminished, and this road with advancing civilization it still follows. The smaller and less frequent the functional demand on them, the weaker and smaller in course of time tend to become the muscles of mastication, the jaws, the teeth, the expanse of the zygomatic arches, and hence the smaller the face in all directions, except possibly in the nasal height which is subject to some separate influences.

TABLE 134

HEIGHT BREADTH	HEIGHT BREADTH	HEIGHT BREADTH
High and narrow	Medium and narrow	Low and narrow
High and medium	Medium and medium	Low and medium
High and broad	Medium and broad	Low and broad

Independently of functional influences which in time have produced changes of evolutionary significance, the face is subject to the influences of the form of the head (vault), and to changes in stature. The broader the head, the broader in general tends to be the face, and vice versa; and the taller the stature the larger in all dimensions will be the head as well as the face, regardless of other agencies that may be active simultaneously.

In an average-statured civilized white man of today, the face should be on the average of moderate absolute height, with very moderate to fairly good breadth, according to the shape of the head; and this in fact is generally the case. But in a tall individual the face will be of considerable height, and in many individuals due to mixture of types and other conditions we will meet with aberrant conditions. Given men or women of equal stature and form of head, the larger the face the more primitive it may be said to be in type, and the reverse. The massive lower jaw does not denote mental but is an expression of muscular energy, and is a retrograde rather than an advanced and desirable morphological condition.

We may now approach the conditions shown by the facial measurements of the Old Americans. They are shown in tables 135 to 143.

TABLE 135

Old Americans, males: Face—menton–crinion

Laboratory series

Number of observations: 147*

General average: 18.45 cm.

1st series of 37—18.5 cm.   4th series of 32—18.2 cm.
2nd series of 35—18.4 cm.   5th series of 21—18.5 cm.
3rd series of 22—18.6 cm.

Minimum: 16.1 cm.   Maximum: 20.7 cm.

TABLE OF FREQUENCIES

	Up to 16.75 cm.	16.76–17.0 cm.	17.1–17.25 cm.	17.26–17.5 cm.	17.51–17.75 cm.	17.76–18.0 cm.	18.1–18.25 cm.	18.26–18.5 cm.	18.51–18.75 cm.	18.76–19.0 cm.	19.1–19.25 cm.	19.26–19.5 cm.	19.51–19.75 cm.	19.76–20.0 cm.	20.1–20.25 cm.	Above 20.5 cm.
Number of cases.....	2	5	8	7	11	17	6	29	14	17	6	3	7	7	5	3
Per cent.............	1.4	3.4	5.4	4.8	7.5	11.6	4.1	19.7	9.5	11.6	4.1	2.0	4.8	4.8	3.4	2.0

* In fully 100 subjects the loss of hair over the forehead made a correct measurement impossible.

TABLE 136

Old Americans, females: Face—Menton-crinion

Number of observations: 206

General average: 17.53 cm.

1st series of 49—17.34 cm.   3rd series of 49—17.64 cm.
2nd series of 49—17.52 cm.   4th series of 59—17.43 cm.

Minimum: 15.5 cm.   Maximum: 19.5 cm.

TABLE OF FREQUENCIES

	15.5–15.75 cm.	15.76–16.0 cm.	16.1–16.25 cm.	16.26–16.5 cm.	16.51–16.75 cm.	16.76–17.0 cm.	17.1–17.25 cm.	17.26–17.5 cm.	17.51–17.75 cm.	17.76–18.0 cm.	18.1–18.25 cm.	18.26–18.5 cm.	18.51–18.75 cm.	18.76–19.0 cm.	19.1–19.25 cm.	19.26–19.5 cm.
Number of cases.....	3	8	8	8	7	24	14	29	15	32	17	20	6	9	3	3
Per cent.............	1.5	3.9	3.9	3.9	3.4	11.6	6.8	14.1	7.3	15.5	8.2	9.7	2.9	4.4	1.5	1.5

The principal notes that may be made on these tables, and figures 22 to 26, are the following:

The distribution of the total as well as the lower facial height is large and irregular. If we reduce the number of subdivisions, the series as well as curves appear more regular, but this is merely covering the conditions. The irregularity in the distribution of these two measurements is greater than that in any other dimension of the head or face and can only indicate unsettled conditions.

The distribution of the facial breadth is perceptibly more simple and more regular than that of either of the heights of the face.

TABLE 137

Old Americans, males: Face—Menton-nasion

Number of observations: 247
General average: 11.93 cm.

1st series of 50–11.96 cm. 4th series of 50—11.86 cm.
2nd series of 50—11.97 cm. 5th series of 50—11.89 cm.
3rd series of 47—11.92 cm.

Minimum: 10.4 Maximum: 13.4 cm.

	TABLE OF FREQUENCIES												
	10.4-10.5 cm.	10.51-10.75 cm.	10.76-11.0 cm.	11.1-11.25 cm.	11.26-11.5 cm.	11.51-11.75 cm.	11.76-12.0 cm.	12.1-12.25 cm.	12.26-12.5 cm.	12.51-12.75 cm.	12.76-13.0 cm.	13.1-13.25 cm.	13.26-13.4 cm.
Number of cases.	5	5	12	23	29	21	49	23	36	14	16	9	5
Per cent............	2.0	2.0	4.9	9.3	11.7	8.5	19.8	9.3	14.6	5.7	6.5	3.6	2.0

TABLE 138

Old Americans, females: Face—Menton-nasion

Number of observations: 210
General average: 11.09 cm.

1st series of 50—11.2 cm. 3rd series of 50—11.15 cm.
2nd series of 50—11.0 cm. 4th series of 60—11.1 cm.

Minimum: 9.8 cm. Maximum: 13.2 cm.

	TABLE OF FREQUENCIES												
	9.8-10.0 cm.	10.1-10.25 cm.	10.26-10.5 cm.	10.51-10.75 cm.	10.76-11.0 cm.	11.1-11.25 cm.	11.26-11.5 cm.	11.51-11.75 cm.	11.76-12.0 cm.	12.1-12.25 cm.	12.26-12.5 cm.	12.51-12.75 cm.	12.76-13.0 cm.	13.1-13.2 cm.
Number of cases...........	6	8	19	21	47	34	34	12	20	6	2			1
Per cent.................	2.9	3.8	9.0	10.0	22.4	16.2	16.2	5.7	9.5	2.9	0.9			0.5

The distribution of the two indices is fairly good, particularly in the females, but it should be noted that the subdivisions are rather large, so that many smaller irregularities are doubtless obscured.

The above facts lead to the conclusion that the variability of the facial parts in the Old Americans is still considerable, being even more marked than that of the vault of the head, and that a definite American facial type

TABLE 139

Old Americans, males: Breadth of face (diameter bizygomatic maximum)

Number of observations: 247

General average: 13.86

1st series of 50—13.92 cm.   4th series of 50—13.79 cm.

2nd series of 50—13.84 cm.   5th series of 50—13.85 cm.

3rd series of 47—13.89 cm.

Minimum: 12.7.   Maximum: 15.2 cm.

	TABLE OF FREQUENCIES									
	12.7–13.0 cm.	13.1–13.25 cm.	13.26–13.5 cm.	13.51–13.75 cm.	13.76–14.0 cm.	14.1–14.25 cm.	14.26–14.5 cm.	14.51–14.75 cm.	14.76–15.0 cm.	15.1–15.2 cm.
Number of cases..................	12	17	33	37	69	34	22	14	7	2
Per cent.........................	*4.9*	*6.9*	*13.4*	*15.0*	*27.9*	*13.8*	*8.9*	*5.7*	*2.8*	*0.8*

TABLE 140

Old Americans, females: Breadth of face (diameter bizygomatic maximum)

Number of observations: 210

General average: 12.99 cm.

1st series of 50—13.02 cm.   3rd series of 50—13.0 cm.

2nd series of 50—12.96 cm.   4th series of 60—12.92 cm.

Minimum: 12.0 cm.   Maximum: 14.6 cm.

Relation to males as 94.3 to 100

	TABLE OF FREQUENCIES									
	12.0–12.25 cm.	12.26–12.5 cm.	12.51–12.75 cm.	12.76–13.0 cm.	13.1–13.25 cm.	13.26–13.5 cm.	13.51–13.75 cm.	13.76–14.0 cm.	14.1–14.25 cm.	14.26–14.6 cm.
Number of cases..................	11	20	31	58	28	40	12	8		2
Per cent.........................	*5.2*	*9.5*	*14.8*	*27.6*	*13.3*	*19.0*	*5.7*	*3.8*		*0.9*

so far as dimensions are concerned cannot as yet be considered as fully established.

The main conditions shown by figures 22–26, etc., are abstracted in table 144.

With the dearth of similar records on either the American or more closely related European peoples, the main value of this table is that of reliable data for future comparisons.   They show the face of the Old Americans of today and by them may be gauged facial changes in the same stock in time to come.

TABLE 141

Old Americans, males: Facial index, total (or physiognomic)

Laboratory series

Number of observations: 147

General average: 75.10

1st series of 37—75.42	4th series of 32—75.65
2nd series of 35—75.37	5th series of 21—73.89
3rd series of 22—74.65	

Minimum: 66.7.   Maximum: 85.7

	TABLE OF FREQUENCIES							
	66.7–67.5	67.6–70.0	70.1–72.5	72.6–75.0	75.1–77.5	77.6–80.0	80.1–82.5	82.6–85.7
Number of cases............	1	12	33	25	38	22	12	4
Per cent...................	*0.7*	*8.2*	*22.4*	*17.0*	*25.8*	*15.0*	*8.2*	*2.7*

TABLE 142

Old Americans, females: Facial index, total (or physiognomic)

Number of observations: 206

General average: 74.08

1st series of 49—74.28	3rd series of 49—74.02
2nd series of 49—74.08	4th series of 49—74.3

Minimum: 67.0.   Maximum: 85.88

	TABLE OF FREQUENCIES							
	67.0–67.5	67.6–70.0	70.1–72.5	72.6–75.0	75.1–77.5	77.6–80.0	80.1–82.5	82.6–85.88
Number of cases............	3	23	43	56	42	25	9	5
Per cent...................	*1.5*	*11.2*	*20.9*	*27.2*	*20.4*	*12.1*	*4.4*	*2.4*

Aside of this, however, they reveal interesting relations of the facial parts in the two sexes.   The female:male ratio of the total height of the face (to hair line) as well as that of the face breadth, and consequently that of the total or physiognomic facial module (mean diameter), is exactly the same (93.6), showing the face as a whole to be of the same form in the two sexes.   But the female:male ratio in the lower facial height (to nasion) is somewhat less indicating that the inferior part of the face in the females is relatively low.   This fact will be seen even better when we compare the main facial dimensions in the two sexes with stature.

Another interesting lot of conditions revealed by our figures relates to the differences shown by the several groups of the Old American males.   The facts are given in tables 145 and 146.   In considering them it should be remembered that the laboratory group comprises almost exclusively men in professional, business and clerical vocations, with few artisans and no

TABLE 143

Old Americans: Facial index, lower (or anatomic)

Laboratory series

Males	Females
Average: 86.08	Average: 85.30
1st 50—86.01 3rd 47—85.84	1st 50—85.9 3rd 50—85.65
2nd 50—86.55 4th 50—85.99	2nd 50—84.85 4th 60—85.25
5th 50—85.96	
Minimum: 73.3. Maximum: 98.5	Minimum: 74.2. Maximum: 99.3

LABORATORY	TABLE OF FREQUENCIES										
	73.3–75.0	75.01–77.5	77.51–80.0	80.01–82.5	82.51–85.0	85.01–87.5	87.51–90.0	90.01–92.5	92.51–95.0	95.01–97.5	97.51–100.0
Males (247):											
Number of cases..........	2	9	23	24	43	49	52	18	15	10	2
Per cent.................	*0.8*	*3.6*	*9.3*	*9.7*	*17.4*	*19.8*	*21.0*	*7.3*	*6.1*	*4.1*	*0.8*
Females (210):											
Number of cases..........	2	9	14	27	40	49	41	22	3	2	1
Per cent.................	*1.0*	*4.3*	*6.7*	*12.8*	*19.1*	*23.3*	*19.5*	*10.5*	*1.4*	*1.0*	*0.5*

laborers; that the southern " engineers" were mechanics though not a few of them with higher education; and that the Tennessee highlanders were exclusively non-educated or but poorly schooled farmers and woodsmen.

The measurements show that in the laboratory group the average face measurements and particularly the lower facial height are lower than those of any of the other groups; that the Tennessee highlanders come next; and that the "engineers," both southern and of mixed-states parentage have the largest faces.   The relative values of the measurements, however, remain much the same in the four groups, so that the facial indices are close together though not quite identical; due to the reduced lower facial height the laboratory men show a slightly higher morphologic and lower physiognomic index than the two other groups.

TABLE 144

Old Americans: The face

(Whole series)

Size

	MALES						FEMALES					
	Height							Height				
Number of subjects	To Nasion	To Crinion	Breadth: diameter bi-zygomatic maximum	Facial module* mor-phologic	Facial module mor-phologic vs. stature†	Facial morphologic vs. cephalic module‡	Number of subjects	To Nasion	To Crinion	Breadth: diameter bi-zygomatic maximum	Facial module mor-phologic	Facial module mor-phologic vs. stature	Facial morphologic vs. cephalic module
(726)	12.15	18.74	13.87	13.01	74.65	79.68	(210)	11.09	17.54	12.99	12.04	74.40	77.28

Shape

MALES		FEMALES	
Facial index		Facial index	
Morphologic	Physiognomic	Morphologic	Physiognomic
87.60	74.12	85.39	74.08

Female *vs.* male (male = 100)

STATURE	FACE HEIGHT TO NASION	FACE HEIGHT TO CRINION	BREADTH	FACIAL MODULE		FACIAL MORPHO-LOGIC MODULE vs. STATURE	FACIAL MORPHO-LOGIC vs. CEPHALIC MODULE	FACIAL INDEX	
				Physiog-nomic§	Morpho-logic			Morpho-logic	Physiog-nomic
92.9	91.3	93.6	93.6	93.6	92.5	99.7	97.0	97.5	99.9

* $\dfrac{\text{Height to Nasion} + \text{Breadth}}{2}$. Note: Total height of face (to crinion) impracticable for this purpose on account of the many cases where due to loss of hair it cannot be secured.

† $\dfrac{\text{FM} \times 1000}{5}$.

‡ $\dfrac{\text{FM} \times 100}{\text{CM}}$.

§ $\dfrac{\text{F Height to Crinion} + \text{Breadth}}{2}$.

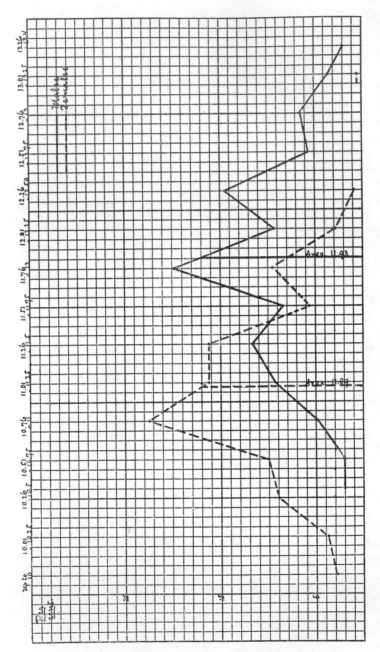

FIG. 22. OLD AMERICANS: LOWER HEIGHT OF FACE (MENTON-NASION)—LABORATORY SERIES: MALES 247, FEMALES 210

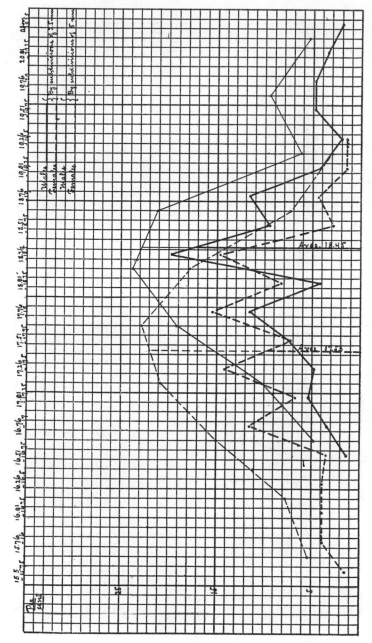

FIG. 23. OLD AMERICANS: TOTAL HEIGHT OF THE FACE (MENTON-CRINION)—LABORATORY SERIES: MALES 147, FEMALES 206

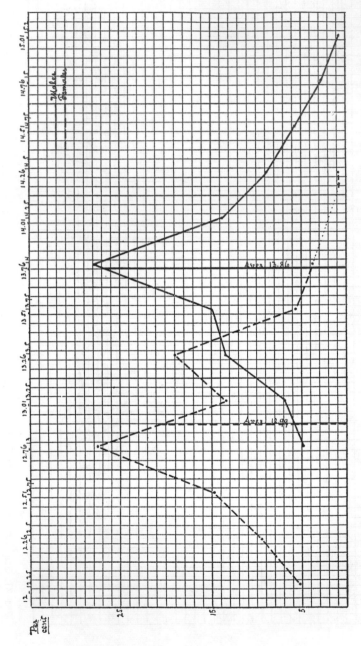

FIG. 24. OLD AMERICANS: BREADTH OF FACE (DIAM. BIZYGOMATIC MAXIMUM)—LABORATORY SERIES: MALES 247, FEMALES 210

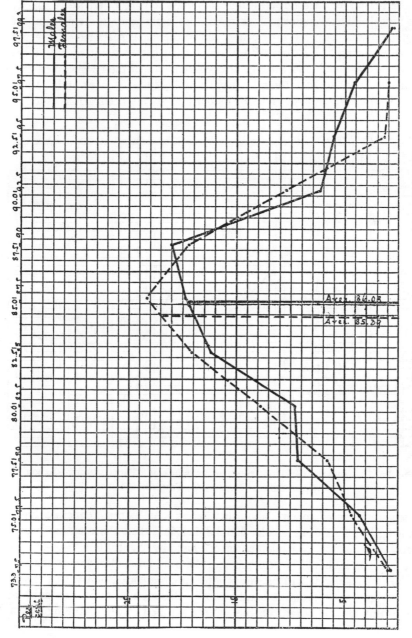

FIG. 25. OLD AMERICANS: LOWER (OR ANOTOMIC) FACIAL INDEX—LABORATORY SERIES: MALES 247, FEMALES 210

The reason for these group differences may be partly hereditary, partly functional. The "engineers" or mechanics come very largely from the farming or manually working classes where the facial parts have preserved a greater strength; but they also, through their better facilities and higher earnings, command, and through the requirements of their work, consume, abundant food, so that their jaws have probably been more active functionally than those of the men of indoor and sitting occupations, such as

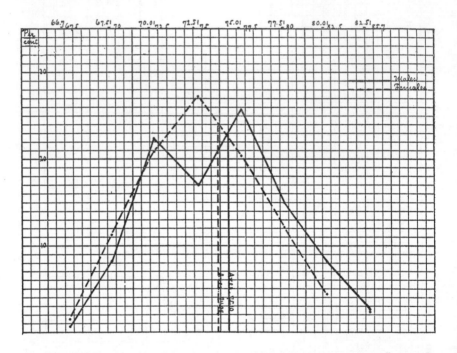

FIG. 26. OLD AMERICANS: THE TOTAL OR PHYSIOGNOMIC FACIAL INDEX—LABORATORY SERIES: MALES 147, FEMALES 206.

mostly represented in our laboratory series. As to the Tennessee highlanders, their somewhat smaller facial dimensions than those of the "engineers" may possibly be explained on one hand by slightly less "work;" but in this group it should be remembered, the head is smaller, and as the size of the face stands as will be shown later in close correlation with the size of the vault, the somewhat smaller face in this group may in the main be due to this reason. Light on the subject will be thrown by the figures in table 146.

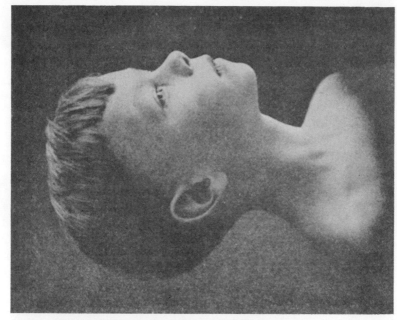

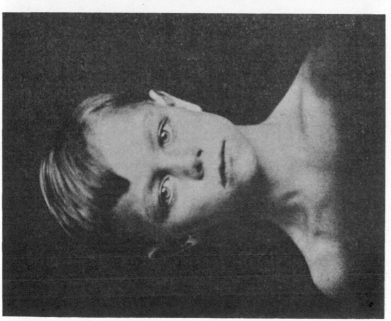

WILLIAM HUBERT AARON
(Washington, D. C.)

Age 6 years.   American ancestry on both sides to 8th generation

TABLE 145

Old Americans: Dimensions of face

Males

GROUP	NUMBER OF SUBJECTS	HEIGHT Menton nasion	HEIGHT Menton crinion	BREADTH: DIAMETER BIZYGOMATIC MAXIMUM	FACIAL INDEX Morphologic	FACIAL INDEX Physiognomic
All....................................	(726)	12.15	18.74	13.87	87.6	74.0
Laboratory (All states)................ {	(247)	11.925	(147)* 18.45	13.86	86.03	(148)* 75.1
Drafted "Engineers," Southern States......	(256)	12.39	18.99	13.96	88.7	73.6
Drafted "Engineers," other and mixed states...............................	(91)	12.36	18.89	13.98	88.4	73.9
Tennessee Highlanders....................	(132)	12.04	18.52	13.65	87.75	73.9
Laboratory group *vs.* { Southern Engineers (per cent)..		−3.68	−2.64	−0.79	−2.85	+1.80
Tennessee Highlanders (per cent).....................		−1.00	−0.38	+1.52	−1.96	+1.60

* Due to loss of hair in others the measurement could only be taken on the number of individuals here stated.

TABLE 146

Old Americans: Size of face vs. size of head

	MALES Morphologic facial module*	MALES Cephalic module†	MALES Stature	MALES Facial module-cephalic module‡ index	FEMALES Morphologic facial module	FEMALES Cephalic module	FEMALES Stature	FEMALES Facial module-cephalic module index
All......................	13.01	16.33	174.32	79.67	12.04	15.58	161.84	77.28
Laboratory (All states).....	12.89	16.40	174.44	78.60				
Southern "Engineers".......	13.17	16.37	174.26	80.46				
Tennessee Highlanders......	12.84	16.07	174.29	79.93				

* Mean lower facial diameter: $\dfrac{\text{(FH (to Nasion)} + \text{FB}}{2}$

† Mean head diameter: $\dfrac{L + B + H}{3}$

‡ Morphological *vs.* cephalic module: $\dfrac{FM \times 100}{CM}$

Note: All indices are calculated from the totals, not the averages.

The differences in the size of the face among the Old Americans may be expressed most readily by the morphologic facial module, and its relations to head size and stature (table 146).

The figures in table 146 only accentuate the facial differences in the three groups of male Old Americans. In the Laboratory group the face is smaller, in the "engineers" larger than the general average, both absolutely and in relation to the size of the head. In the highlanders, the face, rather small absolutely, relatively to head size is above the general average and therefore relatively larger than that in the Laboratory series, coming close to that of the mechanics. The stature being much alike in the three groups is not instrumental in these differences.

From all this it is plain that the absolutely slightly subaverage size of the face in the highlanders is in the main due to their smaller head; while in the "engineers" the both absolutely and relatively large face can only be connected with functional causes, the effects of which may have been inherited or acquired.

That the differences presented by the "engineers" are not territorial, will be seen conclusively in the table in which the "engineers" have been divided into two groups, namely, those born in the southern states and those of the more northern and eastern states, including those whose parents were born in separate states. The facial dimensions as well as indices in these groups are practically identical.

Influence of age

In studying the head it has been seen that the vault enlarges slightly in all its principal diameters up to or near middle life. So far as the face is concerned the conditions are similar but the changes are of different degree in the two sexes.

Taking the 25 youngest and 25 oldest males with the 20 youngest and 20 oldest females, both of the Laboratory group which is most suitable for such comparisons, conditions are found as follows:

In the absolute measurements, in the males, the face of the oldest is somewhat higher as well as slightly broader than that of the youngest. In the females similar conditions prevail, the absolute values being slightly greater in the elderly.

The simple measurements, however, are inadequate in these cases, due to the fact that the young and the old in the females differ very appreciably in stature with which, as will be shown later, facial dimensions stand in important correlation. Reducing the measurements to their ratios of stature, we find the following conditions:

TABLE 147

Old Americans: Face in relation to age

Laboratory series

	STATURE	FACE HEIGHT To nasion	FACE HEIGHT To crinion	FACE BREADTH	FACIAL MODULE MORPHOLOGIC	FACIAL INDEX Morphologic	FACIAL INDEX Physiognomic
Males							
(25) youngest....................	173.8	11.60	18.28*	13.76	12.678	84.33	74.74
(25) oldest.......................	174.6	12.02	18.15†	13.82	12.900	83.33	77.55
Percental relation of above measurements to stature:							
Youngest....................		6.68	10.47	7.92	7.295		
Oldest......................		6.88	10.58	7.92	7.387		
In favor of youngest (per cent)..						1.0	
Corrected‡						...	
In favor of oldest (per cent)....		(0.20)	0.11		(0.09)		2.8
Corrected...................		2.9	1.04		1.2		
Females							
(20) youngest....................	164.5	11.05	17.55	12.96	12.0	85.4	74.0
(20) oldest.......................	159.3	11.09	17.54	13.05	12.07	85.0	74.6
Percental relation of above measurements to stature:							
Youngest....................		6.72	10.67	7.88	7.30		
Oldest......................		6.96	11.01	8.19	7.58		
In favor of youngest (per cent)..						0.47	0.8
Corrected‡						....	...
In favor of oldest (per cent)....		(2.4)	(3.4)	(3.1)	(2.8)		
Corrected...................		3.4	3.1	3.8	3.7		

* Twenty-one cases; in 4 there where was some loss of hair.

† But 4 cases in which hair-line was not affected by loss of hair; the stature ratio is based on the stature of these four.

‡ Higher figures taken as 100.

Males: The oldest show a slightly greater relative height than the youngest, while the breadth ratios are identical. As to the total facial height, due to some loss of hair over the forehead in nearly all the elderly adults the number of cases is not sufficient for a valid comparison.

TABLE 148

Old Americans: Facial measurements and indices, and age
Laboratory series

		MALES (247)					FEMALES (210)				
		Up to 29 years	30–39 years	40–49 years	50–59 years	About 59 years	Up to 29 years	30–39 years	40–49 years	50–59 years	Above 59 years
Facial height to nasion	Number	(91)	(63)	(47)	(34)	(12)	(73)	(71)	(36)	(27)	(3)
	Average	11.67	12.05	12.11	12.12	11.92	11.03	11.15	11.10	11.07	11.37
	Ratio of stature	6.70	6.89	6.93	6.95	6.82	6.78	6.88	6.83	6.95	6.85
Facial height to crinion	Number	(74)	(43)	(20)	(8)	(2)	(73)	(71)	(35)	(24)	(3)
	Average	18.26	18.79	18.45	18.69	17.60	17.44	17.57	17.63	17.58	17.53
	Ratio of stature	10.50	10.74	10.54	10.76	9.97	10.73	10.85	10.86	11.05	10.56
Diameter bizygomatic maximum	Number	(91)	(63)	(47)	(34)	(12)	(73)	(71)	(36)	(27)	(3)
	Average	13.80	13.92	13.80	13.97	13.82	12.93	13.0	13.06	12.99	13.40
	Ratio of stature	7.92	7.96	7.91	8.03	7.91	7.95	8.03	8.04	8.16	8.07
Facial module morphologic	Number	(91)	(63)	(47)	(34)	(12)	(73)	(71)	(36)	(27)	(3)
	Average	12.73	13.0	12.96	13.05	12.87	11.98	12.14	12.08	12.03	12.38
	Ratio of stature	7.31	7.43	7.43	7.50	7.36	7.37	7.50	7.37	7.55	7.45
Facial module physiognomic	Number	(74)	(43)	(20)	(8)	(2)	(73)	(71)	(35)	(24)	(3)
	Average	16.01	16.39	16.09	16.34	15.75	15.18	15.29	15.78	15.29	15.47
	Ratio of stature	9.20	9.37	9.2	9.40	8.92	9.34	9.38	9.71	9.55	9.25
Facial index morphologic	Number	(91)	(63)	(47)	(34)	(12)	(73)	(71)	(36)	(27)	(3)
	Average	84.56	86.49	87.73	86.74	86.24	85.28	85.77	85.02	85.26	84.82
Facial index physiognomic	Number	(74)	(43)	(20)	(8)	(2)	(73)	(71)	(35)	(24)	(3)
	Average	75.47	74.45	74.39	74.85	78.98	73.26	73.97	73.97	74.0	76.23

Females: The ratio of the facial dimensions to stature is, in the case of every one of the measurements, quite perceptibly higher in the oldest than in the youngest of the group.

In the males therefore we have in this comparison no indication that relatively to stature the breadth of the face increases with age, while the height augments very moderately; but in the females a slight relative enlargement with age in both facial dimensions appears quite definitely.

The conditions are further shown in table 148 in which the facial measurements are given by periods of age. These records make it plain that, notwithstanding some irregularity, the facial, like the head proportions increase slightly with age in both sexes up to middle life, but that in the sixth decade, again as with the head, there occur for some reason smaller averages which, when the intermediate groups are left out as in the first comparison, mask the changes that have taken place before.

In the Old Americans, therefore, both the head and the face enlarge appreciably during adult life up to approximately middle age. The changes in the face are probably of simple correlative nature, corresponding to those of the vault. Above fifty, both head and face measurements show a decline, though whether this is an age effect or not can not as yet be definitely decided.

Influence of stature

A correlation with stature is an important factor with every measurement of the body and the face makes no exception.

In the case of the head, stature was seen to affect directly and materially the length and height, in less measure the breadth of the vault, and with the face conditions are somewhat similar.

Comparing fair groups of the shortest and tallest individuals of the two sexes in the Laboratory series, groups in which the form of the head happens to be on the average nearly alike and hence but little disturbing, we obtain the following indications:

1. Stature affects all the facial dimensions;

2. On the whole it affects them more in the males than in the females; and

3. It affects them unevenly, both as individual measurements and in the two sexes.

4. Due to the unevenness of the effect on the different dimensions, the facial indices are also modified.

Table 149 shows that of the four groups used in comparison, the two female are wider apart in stature than the male, notwithstanding which the

TABLE 149

Old Americans: Face in relation to stature

Laboratory series

	STATURE	FACE HEIGHT		FACE BREADTH	FACIAL MODULE MORPHOLOGIC	FACIAL INDEX	
		To nasion	To crinion			Morphologic	Physiognomic
Males							
(25) shortest (cephalic index 78.70)	165.09	11.43	17.92*	13.58	12.51	84.16	75.42
(25) tallest (cephalic index 77.93)	184.17	12.14	18.67†	13.99	13.07	86.80	74.32
		+6.2%	+4.2%	+4.1			
Percental relation of above measurements to stature:							
Shortest		6.95	10.86	8.26	7.61		
Tallest		6.59	10.14	7.59	7.09		
In favor of shortest (per cent)		(0.36)	(0.72)	(0.67)	(0.52)		1.46
Corrected‡		5.20	6.63	8.11	6.83	3.04	
In favor of tallest (per cent)	10.36						
Females							
(20) shortest (cephalic index 80.55)	151.3	10.82	17.140	12.795	11.81	84.6	74.6
(20) tallest (cephalic index 79.17)	172.2	11.15	17.775	13.035	12.10	85.5	73.4
		+2.1%	+3.7%	+1.9%			
Percental relation of above measurements to stature:							
Shortest		7.15	11.33	8.46	7.805		
Tallest		6.47	10.32	7.57	7.027		
In favor of shortest (per cent)		(0.68)	(1.01)	(0.89)	(0.78)		1.61
Corrected‡		9.05	8.91	8.95	9.97	1.05	
In favor of tallest (per cent)	12.14						

* 18 subjects.

† 15 subjects.

‡ All figures of upper line reduced to 100 and figures below to proportions of 100.

differences in the facial dimensions are considerably more marked in the males. In the male therefore stature must be assumed to have greater influence on the size of·the face than in the female. No such differences, or at least none so marked, have been noticed in the case of the vault. The figures bearing on this point in the two parts are repeated in table 150.

Considering the fact that in the two female groups here concerned the differences in stature are greater than those in the two male groups (males 10.36, female 12.14 per cent), it may be said that, in the case of the vault, a slightly greater effect of stature is manifested on the height and breadth of the part in the males, while its influence on the length is the same; while in the case of the face the effect of stature in the males is much more pronounced, especially with the lower height and breadth. The main explanation of these differences lies possibly in the fact that the taller men are relatively more athletic and robust than the tall women of the class here

TABLE 150

Percental differences in head and facial dimensions in extremes of stature

Laboratory series

	HEAD			FACE		
	Height	Length	Breadth	Height, lower	Height, total	Breadth
In favor of tallest:						
Males	3.81	2.43	1.47	6.20	4.20	4.10
Females	3.47	2.48	0.78	2.10	3.70	1.90

dealt with. There may also however be a contributing cause relating to a difference in the development with stature of the forehead in the two sexes, as indicated by the figures on the total facial height. We are evidently confronted here with some of the more detailed workings of nature which escape us in rougher studies, and which may be of but little importance in most cases, but among which there occur now and then instances that open a way to new light on our problems.

The percental relations of the various measurements of the face to stature, given in table 149, and their differences, while somewhat more difficult to grasp illustrate even more precisely the above mentioned conditions.

As to the facial indices, it should be noted that the differences in the morphologic index are more marked than those in the physiognomic, which is affected by the behavior of the forehead; and that due to stature alone the morphologic index will be perceptibly higher in the tallest than it is in the shortest individuals of an ethnic unit.

TABLE 151

Old Americans: Correlation of facial dimensions with stature

DIMENSION GROUP	STATURE OF MALES					STATURE OF FEMALES			
	153.0–160.0	160.01–170.0	170.01–180.0	180.01–190.0	Above 190.0	145.0–150.0	150.01–160.0	160.01–170.0	170.01–180.0
Menton-nasion height:									
Laboratory (all states)	11.30	11.71	11.96	12.17					
Southern States	12.20	12.24	12.41	12.53	12.60				
Mixed States	11.90	12.18	12.37	12.81					
Tennessee Highlands		11.59	12.07	12.19					
All (726)	(5) 11.78	(172) 11.94	(443) 12.19	(104) 12.37	(2) 12.60	(3) 10.63 (210) 10.63	(72) 10.93	(115) 11.21	(20) 11.04
Menton-crinion height:									
Laboratory (all states)	18.75	18.11	18.56	18.74					
Southern States	18.0	18.75	19.0	19.25	19.30				
Mixed States		18.89	18.90	19.0					
Tennessee Highlands		18.11	18.62	18.68					
All (558)	(4) 18.47	(126) 18.43	(349) 18.78	(77) 18.98	(2) 19.30	(3) 17.30 (206) 17.30	(71) 17.26	(112) 17.68	(20) 17.72
Diameter Bizygomatic Maximum:									
Laboratory (all states)	(13.85)	13.71	13.90	13.95					
Southern States	(13.55)	13.85	13.95	14.19	14.25				
Mixed States	(13.70)	14.04	13.94	14.20					
Tennessee Highlands		13.49	13.65	13.89					
All (726)	(5) 13.7	(172) 13.76	(443) 13.87	(104) 14.06	(2) 14.25	(3) 12.77 (210) 12.77	(72) 12.86	(115) 13.05	(20) 13.13

The direct correlation of the facial dimensions with stature will be seen conclusively in table 151.   It will be noted that there is a progression with increase in stature in every one of the measurements and in every one of the groups.   The only irregularities occur in groups in which the numbers are so small that the result cannot be regarded as definite.   This evidence simply accentuates the necessity, in the study of facial measurements and especially of any changes in the same due to physiological action, of taking account of both stature and the head dimensions.

The relation of the individual facial measurements to stature, and also to the three main head diameters, in the four male groups as well as the

TABLE 152

Old Americans: Relation of facial measurements to stature and the three main diameters of the head

FACE	RATIO	MALES				FEMALES	
		All	Laboratory	Southern "Engineers"	Tennessee Highlanders	All	Females vs. males (M = 100)
Height to nasion........ {	Of stature	6.97	6.84	7.12	6.91	6.85	98.3
	Of head length	61.6	60.3	62.8	61.7	59.6	96.8
	Of head height	87.5	85.3	87.4	88.5	83.3	95 2
Height to crinion ...... {	Of stature	10.75	10.58	10.88	10.63	10.83	100.8
	Of head length	95.0	93.3	95.8	95.0	94.2	99.2
	Of head height	135.0	132.5	136.0	136.1	131.6	97.5
Diameter bizygomatic.. { maximum.......... {	Of stature	7.96	7.95	8.04	7.83	8.03	100.9
	Of head breadth	90.3	89.5	90.8	90.4	87.8	97.2

females, is given in table 152.   The data show considerable uniformity, but also some characteristic differences.

Whatever the dimensions with which the size of the face and each of the diameters separately is compared, the Laboratory series is seen to show sub-average the "engineer" series above-average proportions, while the Tennessee highlanders stand between.   In only one respect are the Tennesseeans slightly below the mean of the Laboratory group, namely in the relation of the breadth of the face to stature.   They have therefore a slightly narrower face than the rest of the Old Americans, which however, as seen from further comparison (Face Breadth *vs.* Head Breadth) is in conformity with and is due to their slightly narrower head.

In contrasting the females with the males in these figures, we see that relatively to stature the dimensions of the female face are inferior to those of the males only in the lower facial height, while they are slightly superior, due to relatively higher forehead and broader head, in the total facial height and facial breadth.

Size of face and head. A comparison of the male and female face dimensions with those of the head in the two sexes can not be adequately gaged from table 152, but it may be observed that the ratios are all inferior for the females to those of stature. What in reality this means, is that the females who are of lower average stature have, as has been seen before, a relatively larger head. If we compare females with males of similar stature the results are much closer. Table 153 is very instructive in this respect.

TABLE 153

Old Americans: Comparison of dimensions of face and head

Laboratory series

STATURE GROUPS	MALES					FEMALES				
	Menton-nasion		Menton-crinion		Diameter bizygomatic maximum ratio of head breadth	Menton-nasion		Menton-crinion		Diameter bizygomatic maximum ratio of head breadth
	Ratio of head length	Ratio of head height	Ratio of head length	Ratio of head height		Ratio of head length	Ratio of head height	Ratio of head length	Ratio of head height	
cm.										
150.1–160	61.4	88.2	96.2	138.4	88.4	59.0	83.0	93.2	131.1	87.1
160.1–170	61.1	86.7	94.3	133.7	89.0	60.0	83.8	94.6	132.1	87.9
170.1–180	61.5	87.5	94.7	134.5	89.6	59.0	81.5	94.7	130.8	88.6

Taking the percental relations of facial to head measurements at the principal sub-divisions of stature in our groups, it will be observed that so far as each sex by itself is concerned the relation of the dimensions remains very nearly constant. The correlation therefore between the facial and head measurements is a very close one. The only change is observed in the ratio of facial to cephalic breadth which in both sexes shows a slight but regular increase as stature rises, showing that the higher the stature the broader relatively to the head is the face.

As to the differences between the two sexes they are small, but all in one direction. At every step and with nearly every measurement, the ratio of the facial to head measurements in the female is slightly smaller than that in the males, showing that even if the factor of stature is evened and eliminated, the female face relatively to size of the head shows in all respects except in total facial height, slightly smaller than that of the males.

Facial dimensions and head form

There remain to be considered the relations of the dimensions and form of the face to head form.

Taking the groups of the most dolichocephalic and the most brachyphalic males and females of the Laboratory series, it will be observed (table 154) that the head form has a marked but uneven influence on the measurements of the face and that this influence, while substantially alike, differs slightly in degree in the two sexes.

Reducing the facial measurements to proportions of stature so as to eliminate as far as possible the influence of the latter, it will be noted that the facial measurement least affected by head form is the lower facial height, while the most affected is the facial breadth. This is merely another illustration of the close correlation existing between the breadth of the head and the breadth of the face.

As a result of the just enumerated conditions there are in the two head forms, in both sexes, differences in the facial indices. The morphological index is very appreciably higher, the physiognomic slightly lower in the dolichocephals. The differences are especially marked in the females. They mean that the face of the Old Americans is both absolutely and relatively to stature broader in the brachycephalic than in the dolichocephalic type. The facial breadth correlates strongly with that of the head, regardless of stature or musculature, through the anatomical necessity of wider separation of the zygomatic insertions.

Comparative data

As to comparative data on facial dimensions, there are available a series of more or less complete reports by various workers, and also the measurements secured by the writer or under his direction on twelve groups of recent immigrants to the United States.[46] However, both series are deficient in records on nationalities that would be of the greatest interest for comparison with the Old Americans. Strange as it may seem the writer was unable to find any data of value relating to measurements of the face on the people of Great Britain and other parts of northwestern Europe. Gustav Retzius

[46] It is a pity that the work on the immigrants, which was carried on by the same method and same instruments, could not have been extended to all racial groups coming to the States; but possibly this may be done later.

TABLE 154

Old Americans: Face in relation to head form

Laboratory series

	STATURE	FACE HEIGHT		FACE BREADTH	FACIAL MODULE MORPHOLOGIC	FACIAL INDEX	
		To nasion	To crinion			Morphologic	Physiognomic
Males							
(25) most dolichocephalic (cephalic index 73.22)	176.1	11.78	18.25*	13.58	12.68	84.48	74.68
(25) most brachycephalic (cephalic index 84.64)	173.4	11.66	18.21†	14.02	12.84	83.17	74.81
Percental differences in favor of the brachycephals‡	−1.53	−0.85	−0.22	+3.14	+1.25	−1.55	+0.17
Percental relation of above measurements to stature:							
Most dolichocephalic		6.69	10.24	7.72	7.20		
Most brachycephalic		6.73	10.50	8.09	7.41		
In favor of dolichocephals (per cent)							
In favor of brachycephals (per cent)		(0.04)	(0.26)	(0.37)	(0.21)		
Corrected‡		0.59	2.48	4.57	2.83		
Females							
(15) most dolichocephalic (cephalic index 74.01)	161.6	11.04	17.39	12.70	11.87	87.0	73.2
(20) most brachycephalic (cephalic index 84.71)	161.2	11.16	17.72	13.34	12.25	83.7	75.5
Percental differences in favor of the brachycephals‡	−0.25	+1.08	+1.86	+4.80	+3.10	−3.79	+3.05
Percental relation of above measurements to stature:							
Most dolichocephalic		6.83	10.76	7.86	7.35		
Most brachycephalic		6.92	10.99	8.28	7.6		
In favor of dolichocephals (per cent)							
In favor of brachycephals (per cent)		(0.9)	(2.3)	(4.2)	(2.5)		
Corrected‡		1.3	2.1	5.1	3.3		

* 14 subjects.
† 17 subjects.
‡ Highest figures taken as 100.

In *"Antropologia Suecica"* gives the distribution of the facial index of the Scandinavians, but without any details as to the actual measurements. There are, it is true, fairly numerous French records or records of measurements taken according to the French method; but in these cases the height of the face is taken up to the ophryon (point above the glabella), which makes any comparison of either the facial height or the facial index impossible. There are also German records, but they are not adequate for our purposes.

The largest number of records of facial dimensions in literature are on people of other than the white races; and among the whites on people of mostly other than Nordic stock and its relations. The data that it was possible to locate are given in table 155, and as the crude figures would have but little value there are added a few calculations. Practically all the groups in the series with the exception of the Egyptians and a portion of the Jews and Germans are brachycephalic groups. All of the groups also with one small exception present lower stature—in some cases very considerably lower—than the Old Americans. Notwithstanding this it may be observed that in the lower facial height (up to nasion) the Americans are equalled and even exceeded by several of the groups, and this is even more true of the breadth of the face. It is only in the total or physiognomic height of the face that the Old Americans range perceptibly above all the other groups. When we come to compare the facial module in these different groups with stature, it will then be seen that in every one of the groups with two minor exceptions the face of the Europeans is relatively larger than that of the Old Americans.

When we compare the facial dimensions of the Old Americans with those of the immigrants into this country made with the same instruments and by the same method, there may be observed the following:

The absolute lower facial height (to nasion) in the Old Americans is slightly inferior only to that of the small group of English, and shows almost identical with that of the Irish. The Armenians also come very near in this respect but in all the other groups the dimension is perceptibly lower. If, however, this dimension is taken in its relation to stature, the Americans are found lowest in the scale. They show in other words a face absolutely rather high, but relatively to the stature lower than that of any of the groups which are available for comparison; and the same conditions appear in connection with the total facial height (menton-crinion diameter).

As to facial breadth, the conditions are different. Here the Old Americans stand almost at the base of the ladder even in the absolute measurement, and very markedly so when the measurement is compared with stature.

TABLE 135

Facial measurements and indices: Comparative data from literature*

Males

GROUP	FACIAL HEIGHT		DIAMETER BIZYGOMATIC MAXIMUM	FACIAL INDEX		FACIAL MODULE		STATURE	FACIAL MODULE vs. STATURE		AUTHOR
	To Nasion	To Crinion		Morphologic	Physiognomic	Morphologic	Physiognomic		Morphologic	Physiognomic	
Egyptians (oasis of Kharga)	11.35	17.60	13.15	86.3	74.7	12.25	15.32	163.8	74.8	93.5	Hrdlička
Jews, Polish	12.0	18.4	13.6	88.2	73.7	12.80	15.98	161.0	79.5	nr. 99.0	Elkind
Jews, Warsaw			13.55					nr. 161.2			Tschepourkovsky
Jews, of White Russia	11.8		13.6	86.8		12.70					Jakowenko
Jews, of South Russia	11.9		13.8	87.5		12.85		165.1	77.8		Weissenberg
Russians, Great	12.2	18.3	13.7	88.4	74.9		16.0	166.0		96.4	Galai
Russians, Great		18.2	14.0		76.7		16.10	165.7		96.0	Ivanovski
Russians, White		18.3	13.8		75.4	13.0	16.05	nr. 165.0		nr. 97.2	Roshdestvenski
Russians, White		18.5	14.1		76.4		16.30	166.7		97.8	Ivanovski
Russians, Little					77.2						Ivanovski
Poles		18.3	14.05		76.9		16.20	164.1		98.7	Baronas
Lithuanians	11.6	18.5	13.9	82.3	75.1		16.20	165.6		97.8	Weisbach
"Northern Slavs"		17.9	14.1		78.8	12.85	16.0	167.1	76.9	95.8	Weisbach
Czechs		18.2	14.0		76.8		16.10	166.5		96.5	Weisbach
Serbians (Herzegovina)		18.2	14.4		78.9		16.30	175.2		93.0	Weisbach
Germans†	12.3	18.6	14.0	87.8	75.3	13.15	16.20	nr. 167.0	nr. 78.7	nr. 97.0	Weissenberg
Germans, Baden	12.1		14.1	85.1		13.10		166.2	78.8		Fischer
Armenians		18.3	14.3		78.2		16.30	167.1		97.5	Ivanovski
Old Americans	12.15	18.74	13.87	87.5	74.3	13.01	16.30	174.3	74.6	93.5	Hrdlička
†100 German females	11.5	17.5	13.2	87.1							Weissenberg

* Data mainly from Weissbach (Körpermessung v. Menschenrassen), Ivanovski (Naselenie Sara), Martin (Lehrbuch). French data are based generally on the menton-ophryon height and are therefore not directly comparable. Even as late as 1920, Pittard, in his "Les peuples des Balkans" employs the menton-ophryon height which renders his otherwise valuable data unutilizable. English data that could be used for comparison are wanting.

TABLE 156

Facial measurements and indices: Comparative data

Males

GROUP	NUMBER OF SUBJECTS	FACE HEIGHT				BREADTH			FACIAL MODULE		FACIAL MODULE vs. CEPHALIC MODULE		FACIAL MODULE vs. STATURE		FACIAL INDEX	
		Menton-nasion	Relation to stature	Menton-crinion	Relation to stature	Diameter bizygomatic maximum	Relation to stature	Relation to head breadth	Morphologic	Physiognomic	Morphologic	Physiognomic	Morphologic	Physiognomic	Morphologic	Physiognomic
Old Americans	726	12.15	69.7	18.74	107.5	13.87	79.6	90.3	13.01	16.30	79.7	99.8	74.6	93.5	87.5	74.3
Laboratory series	(247)	(11.93)	(68.4)	(18.45)	(105.8)	(13.86)	(79.45)	(89.5)	(12.89)	(16.15)	(78.6)	(98.5)	(73.9)	(92.6)	(86.1)	(75.1)
English	20	12.19	71.6	18.53	108.9	13.85	81.4	91.1	13.02	16.19	81.02	100.7	76.5	95.1	88.1	74.7
Irish	35	12.1	70.5	18.90	110.1	13.80	80.4	90.2	12.95	16.35	79.9	100.9	75.5	95.3	87.7	73.0
Armenians	25	12.02	71.8	18.03	107.7	14.06	84.0	90.7	13.04	16.04	82.5	101.6	77.8	95.8	85.5	78.0
Poles	50	11.8	69.2	18.3	107.3	14.3	83.9	91.1	13.05	16.30	81.4	101.7	76.6	95.7	82.5	78.1
Russians	50	11.71	68.9	18.06	106.3	14.1	83.0	91.0	12.90	16.08	81.1	101.1	76.0	94.7	83.0	78.1
Russian Jews	50	11.7	71.1	18.2	110.6	13.9	84.4	89.7	12.80	16.05	80.5	100.9	77.7	97.5	84.2	76.4
North Italians	50	11.7	69.0	18.2	107.3	14.2	83.7	90.5	12.95	16.20	80.7	100.9	76.4	95.5	82.4	78.0
Croatians	50	11.6	67.6	18.1	105.5	14.3	83.2	91.1	12.95	16.20	81.04	101.4	75.5	94.4	81.1	79.0
South Italians	50	11.55	70.7	18.0	110.2	13.9	85.1	92.0	12.72	15.95	80.0	100.3	77.8	97.6	83.1	77.2
Rumanians	50	11.5	68.2	18.0	106.7	14.2	84.2	90.5	12.85	16.10	80.8	101.3	76.2	95.4	81.0	78.1
Greeks	50	11.5	68.3	17.9	106.4	13.9	82.6	92.0	12.70	15.90	79.9	100.0	75.5	94.5	82.7	77.6
Hungarians	50	11.5	69.1	17.8	106.9	14.1	84.7	90.4	12.80	15.95	81.01	100.9	76.3	95.8	81.6	79.2
Mean deviation		0.22	1.14	0.25	1.33	0.15	1.24	0.52	0.10	0.12	0.58	0.42	0.72	0.80	2.10	1.50

225

The face of the Old Americans may therefore be characterized as absolutely rather high but of only a moderate breadth; while when compared with stature it is seen to be relatively rather low and especially narrow.

The facial indices reflect at least in part the above conditions. Except in the English and Irish who are very close, the morphologic facial index in the Old Americans is higher and the physiognomic lower, and that in both cases very plainly so, than in any of the groups with which it can here be compared. Both of these indices express the relative facial narrowness of the Americans of the old stock.

The facial modules show the face of the Old Americans in its totality to be absolutely fairly large but to be relatively smaller than that of any of the other groups when compared with the size of the head (expressed by the cephalic module), or the stature.

All of these conditions are even more accentuated if we use for comparison instead of the whole Old American male group only that of the Laboratory, which represents on the whole a higher social group than the remainder. The face here relatively is even more delicate.

There is only one interpretation that may be given to the above facts which is that improved social conditions, in other words better prepared and more nourishing food, necessitating less action of the teeth and jaws with their muscles, tends towards a further reduction of the facial features even though these in their necessary correlation with stature and head dimensions may remain absolutely of fair size. Had there been no reduction of the jaws in the Old Americans their face, with their tall stature and good size of head, would be not only materially larger but especially broader than it now is in actuality.

Summary of results relating to mean facial measurements

The face of the Old Americans shows extensive and somewhat irregular individual variation in length and height, less so in breadth. A distinctive American facial type so far as dimensions are concerned cannot as yet be considered as fully established.

In general the face as a whole (physiognomy) is of the same form in the two sexes; but the anatomic face (to nasion) differs somewhat, being relatively slightly lower in the females; as a result of which the physiognomic index is almost the same in the two sexes, but the morphologic is higher in the males.

The facial proportions, aside of the forehead, differ somewhat in the several groups of males, being both absolutely and relatively to stature smallest, especially in the lower facial height, in the Laboratory group,

TWO TYPES OF OLD AMERICAN BOYS
(Washington, D. C.)

largest in the southern "engineers" and intermediate in the Tennessee highlanders. The smaller face in the highlanders than in the "engineers" is due essentially to their smaller head. The larger face in the "engineers" can only be due to functional causes, inherited or acquired.

The facial indices are practically identical in the "engineers" and highlanders, but the morphologic index, due to their relatively lesser lower facial height, is lower, while the physiognomic index, due to their relatively also somewhat narrower face, is higher in the Laboratory group than in the two others.

Influence of age. As with the head, so in the face, the dimensions keep on enlarging slightly during adult life up to approximately middle age, after which there appears some diminution. The changes with age in the face affect all the diameters and are probably of a correlative nature with those of the head.

Influence of stature. Increase in stature causes increase in the dimensions of the head and largely in correlation with this also an increase in the dimensions of the face, though the augmentations in the three main diameters of the face are not entirely harmonious.

Stature has more influence on the facial measurements in the males than in the females.

The morphologic index of the face is higher, the physiognomic somewhat lower in the tallest than in the shortest individuals of a given group, both sexes.

The correlation between facial and head measurements is a close one at all statures.

In the females the ratio of facial to head measurements, except as to the forehead, is throughout all stature groups slightly smaller than it is in the males.

Influence of head form. Head form (cephalic index) has a marked but uneven influence on the measurements of the face; and this influence, while substantially of the same nature, differs slightly in the two sexes.

The measurement least affected by head form is the lower facial height; that most affected is the facial breadth.

As we proceed from dolicho- to brachycephaly the morphological index of the face grows appreciably higher; the changes in the physiognomic index are smaller.

Special. In all studies of facial dimensions it appears necessary to take account at the same time of both the stature and the measurements of the head.

Comparative. In comparison with the face of various Europeans and a

series of groups of recent immigrants to the United States, that of the Old
Americans, while absolutely of fair dimensions, especially in height, relatively to head size and stature shows a moderate reduction in height with
marked reduction in breadth.   This is particularly true of the Laboratory
or higher social group of the Old Americans.

FACIAL CONSTITUENTS

The forehead

Descriptive.   There is a universal, ingrained notion that a low, as well
as a sloping, forehead means low intelligence or greater "brutality," and
vice versa.   This view is intimately connected on one hand with the view
that the frontal lobes of the brain are the main seat of intelligence, and on
the other with observations of low or slanting foreheads in idiots and here
and there in brutal men and criminals as well as in at least some savages,
in man of antiquity, in the anthropoid apes and in general in lower animals.
Painters, sculptors, novelists have contributed greatly towards the estab-
lishment of this notion, until it became so deep rooted as to be almost
instinctive.   Nor is it without some real foundation; yet the subject is not
as simple as has been assumed.

The sloping forehead, if we except pathological brains, is generally due
to a greater than usual development of the frontal sinuses or the supraorbital
region; in other words it is not the upper part of the forehead that is de-
pressed but the lower part that has been carried forward more than usual,
that has given more or less of an external slope to a forehead which inwardly,
together with the fore part of the brain, may be quite normal.   Such a
forehead may naturally and does in known instances co-exist with a brain
of high qualities.

As to height, a forehead may be high simply because of an accidental
compression in infancy of the back of the skull, for which it helps to com-
pensate.   High foreheads are well known among certain Indians (*e.g.*,
the Pueblos, Navaho, etc.) where occipital flattening is favored, that have
no brain value.   A low or high forehead under normal conditions is of more
meaning, unless the former be due to mere variation in the forward extension of the hair, or the latter to its loss as happens very often.   A rather low
forehead may also go with a low vaulted but broad skull and high forehead
with a high skull without any relation to brain quality.   Only in cases
where the forehead is distinctly low, or distinctly high as well as broad for a
given type of head, is there some justification for judging from it as to the
brain of the individual.

As to the visual effect of the height of the forehead, the figures in table 157 show that in nearly nine-tenths of the male and over four-fifths of the female Old Americans, the forehead gave the impression of "medium;" in approximately one-eleventh of the males and one-ninth of the females it impressed one as lower than medium; while in a little over three per cent of the males and nearly nine per cent of the females it appeared above medium to high. The more frequent occurrence of relatively high foreheads in the females has already been noticed in our dealing with the face and will be well seen when we come to deal with the measurements of the part.

Detailed visual observations on the forehead in the Old Americans indicate, therefore, that where no hair has been lost the forehead is seldom sub-medium, and in the males also seldom markedly above medium in height; that in the females an above-medium height is more frequent; and that as a rule the forehead appears neither markedly broad nor narrow.

TABLE 157

Old Americans: Forehead

	MALES	FEMALES
	per cent	*per cent*
Low to submedium....................................	8.7	10.7
Medium..	88.0	80.7
Above medium to high...............................	3.3	8.7
Upright..	97.3	98.0
Slightly to moderately sloping.........................	2.7	2.0
Pronounced slope......................................		

As to inclination, the forehead in the Old Americans was found to be generally upright, a slight to moderate slope being present in only a very few individuals. The actual records are in table 157.

In this place and before we approach the measurements of the forehead, a few words may be said also about the supra-orbital ridges.

Supra-orbital ridges. In approximately two-thirds of the males and a little over one-third of the females these ridges were found about as average in the general American population or white people at large; in nearly one-fourth of the males and over one-half of the females they were sub-medium to slight, while in more than seven per cent of the females they were absent or very nearly so even to palpation. In only one-tenth of the males were these ridges above medium to pronounced and in only four per cent were they above medium for the sex in the females. All of which shows a plain tendency towards diminution of these ridges in the Old Americans. Table 158 gives the records.

Measurements of the forehead. The matter of actual dimensions of the forehead has, so far as its height is concerned, been involved in the measurements of the total height of the face, and there were indications that the part presents interesting sex differences. We may now approach the measurements of both height and breadth of the forehead directly. Tables 159 and 160 show the main values and individual variation in the height.

All that needs to be remarked about these tables and figure 27 is as follows:

1. The individual variation in forehead height is fairly large, and appreciably greater in the males than in the females.

2. The forehead of the female is in height remarkably close to that of the male (98.02 per cent).

3. The dispersion of the measurement, and as a result also the curves, are remarkably regular, particularly so in the females of which in this case there are a larger number.

Sex groups. The next point of interest to inquire into, is the differences in the height of the forehead in the two sexes, and in the several groups of Old Americans that are represented in our series, for which purpose it will be necessary to show also the relative values of the measurement (table 161).

The females are seen to have relatively higher forehead than the males, particularly when compared to height of face and size of head—due probably in the main to somewhat higher hair insertion. The Laboratory group show the highest, the "engineers" the lowest forehead in relation to the total height of the face; in reality however it is the lower part of the face that differs, being subaverage in the Laboratory and above average in the "engineer" series, while the forehead remains almost identical in the two groups. The Tennessee group, notwithstanding their backwardness, have a forehead both absolutely and relatively to stature much like the rest of the Old Americans, and to their somewhat smaller head it shows even a higher relation. There is little in all this that would sustain the notion that—except perhaps in a very general way or in special cases—the height of the forehead within a group such as ours could be used as an index of intelligence.

Relation to age. A study of the effects of age upon the height of the forehead is frequently interfered with in the Old Americans, more particularly the males, by loss of hair over the forehead. Such a loss was present, as has been shown before, in fully two-fifths of the males examined. With the females this proportion is much smaller but even so there is some interference. Judging however indirectly from the slight growth in the size of both the head as well as the face during the adult period, it seems safe

TABLE 158

Old Americans: Supra-orbital ridges

	MALES	FEMALES
	per cent	*per cent*
None..		7.3
Slight...	5.3	
Submedium (for the sex)............................	18.0	50.7
Medium...	65.3	38.0
Above medium.....................................	8.0	4.0
Pronounced.......................................	3.3	

TABLE 159

Old Americans, males: Height of forehead (nasion-crinion)

Number of observations: 148
General average: 6.58 cm.
1st series of 73—6.58 cm.
2nd series of 54—6.53 cm.
3rd series of 20—6.70 cm.
Minimum: 5.1 cm.   Maximum 8.3 cm.

TABLE OF FREQUENCIES

	5.0–5.2 cm.	5.3–5.5 cm.	5.6–5.8 cm.	5.9–6.1 cm.	6.2–6.4 cm.	6.5–6.7 cm.	6.8–7.0 cm.	7.1–7.3 cm.	7.4–7.6 cm.	7.7–7.9 cm.	8.0–8.2 cm.	8.3–8.5 cm.
Number of cases..........	2	3	10	13	30	32	35	10	10	2	0	1
Per cent.................	*1.3*	*2.0*	*6.7*	*8.8*	*20.2*	*21.6*	*23.6*	*6.7*	*6.7*	*1.3*		*0.7*

TABLE 160

Old Americans, females: Height of forehead (nasion-crinion)

Number of observations: 207
Average: 6.45 cm. (1st 49—6.37; 2nd 49—6.50; 3rd 49—6.50; 4th 60—6.41 cm.)
Minimum: 5.2 cm.   Maximum: 7.8 cm.

TABLE OF FREQUENCIES

	5.0–5.2 cm.	5.3–5.5 cm.	5.6–5.8 cm.	5.9–6.1 cm.	6.2–6.4 cm.	6.5–6.7 cm.	6.8–7.0 cm.	7.1–7.3 cm.	7.4–7.6 cm.	7.7–7.8 cm.	7.9 cm.
Number of cases..............	3	12	19	34	36	36	33	26	5	2	1
Per cent.....................	*1.4*	*5.8*	*9.2*	*16.4*	*17.4*	*17.4*	*16.1*	*12.6*	*2.4*	*0.9*	*0.5*

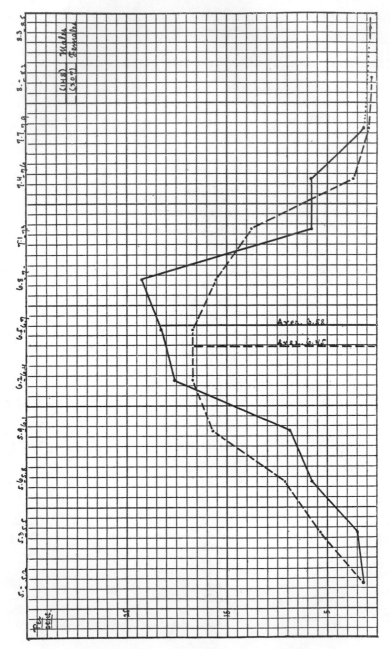

FIG. 27. OLD AMERICANS: HEIGHT OF THE FOREHEAD—LABORATORY SERIES

to conclude that the forehead also undergoes a slight increase in height (as well as breadth) during the adult period in this class of people. As a matter of fact the height of the forehead-stature ratio in the 20 youngest females is 3.94, in the 20 oldest ones 4.03, showing an appreciable relative excess for the old.

Effects of stature. As the whole face so the forehead stands in a fairly close correlation with stature. This fact is especially well shown in table 162. There are some irregularities here and there due probably to insufficient numbers, but on the whole the higher the stature the higher also is the forehead. Yet the correlation is not a direct one; the stature has nothing to do with the forehead, but stature has a direct effect upon the size of the head and the height of the forehead goes largely with this. The correlation of the height of the forehead with that of the rest of the face

TABLE 161

Old Americans: Height of forehead in the several groups and the two sexes

	MALES					FEMALES	LABORATORY SERIES FEMALES *vs.* MALES (M = 100)
	All	Laboratory	Southern "Engineers"	Tennessee Highlands			
Height, nasion to hair line..........	6.59	6.58	6.594	6.57		6.45	98.02
Percental relation to total height of face............................	35.17	35.7	34.7	35.5		36.8	103.1
Percental relation to stature........	3.78	3.77	3.77	3.77		3.80	100.8
Percental relation to size of head (cephalic module)..............	40.36	40.1	40.3	40.9		41.4	103.2

when the stature is equal is probably small, if any; they are both concomitantly affected by the size of the head and indirectly by stature, but otherwise they have little if any interdependence.

Comparative. After what was just shown it will not be astonishing to find that the forehead differs but little between the Old Americans and the different white immigrants who reach this country. It is in fact remarkably alike in all the groups barring the Armenians[47] who, doubtless as a result of the vicissitudes of their existence under the Turkish rule, are somewhat backward in this respect as they are in the smaller size of the head and relatively larger size of the face. It is odd indeed that these people, representatives of whom all over the Near East have such a general high reputation for their business abilities, should make so poor a showing so far as

[47] All from Asia Minor.

head development is concerned in contrast with other immigrants; but probably no white people have on the whole had less chance to develop their intellectual faculties. It will be of the utmost interest to watch their progress in the totally new environment to which they have been transplanted. On the other hand an unexpectedly good showing as to size of head and especially that of forehead, difficult to understand clearly, is made by the southern Italians. In this case corroboration on further series is very desirable.

TABLE 162

Old Americans: Height of forehead, and its relation to stature

	STATURE					
	145.0–150.0	150.01–160.0	160.01–170.0	170.01–180.0	180.01–190.0	Above 190.0
All: Males..................		(4)* 6.55	(125) 6.50	(350) 6.59	(107) 6.68	(2) (6.70)
Females..............	(3) 6.66	(72) 6.34	(111) 6.47	(20) 6.68		
Laboratory..............		(1) (7)	(36) 6.48	(89) 6.58	(22) 6.72	
Southern "Engineers".......		(3) (6.12)	(64) 6.53	(182) 6.60	(71) 6.68	(2) (6.70)
Tennessee Highlanders......			(25) 6.42	(79) 6.59	(14) 6.64	

* Number of individuals.

Breadth of forehead. The forehead is characterized also by its breath and logically this should be measured as it is taken visually, at its maximum. Unfortunately however, there are no satisfactory landmarks for such a measurement and so we take the diameter frontal minimum, which is the breadth between the most closely approaching points on the temporal lines or ridges. This gives the lowermost breadth of the frontal squama, which due to its strength and conformation is probably the least readily affected part of the frontal by any physiological changes in the size of the brain, and therefore is not as valuable as would be the breadth maximum;

TABLE 163

Height of forehead vs. height of head and stature: Comparative data

GROUP	HEIGHT OF FOREHEAD	HEIGHT OF FACE (TO CRINION)	HEIGHT OF HEAD	SIZE OF HEAD (CEPHALIC MODULE)	STATURE	HEIGHT FOREHEAD-HEIGHT FACE INDEX*	HEIGHT FOREHEAD-HEIGHT HEAD INDEX†	HEIGHT FOREHEAD-HEIGHT CEPHALIC MODULE INDEX‡	HEIGHT FOREHEAD-STATURE INDEX§
Males:									
Old Americans (all)	6.59	18.74	13.88	16.33	174.32	35.17	47.48	40.36	37.8
Old Americans (females)	(6.45)	(17.54)	(13.32)	(15.57)	(161.84)	(36.77)	(46.17)	(41.4)	(38.0)
Armenians	6.02	18.03	13.7	15.77	167.4	33.4	43.9	38.2	36.0
Hungarians	6.3	17.80	13.8	15.80	166.5	35.4	45.7	39.9	37.8
English	6.35	18.53	13.7	16.07	170.2	34.3	46.4	39.5	37.3
Russians	6.35	18.06	13.7	15.93	169.8	35.2	46.4	39.9	37.4
Greeks	6.4	17.9	13.8	15.87	168.3	35.8	46.4	40.3	38.0
Croatians	6.5	18.1	13.8	15.98	171.6	36.5	47.1	40.6	37.9
Russian Jews	6.5	18.2	13.4	15.90	164.6	35.7	48.5	40.9	39.5
Northern Italians	6.5	18.2	13.75	16.05	169.6	35.7	47.3	40.5	38.3
Poles	6.5	18.3	13.7	16.03	170.4	35.4	47.4	40.55	38.1
Rumanians	6.5	18.0	13.8	15.93	168.7	36.1	47.4	40.8	38.5
Southern Italians	6.55	18.0	13.6	15.93	163.4	36.4	48.2	41.1	40.1
Irish	6.6	18.9	13.6	16.18	171.6	34.9	48.5	40.8	38.5
Mean deviation (of series, males)	0.11	0.25	0.88	0.12	2.28	0.61	0.91	0.49	0.70

* $\dfrac{\text{Height of forehead} \times 100}{\text{Height of face (menton-nasion)}}$

† $\dfrac{\text{Height of forehead} \times 100}{\text{Height of head}}$

‡ $\dfrac{\text{Height of forehead} \times 100}{\text{Mean head diameter (cephalic module)}}$

§ $\dfrac{\text{Height of forehead} \times 1000}{\text{stature}}$

nevertheless it is a character of some significance and the measurement is easily secured.

The diameter frontal minimum was taken on the Laboratory series only (table 164).

The breadth of the forehead is seen to lack the relative superiority in the female that was shown by the height, and to agree very closely with the size of the head.

TABLE 164

Old Americans: Breadth of forehead

MALES		FEMALES		FEMALES vs. MALES (M = 100)				
Number of subjects	Diameter frontal minimum	Number of subjects	Diameter frontal minimum	Forehead		Size of head	Size of face	Stature
				Breadth	Height			
(247)	10.59	(210)	10.12	95.6	98.9	95.0	93.0	92.8

TABLE 165

Old Americans, males: Face-diameter frontal minimum

Number of observations: 247

General average: 10.59 cm.

1st series of 50—10.7 cm. 4th series of 50—10.5 cm.

2nd series of 50—10.5 cm. 5th series of 50—10.5 cm.

3rd series of 47—10.5 cm.

Minimum: 9.3 cm. Maximum: 11.9 cm.

	TABLE OF FREQUENCIES													
	9.2–9.3 cm.	9.4–9.5 cm.	9.6–9.7 cm.	9.8–9.9 cm.	10.0–10.1 cm.	10.2–10.3 cm.	10.4–10.5 cm.	10.6–10.7 cm.	10.8–10.9 cm.	11.0–11.1 cm.	11.2–11.3 cm.	11.4–11.5 cm.	11.6–11.7 cm.	11.8–11.9 cm.
Number of cases............	1	1	5	7	21	23	46	54	44	22	14	3	5	1
Per cent....................	0.4	0.4	2.0	2.8	8.5	9.3	18.6	21.8	17.7	8.9	5.6	1.2	2.0	0.4

The range and nature of the variation of the measurement are shown in tables 165 and 166, and figure 28. The subseries records and the dispersion of the measurement are remarkably uniform, more so than those of any other dimension so far dealt with, and the range of individual variation is less than that of the height of the forehead.

Diameter frontal minimum, in relation to age, stature and head form. For the sake of conciseness, the relation of the lower frontal breadth to the above factors may be dealt with collectively. The data bearing on the subject are presented in table 167. They show the following conditions:

Age. The oldest subjects, both males and females, give a trifle larger lower frontal breadth than the youngest, which fact is also apparent, particularly in the females, in the relative value of the measurement to stature. When however the diameter is compared with the breadth of head and with that of the face, all age influence disappears or very nearly so. It may be said therefore that, within the adult span of life, while the lower breadth of the forehead may slightly increase, this augmentation simply follows that of the head and face and the relative proportions of the part to breadth of head and breadth of face remain practically identical.

Stature. Stature, at first sight, appears to have a marked influence on the dimension under consideration. While absolutely the inferior frontal breadth is, as could be expected, somewhat smaller in the short than in the tall individuals, relatively it gives a very perceptibly higher value in the

TABLE 166

Old Americans, females: face—diameter frontal minimum

Number of observations: 210

Average: 10.12 cm. (1st 50—10.2; 2nd 50—10.2; 3rd 50—10.1; 4th 60—10.05 cm.)

Minimum: 9.0 cm.   Maximum 11 2 cm.

	TABLE OF FREQUENCIES											
	9.0–9.1 cm.	9.2–9.3 cm.	9.4–9.5 cm.	9.6–9.7 cm.	9.8–9.9 cm.	10.0–10.1 cm.	10.2–10.3 cm.	10.4–10.5 cm.	10.6–10.7 cm.	10.8–10.9 cm.	11.0–11.1 cm.	11.2–11.3 cm
Number of cases..........	1	3	12	20	28	49	38	21	20	14	3	1
Per cent.................	0.5	1.4	5.7	9.5	13.3	23.3	18.1	10.0	9.5	6.7	1.4	0.5

former. But once more when we regard the dimension in its relations to breadth of head and face, the differences nearly disappear, showing that the measurement correlates with the latter and not directly with the stature. Nevertheless there is an indication that in this case stature has some direct effect. The ratio of the lower breadth of the forehead to breadth of head is slightly higher in the tall males, and both this as well as the breadth of forehead: breadth of face ratios are plainly higher in the tall than in the short females.

Some further light on the relation of the lower breadth of forehead and stature in the two sexes is given by the comparisons in table 168.

These figures show also that the forehead in the females is both absolutely and relatively somewhat narrower than that of the males even where the stature is equal, notwithstanding the fact that the female head is more

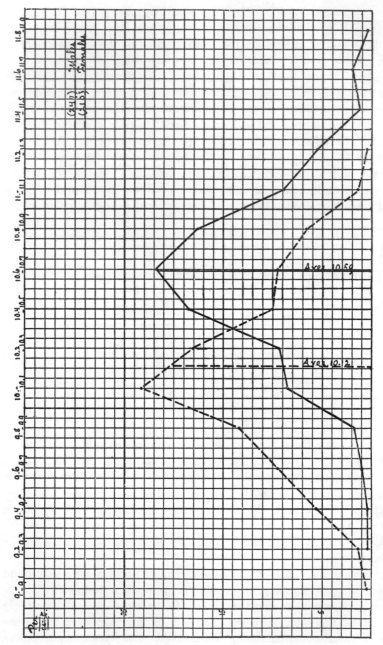

FIG. 28. OLD AMERICANS: DIAMETER FRONTAL MINIMUM—LABORATORY SERIES

TABLE 167

Old Americans: Breadth of forehead, age, stature and head form

Laboratory series

	MALES								FEMALES						
	Stature	Diameter frontal minimum	Ratio to stature	Breadth of head	Ratio of diameter frontal minimum to breadth of head	Breadth of face	Ratio of diameter frontal minimum to breadth of face		Stature	Diameter frontal minimum	Ratio to stature	Breadth of head	Ratio of diameter frontal minimum to breadth of head	Breadth of face	Ratio of diameter frontal minimum to breadth of face
Old Americans: Breadth of forehead and age															
(25) youngest	173.8	10.53	6.06	15.22	69.22	13.76	76.56	(20)	164.5	10.11	6.15	14.86	68.04	12.96	78.05
(25) oldest	174.6	10.60	6.19	15.36	69.01	13.82	76.68	(20)	159.3	10.17	6.39	14.76	68.88	13.05	77.93
Old Americans: Breadth of forehead and stature															
(25) shortest	164.4	10.42	6.34	15.29	68.15	13.58	76.73	(20)	151.3	9.92	6.62	14.70	67.48	12.79	77.56
(25) tallest	184.4	10.64	5.77	15.52	68.56	13.99	76.05	(20)	172.2	10.30	5.98	14.82	69.50	13.03	79.05
Old Americans: Breadth of forehead and head form															
(25) most dolichocephalic	176.1	10.40	5.91	14.94	69.60	13.58	76.56	(15)	161.6	9.89	6.12	14.15	69.88	12.70	77.87
(25) most brachycephalic	173.4	10.64	6.13	16.02	66.41	14.02	75.87	(20)	161.2	10.26	6.37	15.35	66.82	13.34	76.91

brachycephalic. The female forehead among the Old Americans may therefore be characterized as relatively high but slightly narrow (at the level of the diameter frontal minimum). These conditions find combined expression in the forehead index $\dfrac{FhH \times 100}{FhB}$; this index is 63.74 in the females, 62.13 in the males. The indications are that at least the latter feature and possibly both are shared by white women in general.

TABLE 168

Old Americans: Breadth of forehead vs. stature

Laboratory series

	STATURE					
	145.0–150.0 cm.	150.01–160.0 cm.	160.01–170.0 cm.	170.01–180.0 cm.	180.01–190.0 cm.	General average
Males:						
Number of subjects............		(2)	(61)	(147)	(37)	(247)
Diameter frontal minimum.....		(10.25)	10.49	10.62	10.66	10.59
Females:						
Number of subjects............	(3)	(73)	(114)	(20)		(210)
Diameter frontal minimum.....	9.66	10.05	10.15	10.28		10.12
Females *vs.* males (M = 100)			96.8	96.8		95.6
Mean stature of the subjects in each group....... Males		156.1	167.5	175.3	183.4	174.44
Females	147.9	156.15	164.2	172.2		161.84
Percental relation of breadth of forehead to actual mean stature of each group.................. Males		6.57	6.26	6.06	5.81	6.07
Females	6.53	6.44	6.18	5.97		5.91
Differences in favor of males........		0.13	0.08	0.09		0.08

Effects of head form. In this respect there appear some interesting conditions. The lower breadth of the forehead is greater both absolutely as well as relatively to stature in the brachycephalic. This applies to both sexes, and the differences in the values of the measurement as well as the ratio are much alike in the two. When however we come to the ratios of the measurement to breadth of head and that of the face, it is seen that both of these ratios, in both sexes, are larger in the dolicho- than in the brachycephals, indicating that as we pass from the former to the latter condition the lower frontal breadth lags behind the breadth of the head, and in lesser degree also behind that of the face: a fact which may be of some significance in studies on the nature of brachycephaly.

Comparative. Available data on the diameter frontal minimum in the living are scattered and by no means common.   Those on the skull are much

TABLE 169

	MALES	FEMALES	FEMALE TO MALE
Old Americans..........................	*10.59*	*10.12*	*95.6*
Polish Jews (Elkind).....................	10.6	10.2	*96.2*
White Russian Jews (Jakovenko)..........	10.6	10.1	*95.3*
Lithuanians (Baronas)....................	11.0*	10.7*	*97.3*
Kharga Oasis Egyptians (Hrdlicka)........	10.3		

* Probably too high.

more frequent and a nice series of comparisons of the diameter with the transverse maximum of the head is given by Topinard (Élém. d'Anthrop. gén., p. 692).[48]   Of the data on the living the largest series (on 14 groups) is given by Pittard in his "Les peuples des Balkans" (p. 586), but unfortunately these measurements have evidently not been taken in exactly the standard way for they are all too high, ranging from 11.0 to 11.41

[48] As the relative figures are probably much the same on the skull and on the living the data may here be reproduced:

	RATIO OF DIAMETER FRONTAL MINIMUM TO DIAMETER TRANSVERSE MAXIMUM OF SKULL
Parisians (modern males).....................................	68.8
Parisians (modern females)..................................	68.8
Auvergnats...	66.5
Dutch..	66.0
Homme-Mort Grotto (polished stone).........................	68.6
deBaye Grotto (polished stone)..............................	67.0
Esquimo..	69.7
Chinese..	65.9
Javanese...	64.0
Polynesians..	66.0
African Negroes..	70.0
Hottentots and Bushmen....................................	72.7
New-Caledonians...	71.5
Australians..	76.6
Tasmanians..	69.3
Indian Parias..	69.9

cm., and cannot be used for comparison with our records. The more available data are given in table 169.

The indications are of much sameness rather than of marked differences. The Egyptians were of low stature (163.8 cm.) and hence of small head. There is a need here of measurements on diverse groups by the same method and instruments.

Summary of the main facts relating to the study of the forehead in the Old Americans. Visual observations: The forehead is seldom low and seldom very high, particularly so in the males.

It is generally upright, rarely slightly to moderately sloping.

The supra-orbital ridges are moderately developed, rarely pronounced, much more frequently sub-medium.

Height of forehead: The individual variation in forehead height is fairly large without being excessive; it is greater in the males than in the females.

The female forehead in height is close to that of the male; relatively to the height of face and size of head it exceeds that of the male.

The dispersion of the measurement is very regular.

In the several groups of the males the absolute height of the forehead is much alike.

There is no indication that the height of the forehead is a safe index of intelligence.

In conformity with the rest of the head the forehead increases slightly with age during adult life.

The height of the forehead increases with stature, but is only indirectly correlated with same, the increase following that of the head.

There is but little difference in the height of the forehead of the Old Americans and other groups of whites.

Lower breadth of forehead: The measurement shows but moderate variation, with regular dispersion, in the Old Americans.

The dimension correlates directly with the size of the head, and does not show relative superiority in the females as did the forehead height.

The proportion grows slightly larger during adult life with age, in conformity with the increase in the size of the head as a whole.

The measurement is affected by increase in stature, but to a large extent only through increase in the size of the head.

Head form affects the lower frontal breadth through correlation of the same with the breadth of the head; but the lower breadth of the forehead increases more slowly than that of the head.

Comparative data so far as available show no substantial differences among whites except such as may be due to marked differences in stature.

Henry D. Hooker, Jr.
(New Haven, Conn.)
A good line of American ancestry, both sides

Young Man
Old American of more than 3 generations on each side

The female compared with the male forehead may be characterized as relatively high but slightly narrow.

Like the height so the breadth of the forehead is no safe index of mental powers. All that may be said is that high or broad, or high and broad, forehead goes generally with a large head and brain, which means greater development of the latter and due to this mostly a greater effectiveness.

The eyes

The foremost characteristic of the eyes is their pigmentation, which has already been dealt with.

But the eyes differ also individually and even in groups and races in their prominence, in the inclination and shape of the palpebral openings and in the conformation of the eyelids. Moreover they will or may differ

TABLE 170

Old Americans: Eye-slits

	MALES	FEMALES
	per cent	*per cent*
Horizontal or near (as average in whites)..................	98.0	98.0
External canthi perceptibly to plainly higher..............	2.0	2.0

in these respects in the same individual at different ages, according to health, and even according to the state of the mind.

The majority of these details would require special studies. The only observations that it was practicable to make in the current work on the Old Americans were those on the axis of the palpebral openings or eye-slits. But it may be said in general that in none of the other respects do the Old Americans differ from the prevailing forms among western Europeans.

Eye-slits. Among small children in the Old American families, as among those of other groups of whites, there can be met every now and then a child with a trace more or less marked of the epicanthus, or of an obliquity of the eye-slits with the external canthus a trace higher. Among the adults a perceptible slant to the eyes was found in but two per cent in each of the sexes. The eye-slits therefore, taken as a rule, are horizontal.

The cheek bones

Another important feature of the face, entering largely into its character, is the size and prominence of the cheek bones or malars. The results obtained by their detailed grading in our Laboratory group is quite interesting. Curiously, the males show a considerably larger proportion of sub-medium to very sub-medium grades than the females, and the latter show also a little more than three times as many cases of a relative prominence of these parts. As in so many other respects the female also in these features appears to conserve more of the ancestral conditions. Really large or prominent malars and zygomae were found in no case of the Old Americans.

The nose

Next to the eyes and the forehead the nose is the most important part of the physiognomy, particularly when this is regarded more or less in

TABLE 171

Old Americans: Prominence of the malars and zygomae

	MALES	FEMALES
	per cent	*per cent*
Very submedium......................................	10.7	0.7
Submedium...	36.0	21.3
Medium..	51.3	71.3
Somewhat prominent..................................	2.0	6.7
Prominent...		

TABLE 172

Old Americans: Depression at nasal root

	MALES	FEMALES
	per cent	*per cent*
None..	0.7	3.3
Slight..	1.3	7.0
Submedium...	16.0	20.0
Medium..	81.3	68.3
Pronounced..	0.7	1.3
Wide..	(0.7)	(8.0)

profile. And there is no other part that differs as much individually and racially.

Descriptive characteristics of the nose comprise those of its root, its bridge, its alae and its septum, all of which vary considerably with age, sex, individually and in groups. Detailed notes on these features (except the alae) in the Old Americans gave the following results:

Nasal root. The depression at the nasal root is a feature which at times adds considerably to the character of the face. In the female, where the glabella is less developed and the nasal bridge is mostly lower, the depression is frequently shallower and wider than in the male. The higher the bridge of the nose in either sex the less marked is liable to be the root depression. In the artist's "Greek" nose, as well known, there is no depression whatever at the root of the nose; such cases in reality however are met with but seldom. Among the Old Americans a complete lack of a depression at the nasal root was found but once in 130 men and but once in over thirty-three women. In seventeen per cent of the men and twenty-seven per cent of the women the depression was less to much less than the medium; while in but a few cases of either sex was it pronounced.

Nose bridge. The most common form of the nose (in reality the nasal bridge) in the males is the markedly convex; in the females the concavo-convex or "wavy;" but there is also a fairly large proportion (one in five

TABLE 173

Old Americans: Nose—form of bridge

	MALES		FEMALES	
	per cent		*per cent*	
Concave ⎰Slightly..	4.0 ⎫		3.3 ⎫	
Concave ⎰Moderately.....................................	4.7 ⎬ 8.7		5.3 ⎬ 8.6	
⎱Markedly......................................	0 ⎭		0 ⎭	
Straight or nearly so.....................................	22.0		24.7	
Convex ⎰Slightly..	18.0 ⎫		14.0 ⎫	
Convex ⎰Moderately.....................................	24.0 ⎬ 42.0		17.3 ⎬ 31.3	
⎱Markedly......................................	(0) ⎭		(0) ⎭	
Concavo-convex (wavy).................................	27.3		35.3	

males, one in four females) of straight noses, while in one in approximately each twelve males as well as twelve females, the nose is concave. The general notion that the "Uncle Sam" or American nose is typically convex is, as seen, not borne out by the facts. The feature is very variable (table 173).

The Old American nose, therefore, may be described as variable in form, with a frequent tendency towards more or less convexity. It impresses one as rather long, of moderate breadth, neither "thick" nor too delicate, and of fair but generally not excessive prominence.

Nasal septum: Inclination. The inclination of the septum is a physiognomic character which is directly connected with the growth of the nose. The smaller the development of the organ in a vertical direction the more open is the angle between the septum and the parts below and *vice versa.* An upwardly inclined septum (*i.e.,* its distal end, at the point, higher in a naturally held head than the proximal), is typical of infancy, diminishing gradually with age. But as the nose keeps on growing in the nasion-point length—a growth which lasts with some persons if not all, to old age, the septum becomes at first horizontal and then inclines more or less downwards. The upwardly inclined septum is therefore an infantile, the downwardly inclined septum an old age character; nevertheless the former persists more or less frequently to adult life, while the latter is found occasionally before old age is reached, and the frequency of both differs considerably in different human groups. In the Old American the septum was found to be horizontal, or nearly so, in over one-half of the males and less than one-half in the females; it was inclined upwards, slightly to markedly, in nearly one-third of the males and not far from one-half of the females; and it was inclined downwards more or less in approximately one in nine of the males

TABLE 174

Old Americans: Nose—inclination of septum

		MALES	FEMALES
		per cent	*per cent*
Horizontal or nearly so..............................		56.3	47.6
Inclined upwards	Slightly............................	20.0 ⎫	28.6 ⎫
	Moderately.........................	9.7 ⎬ 32.0	13.8 ⎬ 45.7
	Markedly..........................	2.3 ⎭	3.3 ⎭
Inclined downwards	Slightly............................	8.9 ⎫	6.2 ⎫
	Moderately.........................	2.4 ⎬ 11.7	0.5 ⎬ 6.7
	Markedly..........................	0.4 ⎭	0 ⎭

and one in fifteen of the females.   The females show plainly more approach to the infantile condition, while in the males the nose (tip to nasion) is for much the same average age, relatively longer.

Measurements. While the "physiognomy" is essentially an organ of vision and emotion-expression, as well as an adjunct 'organ' of speech and sex, and the lower part of the face is principally an organ for the intake and trituration of food, the nose in the main is an organ of respiration, and as such is largely subject to other influences than the rest of the facial structures. The air passing through the nose is moistened, warmed and partly filtered of foreign particles, all of which renders it less irritating to the bronchi and lungs. The narrower the nasal cavities are, the more effective they are for these purposes. In the tropics where the air is generally warm and moist and where at the same time the freest possible respiration is needed, the nasal aperture of the natives is, as a rule, broad; in the moderate zones it is prevalently of medium width; while in cold regions it is generally narrow. The broad nose is also mostly short with a more or less low bridge, the narrow nose mostly long and in the white race also frequently rather prominent.

Both the length and breadth of the nose are naturally physiognomic characters of consequence, but their main value is in anthropometry, and their percental relation gives the Nasal Index which is of very material aid in racial classification.

Unfortunately the nasal height on the living is difficult to take accurately due to the indistinctness in most cases of the upper landmark of the measurement. The only remedy for this is a thorough acquaintance with the location of the nasion in the skull and in bodies on the dissecting table. With travelers, etc., who have not gained this the records of nasal height and in consequence also the nasal index can not help but be erroneous and can be used with but little if any confidence.

Nasal and sub-nasal height. The nasal height extends from the naso-frontal articulation (nasion) to the base of the nasal spine, and divides the face proper into two only partly correlated portions, the nasal and the sub-nasal. The latter, of considerable evolutionary importance, will be dealt with separately.

Nasal breadth. This is the normal external breadth of the nasal alae. This measurement, while also important phylogenetically, is subject to considerable ontogenetic modifications, resembling in this respect the dorsum or bridge of the nose.

Nasal index. Due to the numerous individual modifications in nose breadth the index, which is merely the percental ratio of nasal breadth to length, must necessarily reflect these conditions and so be individually of but limited anthropological value; but in averages of appropriate groups it is a very serviceable character in anthropometric determinations, scarcely inferior in value to any of the indices of the skull or head.

Tables 175 to 180 and figures 29 to 31 give the range and distribution of these measurements and index.

Nasal measurements, index, and age. Upon further analysis of the data on the nose in the Old Americans, it appears that a definite influence on the nasal dimensions as well as on the index is exercised by age. The even more marked influence of this factor on the length of the dorsum or free part of the nose has already been noted under "Observations." It will now be seen that the nose grows with age in both length and breadth and that the nasal index becomes higher with age. This means that the enlargement with age is slightly more in breadth than in the proximate (nasion-spine) length; should we measure the dorsal or nasion-nasal point length the conditions

TABLE 175

Old Americans, males: Height of nose

Laboratory series

Number of observations: 247

Average: 5.35 cm. (1st 50—5.35; 2nd 50—5.37; 3rd 47—5.26; 4th 50—5.38;
5th 50—5.37 cm.)

Minimum: 4.3 cm.   Maximum: 6.3 cm.

	TABLE OF FREQUENCIES										
	4.3-4.35 cm.	4.4-4.55 cm.	4.6-4.75 cm.	4.8-4.95 cm.	5.0-5.15 cm.	5.2-5.35 cm.	5.4-5.55 cm.	5.6-5.75 cm.	5.8-5.95 cm.	6.0-6.15 cm.	6.2-6.35 cm.
Number of cases..............	1	4	5	11	36	58	71	40	15	4	2
Per cent......................	0.4	1.6	2.0	4.5	14.6	23.5	28.7	16.2	6.1	1.6	0.8

TABLE 176

Old Americans, females: Height of nose

Number of observations: 210

Average: 4.94 cm. (1st 50—5.01; 2nd 50—4.89; 3rd 50—4.90; 4th 60—4.99 cm.)

Minimum: 4.2 cm.   Maximum: 6.1 cm.

	TABLE OF FREQUENCIES								
	4.2-4.35 cm.	4.4-4.55 cm.	4.6-4.75 cm.	4.8-4.95 cm.	5.0-5.15 cm.	5.2-5.35 cm.	5.4-5.55 cm.	5.6-5.75 cm.	Above 5.75 cm.
Number of cases	7	15	35	44	50	44	11	3	1
Per cent.............	3.3	7.1	16.7	21.0	23.8	21.0	5.2	1.4	0.5

TABLE 177

Old Americans, males: Breadth of nose

Laboratory series

Average: 3.61 cm. (1st 50—3.6; 2nd 50—3.58; 3rd 47—3.6; 4th 50—3.6;
5th 50—3.64 cm.)

Minimum 3.0 cm.   Maximum: 4.3 cm.

	TABLE OF FREQUENCIES													
	3.0-3.05 cm.	3.1-3.15 cm.	3.2-3.25 cm.	3.3-3.35 cm.	3.4-3.45 cm.	3.5-3.55 cm.	3.6-3.65 cm.	3.7-3.75 cm.	3.8-3.85 cm.	3.9-3.95 cm.	4.0-4.05 cm.	4.1-4.15 cm.	4.2-4.25 cm.	4.3-4.35 cm.
Number of cases.........	2	4	13	20	29	35	39	33	30	20	14	1	6	1
Per cent.................	0.8	1.6	5.3	8.1	11.7	14.2	15.8	13.4	12.1	8.1	5.7	0.4	2.4	0.4

TABLE 178

Old Americans, females: Breadth of nose

Number of observations: 210

Average: 3.25 cm. (1st 50—3.25; 2nd 50—3.35; 3rd 50—3.20; 4th 60—3.24 cm.)
Minimum: 2.8 cm. Maximum 3.8 cm.

	TABLE OF FREQUENCIES										
	2.8-2.85 cm.	2.9-2.95 cm.	3.0-3.05 cm.	3.1-3.15 cm.	3.2-3.25 cm.	3.3-3.35 cm.	3.4-3.45 cm.	3.5-3.55 cm.	3.6-3.65 cm.	3.7-3.75 cm.	3.8-3.85 cm.
Number of cases..............	5	10	23	33	33	42	23	25	8	5	2
Per cent.	2.4	4.8	10.9	15.7	15.7	20.0	10.9	11.9	3.8	2.4	0.95

TABLE 179

Old Americans, males: Nasal index

Laboratory series
Number of observations: 247

Average: 67.45 (1st 50—67.38; 2nd 50—66.90; 3rd 47—68.78 4th 50—67.32;
5th 50—67.99)
Minimum: 53.2 Maximum: 90.9

	TABLE OF FREQUENCIES														
	53.2-55.0	55.1-57.5	57.6-60.0	60.1-62.5	62.6-65.0	65.1-67.5	67.6-70.0	70.1-72.5	72.6-75.0	75.1-77.5	77.6-80.0	80.1-82.5	82.6-85.0	85.1-88.5	88.6-90.9
Number of cases.....	1	7	14	31	38	40	36	29	27	11	5	5	1	1	1
Per cent............	0.4	2.8	5.7	12.6	15.4	16.2	14.6	11.7	10.9	4.4	2.0	2.0	0.4	0.4	0.4

TABLE 180

Old Americans, females: Nasal index

Number of observations: 210

Average: 65.98 (1st 50—64.25; 2nd 50—68.3; 3rd 50—65.5; 4th 60—64.95)
Minimum: 50.8. Maximum: 78.7

	TABLE OF FREQUENCIES											
	30.1-52.5	52.6-55.0	55.1-57.5	57.6-60.0	60.1-62.5	62.6-65.0	65.1-67.5	67.6-70.0	70.1-72.5	72.6-75.0	75.1-77.5	77.6-80.0
Number of cases.........	1	5	8	23	29	24	48	25	15	17	7	8
Per cent.................	0.5	2.4	3.8	10.95	13.8	11.4	22.9	11.9	7.1	8.1	3.3	3.8

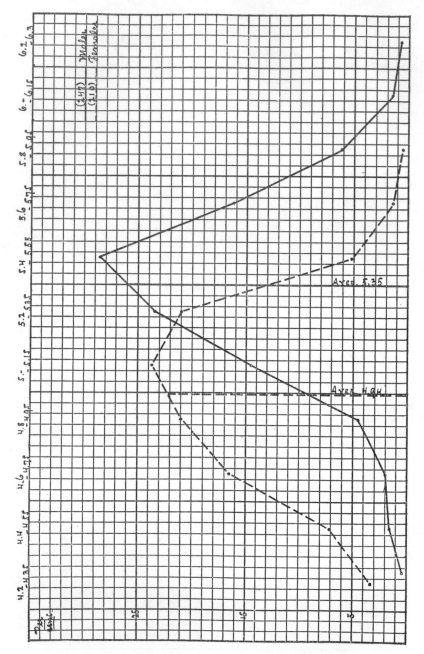

Fig. 29. Old Americans: Height of Nose—Laboratory Series

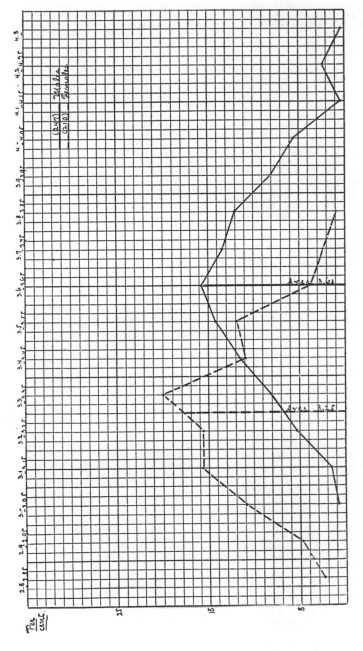

FIG. 30. OLD AMERICANS: BREADTH OF NOSE—LABORATORY SERIES

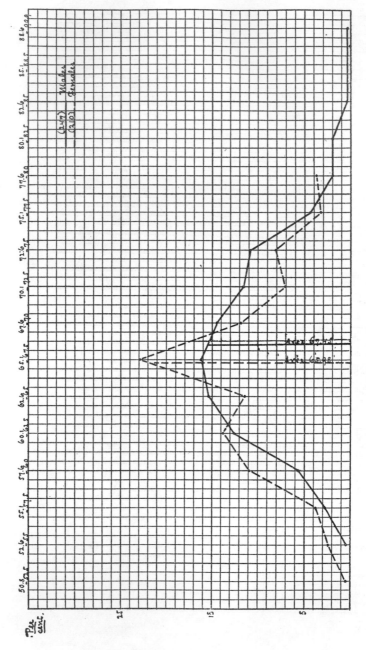

FIG. 31. OLD AMERICANS: NASAL INDEX—LABORATORY SERIES

TABLE 181

*Old Americans: Nasal dimensions and index vs. age**

Laboratory series

		MALES				FEMALES			
		Age	Nose height	Nose breadth	Nasal index		Age	Nose height	Nose breadth	Nasal index
Youngest.............	(25)	24.2	5.23	3.50	67.1	(20)	23.0	4.90	3.15	64.5
General average.......	(247)	42.5	5.35	3.61	67.45	(210)	41.0	4.95	3.25	65.7
Oldest................	(25)	59.5	5.52	3.78	68.6	(20)	57.2	5.07	3.38	66.9

* These comparisons are restricted to the Laboratory series for the reason that there were no elderly men in the other groups.

TABLE 182

Relation of nasal dimensions to height of face and stature at different ages

Laboratory series

		MALES						FEMALES				
	Height of face menton-nasion	Stature	Per cent relation to facial height		Per mille relation to stature		Height of face menton-nasion	Stature	Per cent relation to facial height		Per mille relation to stature	
			Nasal height	Nasal breadth	Nasal height	Nasal breadth			Nasal height	Nasal breadth	Nasal height	Nasal breadth
Youngest..	11.60	173.78	45.1	30.2	30.1	20.1	11.05	164.52	44.3	28.5	29.8	19.1
Average...	11.93	174.44	44.9	30.2	30.7	20.7	11.09	161.84	44.6	29.3	30.6	20.1
Oldest.....	12.02	174.63	45.9	31.4	31.6	21.6	11.09	159.27	45.7	30.5	31.8	21.2

TABLE 183

Old Americans: Nasal dimensions and index vs. stature

Laboratory series

		MALES						FEMALES					
		Age	Nose Height	Nose Breadth	Nose Index	Per mille ratio to stature of Nose height	Per mille ratio to stature of Nose breadth		Age	Nose Height	Nose Breadth	Nose Index	Per mille ratio to stature of Nose height	Per mille ratio to stature of Nose breadth
		years							years					
Shortest......	(25)	33.3	5.19	3.55	68.4	31.6	21.6	(20)	39.4	4.89	3.24	66.3	32.3	21.4
Tallest.......	(25)	37.1	5.51	3.71	67.3	29.9	20.1	(20)	32.6	5.06	3.24	64.0	29.4	18.8

would probably be reversed.   It is of course essentially, though not wholly, the fleshy and cartilaginous nose that keeps on growing, as do other soft parts of the face (ears, mouth, skin, eyelids).   Interesting sexual agreements in the growth of the nose with age will be noted in the lower figures, though in the women the changes in both nasal length and breadth are a trace greater.

Effects of stature.   On comparing the nasal measurements in the shortest and tallest groups from our Laboratory series, as shown in table 183, it is

TABLE 184

Old Americans: Nasal index vs. stature

	STATURE					
	145.0–150.0	150.01–160.0	160.01–170.0	170.01–180.0	180.01–190.0	Above 190.0
Males:						
All (610)...............		(5) (64.3)	(148) 66.6	(365) 65.6	(90) 65.5	(2) (60.0)
Laboratory (247)............		(2) (63.1)	(61) 67.8	(147) 67.7	(37) 67.5	
South (256)............		(2) (66.0)	(62) 66.1	(148) 64.2	(42) 63.8	(2) (60.0)
Mixed States (91).......		(1) (63.4)	(20) 65.1	(61) 63.5	(9) 65.4	
Tennessee (16).........			(5) 67.0	(9) 66.8	(2) (65.7)	
Females:						
All (210)...............	(3) (68.4)	(72) 66.3	(115) 65.9	(20) 64.1		

seen that in the males both height and breadth of the nose are very appreciably higher in the tallest group, but in the females, while there is also a difference in absolute nasal height in favor of the tall, the breadth of the nose in the two extreme stature groups is identical.   The nose height-stature ratio indicates that the correlation of these two measurements in both sexes is a rather weak one; and the same is true of the correlation between stature and nose breadth.

The nasal height, it will be shown later, correlates directly and closely

TABLE 185

Old Americans: Nasal dimensions and index vs. facial dimensions

Laboratory series

		MALES					
		Face		Nose		Nasal: Facial height ratio*	Nasal: Facial breadth ratio
		Menton-nasion height	Diameter bizygomatic maximum	Height	Breadth		
Shortest............	(25)	11.43	13.58	5.19	3.55	*45.40*	*26.13*
Tallest.............	(25)	12.14	13.99	5.51	3.71	*45.37*	*26.52*

		FEMALES					
Shortest............	(20)	10.82	12.795	4.89	3.24	*44.73*	*25.32*
Tallest.............	(20)	11.15	13.035	5.065	3.24	*45.43*	*24.86*

*Ratios determined from totals, not from averages.

TABLE 186

Old Americans: Nasal dimensions and index according to breadth and height of face

Laboratory series

		Facial breadth	Facial height menton-nasion	Nose*			Percental relation of	
				Height	Breadth	Index	Nasal to facial height	Nasal to facial breadth
Narrowest faces....................	(25)	13.05	11.62	5.34	3.51	*65.6*	*46.0*	*28.9*
General average of the series.........	(247)	13.86	11.93	5.35	3.61	*67.45*	*44.9*	*26.0*
Broadest faces.....................	(25)	14.75	12.17	5.41	3.62	*66.9*	*44.5*	*24.6*
Difference between narrowest and broadest† face...................							*3.26*	*14.88*

				FEMALES				
Narrowest faces....................	(25)	12.27	10.81	4.85	3.09	*63.6*	*44.9*	*25.2*
General average of the series.........	(210)	12.99	11.09	4.95	3.25	*65.7*	*44.6*	*25.0*
Broadest faces.....................	(25)	13.74	11.38	4.98	3.34	*67.0*	*43.8*	*24.3*
Difference between narrowest and broadest† face...................							*2.45*	*3.57*

*All indexes and ratios derived from totals.

†Percental difference between the two extreme ratios, the higher = 100.

with the height of the face and is affected by stature only as far as the facial height is affected.

Relation of nasal index to stature. It was seen from the preceding data that the nasal height and, at least in the males, also the breadth increase with stature, or rather with the size of the face which stands in correlation with stature. So much was to be expected. But it could hardly have been anticipated that the relative proportions of the nose change with the height of the body. Nevertheless that such in general is the case is indicated by the following comparisons which show that, barring an occasional exception, the higher the stature the lower is the nasal index. The fact is due to an augmentation with stature of the height of the face and with this of the height of the nose, while the breadth of the nose is less affected (males) or unaffected (females).

TABLE 187

Nasal dimensions and index vs. shape of head

| | | MALES | | | | FEMALES | | |
| | | Nose | | | | Nose | | |
		Length	Breadth	Index		Length	Breadth	Index
Laboratory series:								
Most dolichocephalic....	(25)	5.40	3.59	66.5	(15)	4.90	3.17	64.8
Most brachycephalic....	(25)	5.32	3.52	66.1	(15)	4.91	3.26	66.8
"Engineer" series:								
Most dolichocephalic....	(25)	5.50	3.40	61.9				
Most brachycephalic....	(25)	5.44	3.42	62.9				

Nose and face. We may now inquire into the relations of the dimensions of the nose with those of the face, and the more important comparisons will naturally be those of height with height and breadth with breadth. The results of such comparisons are given in tables 185 and 186. They show that the nasal height correlates directly, closely and very nearly evenly in the two sexes, with the morphological height of the face; but that the correlation of nasal with facial breadth is less marked and unlike in the sexes, though the latter condition may possibly be somewhat accidental.

Nasal measurements, nasal index and form of head. The correlation of the nasal dimensions and index with dolicho- and brachycephaly, has received but inadequate attention in the past, and nothing definite has been established. The absolute measurements on the Old Americans, as given in table 187, would seem to show but little of such correlation. What differ-

·ences appear in the figures are slight and limited to the females and the "engineer" group.

However, as the nasal dimensions are affected directly by age and indirectly by stature, these factors must receive consideration in this connection. Taking the same Laboratory groups as above it is found (table 188) that the influence of age may possibly enter slightly into the case among the males, where one of the groups is nearly a decade older than the other, but its effect on the relative proportions of the nose cannot be material.[49] As to stature, its differences have surely some bearing on the results in the males, but not in the females.

Comparing the nasal with the anatomical facial height in the two headform groups, it is noted that the resulting ratios are almost identical, so

TABLE 188

Old Americans: Nasal dimensions and index vs. head form

Laboratory series

	MALES (247)				FEMALES (210)			
	Cephalic index				Cephalic index			
	Below 75.0	75.01–80.0	80.01–85.0	Above 85.0	Below 75.0	75.01–80.0	80.01–85.0	Above 85.0
	(35)	(151)	(54)	(7)	(20)	(104)	(78)	(8)
Nasal length............	5.42	5.35	5.33	5.39	4.89	5.0	4.90	4.97
Nasal breadth..........	3.61	3.63	3.55	3.60	3.19	3.31	3.21	3.23
Nasal index.............	66.7	67.9	66.6	66.8	65.1	66.1	65.5	65.0

that it may be concluded the height of the nose correlates only with that of the face and is not affected by head-form except and in so far as this may affect the height of the face; and it was seen before when dealing with the facial measurements that the form of the head influences the anatomical height of the face least of all the facial dimensions. The same fact, *i.e.,* an independence of nasal height of head form, is further indicated by its correlation with stature, which gives very nearly the same values in the dolicho- as in the brachycephals of our series.

It is clear therefore that outside of age the nasal height correlates only with the height of the morphologic face which in turn correlates with stature, and that head form alone has but very slight if any effect on the dimension.

With the breadth of the nose matters are somewhat different.

[49] In the two groups of "Engineers" the stature is nearly the same: dolichocephalic 174.9, brachycephalic 174.4.

Brachycephaly means a relatively broad head that generally implies also a relatively broad face, which in turn may be conceived to have an influence on the breadth of the nasal aperture and the external nose. Yet the actual data do not bear out this assumption. It has already been seen that in absolute measurements the breadth of the nose is much the same in the

TABLE 189

Relations in dolicho- and brachycephaly of nasal measurements to facial height and breadth

		Age	Face height	Face breadth	Percental relation of nasal to facial height	Percental relation of nasal to facial breadth
		MALES				
		years				
Most dolichocephalic.........	(25)	41.8	11.78	13.58	*45.5**	*26.6*
Most brachycephalic.........	(25)	33.3	11.68	14.02	*45.6*	*25.1*
		FEMALES				
Most dolichocephalic.........	(15)	34.7	11.07	12.70	*44.4*	*25.0*
Most brachycephalic.........	(20)	31.9	11.17	13.34	*44.0*	*24.4*

Relations in dolicho- and brachycephaly of nasal measurements to stature

		Stature	Per mille relation to stature of	
			Nasal height	Nasal breadth
		MALES		
Most dolichocephalic..........	(25)	176.1	*30.4*	*20.5*
Most brachycephalic..........	(25)	173.4	*30.7*	*20.3*
		FEMALES		
Most dolichocephalic..........	(15)	161.6	*30.3*	*19.6*
Most brachycephalic..........	(20)	161.2	*30.5*	*20.2*

*All ratios calculated from the ratios not from the averages.

most dolicho- and the most brachycephalic in the Laboratory group and is but slightly higher in the brachycephals among the "Engineers" and in the females. Even more conclusive however are the figures in table 189— there is no progression of either the nasal breadth or the nasal index with increasing brachycephaly. Where there are changes they affect both of the nasal measurements. The breadth of the nose correlates to some extent with the breadth of the face, as seen in the additional tables, but the broader

T. D. WOODBRIDGE
(Boston)

Old New England ancestry. No European blood known of on either side since 1650.

WILTON L. PUTNAM
(Goodrich, Colo.)

Seven great grandparents and all following born in U. S. A.

MR. RUSSELL BRADFORD
(University of Virginia)

Long American ancestry on each side

PROFESSOR RICHARD S. LULL
(Yale University)

No admixture of foreign blood known of for at least 6 generations.

faces are on the average also higher and give, too, a greater height of the nose so that matters are equalized and the nasal index is not affected or affected but little.

Group differences. The nasal dimensions and index are not identical in the three groups of males represented in our studies. The differences will be seen in table 190. They are more marked in the breadth than in length. They are due in the main to differences in age.

These figures show that the breadth of the nose, if we take groups of approximately the same age, is almost identical, differing only by from one- to three-tenths of a millimeter. The difference in the index in the southern "Engineers" is due to a greater height of the nose in that group, going, as has been shown before, with a stronger (higher) face. The highlanders, age for age, do not differ materially from the Old Americans of lower lands; but northeastern highlands with their foothills do not present strictly speaking a pronounced or high altitude mountain environment.

TABLE 190

Old Americans: Nasal dimensions and index by groups

Males

	AVERAGE AGE	STATURE	NOSE		
			Length	Breadth	Index
(247) Laboratory......................	42.5	174.44	5.35	3.61	*67.45*
(25) Laboratory, youngest...........	24.2	173.78	5.23	3.50	*67.10*
(347) Southern "Engineers"..........	23.6	174.26	5.40	3.47	*64.40*
(16) Tennessee Highlanders.	26.0	173.65	5.23	3.48	*66.70*

It may therefore be concluded that, while the three groups of male Old Americans that are available for comparison show certain differences in nasal dimensions as well as index, these differences are of functional rather than racial nature. The same social classes at the same age are in all probability substantially alike in nasal features.

Comparative. Data on nasal dimensions and index are almost as common as those on the length, breadth and index of the head; nevertheless there is hardly enough of those which would be of most interest for our purpose, namely those on the British peoples, and of the many others not all are equally dependable due to frequent bias developed by not fully prepared observers in estimating the nasion position.

The records which deserve the first consideration are those on the immigrants taken under the author's direction, and the two measurements as well as the index will with some advantage be considered separately Those on the length are given in table 191.

The actual height of the nose in the Old Americans is seen to be rather marked. The measurement is practically identical in the English and the Americans, and in both of these it is higher than in any of the other groups.

In relation to the lower facial height (to nasion) the Old Americans and the English show slightly above medium conditions. They are in this respect exceeded slightly by the Greeks and somewhat more so by the Russian Jews. In the nine remaining groups the nasal-to-facial height ratio is slightly to moderately less than in the English and Americans. The shortest nose relatively (as well as absolutely) appears in our group of the Russians.

TABLE 191

Old Americans: Nasal height; comparative data

Males

GROUP	HEIGHT		PERCENTAL RELATION OF NASAL HEIGHT TO FACIAL HEIGHT*	PER MILLE RELATION TO STATURE OF NASAL HEIGHT
	Of face to nasion	Of nose		
Old Americans (all)...........	12.18	5.38	44.2	30.9
Old Americans, (females)......	(11.09)	(4.95)	(44.7)	(30.7)
Comparative:				
Russian Jews.............	11.67	5.27	45.2	32.0
Greeks.................	11.52	5.13	44.6	30.5
English.................	12.19	5.40	44.3	31.7
Armenians...............	12.02	5.30	44.1	31.7
Croatians...............	11.59	5.10	44.0	29.7
North Italians............	11.68	5.11	43.7	30.1
Southern Italians.........	11.56	5.02	43.5	30.7
Hungarians..............	11.47	4.97	43.4	29.8
Rumanians...............	11.51	5.03	43.1	29.8
Irish...................	12.09	5.19	42.9	30.2
Poles...................	11.79	5.04	42.7	29.6
Russians................	11.66	4.98	42.7	29.3

* $\dfrac{\text{Nose height} \times 100}{\text{Face height (to Nasion)}}$

The relation of the nasal height to stature is less instructive though not without value. The females show slightly lower ratio or relatively shorter nose than the males. In relation to the other groups of whites the American males occupy again a nearly medium position. In the Jews, English and Armenians, the nasal height relative to stature is somewhat longer, in all the other groups slightly shorter.

The main points in the above, so far as the Old Americans are concerned, are that as compared with a number of groups of recent European immigrants, they show absolutely as well as relatively a somewhat long nose, which is accompanied as will be shown later by a somewhat submedium maxillary or subnasal height of the face. So far as the other groups are concerned the most notable condition is the shortness of the nose in the Russians.

Nasal breadth. As in nasal length so in nasal breadth there is found in the Old Americans a considerable individual variation, but the mean nasal breadth is just about medium for the white race. Absolutely it is a trace higher than in most of the immigrant groups available for comparison, but relatively to stature, size of face or height of nose it is quite moderate.

TABLE 192

Nose breadth: Comparative data

| | AVERAGE BREADTH OF NOSE | PERCENTAL (OR PER THOUSAND) Relation | |
		To size of face (facial module)	To stature
Old Americans:			
Males.................................	3.53	27.3	20.3
Females..............................	(3.23)	(26.8)	(20.0)
North Italians...........................	3.46	26.7	20.4
Rumanians..............................	3.47	27.0	20.0
Irish..................................	3.48	26.9	20.3
English................................	3.48	26.7	20.4
Greeks................................	3.49	27.5	20.8
Russian Jews...........................	3.49	27.3	21.2
Hungarians.............................	3.50	27.4	21.0
Croatians..............................	3.51	27.1	20.4
Poles.................................	3.56	27.3	20.9
Armenians..............................	3.56	27.3	21.3
Southern Italians........................	3.57	28.0	21.85
Russians...............................	3.58	27.8	21.1

In rough figures, eight of the immigrant groups show a nose in the males a trace narrower, but the average difference in none of them amounts to as much as a whole millimeter; while in four of the groups, the Poles, Armenians, Southern Italians and Russians, the nose is slightly broader.

Compared with the mean diameter of the face the breadth of the nose in the Old Americans is once more seen to be very close to the medium. Compared to stature, however, the nasal breadth in the Americans is rather low, being very slightly to perceptibly exceeded in no less than ten of the groups. The longest nose in relation to stature, it is interesting to observe, occurs in the Southern Italians, in whom also the absolute breadth of the nose is close to maximum.

The gist of this is that while absolutely the nose of the Old Americans shows a fair average breadth, relatively to the size of the face and especially to stature, the breadth is slightly submedium.

The Old American nose may therefore be characterized as comparatively somewhat high and somewhat narrow.

Nasal index. The nasal index or percental relation of the breadth to the height of the nose, is a character of considerable anthropological importance, yet it should be borne in mind that it is based on two variable factors, the nasal height and nasal breadth, which are not wholly interdependent and do not stand in perfect correlation. In consequence the actual measurements of the nose should always be given together with the index.

There are numerous data on the nasal index in the living in literature, far more so than in the case of other facial indices or measurements. But they are not absolutely uniform. In studying the records of different observers on the same people it is evident that, as already alluded to, some of the workers had developed a bias, in all probability in locating the nasion, that mars the results. The nasion landmark is not obvious and can be properly located only by those who have had ample observation as to the point on crania. Even more valuable but not always possible are observations through dissection.

Such as they are the data at large show a wide range of nasal indices which, in common with others, have been subdivided into three classes.[50] But these classes have been given occasionally almost fetishistic significance. They are no morphological realities, have no natural lines of demarcation, and have little more value than descriptive conveniences. As with similar subdivisions of other indices they may well be done without and that perhaps with advantage to anthropology. How if taken literally, they can mislead, has been palpably demonstrated on a recent occasion.[51]

Among the whites the mean nasal index ranges[52] from approximately 60 to 73.

Data on the nasal index in living European whites gathered by Topinard, Deniker, Martin and Ivanovsky, are given in table 193; they are regrettably in but a very few cases accompanied by the actual nasal measurements.

[50] Broca: Leptorhiny—index below 69; Deniker up to 70. Mesorhiny—index 69 to 81.9; Deniker up to 70.1 to 85. Platyrhiny—index 90 and above; Deniker above 85.

[51] Dixon's Racial History of Man, Scribner's, 1923.

[52] See Deniker Races of Man, Appendix III; R. Martin, Lehrbuch d. Anthropologie; and A. A. Ivanovsky, Naselenie Zemnovo šara.

TABLE 193

Nasal index in European whites

GROUP	MALES		FEMALES		OBSERVER
	Number of subjects	Average index	Number of subjects	Average index	
Russian Armenians...............	724	62.6			(Various)
French, fair.......................	100	63.0			Collignon
Germans.........................	38	63.5			Weisbach
Letts............................		63.8		63.6	Waeber
Irish............................	102	64.3			Browne
Russian Jews....................	729	64.4			(Various)
Lorraine........................	50	64.6			Collignon
French Catalans.................	30	65.1			Collignon
Anglo-Scotch....................	20	65.1			Beddoe
Old Americans...................	(727)	65.6	(210)	65.2	
Germans, Baden.................		65.7			Fischer
Southern French.................	50	65.7			Collignon
Rumanians......................	26	66.0			Weisbach
Ruthenians......................	26	66.0			Weisbach
French of Normandy.............	160	66.5			Gilbert d'Hercourt
Sardinians......................	88	66.6			Collignon
English.........................	21	67.0			Beddoe
French, in general...............	1000	67.3			Collignon
Greeks..........................		67.6			Pittard
Flemish.........................		67.7		68.3	Houzé
White Russians..................		67.9		63.3	Roshdestvensky
Bulgarians......................		68.1			Pittard
White Russians..................	902	68.3			(Various)
Hungarians......................	20	68.4			Weisbach
Great Russians...................	711	69.0			(Various)
Jews...........................	1510	69.2			Fischberg
Parisians........................	68	69.4			Topinard
Great Russians..................		69.6		67.4	Galai
Rumanians......................		69.9			Pittard
Scotch..........................	10	70.0			Beddoe
Germans (in Russia).............	57	70.6			Dederer
Bretons.........................		71.4		71.7	Topinard
Little Russians..................		71.6		71.6	Bielodied
Serbians........................	64	72.4			(Various)
Lithuanians.....................		72.9		71.1	Brennsohn

Several plainly either exceptional or erroncous smaller series have been omitted.

The Old Americans are seen to occupy in the nasal index a rather low position, their nose, as has already been noted, being rather long and narrow. This appears to even better advantage if we compare their index with that of the immigrant groups, where the measurements were taken by the same instruments and method (table 194).

The English alone show a slightly lower nasal index having a nose even slightly narrower than the Americans; but our group of the English is too small for definite conclusions as to the English in general. In table 194 a small series of "Anglo-Scotch" gave a very slightly lower, another small series of English a somewhat larger index than the Americans; the indications are that the two groups are in this as in many other respects fairly similar, with the Irish not far away. The close affinities throughout of the Irish to both the British and the Americans are quite instructive.

Summary. Visual observations: The depression at the nasal root, in the Old Americans, ranges from medium to sub-medium. As usual it is more frequently sub-medium in the females.

TABLE 194

Nasal index in Old Americans and recent immigrants to the United States

	ENGLISH (10)	OLD AMERICANS (610)	RUSSIAN JEWS (50)	ARMENIANS (25)	IRISH (35)	NORTH ITALIANS (50)	GREEKS (50)	RUMANIANS (50)	CROATIANS (50)	HUNGARIANS (50)	POLES (50)	SOUTHERN STATES (50)	RUSSIANS (50)
Nasal index..........	64.7	65.6	66.5	67.2	67.3	67.7	68.0	69.0	69.0	70.4	70.6	71.1	71.9

The form of the nasal bridge varies greatly. The order of frequency in the males is: convex, concavo-convex, straight, concave; in the females: concavo-convex, convex, straight, concave.

The nose impresses one as rather long, of moderate breadth and not exceptionally molded.

The inclination of the nasal septum varies with age. It is most frequently horizontal, but quite frequently also, particularly in the females, slightly to moderately inclined upwards. Inclination downward (infrequent) is about twice as frequent in the males as in the females.

Measurements: The height of the nose shows a normal range of variation of about the same extent in the two sexes, and normal regular dispersion.

As to breadth the variability is somewhat greater in the males than in the females. The range is fairly moderate, the dispersion quite regular except in a few minor details.

The nasal index varies considerably (nearly 38 points) in the males; less so (28 points) in the females. Its dispersion is much like that of nose breadth, showing slight irregularities in some details.

Influence of age: Both nasal length and nasal breadth increase during adult life with age; but the increase in length exceeds somewhat that in breadth; as a result of which the nasal index also augments moderately as age advances.

Effects of stature: Stature also affects both nasal dimensions as well as the nasal index. Its influence on the nasal measurements is indirect, through its effect on the size of the head and face and it affects particularly the height of the nose; the breadth, particularly in the females, increasing only where there is a substantial increase in the breadth of the face.

The nasal index decreases with rise in stature due to the above conditions.

Nose and face: Nasal height correlates directly, closely and nearly evenly in the two sexes with the anatomical height of the face.

Nasal breadth correlates with the facial breadth, but the relations are less close than those between nasal and facial height.

Influence of form of head: Head form has but slight and indirect, if any, effect on the height of the nose. It has also but little effect on the breadth of the nose and practically none on the nasal index.

Group differences: The nasal dimensions and indices are not identical in the three groups of Old American males; but a study of the differences shows them to be of functional and particularly age rather than racial nature.

Age: For the same class the age influence in the Old Americans is in all probability substantially the same at all periods.

Comparative: Absolutely the nose of the Old Americans is rather high, with moderate breadth.

Relatively to stature, facial dimensions and age, the nasal height in the Old Americans is near the medium of whites in general.

The nasal breadth, fair on the average, is in the Old Americans slightly sub-medium as compared to European immigrants.

The Old Americans' nose is therefore comparatively somewhat high and somewhat narrow, as a result of which the nasal index is slightly below the average of the Europeans in general.

THE SUB-NASAL PORTION OF THE FACE

Prognathism. The face of the Old Americans as a whole is markedly orthognathic. There are, however, a small proportion of males and nearly the same of females in whom the upper alveolar process shows a moderate slant. In the Laboratory series this process in general was marked by its rather subdued proportions. With this alveolar process go medium to sub-medium teeth of frequently rather poor resistance.

Lips. The lips in slightly over nine-tenths of the cases give the impression of being medium or slightly sub-medium; in about one in thirteen in both males and females they are thin; while in a proportion which coincides almost exactly with slight alveolar prognathism the lips were found slightly to markedly above medium. There is no question but that protrusion on the one hand and absorption of the upper alveolar process on

TABLE 195
Old Americans: Alveolar prognathism
Laboratory series

	MALES	FEMALES
	per cent	*per cent*
None..	92.0	93.3
Slight to moderate......................................	8.0	6.7
Marked..	0	0

TABLE 196
Old Americans: Lips
Laboratory series

	MALES	FEMALES
	per cent	*per cent*
Thin...	0.7	0.7
Medium or nearly so.....................................	90.7	92.7
Slightly to moderately above medium.....................	8.6	6.6
Thick..	0	0

the other has a direct connection with the apparent thickness and protrusion of the lips. Lips that could at all be called "thick" have not been observed in the group and are excessively rare in Old Americans in general.

The mouth

Measurements on the mouth were taken only in the Laboratory series, which, however, is sufficiently large to give satisfactory results. The only measurement that is practicable is that of the width; it is the diameter between the most distal points in the corners of the mouth at which the mucous membrane of the orifice joins the skin.   In some cases the distal parts of the upper lip must be slightly pushed up by the observer to get at these points but otherwise there is no difficulty.   The mouth, it is self understood, is to be kept wholly at rest.   The main results of the measurements are given in table 197.

These figures are very interesting.   The actual dimensions are, as will be seen later, rather less than medium for white people.   But they agree more than any other measurement so far considered in their relation to the size (mean diameter) of the face, and both show practically identical sex relation as does the stature, which strongly suggests a close correlation of the three dimensions.   The mouth of the female is not only absolutely but also a trace relatively smaller than that of the males.

TABLE 197

Old Americans: Mouth width

Laboratory series

	OLD AMERICANS				COMPARATIVE*			Female *vs.* male (M = 100)*		
	Average	Percental relation to size of face (facial module)	Per mille relation to stature		Average	Percental relation to size of face (facial module)	Per mille relation to stature	Mouth	Face (facial module)	Stature
Males (247)	5.37	41.5	30.7	Females (210)	4.97	41.3	30.8	92.3	93.0	92.8

* Laboratory series.

The tables of frequencies and the curves of distribution of the measurement (tables 198 and 199 and figure 32) show fairly large individual variation, much alike in extent in the two sexes, with a regularity of dispersion.

Mouth vs. age.   Taking the mouth width in the youngest and the oldest of the Old Americans, there appears in both sexes a rather marked difference in favor of age.   Evidently the mouth, like the nose and other facial parts, grows with age, and the age factor, usually neglected, may account for a good many of the apparent group differences in the feature that have been recorded in anthropological literature.   In the males the difference within the moderate age range of our series is near 9 per cent, in the females as much as 11 per cent, and that notwithstanding the fact that the stature, with which the size of the mouth stands in direct correlation, is higher in the young than in the old groups.   In the young adults, especially in the females, the mouth is therefore both absolutely and relatively to stature smaller than it is later in life, showing that the mouth grows during adult life independently of stature.

Mouth and stature. A comparison of the mouth in the shortest and tallest groups of individuals of our series with the average shows a steady

TABLE 198

Old Americans, males: Width of the mouth

Number of individuals measured: 247

General average: 5.37 cm.

1st series of 50—5.36 cm.	4th series of 50—5.42 cm.
2nd series of 50—5.32 cm.	5th series of 50—5.41 cm.
3rd series of 47—5.36 cm.	

Minimum: 4.5 cm.   Maximum: 6.6 cm.

	TABLE OF FREQUENCIES											
	4.4-4.5 cm.	4.6-4.7 cm.	4.8-4.9 cm.	5.0-5.1 cm.	5.2-5.3 cm.	5.4-5.5 cm.	5.6-5.7 cm.	5.8-5.9 cm.	6.0-6.1 cm.	6.2-6.3 cm.	6.4-6.5 cm.	6.6-6.7 cm.
Number of cases..........	3	4	22	38	40	64	40	18	10	6	1	1
Per cent..................	1.2	1.6	8.9	15.3	16.2	25.8	16.2	7.3	4.0	2.4	0.4	0.4

TABLE 199

Old Americans, females: Width of mouth

Number of observations: 210

Average: 4.95 cm. (1st 50—4.87; 2nd 50—5.0; 3rd 50—4.9; 4th 60—5.02 cm.)

Minimum: 3.9 cm.   Maximum 5.9 cm.

	TABLE OF FREQUENCIES										
	3.8-3.9 cm.	4.0-4.1 cm.	4.2-4.3 cm.	4.4-4.5 cm.	4.6-4.7 cm.	4.8-4.9 cm.	5.0-5.1 cm.	5.2-5.3 cm.	5.4-5.5 cm.	5.6-5.7 cm.	5.8-5.9 cm.
Number of cases..............	1	0	8	20	32	45	42	31	19	10	2
Per cent......................	0.5		3.8	9.5	15.2	21.4	20.0	14.8	9.0	4.8	0.95

increase in the mouth width as stature advances.   Stature has, therefore, a positive influence upon the size of the mouth.   But as stature rises the augmentation in the width of the mouth progresses at a diminishing rate, in consequence of which the mouth-stature ratio is the highest in the shortest and lowest in the tallest individuals.   The mouth, therefore, while absolutely broader in the tall than in the short of both sexes, relatively to stature is larger in the shorter individuals.

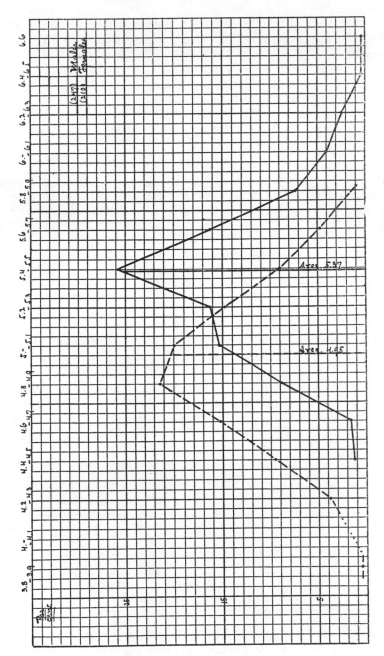

FIG. 32. OLD AMERICANS: WIDTH OF THE MOUTH—LABORATORY SERIES

The correlation of mouth-width with stature in the Laboratory group may also be seen from table 202. The progression is especially nice in the females.

TABLE 200

Width of mouth vs. age

Laboratory series

	MALES		FEMALES		OLD vs. YOUNG (Old = 100)	
	In 25 youngest	In 25 oldest	In 20 youngest	In 20 oldest	Males	Females
Mouth width...............	5.22	5.73	4.63	5.2	*91.1*	*89.0*
Corresponding stature........	176.3	174.5	164.5	159.3		
Mouth width *vs.* stature......	*29.6*	*32.8*	*28.1*	*32.7*		

TABLE 201

Old Americans: The width of the mouth and stature

Laboratory series

		MALES					FEMALES (210)			
		Age	Stature	Mouth	Ratio (S = 1000)		Age	Stature	Mouth	Ratio (S = 1000)
		years					*years*			
Shortest......	(25)	33.3	164.4	5.31	*32.3*	(20)	39.4	151.3	4.94	*32.6*
Average......		42.5	174.4	5.37	*30.7*		41.0	161.8	4.97	*30.8*
Tallest.......	(25)	37.1	184.4	5.45	*29.6*	(20)	33.0	172.2	5.07	*29.4*

TABLE 202

Old Americans: Width of mouth vs. stature

Laboratory series

MALES (247)				FEMALES (210)			
150.01–160.0	160.01–170.0	170.01–180.0	180.01–190.0	145.0–150.0	150.01–160.0	160.01–170.0	170.01–180.0
(2)	(61)	(147)	(37)	(3)	(72)	(115)	(20)
5.20	5.35	5.40	5.40	4.83	4.92	4.96	5.07

The effect of stature on the size of the mouth is naturally not direct, the direct correlation of the mouth being with the size of the face, which in turn is influenced directly by stature. That this is so will be well seen from table 203, in which the breadth of the mouth is compared with the mean facial diameter.

That the correlation of the size of the mouth is primarily with the size of the face as a whole and not with the breadth of the face (which is considerably influenced by the breadth of the head) is shown in table 204.

At a given age, therefore, the relations of stature and the size of the mouth may be expressed as follows: The higher the stature the larger in

TABLE 203

Old Americans: Correlation of breadth of mouth with size of face
Laboratory series

	MALES				FEMALES			
		Facial module (morphologic)	Breadth of mouth	Ratio (F.M. = 100)		Facial module (morphologic)	Breadth of mouth	Ratio (F.M. = 100)
Shortest....................	(25)	12.51	5.31	*42.4*	(20)	11.92	4.94	*41.8*
Tallest....................	(25)	13.07	5.45	*41.7*	(20)	12.14	5.07	*41.9*

TABLE 204

Old Americans: Breadth of mouth vs. breadth of face
Laboratory series

	MALES				FEMALES			
		Breadth of face	Breadth of mouth	Ratio (B.F. = 100)		Breadth of face	Breadth of mouth	Ratio (B.F. = 100)
Narrowest faces............	(20)	13.01	5.22	*40.1*	(25)	12.27	4.82	*39.3*
Broadest faces............	(23)	14.78	5.72	*38.7*	(22)	13.73	5.14	*37.4*

general the face; and the larger the face as a whole the broader is the mouth, the relations between the two remaining much the same for different statures.

Mouth vs. head form. There is no *a priori* reason for expecting any relation between head form and the width of the mouth, and none appears from the data. What little differences there are, are due to differences in stature. (See table 205.)

Comparative. Regrettably no measurements of the mouth have been taken on our series of immigrants. The more important records in literature commence with those of Quetelet (Anthropométrie, 1870) on the Belgians. Measurements of the breadth of the mouth are given on both sexes and year by year up to adult life without, however, any comparisons or conclusions; but as the mean stature for the same groups is also recorded,

TABLE 205

Width of mouth vs. head form

	MALES		FEMALES		DOLICHO- vs. BRACHY-CEPHALIC (D = 100)	
	In 25 most dolicho-cephalic	In 25 most brachy-cephalic	In 20 most dolicho-cephalic	In 20 most brachy-cephalic	Males	Females
Mouth width...............	5.44	5.3	4.93	4.91	*102.6*	*100.4*
Corresponding stature........	174.5	172.6	161.6	161.2		
Mouth width *vs.* stature......	*31.2*	*30.7*	*30.5*	*30.5*		

TABLE 206

Breadth of mouth in Belgians (Quetelet)

AGE	MALES			FEMALES		
	Stature	Breadth of mouth	Mouth vs. stature*	Stature	Breadth of mouth	Mouth vs. stature*
years						
At birth	50.0	2.6	*52.0*	49.4	2.6	*52.0*
1	69.8	3.1	*45.0*	69.0	3.1	*45.0*
2	79.1	3.3	*42.0*	78.1	3.2	*42.0*
5	98.7	3.6	*36.0*	97.4	3.5	*36.0*
10	127.3	4.2	*33.0*	124.9	4.0	*32.0*
15	151.3	4.7	*31.0*	148.8	4.5	*30.0*
20	166.9	5.1	*31.0*	157.4	4.8	*31.0*
30	168.6	5.4	*32.0*	158.0	5.0	*32.0*

* Calculated from Quetelet's figures.

the relation of mouth breadth to stature is readily ascertained. An abstract of the data, given in table 206, shows that at birth the mouth is relatively broad; that its proportion to stature diminishes up to about puberty; and that afterwards up to the thirtieth year it remains constant or changes but little.

To the preceding may be added a few records collected by Rudolf Martin (table 207), and a valuable series of measurements secured by Pittard[53] in the Balkans (table 208).

TABLE 207

Breadth of mouth: Comparative data

GROUP	MALES	FEMALES	MALES *vs.* FEMALES	AUTHOR
Old Americans..........................	*5.37*	*4.97*	*92.3*	
White Russians...........................		4.70		Jakovenko
French...................................	5.30	4.70	88.7	Testut
Belgians*................................	5.40	5.0	92.6	
Germans (Baden)........................		4.72		Fischer
Polish Jews..............................	5.60	4.90	87.5	Elkind

* From Quetelet.

TABLE 208

Breadth of mouth in peoples of the Balkans

	(180) RUMANIANS	(74) JEWS	(68) GERMANS	(61) RUSSIANS	(76) ARMENIANS	(112) ALBANIANS	(48) KURDS	(125) GREEKS	(107) SERBIANS	(5) MONTENEGRINS	(200) BULGARS
Males........................	5.29	5.31	5.42	5.44	5.54	5.60	5.61	5.61	5.67	5.80	5.84
Females......................	4.82										5.25
Females *vs.* Males..............	91.1										89.9

TABLE 209

Mouth vs. stature (S. = 1000); comparative

	OLD AMERICANS	RUMANIANS	RUSSIANS	BELGIANS (QUETELET)	JEWS	GERMANS	KURDS	SERBS	ARMENIANS	ALBANIANS	MONTENEGRINS	GREEKS	BULGARS*
Males..............	30.7	31.0	31.4	32.0	32.1	32.2	32.9	33.2	33.3	33.4	33.6	33.6	35.0
Females...........	30.8	n.31.0		32.0									34.2

* All, except the Belgians, calculated from Pittard's data, from Dobrudja, Rumania.

The mouth of the Old Americans, in contrast with the other groups of whites, is seen to be of but moderate breadth and very nearly like that

[53] 4°, Genève-Paris, 1920.

of the Belgians. Among the fourteen male series available for comparison it is larger than that of but three, slightly to moderately smaller than that of the remaining eleven groups. In the available females the comparison is unsatisfactory, due to probable age differences.

A more correct estimate of the proportions of the mouth, however, in all the groups may be found by contrasting its breadth to stature (table 209).

The mouth in the Old Americans, already absolutely rather sub-medium, gives the lowest value in relation to stature of all the series, notwithstanding the fact that the Americans are of rather high mean age (males 42.5, females 41 years)[54] which has been seen to favor the size of the mouth. This showing may have some connection with the size of the dental arches which in higher civilized man tend to a reduction.

Summary. The face of the Old Americans in general is orthognathic, presenting but occasionally a slight to moderate alveolar protrusion. The lips are usually medium to sub-medium in thickness, seldom somewhat above medium. Thick lips are practically unknown. The sub-nasal height is most moderate in the Laboratory series, somewhat more marked in the Tennessee highlanders, most developed in the southern "Engineers."

The size of the mouth in the Old Americans is moderate for white people.

The sexual differences are practically the same as those in the size of the face and in stature.

Individual variation is fairly large but not excessive; dispersion quite regular.

Age has a well marked effect, the size of the mouth increasing as age advances within the adult life.

The size of the mouth stands in important though indirect correlation with stature; but the increase lags considerably behind that of the stature.

It correlates directly and with much uniformity with the size of the face (morphological).

In short individuals the mouth, though absolutely smaller, relatively to stature is larger than in tall persons.

The size of the mouth correlates only secondarily with the breadth of the face.

Head form has apparently no influence upon the proportions of the mouth.

[54] The age of the subjects in the other series is not known except in that of Quetelet, where it was 30 years.

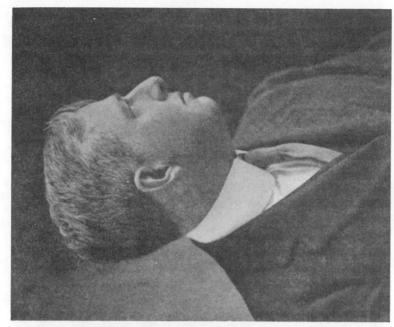

Dr. F. L. Stanton
(New York City)
Old American ancestry, both sides

Comparative: Contrasted with other groups of whites and that particularly in its ratio to stature, the mouth of the Old Americans of the Laboratory series appears to be decidedly moderate.

TABLE 210

Old Americans: Chin

Laboratory series

PROMINENCE	Males	Females	FORM	Males	Females
	per cent	per cent		per cent	per cent
Submedium...........			Rounded..............	80.0	100.0
Medium..............	80.0	96.7	Square..............	19.3	
Above medium........	20.0	3.3	High................	0.7	

TABLE 211

Old Americans: Subnasal height

	MALES				FEMALES
	All (610)	Laboratory (247)	Southern "Engineers" (347)	Tennessee Highlanders (16)	All (210)
Stature................................	174.30	174.44	174.26	173.65	161.84
Facial height to nasion....................	12.12	11.93	12.375	11.81	11.092
Nasal height............................	5.38	5.35	5.40	5.24	4.95
Subnasal height........................	6.74	6.58	6.975	6.57	6.14
Ratio: Subnasal height—facial height.......	*55.61*	*55.24*	*56.36*	*55.63*	*55.37*
Ratio: Subnasal height—stature...........	*3.87*	*3.77*	*4.0*	*3.78*	*3.79*
Mean diameter of head..................	16.33	16.40	16.37	16.07	15.58
Ratio: Subnasal height—mean head diameter................................	*41.27*	*40.12*	*42.61*	*40.88*	*39.41*

The chin

The chin as a rule is of medium, and, in the males, rather above medium prominence (protrusion forward). In no case regarded .in detail could it be described as even sub-medium. In all the females and four-fifths of the males it was found to be rounded while in one-fifth of the males it was square.

Sub-nasal height

The sub-nasal height is essentially the height of the jaws or that part of the face concerned with mastication. It has a widely different function from that of the nasal part and is subject to radically different influences. It is the active mechanical portion of the face and should reflect the demands made upon it in a given group as well as in the individual.

That it does so is shown quite conclusively by its measurements in the Old Americans. Taking our several groups (table 211) we see this portion least developed among the males of the Laboratory series, next in those of the Tennessee highlanders and most in the southern "Engineers." The females agree quite closely with the Laboratory males.

The relative values of the lower facial portion are especially well shown when we contrast this with the size of the head. In this case the females appear in their true position, their sub-nasal height ratio falling even below that of the Laboratory males. The odd condition of the southern mechanics who show decidedly the strongest jaws, and that of the Tennessee highlanders who remain intermediate between the Laboratory group and the "Engineers," is well seen also in this comparison.

Influence of age. The group of the youngest males shows apparently more developed lower jaws than the group of the old. However the differences here are difficult to gauge exactly on account of the wear and loss of teeth in the old. It is nevertheless quite probable that within the Laboratory series the youngest adults were on the whole somewhat more athletic and vigorous than the old. In the females the lower facial portion appears also somewhat stronger both absolutely and relatively to facial height in the young, but relatively to stature conditions are about equal. At all events it is plain that within the age limits of our groups no further devolutionary weakening of the sub-nasal portion of the face is perceptible.

Effects of stature. Absolutely the taller have a larger sub-nasal region than the short. Relatively to facial height there is but little difference in the proportion whatever the stature. But relatively to stature the jaws are larger in the short than in the tall persons. These facts mean that the lower facial height correlates closely with the total facial height and but secondarily with stature.

Influence of head form. The effect of head form on the sub-nasal height of the face appears to be very slight if any, whether we consider the facial dimensions or the ratios.

Influence of nasal height. It remains to be asked what effect on the height of the jaws is exercised by the height of the nose or, in other words, what correlation exists between the maxillary and nasal subdivisions of

TABLE 212

Old Americans: Relation of subnasal height to age, stature and head form

Laboratory series

		MALES					FEMALES			
					Percental relations of subnasal height to					Percental relations of subnasal facial height to
	Age	Stature	Subnasal height	Facial height (menton-nasion)	Stature	Age	Stature	Subnasal height	Facial height (menton-nasion)	Stature
Youngest..........	(25) 24.2	173.78	6.37	54.91	3.67	(20) 23.0	164.52	6.15	55.66	3.74
Oldest.............	(25) 59.5	174.63	6.0	52.08	3.43	(20) 57.2	159.27	6.02	54.28	3.78
Shortest...........	(25) 33.3	164.38	6.24	54.59	3.80	(20) 39.4	151.32	5.93	54.81	3.92
Tallest.............	(25) 37.1	184.40	6.63	54.61	3.60	(20) 32.6	122.20	6.09	54.62	3.54
Most dolicho-cephalic..........	(25) 41.8	176.07	6.42	54.48	3.64	(15) 34.7	161.57	6.14	55.62	3.80
Most brachy-cephalic..........	(25) 33.3	173.43	6.35	54.39	3.66	(20) 31.9	161.18	6.25	56.0	3.88

TABLE 213

Old Americans: Nasal and sub-nasal height in those with shortest and those with longest noses

Laboratory series

		MALES				FEMALES		
		Height of nose	Height of subnasal part	Ratio of nasal to subnasal height (Sbn. H = 100)		Height of nose	Height of subnasal part	Ratio of nasal to subnasal height (Sbn. H = 100)
Lowest nasal height..............	(20)	4.71	6.37	73.96	(20)	4.40	6.10	72.15
Highest nasal height............	(20)	5.90	6.61	89.33	(15)	5.54	6.07	91.22
Per cent of difference............		20.2	3.6	17.2		20.6	−0.5	20.9

the face. The data bearing most closely on this question are given in table 213.

By taking the groups with the smallest and the greatest nasal height, it is found that the sub-nasal height of the face does not follow at all (females) or follows but slightly (males) that of the nasal part of the face. In females with the greatest nasal height the subnasal height is actually absolutely a trace smaller than in those with the shortest noses. The conditions are nicely expressed also by the ratio or index of the nasal to subnasal height. In those with the shortest noses the ratio is very much smaller than in those with the longest, indicating that the nasal height enlarges quite independently, or very nearly so, of the sub-nasal proportions.

The two portions of the lower face, the nasal and maxillary, are two different physiological entities and probably the only correlation that exists between them is that the upper portion follows the lower in strength or weakness.

The subject affords excellent opportunity for further studies.

TABLE 214

Old Americans: Subnasal height vs. bigonial breadth

Laboratory series

MALES						FEMALES					
20 greatest subnasal height			20 lowest subnasal height			20 greatest subnasal height			20 lowest subnasal height		
Sub-nasal height	Bi-gonial breadth	Ratio	Sub-nasal height	Bi-gonial breadth	Ratio	Sub-nasal height	Bi-gonial breadth	Ratio	Sub-nasal height	Bi-gonial breadth	Ratio
7.64	10.75	71.10	5.57	10.59	52.62	6.98	10.0	69.80	5.32	9.74	54.60

Correlation of sub-nasal height with the bigonial breadth of the lower jaw. The sub-nasal height consists of the height of the upper jaw, the teeth and the lower jaw; and reasoning in advance it would seem plausible to expect that whatever affects the development of the lower jaw should be reflected in the sub-nasal proportions. Probably it is. It can hardly be conceived that, in general, a powerfully developed jaw should not be above or one developed weakly below the average in height. But on the living there is no direct means of gaging these facts. As will be seen below it can not be shown by comparing the sub-nasal height with the bigonial breadth of the lower jaw, for this, while influenced by the general development of the bone, correlates also with the breadth of the face and head and is subject to other agencies. As a result when we compare the sub-nasal height with the bigonial diameter there is found but little correspondence. Taking from our Laboratory series 20 males as well as females in whom the sub-nasal height is greatest and equal numbers of those in whom it is smallest, and contrasting all with the corresponding bigonial breadth, it is found that the latter, while larger in the groups with high jaws and *vice versa*, shows on the whole but a limited correlation with the sub-nasal height. (See table 214.)

Comparative. The available records for comparison are those on recent white immigrants to the United States. The principal data are given in table 215. They show that so far as sub-nasal height is concerned the Old Americans differ considerably according to group, the part being less

TABLE 215

Sub-nasal height in Old Americans and immigrants

Males

GROUP*	SUB-NASAL HEIGHT	SIZE OF HEAD (CEPHALIC MODULE)	SUB-NASAL HEIGHT-CEPHALIC MODULE RATIO	LOWER FACIAL HEIGHT (MENTON-NASION)	SUB-NASAL HEIGHT-LOWER FACIAL HEIGHT RATIO	STATURE	SUB-NASAL HEIGHT-STATURE RATIO
Old Americans:							
Laboratory............	6.58	16.40	40.12	11.93	55.24	174.44	3.77
Southern "Engineers"..	6.98	16.37	42.16	12.38	56.36	174.26	4.00
Russian Jews..............	6.39	15.90	40.1	11.67	54.8	164.6	3.89
Greeks....................	6.39	15.87	40.3	11.52	55.4	168.3	3.80
Croatians.................	6.49	15.98	40.6	11.60	56.0	171.6	3.73
Rumanians................	6.49	15.93	40.7	11.51	56.9	168.7	3.85
North Italians............	6.57	16.05	40.9	11.68	56.3	169.6	3.87
Southern Italians..........	6.54	15.93	41.05	11.56	56.5	163.4	4.00
Hungarians................	6.49	15.80	41.1	11.47	56.6	166.5	3.90
Russians..................	6.71	15.93	42.1	11.66	57.5	169.8	3.95
Poles.....................	6.76	16.03	42.2	11.79	57.3	170.4	3.97
English...................	6.79	16.07	42.25	12.19	55.7	170.2	3.99
Armenians.................	6.72	15.77	42.61	12.02	55.9	167.4	4.01
Irish.....................	6.90	16.18	42.65	12.09	57.1	171.6	4.02

* Arranged in order of value of subnasal height—cephalic module ratio.

developed in the Laboratory series, most developed in the southern "Engineers." As a result there is obtained quite a different picture when the immigrants are compared with the former or the latter group of the Americans.

Taking the Old Americans of the Laboratory series, men of clerical, professional and business occupations, it is seen that while absolutely their sub-nasal height would compare with about the average of the immigrants, relatively to the size of the head, height of the face as well as stature it is exceeded by practically all the immigrant groups. In this class of the Old Americans, therefore, the sub-nasal height may be characterized as decidedly reduced.

But if we take the southern "Engineers" for comparison it will be noted that in the development of the sub-nasal portion of the face they exceed most of the immigrants, being surpassed in all the ratios only by the Irish who show the largest development of the sub-nasal parts of all the groups available for comparison.

Of the three ratios by which the relative height of the sub-nasal portion of the face is expressed, the best is perhaps that in which the dimension is compared with the mean diameter of the head, closely followed in value by the ratio which gives us the relation of the lower to total (anatomic) facial height. The ratio to stature, while also useful, gives less satisfactory results, the part correlating more closely with the size of the face and size of the head.

The data here given show the powerful influence even within the same people of function upon the development of the lower jaws. It is quite possible that the southern mechanics have had in their ancestry a large proportion of the "Scotch-Irish" who, if we can judge from the showing of the Irish among our recent immigrants, may have carried and transmitted to their progeny strongly developed jaws; but in the end the cause of the differences in the development of the jaws between the Laboratory and the southern group must rest on a functional basis.

Summary. In the relative development of the sub-nasal portion of the face, the females agree closely with the Laboratory males.

Within the age limits of the groups considered, the influence of age is negative. The youngest of both sexes show actually a slight superiority over the old.

Stature has a positive though probably indirect influence on the height of the sub-nasal portion of the face; but relatively to stature the jaws are larger in the short than in the tall persons.

The height of the jaws is affected but slightly if at all by the form of the head.

The sub-nasal height is influenced but slightly, if at all, by the height of the nasal portion of the face.

The correlation of the sub-nasal height with the bigonial breadth of the lower jaw is limited, the latter being largely influenced by other factors.

On comparison the male Old Americans of the Laboratory series are observed to stand, in sub-nasal height, at the base of the whites available for comparison. On the other hand the southern "Engineers" compare well in this respect with recent immigrants in whom the sub-nasal height is most developed.

The lower facial breadth: Diameter bigonial

The lower facial breadth is the breadth at the maximum external separation of the angles of the lower jaw. It is a feature largely connected with the development of the masseter muscles, or in other words, the use of the lower jaw in mastication, and as such is primarily of physiological rather than morphological value. In general in any people these angles are more subdued in the higher than in the lower classes.

Visual observations. In the Laboratory series of the Old Americans, detailed notes on the angles of the lower jaw show that in one-third of the males and two-fifths of the females the angles ranged from "sub-medium" (as compared with ordinary whites) to "decidedly sub-developed." A record of this nature together with the already discussed subaverage showing of the malars and supraorbital ridges, could probably not be equalled in any comparable group of the more recent American population. Bulging angles, such as not infrequently seen among male immigrants, were wholly absent. The whole lower as well as upper jaw in the Old American stock, such as represented by the Laboratory series, is of moderate proportions. An abstract of the records is given in table 216.

The bigonial diameter. The bigonial diameter is the breadth between the points of maximum separation of the angles of the lower jaw.[55] In the Laboratory series it gave the values shown in tables 217 and 218.

These tables and figure 33 show substantial differences in the range of variation and mode of distribution of the lower facial breadth in the two sexes. In the females the range is moderate, the dispersion regular; in the males the range is considerably larger and the dispersion of the measurement is peculiar. Evidently both the feature itself and the causes underlying its variation are considerably more uniform in the females of our series than in the males.

Differences of sex. Compared *in toto* to stature the bigonial breadth gives but a very slightly higher value in the males than in the females; but this showing is deceptive. It is not due, as will be shown later, to close correlation between the two dimensions, but involves other factors.

Comparing the bigonial breadth in the two sexes to breadth and size of face as well as the size of head, it will be seen (see table 219) that in

[55] It is taken with the points of the *compas d'épaisseur* applied to the bone.

TABLE 216

Old Americans: Prominence of angles of lower jaw

Laboratory series

	MALES	FEMALES
	per cent	*per cent*
Very subdued..	3.3	2.7
Sub-medium...	26.0	36.0
Medium...	57.3	59.3
Slightly to moderately above medium....................	12.7	2.0
Prominent...	0.7	

TABLE 217

Old Americans, males, face: Diameter bigonial

Number of observations: 247

General average: 10.63 cm.

1st series of 50—10.66 cm.   4th series of 50—10.60 cm.

2nd series of 50—10.74 cm.   5th series of 50—10.55 cm.

3rd series of 47—10.61 cm.

Minimum: 9.0 cm. Maximum: 12.6 cm.

TABLE OF FREQUENCIES

	8.9-9.0 cm.	9.1-9.2 cm.	9.3-9.4 cm.	9.5-9.6 cm.	9.7-9.8 cm.	9.9-10.0 cm.	10.1-10.2 cm.	10.3-10.4 cm.	10.5-10.6 cm.	10.7-10.8 cm.	10.9-11.0 cm.	11.1-11.2 cm.	11.3-11.4 cm.	11.5-11.6 cm.	11.7-11.8 cm.	11.9-12.0 cm.	12.1-12.2 cm.	12.3-12.4 cm.	12.5-12.6 cm.
Number of cases..	1	1	1	8	11	24	23	35	19	35	36	16	17	10	5	4	0	0	1
Per cent..	0.4	0.4	0.4	3.2	4.4	9.7	9.3	14.1	7.6	14.1	14.5	6.4	6.8	4.0	2.0	1.6			0.4

TABLE 218

Old Americans, females: Face, diameter bigonial

Number of observations: 210

Average: 9.84 cm. (1st 50—9.86; 2nd 50—9.89; 3rd 50—9.89; 4th 60—9.73 cm.)

Minimum: 8.5 cm. Maximum: 11.3 cm.

TABLE OF FREQUENCIES

	8.5-8.6 cm.	8.7-8.8 cm.	8.9-9.0 cm.	9.1-9.2 cm.	9.3-9.4 cm.	9.5-9.6 cm.	9.7-9.8 cm.	9.9-10.0 cm.	10.1-10.2 cm.	10.3-10.4 cm.	10.5-10.6 cm.	10.7-10.8 cm.	10.9-11.0 cm.	11.1-11.2 cm.	11.3-11.4 cm.
No. of cases..	1	1	6	10	22	32	40	34	30	18	10	4	1	0	1
Per cent......	0.48	0.48	2.86	4.76	10.5	15.2	19.05	16.2	14.3	8.6	4.76	1.9	0.48		0.48

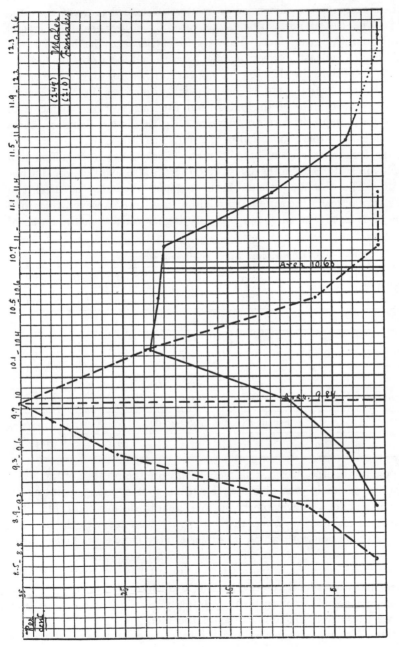

FIG. 33. OLD AMERICANS: DIAMETER BIGONIAL—LABORATORY SERIES

all these respects the dimension is relatively somewhat greater in the males. The closest correlation is indicated here between the bigonial breadth and the mean facial diameter; next between the bigonial and facial breadth and last between bigonial breadth and the size of the head.

Age. Conditions in this respect appear further to differ in the two sexes. In the males there is but a slight difference in the absolute measurements in favor of the oldest; but the ratios of the diameter to stature and breadth of face are identical. In the males, therefore, there is no evidence in this connection of the influence of age.

In the females conditions are different. The youngest set differs considerably in statures from the oldest, and there is also slightly more brachycephaly. The absolute values of the bigonial diameter in these two groups is practically the same. In relation to stature, however, the group of the more aged women shows a plainly higher ratio than the group of

TABLE 219

Old Americans: Diameter bigonial maximum

NUMBER OF SUBJECTS	AVERAGE	PERCENTAL RELATION TO STATURE	RELATION TO BREADTH OF FACE	RELATION TO SIZE OF FACE (FACIAL MODULE MORPHOLOGIC)	RELATION TO SIZE OF HEAD (CEPHALIC MODULE)
Males					
(247)	*cm.* 10.63	6.09	76.7	82.1	64.8
Females					
(210)	9.84	6.08	75.8	81.7	63.2
Female *vs.* male (male = 100)					
	92.6		98.8	99.5	97.5

of the young; in other words, relatively to stature the breadth of the lower jaw at its angles is greater in the old than in the young, pointing to a certain amount of development in this breadth during adult life. On the other hand, when we compare the bigonial diameter with the breadth of face, a dimension with which it correlates very closely, we find a slight excess in the ratio in favor of the young, which however merely indicates that the face (diameter bizygomatic maximum) has also increased with age and that even slightly more than the breadth of the lower jaw. That such an increase in absolute breadth actually takes place has been seen when we considered the proportions of the face.

Stature. Taking the shortest and the tallest groups of our Laboratory

TABLE 220

Old Americans: Diameter bigonial and age, stature and head form

Laboratory series

		MALES							FEMALES					
		Age	Stature	Cephalic index	Diameter bigonial	Diameter bigonial ratio of stature	Breadth of face	Diameter bigonial-face breadth ratio	Age	Stature	Cephalic index	Diameter bigonial	Diameter bigonial ratio of stature	Breadth or face	Diameter bigonial-face breadth ratio
		years							*years*						
Diameter bigonial and age															
Youngest	(25)	24.2	173.8	77.6	10.52	6.05	13.76	76.56 (20)	23.0	164.5	80.3	9.88	6.00	12.96	76.23
Oldest	(25)	59.5	174.6	77.4	10.58	6.06	13.82	76.53 (20)	57.2	159.3	79.5	9.89	6.21	13.05	75.82
Diameter bigonial and stature															
Shortest	(25)	33.3	164.4	78.7	10.35	6.30	13.58	76.20 (20)	39.4	151.3	80.6	9.73	6.43	12.79	76.08
Tallest	(25)	37.1	184.4	77.9	10.70	5.80	13.99	76.47 (20)	32.6	172.2	79.2	10.04	5.83	13.03	77.09
Diameter bigonial and head form															
Most dolichocephalic	(25)	41.8	176.1	73.2	10.53	5.98	13.58	77.53 (15)	34.7	161.6	74.0	9.58	5.93	12.70	75.43
Most brachycephalic	(25)	33.3	173.4	84.6	10.64	6.13	14.02	75.86 (20)	31.9	161.2	84.7	9.97	6.19	13.34	74.74

series of subjects, groups which do not differ materially so far as mean age and mean cephalic index are concerned, it is seen that the absolute measurement is quite appreciably larger in the tall; but relatively to stature the tall have decidedly narrower jaws than the short. This means that the breadth of the lower jaw does not correlate appreciably with stature.

When on the other hand we compare the bigonial diameter with the breadth of the face, we find a very close correlation between the two with

TABLE 221

Old Americans: Diameter bigonial—progression with stature

	145.0–150.0	150.01–160.0	160.01–170.0	170.01–180.0	180.01–190.0	GENERAL AVERAGE
Males................................		(2) 10.0	(61) 10.47	(147) 10.71	(37) 10.63	(249) *10.63*
Females.............................	(3) 9.73	(72) 9.75	(115) 9.87	(20) 10.01		(210) *9.84*
Females vs. Males:......................		*97.5*	*94.3*	*93.5*		*92.6*
Percental relation to true mean stature of each group:						
Males..............................		*6.41*	*6.25*	*6.11*	*5.80*	*6.09*
Females...........................	*6.58*	*6.24*	*6.01*	*5.81*		*6.08*
Difference in favor of males..............		*0.17*	*0.24*	*0.30*		

a slight excess for the bigonial breadth in both of the tallest groups. This indicates that the muscles of mastication and hence the breadth of the lower jaw at its angles are, relatively to facial breadth, slightly more developed in the tall than in the short, which on the whole is quite natural. Further light on the subject will be given by the data in table 221.

This table shows plainly that like all the other diameters of the head as well as face, the bigonial breadth increases progressively in both sexes with stature; but from the lowest figures it is plain that the increase of this lower breadth of the face lags in both sexes quite perceptibly behind the increase in stature so that in the shortest individuals, both males and females, the bigonial breadth while absolutely smaller is relatively to stature larger than it is in the taller persons.

The correlation therefore between stature and the lower facial breadth is a weak one.

If we compare the bigonial diameter-stature ratio in the two sexes when obtained with the true mean stature of each of the stature subdivisions, it appears that in each group the lower jaw relatively to stature is quite perceptibly narrower in the females, and furthermore that the difference appears to show a regular increase as the stature rises, so that in the tall the male bigonial breadth is higher above that of the female than in the short individuals: in other words, as stature increases the bigonial breadth lags behind it in the females more than in the males. The tall men have both absolutely and relatively to stature stronger muscles of mastication than equally tall women.

Influence of head form. The brachycephals, as compared to dolichocephals, have a broader head as well as a broader face, and might therefore *a priori* be expected, everything else being equal, to show also broader jaws. This as a matter of fact seems to be the case to some extent, the brachycephalic Old Americans showing both absolutely and relatively to stature somewhat higher values than the dolichocephals.

But when we examine the relation of the bigonial diameter to the breadth of the face, we find that in both sexes the lower jaw is relatively somewhat broader in the dolichocephals. This difference is more marked in the males than in the females and may in the males be largely connected with the factor of higher stature in the dolichocephals.

What may be said in conclusion is that, due to physiological and anatomical reasons (use and development of the muscles of mastication), the breadth of the angles of the lower jaw correlates most closely with the size and the bizygomatic breadth of the face; that age has no appreciable effect on the dimension; that while increasing with stature it does not increase proportionately nor equally in the two sexes; and that head form appears to influence this lower facial breadth only indirectly.

Comparative data on bigonial breadth in other groups of whites in the living are very scarce; there is little doubt however but that in the Old Americans this dimension with respect to their tall stature is a moderate one and probably below the average of whites in whom the muscles of mastication are strongly developed.

Summary. The breadth and prominence of the angles of the lower jaw in the Old Americans is generally more or less subdued.

The bigonial diameter, of moderate mean value, is more variable in the males than in the females.

Relatively to stature and dimensions of face and head the diameter shows some excess in the males.

The diameter correlates most closely with the mean diameter and breadth of the face.

Age within the adult period shows no effect in the males, but there appears in the present series a slight increase in the proportion with age in the females.

The breadth of the lower jaw does not correlate directly with stature.

In groups of the same stature the lower jaw is relatively narrower in the females and the difference increases as stature rises.

Head form influences the lower facial breadth only secondarily.

TABLE 222

Old Americans: Gonio-frontal index

$$\left(\frac{\text{Diameter bigonial} \times 100}{\text{Diameter frontal minimum}} \right)$$

Males

Laboratory series
Number of observations: 247
Average: 100.4: (1st 50—99.2; 2nd 50—101.2; 3rd 47—99.8; 4th 50—100.2;
5th 50—100.2)
Minimum: 77.9. Maximum: 112.1

	TABLE OF FREQUENCIES						
	112.1–110.1	110.0–105.1	105.0–100.1	100.0–95.1	95.0–90.1	90.0–85.1	85.0–84.0
Number of cases....	7	44	68	88	30	8	2
Per cent............	2.8	17.8	27.5	35.6	12.1	3.2	0.8

Females

Number of observations: 210
Average: 97.2: (1st 50—96.7; 2nd 50—97.3; 3rd 50—98.2; 4th 60—97.9)
Minimum: 81.2. Maximum: 109.3

	TABLE OF FREQUENCIES					
	110.0–105.1	105.0–100.1	100.0–95.1	95.0–90.1	90.0–85.1	85.0–81.2
Number of cases.............	13	39	95	44	17	2
Per cent....................	6.2	18.6	45.2	21.0	8.1	1.0

The gonio-frontal index

This is the percental relation between the bigonial diameter of the lower jaw and the diameter frontal minimum, the latter being taken as 100. This index is merely recorded because some efforts in this direction have been made by a few previous observers. It is of but little value, the two measurements having no direct relation with nor bearing one upon the other. It is, however, of physiognomic significance; the higher it is the narrower is the lower face in relation to the forehead, and *vice versa*. As will be seen from table 222 the index shows a considerable range of individual variation.

Summary. Of physiognomic value only. Quite variable. Shows a face of practically the same breadth above and below in the males, slightly narrower below in the females.

General remarks: Adiposity; Wrinkling

Real adiposity of the face (as well as that of the body) is rare in the Old Americans—it was not present in any of the cases examined. A slight to moderate superabundance of fat in face as well as in body is quite common in those above 45, particularly in the females, but that is not, strictly speaking, obesity.

As to *wrinkling*, there was no case which could be characterized as either premature or excessive; in fact the whole process in the Old Americans appears moderate.

THE EARS

The external ear, however, separate its origin and function, may well be regarded as a component part of the physiognomy, as an adjunct of the face; and it is a feature of considerable evolutionary, as well as racial, developmental and individually variational interest.

In the study of the Old Americans observations on the ear were restricted to the measurements of its maximum length and breadth[56] and the left ear alone was measured, as for a right-handed observer its measurements are easier than would be those of the right ear.

Earlier observations

The only former data on adult white American ears are those of Bean,[57] and relate to 86 ears of morgue subjects; but these ears were measured "after

[56] "The ear. Length maximum. Landmarks: Superiorly—the highest point on the border of the helix; inferiorly—the lowermost point on the lobule. The rod of the compass should be held parallel to the long axis of the ear with its branches tangent to the points indicated; use no pressure. . . . . Breadth. Distance between two lines parallel to the long axis of the ear, one of these lines being tangent to the anterior, the other to the posterior border of the helix." Hrdlička, Anthropometry, Wistar Institute, Philadelphia, 1920.

[57] Bean (Robert Bennett)—Some characteristics of the external ear of American Whites, American Indians, American Negroes, Alaskan Esquimos and Filipinos. Am. J. Anat., September, 1915, XVIII, No. 2.

having been preserved in formalin" for from a few weeks to several years, which disadvantage is coupled with that of a lack of data as to ancestry, stature and age. The results on 67 of these ears that were tabulated by Bean are shown in table 223.

The data agree, as will be seen, fairly closely with those on the Tennessee highlanders of our series, though the breadth is slightly greater and hence the index slightly higher. The right ear is appreciably longer as well as

TABLE 223

Ears of New Orleans morgue subjects (Bean)

	RIGHT			LEFT		
	Length	Breadth	Index	Length	Breadth	Index
67 ears, males*..............	6.49	3.76	*57.9*	6.32	3.68	*58.3*

* In nineteen other cases in which only the right ear was measured, the averages obtained were: Length—6.52; Breadth—3.86; Index—*59.2*.

TABLE 224

Old Americans, males: Height of left ear

Number of observations: 247

General average: 6.69 cm.

1st series of 50—6.57 cm.   4th series of 50—6.70 cm.

2nd series of 50—6.78 cm.   5th series of 50—6.66 cm.

3rd series of 47—6.71 cm.

Minimum: 5.5 cm.   Maximum: 7.8 cm.

	TABLE OF FREQUENCIES										
	5.5 cm.	5.55–5.75 cm.	5.8–6.0 cm.	6.05–6.25 cm.	6.3–6.5 cm.	6.55–6.75 cm.	6.8–7.0 cm.	7.05–7.25 cm.	7.3–7.5 cm.	7.55–7.75 cm.	7.8 cm.
Number of cases..............	2	1	11	25	68	29	57	28	17	4	5
Per cent.....................	*0.8*	*0.4*	*4.5*	*10.1*	*27.5*	*11.7*	*23.1*	*11.3*	*6.9*	*1.6*	*2.0*

slightly broader than the left, with a slightly lower index (due to greater length). Bean shows also that in the whites "the length and breadth of the ear increase with increase of stature, the length relatively more than the breadth, wherefore the physiognomic index of the ear decreases with increase of stature."

Old Americans

The principal data concerning the ear measurements and ear index are given in tables 224 to 229, and figures 34 and 35.

Dr. William T. Wilson
(New York)
Old American, both sides

From these it will be seen that the absolute measurements show but a fair range of individual variation and that this is much alike in the two sexes; but that the variation in the ear index, particularly in the males, is very extensive (males 27, females 20 points).

TABLE 225

Old Americans, females: Height of left ear

Number of observations: 210

General average: 6.1 cm.

1st series of 50—6.07 cm.   3rd series of 50—6.05 cm.

2nd series of 50—6.17 cm.   4th series of 60—6.11 cm.

Minimum: 5.05 cm.   Maximum: 7.25 cm.

	TABLE OF FREQUENCIES								
	5.05–5.25 cm.	5.3–5.5 cm.	5.55–5.75 cm.	5.8–6.0 cm.	6.05–6.25 cm.	6.3–6.5 cm.	6.55–6.75 cm.	6.8–7.0 cm.	7.05–7.25 cm.
Number of cases.....	1	13	32	48	45	43	15	10	3
Per cent.............	*0.5*	*6.2*	*15.2*	*22.9*	*21.4*	*20.5*	*7.1*	*4.8*	*1.4*

TABLE 226

Old Americans, males: Breadth of left ear

Number of observations: 247

General average: 3.79 cm.

1st series of 50—3.68 cm.   4th series of 50—3.82 cm.

2nd series of 50—3.82 cm.   5th series of 50—3.84 cm.

3rd series of 47—3.78 cm.

Minimum: 3.05 cm.   Maximum: 4.6 cm.

	TABLE OF FREQUENCIES															
	3.0–3.05 cm.	3.1–3.15 cm.	3.2–3.25 cm.	3.3–3.35 cm.	3.4–3.45 cm.	3.5–3.55 cm.	3.6–3.65 cm.	3.7–3.75 cm.	3.8–3.85 cm.	3.9–3.95 cm.	4.0–4.05 cm	4.1–4.15 cm.	4.2–4.25 cm.	4.3–4.35 cm.	4.4–4.45 cm.	4.5 cm. and Above
Number of cases....	1	1	1	4	12	18	38	34	41	36	23	18	11	4	4	1
Per cent..........	*0.4*	*0.4*	*0.4*	*1.6*	*4.9*	*7.3*	*15.4*	*13.8*	*16.6*	*14.6*	*9.3*	*7.3*	*4.5*	*1.6*	*1.6*	*0.4*

As to the dispersion of the measurements, which is seen at a glance in the curves, it is noticeable that while the females show considerable regularity, the males in both the height and breadth of the ear give two separate modes which can hardly be without significance though the nature of this may not be easily determined.

TABLE 227

Old Americans, females: Breadth of left ear

Number of observations: 210

Average: 3.47 cm. (1st 50—3.45; 2nd 50—3.49; 3rd 50—3.4; 4th 60—3.52 cm.)

Minimum: 2.9 cm.   Maximum: 4.2 cm.

	TABLE OF FREQUENCIES													
	2.9–2.95 cm.	3.0–3.05 cm.	3.1–3.15 cm.	3.2–3.25 cm.	3.3–3.35 cm.	3.4–3.45 cm.	3.5–3.55 cm.	3.6–3.65 cm.	3.7–3.75 cm.	3.8–3.85 cm.	3.9–3.95 cm.	4.0–4.05 cm.	4.1–4.15 cm.	4.2–4.25 cm.
Number of cases..........	3	7	7	12	32	42	32	27	26	13	6	2	0	1
Per cent.................	1.4	3.3	3.3	5.7	15.2	20.0	15.2	12.8	12.4	6.2	2.9	1.0		0.5

TABLE 228

Old Americans, males: Left ear index

Number of observations: 247

General average: 56.7

1st series of 50—56.09	4th series of 50—57.14
2nd series of 50—56.43	5th series of 50—57.84
3rd series of 47—56.67	

Minimum: 44.9.   Maximum: 71.5.

	TABLE OF FREQUENCIES									
	Up to 50.0	50.01–52.50	52.51–55.0	55.01–57.50	57.51–60.0	60.01–62.50	62.51–65.0	65.01–67.50	67.51–70.0	70.01 and over
No. of cases.............	7	19	49	72	61	26	11	0	0	2
Per cent.................	2.8	7.7	19.8	29.2	24.7	10.5	4.5			0.8

TABLE 229

Old Americans, females: Left ear index

Number of observations: 210

General average: 56.9

1st series of 50—56.07	3rd series of 50—56.65
2nd series of 50—56.67	4th series of 60—57.92

Minimum: 46.8.   Maximum: 66.7.

	TABLE OF FREQUENCIES								
	46.8–47.5	47.51–50.0	50.01–52.5	52.51–55.0	55.01–57.5	57.51–60.0	60.01–62.5	62.51–65.0	65.01 and over
No. of cases.........	1	6	15	48	50	52	20	10	8
Per cent.............	0.5	2.9	7.1	22.9	23.8	24.8	9.5	4.8	3.8

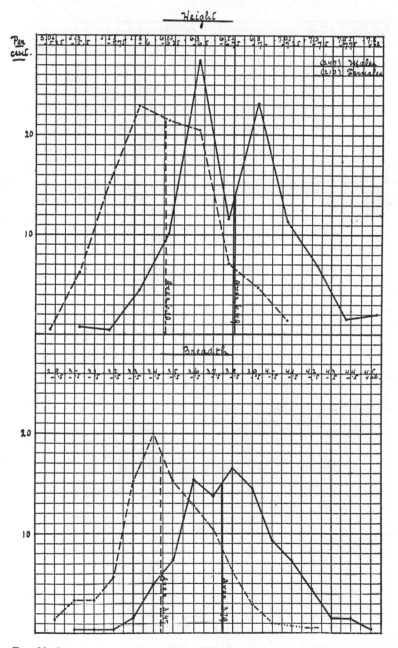

FIG. 34. OLD AMERICANS: DIAMETER OF EARS—LABORATORY SERIES—LEFT EAR

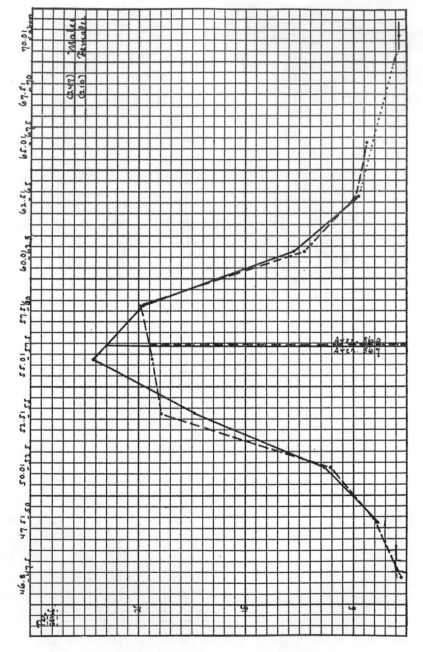

Fig. 35. Old Americans: Left Ear Index—Laboratory Series

In the ear index the irregularity of the measurements in the males has been entirely obscured while the female curve reflects the broad summit (or large aggregation about the average) seen in the curve of the female height of the ear.

A very remarkable condition shown by the curves of the absolute measurements of the index is that while the sex curves show an ample separation with both height and breadth of the ear, they overlap each other to a very large extent in the case of the index. The ear form as expressed by the average ear index is in fact almost identical in the two sexes, which is a unique condition in the whole series of measurements taken on the Old Americans.

Group variation

Outside of the Laboratory group the only other series of ear measurements that it was practicable to secure were those on 100 Tennessee highlanders. The average measurements and index obtained on these as compared with the Laboratory group are given in table 230.

TABLE 230

Old Americans: Dimensions and index of left ear in groups, males

	LEFT EAR			MEAN DIAMETER (EAR MODULE)	EAR LENGTH *vs.* STATURE (S = 10·0)	MEAN EAR DIAMETER *vs.* STATURE	MEAN AGE IN YEARS
	Length	Breadth	Index				
Laboratory................	6.69	3.79	56.7	5.240	33.4	30.0	42.5
Tennessee highlanders.......	6.42	3.65	56.9	5.035	36.8	28.9	25.1

These data show some features of considerable interest. While the ear index in the two groups is practically the same, the ear of the Tennessee highlander is very perceptibly smaller. This relative smallness of the ear in our mountaineers seemed at first hard to explain. The highlanders, as shown before, were seen to possess a somewhat smaller head than those of the Laboratory series and possibly the ears may stand in some correlation with this. But the essential difference between the Tennessee and the Laboratory series is in the age. The average age of the latter is 42.5 years, that of the former 25.1 years. The Laboratory subjects were men of all ages between 24 and 60; the highlanders were drafted young men presenting themselves for examination for the army and ranging from 23 to 33 years. The growth of the ear, as will be shown later, is not fully accomplished by the twenty-fifth year, progressing in fact slowly to late age. It is thus the factor of age which accounts for the difference in the size of the ears of the two series. The actual measurements of the ear in the youngest of the Laboratory series averages: length, 6.42; breadth, 3.61; mean diameter, 5.01; as compared with the highlanders': length, 6.42; breadth, 3.65; mean diameter, 5.03. The measurements are practically identical.

The effects of age

As in the case of the head, face and other parts of the body, the ear has not finished its growth by the time the adult stage of life is reached, but keeps on increasing slightly in dimensions up to old age. That a quite perceptible augmentation in the size of the ear takes place up to 60 is shown by table 231. Taking the group of the youngest and that of the oldest of

TABLE 231

Old Americans: The ear and age

Laboratory series

| | MALES | | | | | FEMALES | | | | |
| | | | Left ear | | | | | Left ear | | |
	Age	Stature	Height	Breadth	Index	Age	Stature	Height	Breadth	Index
Youngest..............	(25)	24.2	173.8	6.40	3.69	57.7	(20)	23.0	164.5	6.01	3.37	56.1
Per mille proportion of stature..............				36.8	21.2					36.5	20.5	
Oldest................	(25)	59.5	174.6	7.14	4.0	55.9	(20)	57.2	159.3	6.42	3.60	56.2
Per mille proportion of stature..............				40.9	22.9					40.3	22.6	

our series, it is seen that the oldest show an ear that is both higher and broader than that of the youngest adults. Moreover the data show plainly that the growth of the ear takes place independently of stature so that the ratios of ear measurements to stature are very appreciably higher in the older than in the younger. Still further the data show that there has been in the males a greater increase with age in the height of the ear than in its breadth, so that the ear height-stature ratio in this sex has undergone both absolute and relative augmentation; but in the females there is no such difference; the two measurements have increased in the same proportion and the index remains practically identical.

The facts relating to ear growth with age during the adult period will appear to further advantage in table 232, in which the ear dimensions and index are given by decades of age. These data are not affected, or affected but slightly by stature which, with the exception of one of the decades in the females, shows but slight differences; and both the length and the breadth of the ear are seen gradually to increase as age advances. Here again the ear index shows a tendency to decrease with age due to a somewhat greater relative augmentation in ear height than ear breadth; though a few irregularities are observed due undoubtedly to insufficient numbers in some of the categories.

TABLE 232

Old Americans: Ear dimensions and index by age

Laboratory series

	MALES					FEMALES				
	24–29 years	30–39 years	40–49 years	50–59 years	Above 59 years	22–29 years	30–39 years	40–49 years	50–59 years	Above 59 years
Ear:	(91)	(63)	(47)	(34)	(12)	(73)	(71)	(36)	(27)	
Length....	6.49	6.56	6.87	7.05	7.13	6.03	5.99*	6.23	6.40	
Breadth...	3.71	3.79	3.80	3.90	4.05	3.43	3.45	3.53	3.56	
Index.....	*57.2*	*57.8*	*55.3*	*55.3*	*56.8*	*56.9*	*57.6*	*56.7*	*55.6*	
Stature........	174.1	175.0	174.5	174.0	174.8	162.6	162.0	162.4	159.2	
Ear module (mean diameter)...	5.10	5.17	5.33	5.47	5.59	4.73	4.72	4.88	4.98	
Per mille ratio of ear module to stature......	*29.3*	*29.6*	*30.6*	*31.5*	*32.0*	*29.1*	*29.2*	*30.0*	*31.3*	

* A chance aggregation of low ears.

Influence of stature

Stature too has a material influence on the ear dimensions; the higher the stature the larger in the main will be the ear in both height and breadth. But the ratio of these measurements to stature shows that the increase in the ear dimensions as stature rises does not keep pace with the augmentation in the latter with the result that in the tallest of our series the ear-stature ratios are appreciably smaller than they are in the shortest individuals, and this difference is larger in the females than in the males.

It appears also that as stature rises the length of the ear increases at a slightly greater rate than the breadth, with the result that as we proceed from the shortest to the tallest the ear index diminishes. (See table 233.)

THE OLD AMERICANS

TABLE 233

Old Americans: The ear and stature
Laboratory series

	MALES						FEMALES				
			Left ear						Left ear		
	Age	Stature	Height	Breadth	Index		Age	Stature	Height	Breadth	Index
Shortest..........	(25)	33.3	164.4	6.46	3.69	57.2	(20)	39.4	151.3	5.99	3.38	56.5
Per mille proportion of stature....				39.3	22.4					39.6	22.3	
Tallest............	(25)	37.1	184.4	6.92	3.89	56.2	(20)	33.0	172.2	6.34	3.44	54.3
Per mille proportion of stature....				37.5	21.1					36.8	20.0	

Ear and head form

A possible correlation between the dimensions of the ear and the form of the head is an open question. If dolicho- and brachycephaly were fundamental racial characters and denoted true long segregated morphological types, then there might be a substantial difference; but if they represent mere and recurring variation of one type then the ears as well as other organs should, whatever the head form, be much alike. The actual conditions in our Laboratory series are shown in table 234.

TABLE 234

Ear dimensions vs. head form

	MEAN AGE	MEAN STATURE	MEAN CEPHALIC INDEX	LEFT EAR				EAR vs. STATURE (S = 1000)		
				Length	Breadth	Mean diameter	Index	Length	Breadth	Mean diameter
Males:										
25 most dolichocephalic...	34.6	174.5	73.2	6.68	3.87	5.275	57.93	38.3	22.2	30.2
25 most brachycephalic....	33.3	172.6	84.6	6.50	3.76	5.13	57.85	37.7	21.8	29.7
Females:										
15 most dolichocephalic...	34.7	161.57	74.0	6.02	3.58	4.80	59.50	37.3	22.15	29.7
20 most brachycephalic....	32.0	161.6	84.7	6.06	3.45	4.755	56.93	37.5	21.35	29.4

The differences that appear in these comparisons after the effects of stature are discounted, are small yet not wholly insignificant.   In the males, the ear in the most dolichocephalic of our series is both higher and broader, in the females broader than that of the brachycephals and the ear index is a trace higher in the more narrow-headed in the males, appreciably higher in the females, than it is in the broad-headed.   The narrower the head therefore, the larger and relatively broader, both however within very modest limits, may be said to be the ear, and *vice versa;* which would seem to point to the significance of the two extremes of head form as long established variations, though not fundamentally different types.

It will be interesting to see if this peculiarity, which in our series affects both the males and the females, will be corroborated on other series. Anthropometry reveals a host of minor organic "behaviors" of similar nature for which it is mostly hard to account and which seem to have little if any practical value to the organism, but which may nevertheless be widespread in a race or even the whole human family, demonstrating very close fundamental relations.

Comparative

The ear in general is known to be absolutely as well as relatively small in the negro and large in many people of the yellow-brown race, while the whites occupy an intermediate position.

Literature on the external ear is richer than that on many another organ. In this country Bean, who has been already quoted in these connections, has made extensive studies of it in children, students and the negro as well as in the Filipinos.[58]   As to white adults we have the nice series of ear measurements by Pittard[59] on the peoples of the Balkans, besides fairly numerous more restricted records.   And the records are generally comparable as to the ear length, which can be measured in only one way.   The ear breadth, however, has not been taken exactly alike by all the observers, though the differences, with the consequent difference in the index, are not

---

[58] Filipino Ears; I. A classification of ear types.   Philippine J. Sci., 1909, IV, Sec. A, 27–53; II. Ears from Malecon Morgue.   *Ibid.*   1910, V, Sec. D, 191–195; III. Negrito. *Ibid.*   1911, VI, Sec. D, 107–125; IV. Ilongot and Mangyan.   *Ibid.*   1913, VIII, 357– 358.   The ear as a morphologic type in racial anatomy.   Verh. d. VIII Intern. Zool. Kong. zu Graz, 921–925.   Some ears and types of men.   Am. Anthrop., 1915, XVII, 529–533.   Some characteristics of the external ear of American whites, American Indians, American negroes, Alaskan Esquimos and Filipinos.   Am. J. Anat., 1915, XVIII, 201– 225.

[59] Pittard (Eugène)—Les peuples des Balkans, 4to, 1920.

very material; and some have measured the left and others the right ear, which is also of no great importance.

Contrasted with that of the immigrants, measured in precisely the same way, the ear of the Old Americans shows the differences given in table 235.

Among the immigrants those who come nearest in size of the ear as related to stature to the Old Americans, as in so many other respects, are seen to be the English, the Irish being slightly more distant. The smallest ears absolutely are found in the low-statured Southern Italians; the smallest ears

TABLE 235

Ear in the Old Americans and immigrants

	LEFT EAR				EAR LENGTH vs. STATURE (S = 1000)	MEAN EAR DIAMETER vs. STATURE	MEAN AGE IN YEARS
	Length	Breadth	Index	Mean diameter (ear module)			
Old Americans ⌠Males.............	6.69	3.79	56.7	5.240	38.4	30.0	42.5
(Laboratory) ⌡Females..........	(6.10)	(3.47)	(56.85)	(4.785)	(37.7)	(29.6)	41.0
Tennessee Highlanders...........	6.42	3.65	56.9	5.035	36.8	28.9	25.1
English.......................	6.57	3.68	56.0	5.125	38.6	30.1	29.3
Irish.........................	6.47	3.64	56.3	5.055	37.7	29.5	30.2
Croatians.....................	6.47	3.64	56.3	5.055	37.7	29.5	35.3
North Italians.................	6.42	3.63	56.5	5.025	37.9	29.6	33.9
Hungarians....................	6.39	3.58	56.1	4.985	38.4	29.9	35.6
Greeks........................	6.38	3.65	57.1	5.015	37.9	29.8	33.9
Russian Jews..................	6.35	3.67	57.7	5.010	38.6	30.4	31.5
Rumanians....................	6.32	3.61	57.1	4.965	37.5	29.4	36.5
Russians......................	6.31	3.60	57.1	4.955	37.2	29.2	32.0
Poles.........................	6.29	3.61	57.5	4.950	36.9	29.0	30.2
Armenians.....................	6.29	3.66	58.2	4.975	37.6	29.7	29.7
South Italians.................	6.20	3.62	58.5	4.910	37.9	30.0	30.4

relatively to stature show curiously again in the Poles and the Russians. These two groups of Slavs have been seen to be physically throughout very near to each other.

The ear index shows a remarkable uniformity in the groups here given, with the Old Americans, both Laboratory and Tennessee, close to the medium. The relatively narrowest ears appear in the English and the Hungarians; the broadest in the Armenians and Southern Italians.

As to comparative data from literature, between the earliest records of Quetelet (Anthropométrie, Bruxelles, 1870) and the latest of Pittard (Les peuples des Balkans, 1920), there are numerous reports on ear measurements, nevertheless the subject is by no means fully covered even in the white race alone.   More particularly there is a dearth of records on the ear of the British peoples, but in other large European groups data are equally more or less wanting; and where they do occur there is seldom a possibility of contrasting them with age and other important factors.   The ear length has, however, frequently been compared with stature.

The earliest generally useful data though limited to ear length are those of Quetelet on Belgians; an abstract of them is given in table 236 (the original gives the measurements by single years).

Topinard (1885) gives the ear index (later distinguished as "physiognomic") and ear module (mean diameter).   Weisbach (1878), Karutz

TABLE 236
Ear length: In Belgians (Quetelet)

	MALE			FEMALE		
Age	Stature	Ear length	Ear length *vs.* stature (S = 1000)	Stature	Ear length	Ear length *vs.* stature (S = 1000)
years						
At birth	50.0	3.5	*70.0*	49.4	3.5	*70.0*
1	69.8	4.6	*67.0*	69.0	4.6	*67.0*
2	79.1	4.9	*63.0*	78.1	4.8	*63.0*
5	98.7	5.1	*52.0*	97.4	5.0	*52.0*
10	127.3	5.5	*44.0*	124.9	5.4	*43.0*
15	151.3	5.8	*39.0*	148.8	5.5	*38.0*
20	166.9	6.1	*37.0*	157.4	5.8	*37.0*
30	168.6	6.2	*37.0*	158.0	5.9	*37.0*

(1897, 1900), Wilhelm (1892) and others publish more or less extensive measurements of the ear.   Schwalbe (1900) adds some measurements and the "morphological" ear index.   Daffner (1902) gives new observations of developmental character on the ear.   Bean (1909 onward) repeatedly calls attention to the morphological as well as racial significance of the ear differences both in size and shape.   Finally Pittard in his large work on the peoples of the Balkans, gives the most ample data on the adult ear obtained so far by a single worker (15 groups).   He directly compares the average length of the ear with average stature in the fifteen Balkan ethnic groups to which his observations extend, without reducing the figures to percental or per-mille proportions (length of ear-stature index)[60] and without taking account of the age factor.

[60] Except in the instance of the Bulgars (p. 190), where he gives the relation to stature of the length and breadth of the ear in the two sexes of this people.

TABLE 237

Ear dimensions and index in whites: Comparative data from literature

Arranged by length, in ascending order

GROUP	MALES								FEMALES								AUTHOR
	Number of subjects	Mean age	Mean stature	Ear				Ear module vs. stature	Number of subjects	Mean age	Mean stature	Ear				Ear module vs. stature	
				Length	Breadth	Index	Module (mean diameter)					Length	Breadth	Index	Module (mean diameter)		
		years								years							
Old Americans (Laboratory)	247	42.5	174.4	6.69	3.79	56.7	5.24	30.0	210	41	161.8	6.10	3.47	56.85	4.785	29.6	
Russians (Dobrudja)	61		173.2	6.63	3.56	53.7	5.095[2]	29.4[2]									Pittard[1]
"Semites" (newer data)				6.60													Karutz[4]
Germans				6.58	(4.13)[6]	(62.8)[6]			102			6.06	3.61	59.6	4.835		Daffner[5]
Alsatians and Germans	109		168.4	6.57	3.97	60.5	5.27	30.0				6.19	3.62	59.0	4.905		Schwalbe[7]
Germans (Dobrudja)	68		166.1	6.50	3.62	55.7	5.06	30.0									Pittard
Armenians[8]	76			6.41	3.66	57.0	5.035	30.3									Pittard
"Semites" (older data)				6.40													Karutz[3]
"Arians"				6.40													Karutz[3]
"Arians"				6.39													Karutz[4]
Serbians	107		170.9	6.38	3.54	55.5	4.96	29.0									Pittard
Albanians	112		167.8	6.37	3.61	56.6	4.99	29.7									Pittard
Jews	74		165.6	6.37	3.56	55.8	4.965	30.0									Pittard
Greeks	125		167.0	6.35	3.59	56.5	4.97	29.8									Pittard
Montenegrins	5		172.8	6.34	3.40	53.6	4.87	28.2									Pittard
Bulgars	200		166.7	6.31	3.69	57.9	5.0	30.0	51		153.6	5.76	3.33	57.9	4.545	29.6	Pittard

	No.							Source
"Europeans"	8		6.31	3.43	*54.0*	4.87		Topinard[9]
Kurds	48	170.7	6.23	3.64	*58.4*	4.985	*29.2*	
Rumanians	151	166.5	6.16	3.53	*57.5*	4.845	*29.1*	Pittard
Great Russians	.		6.14					Vorobjev[10]

[1] Pittard (Eugène)—Les peuples des Balkans. 4°, 1920.
[2] Calculated from Pittard's averages.
[3] Karutz (Eug.)—Studien über die Form des Ohres. Z. f. Ohrheilk., 1897, XXX and XXXI.
[4] Ein Beitrag zur Anthropologie des Ohres. Arch. f. Anthrop., 1900, XXVI, 733–746.
[5] Daffner (Franz)—Das Wachstum des Menschen. 8°, 2nd ed., Leipz., 1902, 372.
[6] Probably an error; does not conform with other data on Germans, nor with its own female series.
[7] Schwalbe (Gustav)—Beiträge zur Anthropologie des Ohres. Virchow's Festschrift, 1891, 123–4.
[8] All Pittard's groups are from Dobrudja (Rumania).
[9] Topinard (P.)—Eléments d'Anthropologie gén., Paris, 1885, 1004.
[10] Quoted by Martin (Lehrb. d. Anthrop.). Value differs greatly from that of Pittard as well as ours.

Note. Weisbach (A.), in his "Körpermessungen verschiedener Menschenrassen," Sep. fr. Z. f. Ethnol., 1877, 8°, Berl., 1878, gives measurements of the length of the ear on 4 groups of whites, but his series include some immature subjects.

The more available data are given in table 237. From them the writer has deduced the mean diameter of the ear which for comparisons as to size is preferable to the length alone, and calculated the relation of this to stature.

From all these comparisons it is seen that the ear in the Old Americans, particularly the males, is absolutely about the longest, and very nearly if not quite, also the broadest. In the females, though the ear is still long, the differences are much less apparent, but regrettably there are only a very few groups available for comparison and these include the two of Germans where it is possible the breadth of the ear was taken in a slightly different way from that of other observers, giving higher values. When, however, the length or especially the mean diameter of the ear is contrasted with stature we find that the American ear is practically identical with that in other groups of whites. That it shows still slightly above the average relative value is doubtless due to the somewhat high mean age of the group.

The justified conclusions are therefore that while the ear in the Old Americans is absolutely long, when stature and age are taken into consideration it is in no way peculiar as compared to other white people.

Summary

The absolute measurements show a fair, the index an extensive variation. The dispersion of the measurements is less regular in the males than in the females.

The ear index is practically identical in the two sexes.

Group variation. There are but two groups available for comparison, that of the Laboratory and Tennessee.

The absolute dimensions of the ear are very perceptibly smaller in the Tennessee men than in those of the Laboratory; but this is found to be wholly the effect of age. For the same age the dimensions are very similar.

Effect of age. Ears grow with age during the adult period. They grow in both dimensions, but more so in length; as a result the ear index tends to decrease with age.

Stature. Stature has a direct effect upon the size of the ears in both height and breadth; but as stature rises the increase in the ear dimensions does not keep pace with the same, with the result that the ear-stature ratios are appreciably smaller in the tall than in the short individuals, the difference being especially marked in the females.

As stature rises the length of the ear increases at a slightly greater rate than the breadth. The result is that the ear index diminishes slightly with rising stature.

Head form. The effects are slight.

The ears in the dolichocephalic males are both slightly higher and broader, in the females broader, than in the brachycephals.

As a result the ear index is a trace higher in the dolichocephalic males; appreciably higher in the dolichocephalic females, than those in the brachycephalic.

Comparative. Absolutely the ear of the Old Americans, particularly the males, is about the longest, and also nearly if not quite the broadest of the whites available for comparison.

Relatively to stature, however, the American ear is very near the average of other whites.

THE CHEST

In measuring the chest for anthropological purposes it is not sufficient merely to take its circumference, yet that is the general procedure. The chest has two distinct diameters, the breadth and depth, and the relation of these diameters changes greatly during development, varies racially and is modified also by environmental conditions as well as certain occupations and habits of the individual.

The two chest diameters can best be measured on the level of the nipples in men and at the corresponding one of the upper border of the 4th costal cartilages in the women. The measurements are taken by broad-branched calipers and recorded at the mean between inspiration and expiration.[61] The mean of the two gives the mean chest diameter or *module* which expresses the size of the chest as conveniently as the cephalic and facial modules express the size of the head and face; while the percental relation of the depth to the breadth measurement gives the very useful chest index. The chest index is high in the newborn to diminish materially during childhood. It is influenced by the contents of the chest (lungs and heart), by the external musculature, and by posture, besides other factors.

Previous observations

There are no previous measurements of this nature on American adults, but the writer has published a series of data secured on white and colored children as well as adolescents.[62] These records showed a gradual decrease

[61] For exact method and instrument see writer's Anthropometry.

[62] Anthropological Investigations on 1,000 White and Colored Children, etc., 8°, New York, 1899, 48–51.

of the chest index with age due to a relatively greater growth in the lateral than in the antero-posterior chest diameter; and they showed also, that the index at all ages was appreciably higher in the colored children (particularly the males) than in the white.

Old Americans

Measurements of the chest were restricted to the Laboratory series. The principal results are given in tables 238 to 243, and figures 36 and 37. They show moderate individual variation in the measurements, a marked one in the index. The dispersion of the two diameters is peculiar in that it tapers farther towards the maximum than it does towards the minimum; the distances of the minimum from the average being for the two diameters and in the two sexes respectively 4.7, 4.4, 5.4 and 4.4 points, that from the average to the maximum being 8.9, 8.2, 8.6 and 6.3 points.

The curves of dispersion are fairly regular and well apart for the two sexes, particularly those of the chest breadth.

The data and curves of the index, however, show an interesting condition —the index in the females exceeds that of the males. This is found to be due to a greater development of the male thorax in breadth. In depth the female chest stands to that of the male as 92.3, in breadth as 89.4, in index as 103.2 to 100. As the stature relation between the two sexes is as 92.8 to 100 which is very close to that of the chest breadth, it must be concluded that the condition underlying the above showing is a relative narrowness of the chest in the females. It is not possible to tell at this moment how the Old American females compare in this respect with others, but there are indications that the condition is not peculiar to, though possibly somewhat accentuated in, the Americans.

Chest and age

Remarkable and unexpected differences in the chest appear when our data are analyzed as to age. It not only becomes evident that the chest increases in size with age after supposedly full growth has been reached, but also that it increases unevenly. It grows during adult life moderately in breadth, but more markedly in depth, particularly so in the males, thus reversing the conditions during childhood and adolescence. The chest in the young adults is flatter than in those after fifty, which is very clearly expressed by the chest index; and the chest of the females is relatively narrower than that of the males at all ages.

FAMILY OF DR. WALTER HOUGH
(Washington, D. C.)
All old Americans, both sides

TABLE 238

Old Americans, males: Chest-diameter lateral

Number of observations: 246

Average: 29.76 cm. (1st 50—29.64; 2nd 50—30.20; 3rd 46—29.93; 4th 50—29.34; 5th 50—29.69 cm.)

Minimum: 25.1 cm.   Maximum: 38.9 cm.

	TABLE OF FREQUENCIES										
	25.1–26.0 cm.	26.1–27.0 cm.	27.1–28.0 cm.	28.1–29.0 cm.	29.1–30.0 cm.	30.1–31.0 cm.	31.1–32.0 cm.	32.1–33.0 cm.	33.1–34.0 cm.	34.1–35.0 cm.	35.1 cm. and above
Number of cases..............	8	12	28	38	63	34	31	20	8	1	3
Per cent......................	*3.2*	*4.9*	*11.3*	*15.4*	*25.6*	*13.8*	*12.6*	*8.1*	*3.2*	*0.4*	*1.2*

TABLE 239

Old Americans, females: Chest, diameter lateral

Number of observations: 175

Average: 26.62 cm. (1st 16—26.3; 2nd 49—26.6; 3rd 50—27.2; 4th 60—26.2 cm.)

Minimum: 22.2 cm.   Maximum: 34.8 cm.

	TABLE OF FREQUENCIES												
	22.1–23.0 cm.	23.1–24.0 cm.	24.1–25.0 cm.	25.1–26.0 cm.	26.1–27.0 cm.	27.1–28.0 cm.	28.1–29.0 cm.	29.1–30.0 cm.	30.1–31.0 cm.	31.1–32.0 cm.	32.1–33.0 cm.	33.1–34.0 cm.	34.1–36.0 cm.
Number of cases.....	4	13	18	38	39	24	17	11	7	2	1		1
Per cent..............	*2.3*	*7.4*	*10.3*	*21.7*	*22.3*	*13.7*	*9.7*	*6.3*	*4.0*	*1.1*	*0.6*		*0.6*

TABLE 240

Old Americans, males: Chest—diameter antero-posterior

Number of observations: 246

Average: 21.70 cm. (1st 50—21.54; 2nd 50—22.01; 3rd 46—22.16; 4th 50—21.48; 5th 50—21.35 cm.)

Minimum: 16.3 cm.   Maximum: 30.3 cm.

	TABLE OF FREQUENCIES														
	16.3–17.0 cm.	17.1–18.0 cm.	18.1–19.0 cm.	19.1–20.0 cm.	20.1–21.0 cm.	21.1–22.0 cm.	22.1–23.0 cm.	23.1–24.0 cm.	24.1–25.0 cm.	25.1–26.0 cm.	26.1–27.0 cm.	27.1–28.0 cm.	28.1–29.0 cm.	29.1–30.0 cm.	30.1–30.5 cm.
Number of cases.......	1	1	13	32	51	58	41	19	10	8	5	4	1	1	1
Per cent..............	*0.4*	*0.4*	*5.3*	*13.0*	*20.7*	*23.6*	*16.7*	*7.7*	*4.0*	*3.2*	*2.0*	*1.6*	*0.4*	*0.4*	*0.4*

TABLE 241

Old Americans, females: Chest—diameter antero-posterior

Number of observations: 175

Average: 20.03 cm. (1st 16—20.85; 2nd 49—20.2; 3rd 50—20.2; 4th 60—19.38 cm.)

Minimum: 15.6 cm.   Maximum: 26.3 cm.

	15.6-16.0 cm.	16.1-17.0 cm.	17.1-18.0 cm.	18.1-19.0 cm.	19.1-20.0 cm.	20.1-21.0 cm.	21.1-22.0 cm.	22.1-23.0 cm.	23.1-24.0 cm.	24.1-25.0 cm.	25.1-26.0 cm.	26.1-26.3 cm.
Number of cases..........	2	3	25	35	33	26	28	5	11	6		1
Per cent.................	1.2	1.7	14.3	20.0	18.8	14.9	16.0	2.9	6.3	3.4		0.6

TABLE 242

Old Americans, males: Chest index

Number of observations: 246

Average: 72.93 (1st 50—72.73; 2nd 50—72.81; 3rd 46—73.96; 4th 50—73.27; 5th 50—71.97)

Minimum: 55.82.   Maximum: 88.6

	55.8-60.0	60.1-62.5	62.6-65.0	65.1-67.5	67.6-70.0	70.1-72.5	72.6-75.0	75.1-77.5	77.6-80.0	80.1-82.5	82.6-85.0	85.1-87.5	87.6-88.6
Number of cases.....	(1)	(5)	(8)	(22)	(38)	53	41	34	17	13	8	4	2
Per cent.............	0.4	2.0	3.2	8.9	15.4	21.5	16.7	13.8	6.9	5.3	3.2	1.6	0.8

TABLE 243

Old Americans, females: Chest index

Number of observations: 175

General average: 75.30

1st series of 16—79.22   3rd series of 50—74.30

2nd series of 49—76.07   4th series of 60—74.90

Minimum: 57.8.   Maximum: 91.49.

	Below 60.0	60.1-62.5	62.6-65.0	65.1-67.5	67.6-70.0	70.1-72.5	72.6-75.0	75.1-77.5	77.6-80.0	80.1-82.5	82.6-85.0	85.1-87.5	87.6-90.0	90.1-91.5
Number of cases..........	1	2	4	7	18	22	25	36	27	15	11	3	3	1
Per cent.................	0.6	1.2	2.3	4.0	10.3	12.5	14.3	20.5	15.4	8.5	6.3	1.8	1.8	0.6

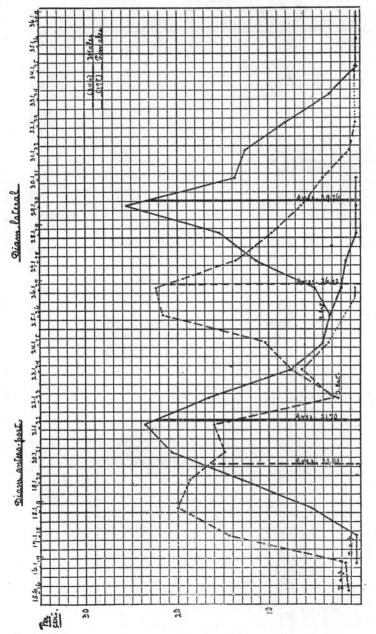

FIG. 36. OLD AMERICANS: CHEST DIAMETERS—LABORATORY SERIES

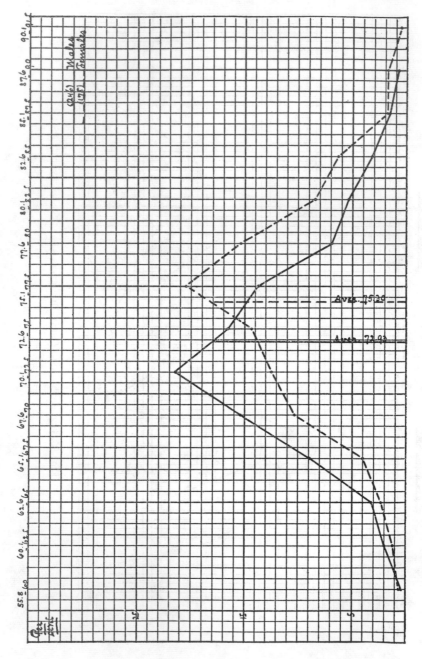

FIG. 37. OLD AMERICANS: CHEST INDEX—LABORATORY SERIES

Chest vs. stature

The correlation of chest dimensions with stature is positive and direct. It appears clearly in the Old Americans. But the relation of the breadth to depth, and hence the thoracic index, remain much the same; neverthe-

TABLE 244

Old Americans: Chest vs. age

Laboratory series

		MALES					FEMALES			
		Breadth	Depth	Mean diameter	Index		Breadth	Depth	Mean diameter	Index
Youngest...............	(25)	29.03	20.61	24.82	70.99	(25)	26.10	19.34	22.72	74.10
General average.........	(247)	29.76	21.70	25.73	72.93	(210)	26.62	20.03	23.33	75.30
Oldest	(25)	29.92	23.03	26.47	76.97	(25)	26.82	20.96	23.89	78.15
Young *vs.* Old (Old=100)		97.0	89.5	93.8	93.2		97.3	92.3	95.1	94.8

TABLE 245

Old Americans: Chest and extremes of stature

Laboratory series

				MALES				
		Age	Stature	Chest			Percental proportion of stature	
				Breadth	Depth	Index	Breadth	Depth
Shortest................	(25)	33.3	164.4	28.9	20.9	72.5	17.6	12.7
Tallest.................	(25)	37.1	184.4	30.1	22.0	73.1	16.3	11.9
Percental difference in favor of tallest...............			10.8	4.0	5.0	0.8	−7.4	−6.3
				FEMALES				
Shortest................	(20)	39.4	151.3	25.4	19.5	76.7	16.8	12.9
Tallest.................	(20)	33.0	172.2	27.4	20.9	76.3	15.9	12.1
Percental difference in favor of tallest...............			12.1	7.3	6.7	−0.5	−5.4	−6.2

less in the tallest of both sexes the chest shows slightly deeper than in those of low stature.

Table 245 gives the chest dimensions and index in the shortest and tallest of the Laboratory groups. The tall have a chest absolutely broader as well as deeper, but relatively to stature the thorax of the short is more ample. The increase with stature in the two dimensions is nearly alike. The chest index is a trace higher (thorax relatively slightly deeper) in the tall males, a trace lower (thorax relatively slightly narrower) in the tall females. Throughout, the chest of the females is relatively to stature quite palpably narrower but a trace deeper than that of the males.

TABLE 246

Old Americans: Chest vs. stature

Laboratory series

	STATURE				
	145.0–150.0	150.01–160.0	160.01–170.0	170.01–180.0	180.01–190.0
Diameter lateral					
Males......................		(2) (29.0)	(60) (29.34)	(147) 29.82	(37) 30.24
Ratio*....................		(18.6)	(17.5)	17.0	16.5
Females..................	(3) (25.13)	(59) 26.15	(97) 26.81	(15) 27.45	
Ratio.....................	(15.6)	16.7	16.3	16.0	
Diameter antero-posterior					
Males......................		(21.45)	21.45	21.67	22.22
Ratio.....................		(13.7)	12.8	12.4	12.1
Females..................	(18.43)	19.74	20.12	20.88	
Ratio.....................	(12.5)	12.6	12.3	12.1	
Chest index					
Males......................		(73.9)	73.2	72.7	73.4
Females..................	(73.3)	75.6	75.2	76.3	

* Per cent of true mean stature.

The data in table 246 give the chest measurement and index by stature-groups of 10 cm.; but as the mean stature of each subdivision differs more or less from the mean of that subdivision there are added percental proportions of the measurements in the actual statures. What is most plain from these figures is that while the chest dimensions absolutely increase as stature rises and that at a fairly even rate, this rate of increase is slower than that of stature, as a result of which the ratio between both chest diameters and stature steadily diminishes. And this diminution is throughout slightly more marked in the males than in the females.

Chest and type of head

Curiously, there appears to exist a slight difference in the chest of the dolicho- and the brachycephals. The difference is small yet alike in the two sexes, which speaks against its being accidental. It concerns the depth of the chest. The breadth in the two types is practically identical, but the depth is a trace greater in the dolichocephals, resulting in a higher chest index. When, however, the chest measurements in the two groups are contrasted with the stature it becomes plain that the chest in the taller dolichocephals is relatively slightly narrower as well as deeper than that in the shorter brachycephals, but that in all likelihood it is the stature and not the head type that is here influential. So far, therefore, as a correla-

TABLE 247

Chest and head form

				MALES				
		Cephalic index	Stature	Chest			Relation to stature	
				Breadth	Depth	Index	Breadth	Depth
Most dolichocephalic........	25	73.2	174.5	29.53	21.52	*72.9*	*16.92*	*12.33*
Most brachycephalic........	25	84.6	172.6	29.43	21.04	*71.5*	*17.05*	*12.19*
				FEMALES				
Most dolichocephalic........	15	74.0	161.6	26.59	20.43	*76.8*	*16.45*	*12.64*
Most brachycephalic........	20	84.5	161.7	26.54	19.54	*73.6*	*16.43*	*12.10*

tion between chest dimensions and head form is concerned, the evidence is rather negative. No such correlation appears plainly, either, in the immigrant series.

Comparative

Racial standards of the chest measurements here dealt with remain still to be established. The immigrants measured in the same way and with the same instruments, gave the values[3] shown in table 248.

These figures show some noteworthy conditions. The Old American males show both absolutely and relatively to stature a chest of good size. But when the individual diameters and the chest index are observed, it is seen that the chest of the Americans is very perceptibly broader but less deep than that in any of the groups available for comparison. The chest

[3] Immigrant groups arranged in descending order on basis of stature.

of the Old Americans of the clerical, professional and leisure classes, as represented by the Laboratory series, may therefore be characterized as relatively broad but slightly shallow. The fact is expressed very convincingly by the chest index which in the Americans is well below that of any of the other series. Of course there are many individual exceptions in our subjects as may be noted in the adjoined seriation, but there are also chests that are decidedly "flat." The whole showing is probably connected with predominantly sedentary occupations and lack of muscular labor. Similar

TABLE 248

Chest dimensions in the Old Americans and in immigrants

	CHEST AT NIPPLE HEIGHT				RELATIVELY TO STATURE (S. = 100)			
	Diameter lateral	Diameter antero-posterior	Mean diameter (chest module)	CHEST INDEX	Stature	Diameter lateral	Diameter antero-posterior	Mean diameter
Old Americans:								
Males............	29.7	21.7	25.7	72.9	174.4	17.06	12.44	14.75
Females..........	(26.6)	(20 0)	(23.3)	(75.3)	(161.8)	(16.44)	(12.38)	(14.41)
Irish.................	28.0	21.35	24.7	76.2	171.6	16.31	12.44	14.37
Croatians..............	27.1	22.1	24.6	81.5	171.6	15.79	12.87	14.33
Poles.................	27.5	21.7	24.6	78.9	170.4	16.13	12.73	14.43
English................	28.0	22.0	25.0	78.6	170.2	16.45	12.93	14.69
Russians..............	27.8	22.6	25.2	81.3	169.8	16.37	13.31	14.84
North Italians..........	27.5	21.4	24.45	77.8	169.6	16.21	12.61	14.41
Rumanians.............	26.9	21.4	24.17	79.7	168.7	15.94	12.68	14.33
Greeks.................	27.6	21.9	24.75	79.3	168.3	16.39	13.01	14.70
Armenians.............	26.75	21.25	24.0	79.4	167.4	15.98	12.69	14 33
Hungarians............	27.45	22.0	24.72	80.1	166.5	16.49	13.21	14.84
Russian Jews..........	25.9	20.9	23.4	80.7	164.6	15.74	12.70	14.22
South Italians..........	27.3	21.0	24.15	76.9	163.4	16.71	12.85	14.78

measurements on the "engineers," the importance of which was not fully appreciated at the time, would have been very valuable in this connection.

The immigrants themselves show marked differences in the chest. That of the Russians is the deepest, that of the Irish as shallow but less broad than that of the Americans. That of the Russian Jews, both absolutely and relatively to stature, is the worst developed.

Summary

The two diameters of the chest (breadth and depth at the height of the nipples) are superior in value to the circumference.

In the Old Americans they show moderate individual variation with fairly regular dispersion.

The percental relations of the two diameters gives the chest index, which varies more than either one of the measurements on which it is based; its dispersion, however, is also fairly regular, though differing somewhat in type in the two sexes.

The chest index of the females exceeds that of the males, due to the relative narrowness of chest in the former.

Influence of age.   The chest grows perceptibly during adult life both in breadth and depth, but the increase in the antero-posterior exceeds that in the lateral diameter, particularly in the males.   This is the reverse of the conditions existing in childhood and adolescence, when the breadth of the chest increases more rapidly than the depth.

As a result of the preceding the chest index increases with age during the adult period, especially so in males.

Effect of stature.   The chest dimensions correlate directly with stature, but they increase at a lesser rate than does the stature.

The rate of increase in the two diameters with stature is much the same, as a result of which the chest index is but little affected by stature.

The chest of the females relatively to stature is narrower but a trace deeper than that of the males.

Type of head.   Discounting stature and age there remains no appreciable influence on the size or shape of the thorax which could be attributed to dolicho- or brachycephaly.

Comparative.   The chest of the Old American males as compared to that of recent immigrants (in general artisans and laborers) is both absolutely and relatively to stature of good size, but relatively not quite as deep. As a result the chest index in the Americans is below that of any of the immigrant groups.

These differences can doubtless be attributed to differences in occupation.

THE HAND

The hand is of interest evolutionally, developmentally, physiologically and probably racially, as well as in respect to sex, age and family peculiarities.   It has been the subject of numerous observations, yet, as with so many other organs, there is no comprehensive study of the part.

Measurements of the hand, more particularly those of its length, were long practised by the artists who eventually were followed by anthropologists; but the more serious efforts of the latter in this direction date barely back to the late 'sixties.

The two logical measurements of the hand are naturally its length and breadth, and the former was found to be quite easy, but a difficulty was encountered with the breadth measurement. Following Topinard (Elém. d'Anthrop. gén., p. 1135) this was to be taken indirectly by "projection," *i.e.*, on the drawn outline of the hand, either across the knuckles (metacarpo-phalangeal articulations), or from the point of the angle between the thumb and the palm across the latter at right angles to the length. The former method is also given by Martin (Lehrb. d'Anthrop., p. 147), who defines it as "the diameter between the median and lateral metacarpal, with fingers extended and measured over the dorsum of the hand."

To the writer, neither of the above methods has given full satisfaction. As with the foot and other parts of the body the object is really to obtain the maximum breadth of the part at right angles to the length, the two giving us a right quadrangle, the absolute as well as the relative proportions or "index" of which are used for comparison. The maximum breadth of the hand can however not be obtained by either of the mentioned procedures. It could be best obtained by a sliding caliper with unevenly long branches, the shorter of which would be applied to the outer (radial) line of the index finger and palm, as far as the thumb, while the longer branch would be brought into touch with the ulnar edge of the palm at its maximum, the two branches being held parallel to the long axis of the hand. This would however require a special instrument which could hardly be used for any other purpose; the writer has therefore adopted the following method[14] which secures practically the same result without any difficulty:

Instrument: The sliding compass. Method: With hand in full extension, apply fixed branch of compass to the angle formed by the tumb and the radial side of the palm, and if necessary compress skin lightly until the point on which the instrument rests is in straight line with the radial surface of the forefinger and palm. The rod of the compass lies applied across the palm, and the moving branch is brought to a point on the ulnar side of the palm midway between the basal (metacarpo-phalangeal) groove of the little finger and the line limiting the hypothenar eminence.

The most satisfactory way of taking this measurement is for the observer to place his left hand under that of the subject so that the tip of his medius is just below the junction of the thumb and palm, and his thumb is on the palm itself. The point of the movable branch of the compass is now applied to the ball of the observer's medius, is brought with this to the required position in the palm-thumb angle of the subject's hand, and the fixed branch is brought slowly to the requisite point of the ulnar side of the palm. This latter point may be marked beforehand, but its location can be easily estimated. The breadth thus obtained is nearer the maximum, more logical and easier to take than would be that at strictly right angles to the length and is much more characteristic than the breadth across the metacarpo-phalangeal articulations.

---

[64] Anthropometry, Wistar Institute, Philadelphia, 1920.

As to length, that is taken as follows:

The length of the hand in the living extends from the middle of the line connecting the proximal limits of the thenar and hypothenar eminences, to the end of the medius, with the hand in full extension. Instrument, sliding compass. Method: Take a sheet of blotting paper, apply its edge to points just given (which if indistinct can easily be ascertained by flexing the hand upon the forearm), mark mid-point with aniline pencil, and secure measurement with hand in full extension.

Previous observations on Americans

There are no such observations.

Old Americans

The writer measured the left hand in all the subjects of the Laboratory series. It was not practicable to extend these measurements to those outside of the Laboratory.

TABLE 249

Old Americans, males: Length of left hand

Number of individuals measured: 247

General average: 19.28 cm.

1st series of 50—19.11 cm.	4th series of 50—19.39 cm.
2nd series of 50—19.37 cm.	5th series of 50—19.31 cm.
3rd series of 47—19.21 cm.	

Minimum: 17.2 cm.   Maximum: 22.3 cm.

	TABLE OF FREQUENCIES										
	17.2–17.5 cm.	17.6–18.0 cm.	18.1–18.5 cm.	18.6–19.0 cm.	19.1–19.5 cm.	19.6–20.0 cm.	20.1–20.5 cm.	20.6–21.0 cm.	21.1–21.5 cm.	21.6–22.0 cm.	22.1–22.3 cm.
Number of cases.............	7	12	30	49	62	46	22	16	1	1	1
Per cent.....................	*2.8*	*4.8*	*12.1*	*19.8*	*25.0*	*18.5*	*8.9*	*6.4*	*0.4*	*0.4*	*0.4*

The principal results are given in tables 249 to 254, and figures 38 to 40. They present some interesting conditions.

Both the length and the breadth of the hand are seen to show a fair individual variation. In length this is about equal in the two sexes; in breadth the females vary less than the males; and this is also true of the hand index.

The distribution of the measurements is remarkably regular for the length, particularly so in the females. As to breadth, the conditions shown at a glance by the chart are peculiar. The type of the curve in the males and females differs considerably, more so than with any other measure-

TABLE 250

Old Americans, females: Length of left hand

Number of observations: 210

Average: 17.34 cm. (1st 50—17.5; 2nd 50—17.2; 3rd 50—17.5; 4th 60—17.3 cm.)

Minimum: 15.2 cm.   Maximum: 19.8 cm.

	TABLE OF FREQUENCIES									
	15.2–15.5 cm.	15.6–16.0 cm.	16.1–16.5 cm.	16.6–17.0 cm.	17.1–17.5 cm.	17.6–18.0 cm.	18.1–18.5 cm.	18.6–19.0 cm.	19.1–19.5 cm.	19.6–19.8 cm.
Number of cases.........	1	4	21	47	61	44	21	7	1	3
Per cent.................	0.5	1.9	10.0	22.4	29.0	21.0	10.0	3.3	0.5	1.4

TABLE 251

Old Americans, males: Breadth of left hand

Number of individuals measured: 247

General average: 9.18 cm.

1st series of 50—9.11 cm.   4th series of 50—9.22 cm.

2nd series of 50—9.19 cm.   5th series of 50—9.24 cm.

3rd series of 47—9.12 cm.

Minimum: 7.7 cm.   Maximum: 11.0 cm.

	TABLE OF FREQUENCIES												
	Below 8.2 cm.	8.3–8.4 cm.	8.5–8.6 cm.	8.7–8.8 cm.	8.9–9.0 cm.	9.1–9.2 cm.	9.3–9.4 cm.	9.5–9.6 cm.	9.7–9.8 cm.	9.9–10.0 cm.	10.1–10.2 cm.	10.3–10.4 cm.	10.5 cm. and above
Number of cases.............	1	9	12	32	43	46	32	38	20	10	0	3	1
Per cent....................	0.4	3.6	4.8	12.9	17.4	18.6	12.9	15.3	8.1	4.0		1.2	0.4

TABLE 252

Old Americans, females: Breadth of left hand

Number of observations: 210

Average: 7.87 cm. (1st 50—7.9; 2nd 50—7.9; 3rd 50—7.85; 4th 60—7.82 cm.)

Minimum: 6.9 cm.   Maximum: 8.6 cm.

	TABLE OF FREQUENCIES								
	6.9–7.0 cm.	7.1–7.2 cm.	7.3–7.4 cm.	7.5–7.6 cm.	7.7–7.8 cm.	7.9–8.0 cm.	8.1–8.2 cm.	8.3–8.4 cm.	8.5–8.6 cm.
Number of cases.....	2	5	10	30	44	63	35	13	7
Per cent.............	0.95	2.4	4.8	14.3	21.0	30.0	16.7	6.2	3.3

ments recorded. That of the females indicates exceptional uniformity; that of the males shows greater variability as well as some irregularity.

Furthermore, the curves are extraordinarily far apart, so much so that they intersect only to a small degree. This means that the breadth of the hand in the Old American males is very different from that of the females.

TABLE 253

Old Americans, males: Hand index

Number of observations: 247

Average: 47.64 (1st 50—47.73; 2nd 50—47.73; 3rd 47—47.53; 4th 50—47.57; 5th 50—47.89)

Minimum: 37.7   Maximum: 54.2

	TABLE OF FREQUENCIES									
	Below 44.0	44.1–45.0	45.1–46.0	46.1–47.0	47.1–48.0	48.1–49.0	49.1–50.0	50.1–51.0	51.1–52.0	52.1–52.6 and above
Number of cases.........	6	10	19	50	63	52	31	10	4	2
Per cent...............	2.4	4.0	7.7	20.2	25.5	21.1	12.6	4.0	1.6	0.8

TABLE 254

Old Americans, females: Hand index

Number of observations: 210

Average: 45.39 (1st 50—45.14; 2nd 50—45.76; 3rd 50—45.1; 4th 60—45.6)

Minimum: 40.5.   Maximum: 50.0

	TABLE OF FREQUENCIES									
	40.5–41.0	41.1–42.0	42.1–43.0	43.1–44.0	44.1–45.0	45.1–46.0	46.1–47.0	47.1–48.0	48.1–49.0	49.1–50.0
Number of cases.........	5	4	11	24	43	54	42	13	11	3
Per cent...............	2.4	1.9	5.2	11.4	20.5	25.7	20.0	6.2	5.2	1.4

The explanation is that the females of the class measured have done but little manual work in their lives, while many of the men have done more. In other words, the differences expressed by the chart are largely differences of a functional nature.

As a result of the just mentioned conditions the curves showing the hand index are also rather wide apart, but otherwise they are quite regular and similar in type. Evidently while the hand in a good many of the males

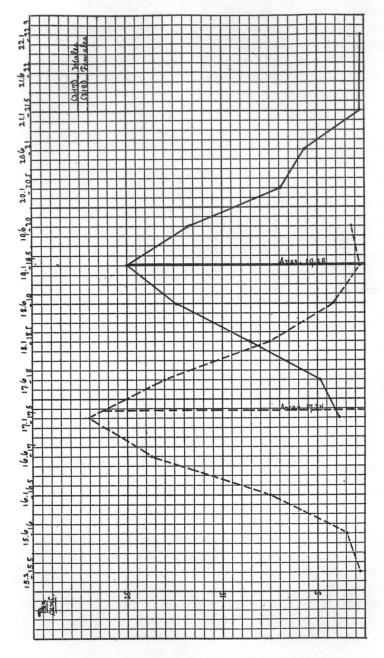

FIG. 38. OLD AMERICANS: LENGTH OF LEFT HAND—LABORATORY SERIES

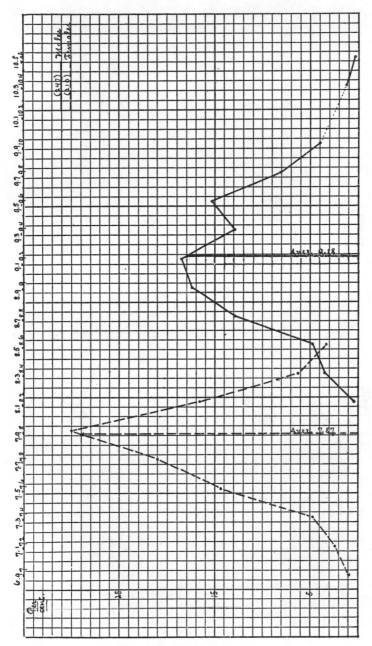

Fig. 39. Old Americans: Breadth of Left Hand—Laboratory Series

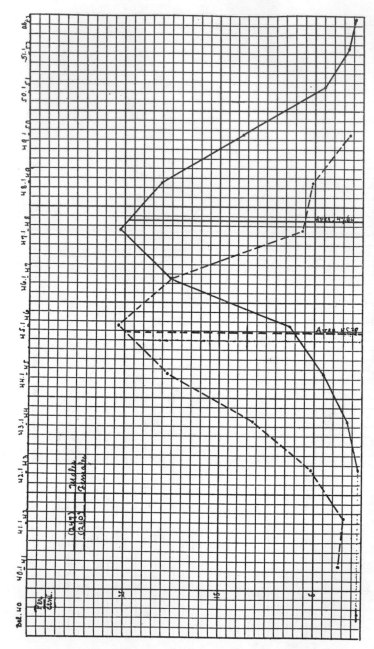

FIG. 40. OLD AMERICANS: LEFT HAND INDEX—LABORATORY SERIES

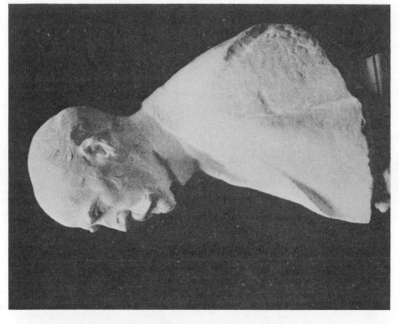

WILLIAM H. HOLMES
(Washington, D. C.)

Old American ancestry on both sides, of mainly English but
partly also "Pennsylvania Dutch" (German) derivation.

WILLIAM H. HOLMES
(Washington, D. C.)
(Side view from a very good bust)

has been modified by work, the modification in this class (mostly clerical, professional and leisured) has not progressed towards any specialization of form.

The male hand is merely broader and stouter. This is shown well by the sex relation of the hand measurements. The length of the female hand is to that of the male as 90, the breadth as 86.5, the index as 95.3 to 100.

Hand and age

As so many other parts of the body, so also the hand grows moderately even after adult life has been reached; and the growth proceeds slightly, as table 255 will show, even in the women who do but little manual labor.

TABLE 255

Hand and age

			MALES				
		Stature	Left hand			Hand module (mean diameter)	Relation of module to stature
			Length	Breadth	Index		
Youngest.......	25	176.3	19.12	9.04	*47.3*	14.08	*79.9*
Oldest.........	25	174.5	19.20	9.16	*47.7*	14.18	*81.3*
			FEMALES				
Youngest......	20	164.5	17.09	7.83	*45.8*	12.46	*75.7*
Oldest.........	20	159.3	17.15	7.82	*45.6*	12.485	*78.4*

Age alone, however, does not appear to have any influence on the form of the hand or hand index, this being practically the same in the youngest as well as the oldest of our groups.

Hand and stature

Stature appears to have a direct and marked effect on both the length and the breadth of the hand.

Taking the shortest and tallest groups of our series, in the males both the length and breadth follow stature fairly closely; the breadth nevertheless shows a slight retardation so that the hand in the tallest is relatively a trace narrower than it is in the shortest individuals, which is well expressed by the hand index.

In the females the increase in the hand length is less close to that in stature than in the males; and the breadth of the hand has increased much less than it has in the males, as a result of which the tallest group of the females shows a hand index 4.3 per cent lower than the group of the shortest individuals. These conditions are well shown in table 256.

TABLE 256

Old Americans: Hand and extremes of stature

Laboratory series

| | | | MALES | | | | |
| | | | Left hand | | | Percental relation to stature of | |
		Stature	Length	Breadth	Index	Head length	Head breadth
Shortest..............................	(25)	164.4	18.18	8.74	48.1	11.06	5.32
Tallest................................	(25)	184.4	20.16	9.59	47.6	10.93	5.20
Percental difference in favor of tallest.....		10.8	9.0	8.9	−0.9	−1.2	−2.3
			FEMALES				
Shortest..............................	(20)	151.3	16.54	7.73	46.7	10.93	5.11
Tallest................................	(20)	172.2	18.23	8.15	44.7	10.59	4.73
Percental difference in favor of tallest.....		12.1	9.3	5.2	−4.3	−3.1	−7.4

TABLE 257

Old Americans: Hand and stature

Laboratory series

| | STATURE | | | | |
	145.0–150.0	150.01–160.0	160.01–170.0	170.01–180.0	180.01–190.0
Males:					
Hand:					
Length........................		(2)	(61)	(147)	(37)
		17.85	18.54	19.39	20.14
Breadth.......................		8.65	8.90	9.09	9.58
Index..........................		48.46	48.0	47.52	47.56
Females:					
Hand:					
Length........................	15.66	16.95	17.50	18.25	
Breadth.......................	7.23	7.77	7.90	8.14	
Index..........................	46.17	45.87	45.15	44.59	

Some further light on the subject may be thrown by ascertaining the dimensions of the hand in stature groups of 10 cm. (table 257).

This, together with the preceding data shows that, other factors not interfering too much, the taller the stature the longer as well as broader is the hand, but that the breadth lags behind the length so that progressively the hand index becomes lower.

This correlation of hand index with stature will need to be borne in mind in future racial comparisons, in fact as it becomes clearer and clearer that the factors of stature, age and occupation are capable of materially affecting the proportions of the human body even after the adult stage has been reached, they must be paid due attention in all first-class anthropological work of the future.   The mass of our data from the past are really only accidentally strictly comparable.

Hand and type of head

There is a prevalent old notion that dolichocephaly and brachycephaly are accompanied by correlated features in the rest of the body, and that among other correspondences a relatively long and narrow hand as well as foot are usually associated with the former, a relatively broader and shorter one with the latter.   In visual observation matters are not so simple nor always well pronounced, yet at large the above rule seems to hold true. When, however, the hand and foot are subjected to careful measurements and when these measurements are dealt with in their relation to stature, age and function as in the case of the Old Americans, matters appear different. The Americans present the conditions shown in table 258.

This table is quite instructive.   We deal here, especially in the females, with hands that have been but little or not more than moderately affected by muscular work.   And the first striking fact is that in the females where the stature of the two extreme groups so far as head form is concerned happens to be equal, the dimensions of the hand, both absolute and relative, as well as the hand index, are very nearly identical; there is a bare trace of an excess in size in favor of the dolichocephals.   There is therefore but a very slight or no difference in the hands of the Old American females whatever the type of the head, and so far at least as their group is concerned there appears to be but a very faint or no connection or correlation between the type of head and the form or size of hand.

In the males also the form of the hand (hand index) is almost the same in the two groups, the difference of five-tenths of a point which appears being too slight to be given any weight.   In the actual dimensions, however, the hand of the dolichocephals is both absolutely and relatively to stature perceptibly larger than that of the brachycephals. The cause of this is not apparent but there is a strong presumption that it may be of a functional nature and hence accidental.

TABLE 258

Old Americans: Hand vs. head type

	MEAN STATURE	HAND				HAND VS. STATURE		
		Length	Breadth	Mean diameter	Index	Length (S. = 100)	Breadth (S. = 1000)	Mean diameter (S. = 1000)
Males:								
25 most dolichocephalic (cephalic index *73.2*)	174.5	19.72	9.28	14.50	47.1	11.30	53.2	83.1
25 most brachycephalic (cephalic index *84.6*)	172.6	19.08	9.08	14.08	47.6	11.05	52.6	81.6
Females:								
15 most dolichocephalic (cephalic index *74.0*)	161.57	17.19	7.87	12.53	45.8	10.64	48.7	77.6
20 most brachycephalic (cephalic index. *84.7*)	161.6	17.19	7.82	12.51	45.5	10.58	48.4	77.4

*Calculated from Quetelet's figures.

Comparative

Earlier data on the dimensions of the hands are not very adequate. In some cases they are limited to the length, while in others breadth is given but it was taken by other methods and hence is not equivalent to our measurements. As a result the length alone can here be considered.

The earliest records of importance are once more those of Quetelet,[65] on an unstated number of Belgians. As in the case of all the data of this author they are given by single years of age, but may be conveniently contrasted as seen in table 259.

In addition to the above Quetelet (page 301) mentions the average of hand length in ten Belgian soldiers as 19.6 cm. Weisbach in 1877,[66] gives among many other measurements also the proportions of the length of hand

[65] Anthropométrie. Bruxelles, 1870.

[66] Weisbach (A.)—Körpermessungen verschiedener Menschenrassen. Sep. fr. Z. f. Ethnol., 1877, 8°, Berlin, 1878.

to stature, but not the hand length itself. Topinard, in 1885 (Elém. d'Anthrop. gén., 1030), adds the relative hand length of 100 Parisians, and Martin (Lehrb. d'Anthrop., 301–302) that of several other groups reported by different authors,[67] again without the absolute measurements. These records, as far as they go, are shown in tables 260 to 262.

TABLE 259

Length of hand in Belgians (*Quetelet*)

AGE	MALES			FEMALES		
	Stature	Length of hand	Relation of hand to stature* (S. = 100)	Stature	Length of hand	Relation of hand to stature
years						
At birth	50.0	6.1	*12.2*	49.4	6.0	*12.2*
1	69.8	8.4	*12.0*	69.0	8.3	*12.0*
2	79.1	9.3	*11.8*	78.1	9.2	*11.8*
5	98.7	11.3	*11.5*	97.4	11.2	*11.5*
10	127.3	14.3	*11.2*	124.9	13.7	*11.0*
15	151.3	17.1	*11.3*	148.8	16.7	*11.2*
20	166.9	18.8	*11.3*	157.4	17.6	*11.2*
30	168.6	19.0	*11.3*	158.0	17.7	*11.2*

* Calculated from Quetelet's figures.

TABLE 260

Hand length vs. stature in various groups of whites, from literature

	LITTLE RUSSIANS	POLISH JEWS	WHITE RUSSIANS	PARISIANS (PAPIL-LAUT)	JEWS	FRENCH (GODIN)	GERMANS (OF BADEN)	SOUTH RUSSIAN JEWS
Males.....	*10.9*	*10.9*	*11.0*	*11.1*	*11.1*	*11.2*	*11.2*	*11.2*
Females...		*10.9*			*11.2*		*11.0*	

	BELGIANS (QUETE-LET)	FRENCH (OF NOR-MANDY)	(100) PARISIANS (TOPI-NARD)	(26) RUMAN-IANS (WEIS-BACH)	(24) NORTHERN SLAVS (WEIS-BACH)	(20) MAGYARS (WEIS-BACH)	(20) JEWS (WEIS-BACH)	LITHUAN-IANS
Males.....	*11.3*	*11.4*	*11.6*	*11.6*	*11.7*	*11.7*	*11.8*	*11.9*
Females...	*11.3*							*12.2*

These figures show beautifully, on one hand the close correlation of hand length with stature, with slighter effects of function; and on the other a

[67] Nothing regrettably on hand or foot is given by Ivanovsky or Pittard. There are, however, data on other peoples than whites, which need not be dealt with in this connection.

TABLE 261

Left hand in the Old Americans

	MALES						FEMALES				
Length	Breadth	Module (mean diameter)	Index	Length *vs.* stature (S. = 100)	Mean diameter *vs.* stature (S. = 1000)	Length	Breadth	Module (mean diameter)	Index	Length *vs.* stature (S. = 100)	Mean diameter *vs.* stature (S. = 1000)
19.28	9.18	14.23	47.6	11.1	81.6	17.34	7.87	12.11	45.4	10.7	74.8

TABLE 262

The hand in the immigrants

(In order of length)

	OLD AMERICANS (247)	IRISH (35)	POLES (50)	ENGLISH (10)	NORTH ITALIANS (50)	CROTIANS (50)	RUMANIANS (50)
Length	19.28	19.3	19.25	19.1	18.9	18.8	18.8
Breadth	9.18	9.4	9.5	9.4	9.4	9.3	9.2
Mean diameter	14.23	14.35	14.32	14.25	14.15	14.05	14.0
Index	47.6	48.7	49.35	49.2	49.7	49.5	48.9
Hand length *vs.* stature	11.05	11.2	11.3	11.2	11.15	11.0	11.15
Breadth of hand *vs.* stature	52.6	54.8	55.8	55.2	55.4	54.2	54.5
Mean diameter of hand *vs.* stature (S = 1000)	81.6	83.6	84.0	83.7	83.4	81.9	83.0

	ARMENIANS (25)	RUSSIANS (50)	HUNGARIANS (50)	GREEKS (50)	SOUTH ITALIANS (50)	RUSSIAN JEWS (50)
Length	18.8	18.7	18.7	18.7	18.6	18.5
Breadth	9.2	9.3	9.4	9.3	9.2	9.0
Mean diameter	14.0	14.0	14.05	14.0	13.9	13.75
Index	48.9	49.7	50.3	49.7	49.5	48.65
Hand length *vs.* stature	11.2	11.0	11.2	11.1	11.4	11.25
Breadth of hand *vs.* stature	55.0	54.8	56.5	55.3	56.3	54.7
Mean diameter of hand *vs.* stature (S. = 1000)	83.6	82.6	84.4	83.2	85.1	83.5

marked correlation of hand breadth with function, that is, muscular work. The American hand, while absolutely long, relatively to stature is shorter than that of nearly all the other groups, but it is above all both absolutely and relatively narrower. The hand index within the range of the white race is evidently essentially an index of physiological importance.

The Old American hand, while absolutely of good size, relatively to stature is seen to be submedium for whites, and that particularly in breadth and especially in the women. But these are hands of men and particularly women who, it may be repeated, have on the whole done but little hard manual labor. Whenever a man was measured who has done such labor his hands were distinctly larger than the average, especially in breadth and thickness. A very instructive comparison in this connection will be that with the immigrants, a large majority of whom belonged to the hand-working classes, and who were measured in exactly the same way as the Old Americans.

Summary

The hand more than other parts of the body is subject to functional modifications which affect its dimensions.

It has not been studied previously in Americans.

In the Old Americans (Laboratory) the dimensions of the hand show only a fair individual variation.

The variation in the length is about equal in the two sexes; in breadth and hand index it is more marked in the males.

The dispersion of the measurements is quite regular for the length, especially in the females; in breadth the females show much uniformity, the males some irregularity.

The averages of hand breadth in the two sexes are exceptionally far apart, more so than those of any other measurement recorded, due to the narrowness of the female hand.

These differences are of a functional nature.

Age. As with the other parts of the body the hand keeps on growing slightly during adult life, even in those who do but little manual labor.

Age does not perceptibly affect the hand index.

Stature. The dimensions of the hand correlate directly and positively with stature.

This is especially true of hand length, the breadth showing a slight retardation so that the hand index diminishes slightly as stature rises.

In the females the correlation of hand dimensions with stature is less marked than in the males, especially in the case of hand breadth.

Type of head. Dolicho- and brachycephaly in the Old Americans appears to have no material effect on the size or shape of the hand.

Comparative. Contrasted with that of other whites the hand in the Old Americans is absolutely longer, but relatively to stature shorter, than that of nearly all the groups available for comparison. In breadth it is both absolutely and relatively narrower, and as a result of this has also the lowest index.

These differences are in all probability of a functional nature.

THE FOOT

The foot possesses an extraordinary evolutionary interest, for in the first place in the course of man's ascent it had to become adapted to the upright posture, and in the second it has lost nearly all its ancestral functions of a

TABLE 263

Old Americans: Variability of feet and hands

	MALES			FEMALES		
	Ratio of variation*			Ratio of variation		
	Length	Breadth	Index	Length	Breadth	Index
Hand..........	26.45	35.95	24.14	26.51	21.60	20.94
Foot..........	26.80	30.56	28.63	24.86	31.10	25.69

* $\dfrac{\text{Average} \times 100}{\text{Range of Variation (minimum to maximum)}}$.

hind hand. In civilized man that is further being supplemented by its encasement since childhood into the shoe and by the predominantly sedentary habits that go with modern life. Its work is now almost entirely restricted to supporting the weight of the body, and to acting in walk as an adjunct lever to the leg.

The foot, like the hand, has been extensively measured by the artist, for industrial purposes and also in anthropometry; but as with the hand the scientific results have hitherto remained rather indefinite.

The measurements of the foot comprise principally its greatest length and greatest breadth, and they are of the easiest. There has developed only one uncertainty, namely whether pressure or no pressure should be applied on the foot when being measured. In the Bertillon identification system the foot has been measured with the body weight applied to it, which cannot but partly deform it. For anthropological purposes, the only suitable method can be that in which the foot preserves its natural proportions, which in the writer's practice is secured by laying it on the bench used for measuring the height sitting while the weight of the body is supported by the foot on which the subject stands. The measurements are taken on the left foot which on the whole is probably less affected functionally and by injuries, by the aluminum broad-branched compass which is employed for the chest diameters.

Earlier data on Americans

There are none.

Old Americans

The feet were measured in all the subjects of the Laboratory series. They were found generally normal, only two subjects presenting conditions which necessitated elimination. Flat feet were infrequent.

TABLE 264

Old Americans, males: Length of left foot

Number of individuals measured: 246

General average: 26.12 cm.

1st series of 50—26.04 cm. 4th series of 50—26.20 cm.
2nd series of 49—26.15 cm. 5th series of 50—26.09 cm.
3rd series of 47—26.11 cm.

Minimum: 22.6 cm.   Maximum: 29.6 cm.

TABLE OF FREQUENCIES

	22.6-23.0 cm.	23.1-23.5 cm.	23.6-24.0 cm.	24.1-24.5 cm.	24.6-25.0 cm.	25.1-25.5 cm.	25.6-26.0 cm.	26.1-26.5 cm.	26.6-27.0 cm.	27.1-27.5 cm.	27.6-28.0 cm.	28.1-28.5 cm.	28.6-29.0 cm.	29.1-29.5 cm.	29.6 cm.
Number of cases.......	1	2	5	13	17	38	43	46	34	22	9	10	3	2	1
Per cent..............	0.4	0.8	2.0	5.3	6.9	15.4	17.4	18.7	13.8	8.9	3.6	4.1	1.2	0.8	0.4

The main facts obtained by the measurements are given in tables 264 to 269, and figures 41 to 43. They partly agree, partly disagree with conditions found in the hands. The range of individual variation in the two parts differs in an interesting way. In the males, the variability in the length of the foot and hand is about equal, but the breadth varies less and the index more in the foot; in the females, the length varies more in the hand, the breadth and index more in the foot.

The dispersion of the measurement and index of the foot appears to be somewhat less regular than that of the hand (table 263). This is particularly true of the breadth of the foot in the females, in which there was

TABLE 265

Old Americans, females: Length of left foot

Number of observations: 210

Average: 23.32 cm. (1st 50—23.4; 2nd 50—23.2; 3rd 50—23.4; 4th 60—23.3 cm.)

Minimum: 20.8 cm.   Maximum: 26.6 cm.

	TABLE OF FREQUENCIES												
	20.8-21.0 cm.	21.1-21.5 cm.	21.6-22.0 cm.	22.1-22.5 cm.	22.6-23.0 cm.	23.1-23.5 cm.	23.6-24.0 cm.	24.1-24.5 cm.	24.6-25.0 cm.	25.1-25.5 cm.	25.6-26.0 cm.	26.1-26.5 cm.	26.6 cm.
Number of cases.....	1	6	11	26	37	50	31	20	20	6	1	0	1
Per cent.............	*0.5*	*2.9*	*5.2*	*12.4*	*17.6*	*23.8*	*14.8*	*9.5*	*9.5*	*2.9*	*0.5*		*0.5*

TABLE 266

Old Americans, males: Breadth of left foot

Number of individuals measured: 245

General average: 9.49 cm.

1st series of 50—9.51 cm.	4th series of 50—9.45 cm.
2nd series of 49—9.54 cm.	5th series of 49—9.34 cm.
3rd series of 47—9.60 cm.	

Minimum: 8.2 cm.   Maximum: 11.1 cm.

	TABLE OF FREQUENCIES															
	8.1-8.2 cm.	8.3-8.4 cm.	8.5-8.6 cm.	8.7-8.8 cm.	8.9-9.0 cm.	9.1-9.2 cm.	9.3-9.4 cm.	9.5-9.6 cm.	9.7-9.8 cm	9.9-10.0 cm.	10.1-10.2 cm.	10.3-10.4 cm.	10.5-10.6 cm.	10.7-10.8 cm.	10.9-11.0 cm.	11.1-11.2 cm.
Number of cases....	1	1	13	14	22	30	38	40	31	17	16	8	7	5	0	2
Per cent...........	*0.4*	*0.4*	*5.3*	*5.7*	*8.9*	*12.2*	*15.5*	*16.3*	*12.6*	*6.9*	*6.5*	*3.3*	*2.8*	*2.0*		*0.8*

TABLE 267

Old Americans, females: Breadth of left foot

Number of observations: 210

Average: 8.35 cm. (1st 50—8.45; 2nd 50—8.35; 3rd 50—8.4; 4th 60—8.29 cm.)

Minimum: 7.2 cm.   Maximum: 9.8 cm.

	TABLE OF FREQUENCIES													
	7.1-7.2 cm.	7.3-7.4 cm.	7.5-7.6 cm.	7.7-7.8 cm.	7.9-8.0 cm.	8.1-8.2 cm.	8.3-8.4 cm.	8.5-8.6 cm.	8.7-8.8 cm.	8.9-9.0 cm.	9.1-9.2 cm.	9.3-9.4 cm.	9.5-9.6 cm.	9.7-9.8 cm.
Number of cases..........	1	4	9	12	33	30	34	28	34	14	5	3	0	3
Per cent.................	*0.5*	*1.9*	*4.3*	*5.7*	*15.7*	*14.3*	*16.2*	*13.3*	*16.2*	*6.7*	*2.4*	*1.4*		*1.4*

evidently a good deal of difference of a functional nature in the women that were studied. A good many of these were of sedentary occupations who have done relatively little of walking or standing in their lives.

The irregularity in the distribution of the breadth of the foot in the females is shown also in the index the curve of which is of a peculiar character.

TABLE 268

Old Americans, males: Foot index

Number of observations: 245

Average: 36.33 (1st 50—36.56; 2nd 49—36.50; 3rd 47—37.80; 4th 50—36.09; 5th 49—35.78)

Minimum: 30.7. Maximum: 41.1

	TABLE OF FREQUENCIES											
	30.7–31.0	31.1–32.0	32.1–33.0	33.1–34.0	34.1–35.0	35.1–36.0	36.1–37.0	37.1–38.0	38.1–39.0	39.1–40.0	40.1–41.0	41.1–41.5
Number of cases..........	1	1	4	15	27	51	73	34	20	17	1	1
Per cent.................	0.4	0.4	1.7	6.1	11.0	20.8	29.8	13.9	8.2	6.9	0.4	0.4

TABLE 269

Old Americans, females: Foot index

Number of observations: 210

Average: 35.84 (1st 50—36.13; 2nd 50—35.91; 3rd 50—35.75; 4th 60—35.51)

Minimum: 31.2. Maximum: 40.47

	TABLE OF FREQUENCIES									
	31.2–32.0	32.1–33.0	33.1–34.0	34.1–35.0	35.1–36.0	36.1–37.0	37.1–38.0	38.1–39.0	39.1–40.0	40.1–40.5
Number of cases.........	1	14	20	42	43	36	28	17	8	1
Per cent.................	0.5	6.7	9.5	20.0	20.5	17.1	13.3	8.1	3.8	0.5

Feet and age

The influence of age on foot dimensions is much less plain than that of stature and can conclusively be shown only where the data are controlled by the latter (see table 270).

It is seen that age has some influence on the size of the foot, even though this influence is considerably less than that of stature. The foot in the oldest men, notwithstanding the fact that they are shorter, is both a trace longer as well as broader than that of the young, while in the older females

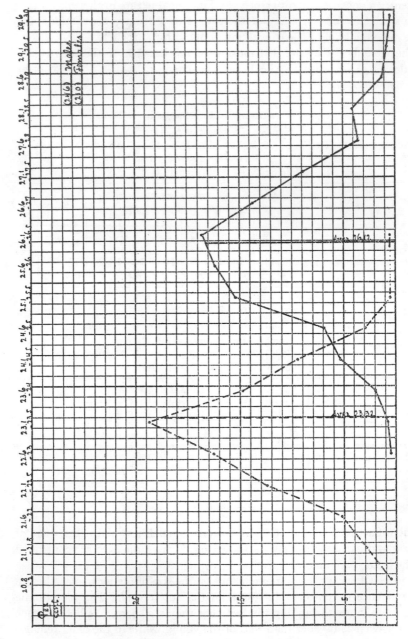

Fig. 41. Old Americans: Length of Left Foot—Laboratory Series

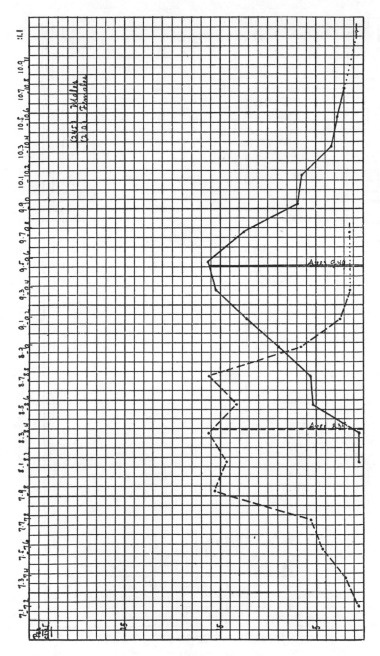

FIG. 42. OLD AMERICANS: BREADTH OF LEFT FOOT—LABORATORY SERIES

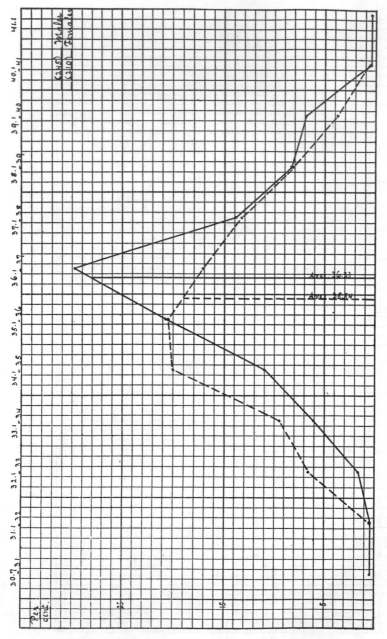

FIG. 43. OLD AMERICANS: LEFT FOOT INDEX—LABORATORY SERIES

the foot is a trace broader than that in the younger.   Relatively to stature the foot in the old of both sexes in both dimensions shows higher values.

The foot, therefore, like the hand and many other parts of the body, continues on the average to grow slightly during adult life; and as with the hand this growth as shown by the index is practically symmetrical.   The very slight excess of the index in the old indicating a very slightly greater relative breadth of the foot, may be due to other factors.

TABLE 270

Old Americans: Foot and age

Laboratory group

| | | MALES | | | | | | | |
| | | | Foot | | | | Foot *vs.* stature | | |
	Mean stature	Length	Breadth	Mean diameter	Index	Length (S. = 100)	Breadth (S. = 1000)	Mean diameter (S. = 1000)
Youngest............	(25)	176.3	25.88	9.31	17.595	36.0	*14.6*	*52.8*	*99.8*
Oldest.............	(25)	174.5	26.14	9.54	17.840	36.5	*15.0*	*54.7*	*102.3*
		FEMALES							
Youngest............	(20)	164.5	23.07	8.22	15.645	35.6	*14.0*	*50.0*	*95.1*
Oldest.............	(20)	159.3	22.99	8.26	15.625	35.9	*14.4*	*51.8*	*98.1*

Feet and stature

An analysis of our data shows that the advance of the foot with stature in length as well as in breadth is very apparent in both sexes; and the increase in the two dimensions is quite harmonious, so that their interrelation (foot index) remains much alike.   The slight differences observed in the indices in the females may be due to a faint tendency of the length to increase proportionately more than the breadth, but may also be connected simply with differences in age and function.   (See tables 271 and 272.)

Feet and head form

Nothing definite, either positively or negatively, has as yet been established on this point, and nothing conclusive can be arrived at without considering all data bearing on the question also in relation to age and stature of the subjects examined.   The data on the Old Americans in this respect are shown in table 273.

TABLE 271

Old Americans: Foot and extremes of stature

Laboratory series

			MALES				
		Stature	Left foot			Percental relation to stature of	
			Length	Breadth	Index	Foot length	Foot breadth
Shortest........................	(25)	164.4	24.76	9.02	36.3	15.06	5.49
Tallest.........................	(25)	184.4	27.34	10.01	36.6	14.83	5.43
Percental difference in favor of tallest		10.8	9.4	9.9	0.8	−1.5	−1.1
			FEMALES				
Shortest........................	(20)	151.3	22.30	8.09	36.3	14.74	5.35
Tallest.........................	(20)	172.2	24.48	8.72	35.6	14.21	5.06
Percental difference in favor of tallest		12.1	9.1	7.2	−1.9	3.6	5.4

TABLE 272

Old Americans: Foot vs. stature

Laboratory series

	STATURE				
	145.0–150.0	150.01–160.0	160.01–170.0	170.01–180.0	180.01–190.0
Males:					
Foot length.................		(2)	(60)	(146)	(37)
Foot breadth..............		(24.65)	25.14	26.23	27.37
Foot index................		(9.15)	9.18	9.50	9.97
		(37.1)	36.5	36.2	36.4
Females:	(3)	(72)	(114)	(20)	
Foot length.................	(21.27)	22.67	23.61	24.46	
Foot breadth..............	(7.43)	8.29	8.35	8.69	
Foot index................	(34.9)	36.6	35.4	35.5	

The mean ages of the groups in the above series being nearly equal, the influence of this factor may be regarded as negligible; and in the females there is also nearly an identity of stature, so that correlation with the form of the head, if any exists, ought to appear there quite plainly. What actually shows in the females is that in the brachycephals the foot is ab-

PROFESSOR FRANKLIN B. DEXTER
(Librarian Yale University)
Sixth generation pure New England blood on both sides

MR. SAMUEL GROB
(Annapolis, Md.)
All ancestors born in U. S. A. for three, and some on father's side for five generations. Swiss and Pennsylvania Dutch originally.

solutely as well as relatively to stature slightly larger, and that compared to its length it is also, though only by a mere trace, broader than in the dolichocephals.   In the males the foot is both absolutely and relatively to stature slightly longer in the dolichocephals, but though absolutely the same, relatively to stature it is slightly broader in the brachycephals.   It may therefore be said that in the brachycephals the foot tends slightly to an excess in breadth, in dolichocephals possibly to a slight excess in length, though in our series this last is only apparent in the males.   A slight correlation of the foot with head form seems therefore to exist, but in the groups under consideration it is too weak to be of much significance.

TABLE 273

Old Americans: Feet vs. head form

Laboratory group

	Mean cephalic index	Mean stature	Mean age	Foot				Foot in relation to stature		
				Length	Breadth	Mean diameter	Index	Length (S. = 100)	Breadth (S. = 1000)	Diameter (S. = 1000)
MALES										
			years							
Most dolichocephalic...	(25)	73.2	174.5	34.6	26.37	9.41	17.89	35.7	15.1	53.9	102.6
Most brachycephalic...	(25)	84.6	172.6	33.3	25.49	9.41	17.45	36.9	14.8	54.5	101.1
FEMALES										
Most dolichocephalic...	(15)	74.0	161.6	34.7	23.04	8.15	15.595	35.4	14.3	50.45	96.5
Most brachycephalic...	(20)	84.7	161.2	32.0	23.39	8.32	15.855	35.6	14.5	51.6	98.4

Comparative

Of older anthropometric data on the foot the first more noteworthy ones are those of Quetelet which, as with the hand, show the development of the part from birth up to the thirtieth year (table 274).

For our purposes the only part of the above data that is of direct concern is that on the adults; nevertheless it may be noted that from birth to ten years and especially at one year of age the foot is relatively broad and short, and that it becomes gradually relatively longer until after the time of puberty, after which its form becomes more stationary.   The changing relations of the foot length and module to stature are also interesting.

The foot in the Old Americans and that in the twelve series of immigrants who were measured by the same methods, gave dimensions as shown in table 275.

These figures show that, absolutely, the foot of the clerical, professional and at-ease Old Americans is of about medium length, but that, just as the hand, it is narrower than that in any of the groups used for comparison. The foot in general nearest to it is the English, with the Irish not far off,

TABLE 274

Foot in Belgians (Quetelet)

AGE	Stature	Foot			Module* (mean diameter)	Relation of length to stature	Relation of module to stature
		Length	Breadth	Index*			
	MALES						
years							
At birth	50.0	7.5	3.0	*40.0*	5.25	*15.0*	*10.5*
1	69.8	10.7	4.8	*44.9*	*7.75*	*15.3*	*11.1*
2	79.1	12.2	5.1	*41.8*	8.65	*15.5*	*10.9*
5	98.7	15.7	5.9	*37.6*	10.80	*15.9*	*10.9*
10	127.3	20.4	7.3	*35.8*	13.85	*16.1*	*10.9*
15	151.3	24.5	8.7	*35.5*	16.60	*16.2*	*10.9*
20	166.9	26.4	9.5	*36.0*	17.95	*15.8*	*10.8*
30	168.6	26.4	9.6	*36.4*	18.0	*15.7*	*10.7*
	FEMALES						
At birth	49.4	7.4	3.0	*40.5*	5.20	*15.0*	*10.5*
1	69.0	10.5	4.7	*44.8*	7.60	*15.2*	*11.0*
2	78.1	12.0	5.0	*41.7*	8.50	*15.4*	*10.9*
5	97.4	15.2	5.7	*37.5*	10.45	*15.7*	*10.7*
10	124.9	19.7	7.0	*35.5*	13.35	*15.8*	*10.7*
15	148.8	23.0	8.2	*35.7*	15.60	*15.5*	*10.5*
20	157.4	23.6	8.5	*36.0*	16.05	*15.0*	10.2
30	158.0	23.7	8.5	*35.9*	16.10	*14.9*	10.2

* Calculated from Quetelet's figures.

but even these are broader. The explanation can only be of less use: the American child of the class represented by our data does not go barefooted as do in season his poorer European cousins, and the grown-ups use their feet less in walking, standing and stresses due to bodily labor.

The moderate development and particularly the slenderness of the Old American foot becomes, however, most apparent when its dimensions are regarded in their relation to stature. With all things equal the foot of the Americans who are the tallest should be absolutely the largest. As it is the length-stature, mean diameter-stature, and especially the breadth-stature index are all very perceptibly lower than those of any of the other groups. Relatively to stature therefore, the foot of this class of the Old Americans is decidedly submedium, and that particularly in breadth. That it bears much the same relation to other groups of whites will be seen from tables 276 and 277, which give the more available records from literature.

TABLE 275

The foot in the Old Americans and immigrants

(Arranged in the order of length)

GROUP	MEAN AGE	MEAN STATURE	LEFT FOOT				FOOT *vs.* STATURE		
			Length	Breadth	Mean diameter (module)	Index	Length (S. = 100)	Breadth (S. = 1000)	Diameter (S. = 1000)
	years								
Old Americans (Laboratory series):									
Males....................	42.5	174.44	26.12	9.49	17.805	36.3	14.97	54.4	102.1
Females...............	41.0	161.84	23.33	8.36	15.845	35.8	14.42	51.7	97.9
Poles.......................	30.2	170.4	26.65	10.6	18.625	39.8	15.64	62.2	109.3
Croatians..................	35.3	171.6	26.5	10.5	18.50	39.6	15.44	61.2	107.8
Irish.......................	30.2	171.6	26.4	10.0	18.20	37.9	15.38	58.3	106.0
North Italians...............	33.9	169.6	26.4	10.3	18.35	39.0	15.57	60.7	108.2
Russians...................	32.0	169.8	26.2	10.4	18.30	39.7	15.43	61.3	107.8
Hungarians.................	35.6	166.5	26.2	10.3	18.25	39.3	15.74	61.9	109.6
English.....................	29.3	170.2	26.15	10.1	18.125	38.6	15.36	59.3	106.5
Greeks......................	33.9	168.3	26.1	10.2	18.15	39.1	15.51	60.6	107.8
Rumaniaus..................	36.5	168.7	26.0	10.2	18.10	39.2	15.41	60.5	107.3
Armenians..................	29.7	167.4	25.8	10.2	18.0	39.5	15.41	69.0	107.5
Russian Jews...............	31.5	164.6	25.8	9.9	17.85	38.4	15.68	60.1	108.5
South Italians..............	30.4	163.4	25.7	10.3	18.0	40.1	15.73	63.0	110.2

From all the preceding it is plain that like the hand so the foot of the Old Americans of the class represented in our series, while absolutely of fair dimensions, especially in length, relatively to stature is both shorter and especially narrower than that of the Europeans available for comparison. It should be borne in mind however that none of the Europeans, data on whom have been here used, represent the same social classes of people as

TABLE 276

Comparative data on foot from literature

(Arranged by order of length)

	AUTHOR	MEAN AGE	MEAN STATURE	FOOT				RELATION TO STATURE OF		
				Length	Breadth	Mean diameter (module)	Index	Length (S. = 100)	Breadth (S. = 1000)	Mean diameter (S. = 1000)
Males										
		years								
(247) Old Americans, Laboratory series.........		42.5	174.44	26.12	9.49	17.805	36.3	14.97	54.4	102.1
(18) Jews..........	Weisbach	19–66	159.9	25.0	9.5	17.25*	38.0	15.6	59.4	107.9
(26) Rumanians.........	Weisbach	20–25	164.3	25.1	10.2	17.65	40.6	15.3	62.1	107.4
(26) Hungarians.........	Weisbach	19–25	165.8	25.6	10.4	18.0	40.6	15.4	62.7	108.6
(24) Northern Slavs.......	Weisbach	20–26	167.1	26.0	10.7	18.35	41.2	15.6	64.0	109.8
Germans.........	Daffner	30	168.56	26.0	9.9	17.95	38.1	15.4	58.7	106.5
Belgians.........	Quetelet	30	168.6	26.4	9.6	18.0	36.4	15.7	56.9	107.0
Females										
(210) Old Americans, Laboratory series.........		41.0	161.84	23.33	8.36	15.845	35.8	14.42	51.7	97.9
Belgians.........	Quetelet	30	158.0	23.7	8.5	16.10	35.9	14.90	53.8	102.0
(62) Germans.........	Daffner	26		24.42	9.38	16.90	38.4			

* This and the following columns determined from the data of the various authors.

the Americans.   The relatively small size of the foot in the Old Americans as in the case of the hand may in all probability be safely referred to functional causes.   It cannot be regarded as a racial character.

TABLE 277

The foot—further comparative data

(After Topinard and Martin)

| | RELATION TO STATURE | | | |
| | Foot length | | Foot breadth | |
	Males	Females	Males	Females
Old Americans............................	*14.97*	*14.42*	*5.44*	*5.17*
Lithuanians.............................	14.6	14.4	5.9	6.1
Letts..................................	14.6	14.8	5.9	5.8
100 Parisians (Topinard)...................	14.8			
Great Russians..........................	15.0			
French of Normandy.....................	15.6			
South Russian Jews......................	15.7			
Jews..................................	15.9			
Badenese..............................	16.0	15.5		

Summary

Conditions relating to measurements and index of the feet in the Old Americans partly agree, partly disagree with those shown by the measurements and index of the hand.

The variability of both measurements and index is somewhat similar to that of the hands, yet differs: it is greater than that of the hand in the index of both sexes, and especially in the breadth of the foot in the females. The greatest variability is present in the breadth of the male hand and in the breadth of the female foot.

The dispersion of the measurement is fairly regular, especially in the females, in the length of the foot, but shows irregularities, particularly in the females, in the breadth.   The distribution of the foot index in the females gives an odd curve.

Age.   The foot continues to grow slightly during adult life.

The growth is harmonious, as a result of which the index changes but very slightly.

Stature.   The influence of stature is direct and pronounced.   It affects both measurements alike, so that the index remains almost unaffected.

Head form. In brachycephaly, the foot appears to tend slightly to an excess of breadth, in dolichocephaly (males) to an excess of length.

Comparative. Absolutely the foot of the Old Americans, like the hand, is of fair size, especially in length; but relatively to stature it is shorter and especially narrower than that of any other whites available for comparison. As a result of its relative narrowness its index is also lower.

These differences, however, are according to all indications not of racial but of functional nature.

THE LEG

The maximum circumference[68] of the leg is a measurement of racial as well as sex and individual importance. There are whole races that are characterized by slender or stout calf; and the measurement shows modifications of sexual, age and nutritional nature.

There are normally stout calves and slender calves. A stout calf may owe its volume to fat, or muscles, or both. It is not necessarily a strong calf, even when muscular. A relatively slender calf may go with great endurance in walking or running, as it frequently does in the American Indian.

Old Americans

There are no earlier measurements of the leg in the American people.

So far as the Old Americans are concerned, the measurement was taken on 194 males and 64 females of the Laboratory series. The results are shown in tables 278 and 279. They indicate, in brief, a fair range of individual variation, with somewhat peculiar but in such subdivisions as it was necessary to use due to the smaller number of subjects, but mildly irregular dispersion. The female curve is odd, in its absence of subnormals as well as abnormals. The mean values of the measurement as well as its distribution are closely alike, so that it may be said the legs in the male and female Old Americans are practically equal, though in the female they contain more fat, in the male more muscle.

[68] "Instrument: Anthropometric tape. Method: The left foot is placed on a bench, as for measurements of the foot itself, and it is brought forward so that the leg forms a little larger than a right angle with the thigh, to insure relaxation of all muscles. The tape, held between the thumb and fore-finger of each hand is then applied somewhat above what appears to be the maximum bulge of the leg, and is brought snugly around the leg but not tightly enough to cause an impression, and a mental note is made of the measurement. The tape is then moved, with a side to side motion, slightly lower and the measurement is observed again; and the process is repeated until the maximum girth has been determined." Anthropometry, Wistar Institute, Philadelphia, 1920.

Leg vs. age

The influence of age on the development or involution of the calf is marked enough before adult life is. reached and in senility,· but changes in the part during adult life, if any, have not yet been·established.   The Old Americans, Laboratory series, give the records shown in table 280.

TABLE 278

Old Americans, males: Maximum circumference of left leg

Number of observations: 194
Average: 36.1 cm. (1st 50—36.1; 2nd 49—36.1; 3rd 43—36.4; 4th 52—35.8 cm.)
Minimum: 30.2 cm.   Maximum: 45.3 cm.

	TABLE OF FREQUENCIES							
	30.1–32.0 cm.	32.1–34.0 cm.	34.1–36.0 cm.	36.1–38.0 cm.	38.1–40.0 cm.	40.1–42.0 cm.	42.1–44.0 cm.	44.1–46.0 cm.
Number of cases............	13	31	56	54	23	12	2	3
Per cent..................	*6.7*	*16.0*	*28.9*	*27.8*	*11.9*	*6.2*	*1.0*	*1.5*

TABLE 279

Old Americans, females: Maximum circumference of left leg

Number of observations: 64
Average: 35.5 cm. (1st 14—34.6; 2nd 50—35.8 cm.)
Minimum: 30.7 cm.   Maximum: 43.4 cm.

	TABLE OF FREQUENCIES						
	30.1–32.0 cm.	32.1–34.0 cm.	34.1–36.0 cm.	36.1–38.0 cm.	38.1–40.0 cm.	40.1–42.0 cm.	42.1–44.0 cm.
Number of cases....	4	18	16	13	11	1	1
Per cent...........	*6.2*	*28.1*	*25.0*	*20.3*	*17.2*	*1.6*	*1.6*

The leg, it is seen, reaches its optimum development in men after thirty, in women after forty.   After fifty in the men the average rises again, due to increase of obesity in a proportion of the individuals.   After this age uniformity in the leg, as in the whole body, decreases in both sexes, there being an increase of the submedium on one hand and of the stout on the other.

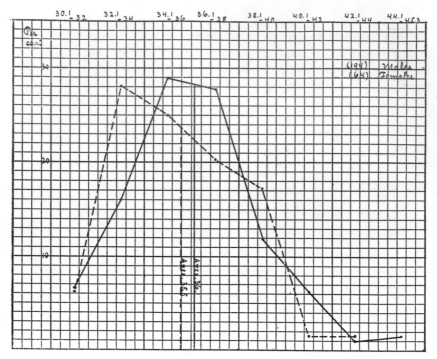

FIG 44. OLD AMERICANS: GIRTH OF LEFT LEG—LABORATORY SERIES

TABLE 280

Old Americans: Girth of leg vs. age

MALES					FEMALES			
24–29 years	30–39 years	40–49 years	50–59 years	Above 59 years	22–29 years	30–39 years	40–49 years	50–59 years
(67)	(51)	(36)	(31)	(9)	(24)	(20)	(19)	(10)
35.3	36.5	36.2	36.6	38.9	35.3	35.5	36.5	35.7

TABLE 281

Old Americans: Girth of leg vs. weight of body

MALES				FEMALES			
	Girth of leg		Girth of leg		Girth of leg		Girth of leg
20 lightest	32.8	20 heaviest	40.75	15 lightest	32.7	15 heaviest	38.5

Weight

The direct influence on the size of the leg of the weight of the body, **is** well shown by table 281. It may be said that, in general, the heavier **the** body the stouter the leg, and *vice versa*.

Effect of stature

A comparison of the leg stoutness in the shortest and tallest groups of the Laboratory series shows the following conditions:

The tall of both sexes have absolutely the stouter legs. Relatively to stature, however, the short have more calf than the tall.

TABLE 282

Old Americans: Circumference of left leg and stature

Laboratory series

		MALES				FEMALES		
		Stature	Circumference	Percental relation to stature		Stature	Circumference	Percental relation to stature
Shortest..................	(21)	164.1	34.8	*21.2*	(10)	152.5	34.7	*22.8*
Tallest...................	(15)	184.2	37.1	*20.1*	(10)	170.8	36.0	*21.1*
Percental differences in favor of tallest................		*10.9*	*6.2*	*−5.0*		*10.7*	*3.6*	*−7.4*

Relatively to stature the legs are stouter in the females than they are in the males, due to more fat; and this is appreciably more the case in the short than in the tall individuals. In other words, the tall of both sexes, but somewhat more so in the females than in the males, are relatively lankier in legs than the short.

The correlation of the size of the leg with stature will be seen even more manifestly in table 283.

Type of head and leg

When the development of the leg is taken, as within a group such as ours it legitimately may, as an index of robustness, it becomes of interest to see if it differs in the dolichocephalic and the brachycephalic strains. Table 284 shows that when stature and age, both of which as has been

TABLE 283

Old Americans: Girth of leg vs. stature

Laboratory series

	STATURE				
	145.0–150.0	150.01–160.0	160.01–170.0	170.01–180.0	180.01–190.0
Males.................{		(2) 34.0	(47) 35.6	(121) 36.3	(24) 36.9
Females...............{	(1) 33.2	(22) 34.5	(36) 35.9	(5) 37.7	

TABLE 284

Old Americans: Girth of leg and head form

Laboratory series

	MALES			
	Mean age	Mean stature	Girth of leg	Girth of leg vs. stature (S. = 100)
18 most dolichocephalic (cephalic index 73.5)	34.1	175.2	35.9	20.5
20 most brachycephalic (cephalic index 83.8).................................	35.5	173.4	35.2	20.3
	FEMALES			
6 most dolichocephalic (cephalic index 74.2).................................	35.0	163.9	36.85	22.5
10 most brachycephalic (cephalic index 84.1).................................	31.7	162.2	35.65	22.0

TABLE 285

Old Americans and immigrants: Circumference of calf

	OLD AMERICANS		SOUTH ITAL-IANS	RUS-SIAN JEWS	RUMAN-IANS	ARME-NIANS	IRISH
	Males	Females					
Girth of leg........................	35.41	35.54	34.35	35.25	35.3	35.8	36.05
Percental relation to stature.........	20.3	21.95	21.0	21.4	20.9	21.4	21.0

	ENGLISH	HUN-GARIANS	NORTH ITAL-IANS	CROA-TIANS	GREEKS	POLES	RUS-SIANS
Girth of leg........................	36.1	36.1	36.4	36.5	36.7	37.3	37.3
Percental relation to stature.........	21.2	21.7	21.5	21.3	21.8	21.9	22.0

seen influence the size of the leg, are taken into consideration, there remains no material difference in the leg development in the two extremes of head form.

Comparative

Records of leg circumstances are scarce. Quetelet (Anthropométrie, p. 433) gives for Belgian men and women thirty years of age the average of 34.3 cm. for males and 32.2 for females, both of which yield the proportion of *20.4* to stature. Martin (Lehrb. Anthrop., p. 322) mentions that the measurement "shows well marked sex and race differences," but gives no data outside of stating that in Europeans the measurement in males is as *20.5*, in females as *22.2* to stature.

The Old Americans (Laboratory series) and the immigrants, show the conditions given in table 285.

These data show plainly that the leg in the Old Americans of the clerical-professional classes is but moderately developed; that it is exceeded by that of practically all the immigrants except those of the lowest stature; and that in relation to stature it gives the lowest value—the highest being that of the agricultural Poles and Russians. The sex difference is quite marked in the Americans, the women showing a calf absolutely about the same but relatively to stature very perceptibly stouter than that of the males. The excess is due of course to more adipose tissue in the female lower limbs.

Summary

The maximum girth of the left leg in the Old Americans (Laboratory) shows a fair range of individual variation, with somewhat odd and, in the females especially, atypical dispersion.

The mean value of the measurement as well as its distribution and curve are closely alike in the two sexes, though of different physiological significance.

Age. The leg reaches its optimum development, on the average, in men after thirty, in women after forty. After fifty the leg in men becomes again somewhat stouter, due to deposition in many of fat. As senility manifests itself in both sexes the calf on the whole commences to decrease, due to loss of fat as well as muscle.

Weight. The weight of the body has a direct influence on the size of the leg, the heavier the body the larger, in general, being the calf and *vice versa*.

Stature. Stature, too, has a direct effect on the size of the leg, though this does not increase proportionately to the increase in stature. Relatively to stature, in consequence, the short have more calf than the tall.

Shape of head. There is no apparent difference in the size of the leg in the dolicho- and brachycephals if the influence of stature, age and weight be excluded.

Comparative. Compared with immigrants, the Old Americans show a leg that is but moderately developed; and when it is taken in relation to the stature the leg in the Old Americans is found to be less stout than that in any of the groups available for comparison. The cause of the difference is in all probability functional (occupational).

Excluding all modifying factors, the leg in the Old Americans would apparently present no racial difference from that of the bulk of the whites.

CHAPTER V

Physiological Observations

In order that physiological observations on any person or any group may be of value, it is necessary to secure the same on only those individuals who are free from pathological as well as other influences that for the time being are capable of modifying the function that is being examined.

The pathological conditions that will affect pulse, respiration, temperature and strength, as well as other functions, are in most cases of a more or less light and temporary character, so much so that at times they are not even specially noticed by the subject. They include above all various derangements of the digestive organs, especially constipation, as well as as slight "colds" and mild infections of other nature, the results of overwork or excesses in any direction.

For the recognition of these disturbing conditions the observer must depend partly upon the statements of those examined, but to these should be added in every case a scrutiny of the tongue, which often tells more than the subject who has been questioned.

In no case where the tongue is perceptibly coated should the observations on pulse, respiration and temperature be included among the normal, even if they should come within the range of variation of the latter.

In addition, pulse, respiration and even temperature will be affected by hunger or a meal taken very shortly before the examination; by mental excitement or unrest; by coffee or other stimulant and tobacco used immediately before coming to the laboratory; by physical exertion; and, so far as respiration and even pulse are concerned, they may be affected in some cases by the consciousness of the subject that they are being examined.

In the case of the Old Americans, all possible care was taken to eliminate these abnormal factors, only those cases being included where the tongue was clean and where other agencies that might affect the observations were absent or immaterial. In addition, in every case a rest of at least twenty minutes was afforded before the examinations were made, and the respiration was counted without the subject's knowledge while the temperature and pulse were being taken. The pulse was counted by quarters of a minute until the true rate was ascertained; and the temperature was taken by a rather slow reliable thermometer placed under the tongue where it was left for five minutes. All these observations were taken with the subject at rest and sitting.

351

The observations of physiological nature were restricted to the Laboratory series, where conditions of normality, rest, etc., could be better determined or controlled. Among the 250 men and 210 women of this series what could be considered as normal pulse was encountered in 184 (73.6 per cent) of the former and 151 (71.9 per cent) of the latter sex, which are very fair proportions; but it should be remembered that these were series out of which all abnormals and unhealthy have already been excluded.

Time

As all of our subjects were examined between the hours of 9 a.m. and 5 p.m., hence after the usual morning minimum and before the late-in-the-day maximum of metabolic activity, and as the forenoon and afternoon cases were nearly equally distributed, the general averages obtained have probably not suffered from the time factor. It was less feasible to regulate the effects of an empty stomach or recent meals, but here again in the general average the conditions probably equalize each other.

Pulse and posture

That the position in which the pulse is taken has an important effect on its frequency, has been shown long ago by Guy.[1] He found the pulse to average, in the lying position, 66.62; sitting, 70.05; and standing 78.9. All the observations on pulse in the Old Americans were taken, as already stated, with the subjects sitting and fully at rest, and the data in literature relate generally to records obtained in similar conditions. An exception to this rule are the occasionally quoted pulse records from the American Civil War, which, in the words of Gould who reports them,[2] in addition to a "limited range of ages" were "most of them taken also in the standing posture."[3] For some unstated reason the observations on 456 drafted men in New York during the World War were also "taken standing."[4]

[1] Guy (Wm. A.)—Guy's Hosp. Rep's., 1838, III, 96. In his article on Pulse, Cyclop. of Anat. and Physiology, 1852, IV, 184, he further reports on 66 men, mean age 27, as giving pulse frequency; lying, 65.62; sitting, 71.12; standing, 81.03; while 50 women, mean age 27, gave pulse: lying 80.24; sitting, 81.98; and standing, 89.26.

[2] Gould (B. A.)—Investigations in the Military and Anthropological Statistics of American Soldiers. 8°, New York, 1869, 523.

[3] "But there are some exceptions to this rule, which our records do not enable us to distinguish from the rest."

[4] Taken under the direction of Dr. Jesse G. M. Bullowa; reported as Comparative Data on Respiration and Circulation among Native and Foreign-Born Males in New York

Variation; dispersion

The records obtained on the pulse in the Old Americans are arranged and charted in tables 286 and 287 and figure 45.

The range of individual variation is seen to be quite large, larger than generally appreciated by medical men; but anthropologically it cannot be regarded as excessive or exceptional.[5]

The dispersion of pulse frequency differs in the two sexes. It is remarkably regular in the males, giving a very good curve. In the females the curve is bi-modal and this corresponds to a similar condition in connection with respiration. There is evidently present some factor in this sex which affects both pulse and respiration and which is absent or subdued in the males; but the exact nature of this factor remains for the present uncertain.

TABLE 286

Old Americans, males: Pulse (per minute)

Number of observations: 184

General average: 70.6

1st series of 44—70.9   4th series of 35—71.0
2nd series of 42—70.2   5th series of 31—72.5
3rd series of 32—68.3

Minimum: 54.0.   Maximum: 86.0

	TABLE OF FREQUENCIES							
	54	55–59	60–64	65–69	70–74	75–79	80–84	85–86
Number of cases............	2	6	29	42	56	34	13	2
Per cent....................	*1.1*	*3.2*	*15.7*	*22.8*	*30.4*	*18.5*	*7.0*	*1.1*

Pulse and sex. The means of what may safely it seems be regarded as the normal pulse in the Old Americans, at rest and in the sitting posture, are 70.6 per minute in the males and 75.5 in the females. The male pulse

City by Clark Wissler, in the Anthrop. Papers of the Am. Mus. Nat. Hist., 1924, XXIII, Part VI, 261–307. In addition this series included a large proportion of sub-adults (166 individuals of 18 to 23 years of age) and some subjects who were not in the best of health (p. 283).

[5] Further elimination of cases would have been quite arbitrary. When the subject declares he or she is well and has been so for some time preceding the examination and there are no indication of heart trouble; when in addition the tongue is clean, there is no mental disturbance and the subject has been comfortably resting for twenty minutes or over, then it is difficult to reject, particularly at the lower part of the scale, whatever record may be obtained, and if an unusual condition is found it is generally acknowledged to be habitual.

is slightly lower than the generally accepted average of 72, probably due to the precautions taken against disturbing factors. The female pulse is just about 5 beats more frequent. The difference is of physiological (metabolic) nature and not due to the difference of the two sexes in stature. The average pulse of the female is more rapid than that of the male at all ages and with all statures. This fact is of course fairly well known though the normal excess, both in general and in special groups, is still somewhat uncertain, differing according to various authors and in various groups between three and ten beats. In the Old Americans of the Laboratory series the difference averages as just seen 5 (4.92) beats, the female pulse standing to that of the male as 107 (106.9) to 100, which is probably very close to the normal average of white people of corresponding classes in general.

TABLE 287

Old Americans, females: Pulse (per minute)

Number of observations: 151

General average: 75.5

1st series of 44—74.64   3rd series of 35—75.71

2nd series of 43—75.44   4th series of 29—77.10

Minimum: 56.0.   Maximum: 92.0

	TABLE OF FREQUENCIES							
	56–59	60–64	65–69	70–74	75–79	80–84	85–89	90–92
Number of cases............	3	5	19	44	37	38	3	2
Per cent...................	*2.0*	*3.3*	*12.6*	*29.1*	*24.5*	*25.2*	*2.0*	*1.3*

Pulse and age. The age of the subject is well known to have an influence on the frequency of the heart beat and numerous students have occupied themselves with the subject, yet the details are not yet fully established. It has been ascertained that, in general, the pulse is most rapid before and within the first year after birth; that it then gradually slows down until the adult stage is reached; that it then remains fairly constant until the onset of senility, after which it again tends to increase. But the various records on the subject show numerous irregularities and probably none of them meet all, or throughout, the requirements of scientific precision. The more conspicuous records are given in table 288.

Tigerstedt (1893)[6], grouping the combined results of Volkman, Guy (Art. Pulse, Todd's Cyclop. of Anat. and Physiol., 1852, 185–9) and Nitsch,

[6] Tigerstedt (R.)—Lehrbuch der Physiologie des Kreislaufer. 1st ed. 8°, Leipzig, 1893, 31–32.

REV. JAMES KING
(Bristol, Tenn.)

One of the ancestors of the noted King family of Old Americans, in Bristol, Tenn. On mother's side from old American stock; father from London. (70 years old when picture taken.)

MRS. JAMES KING, NÉE WILLIAMS
(Bristol, Tenn.)

On both sides for at least 3 generations American. Far back ancestry largely Welsh and French. (70 years old when picture taken.)

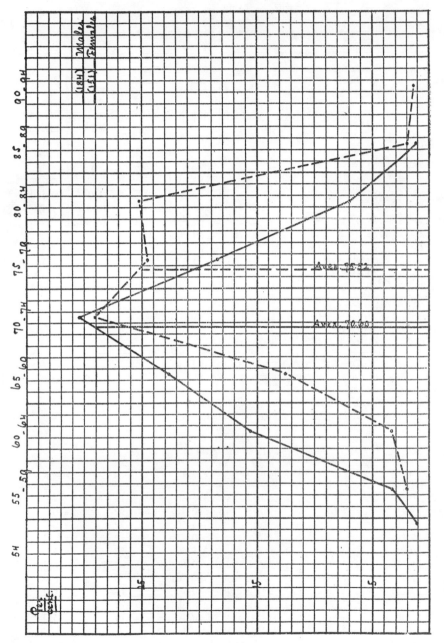

FIG. 45. OLD AMERICANS: PULSE—LABORATORY SERIES

TABLE 288
Pulse and age: in whites

GUY*			QUETELET†			LANDOIS AND STIRLING‡	
Age	Pulse		Age	Pulse		Age	Pulse, male
	Male	Female		Male	Female		
years			years			years	
			0	136.0	135.0	New-born	130–140
						1	120–130
						2	105
						3	100
2–7	97.0	98.0				4	97
			5	88.0		5	94–90
8–14	84.0	94.0				10	About 90
			10–15	78.0		10–15	78
14–21	78.0	82.0	15–20	69.5	78.0	15–20	70
21–28	73.0	80.0	20–25	69.7	77.0	20–25	70
28–35	70.0	78.0	25–30	71.0	72.0	25–50	70
35–42	68.0	78.0	30–50	70.0	74.5	60	74
42–49	70.0 }68.6	77.0 }77.2				80	79
49–56	67.0	76.0				80–90	Over 80
56–63	68.0	77.0					
63–70	70 0	78.0					
71–77	67 0	80.0					
77–84	71.0	82.0					

* Guy (Wm. A.)—Art. Pulse, Cyclop. of Anat. & Physiol., 1852, IV, 184. Pulse taken on healthy individuals with subject sitting and at rest; 25 to 50 observations for each of twelve groups.

† Quetelet (Ad.)—Physique sociale. 8°, 1869, II, 123–4.

‡ Text-book of Physiology. 4th ed., N. Y., 1890, 126.

TABLE 289
Pulse frequency in European whites, by age

AGE	PULSE	SUBJECTS	AGE	PULSE	SUBJECTS
16–17	80	(84)	35–40	72	(144)
17–18	76	(67)	40–45	72	(105)
18–19	77	(48)	45–50	72	(102)
19–20	74	(57)	50–55	72	(42)
20–21	71	(67)	55–60	75	(58)
21–22	71	(54)	60–65	73	(60)
22–23	70	(63)	65–70	75	(51)
23–24	71	(60)	70–75	75	(44)
24–25	72	(44)	75–80	72	(44)
25–30	72	(180)	80 and over	79	(31)
30–35	70	(125)			

gives the data in table 289 on healthy white subjects in the sitting position, but disregarding sex, stature or class (abstracted).

These records do not show a perfect agreement, yet they are much alike in substance. The pulse diminishes up to adult life; it seems quite stationary from about 25 to 55 years of age; and it rises again somewhat thereafter.

The Old Americans who include neither adolescents nor senile subjects would not be expected according to the preceding to show any material pulse difference due to age. What actually appears is shown in table 290.

In the males conditions are somewhat irregular; the lowest pulse rate is nevertheless recorded in the last decade of normal adult life. After that begins senility and the pulse rises. In the females there is a slight but steady diminution in pulse rate up to the sixth decade. The progression of age, after the adult stage has been reached, appears after all

TABLE 290

Old Americans: Pulse vs. age

Laboratory series

	MALES					FEMALES				
	24–29 years	30–39 years	40–49 years	50–59 years	Above 59 years	22–29 years	30–39 years	40–49 years	50–59 years	Above 59 years
Number of subjects...............	(70)	(44)	(37)	(23)	(10)	(48)	(54)	(26)	(22)	(1)
Pulse............................	70.0	70.0	71.6	68.4	72.6	75.5	74.9	74.8	74.3	78.0

not to be without some influence on the pulse which on general physiological considerations seems only natural.

Pulse and stature

The influence of stature on the frequency of heart beats has been studied amongst older authors, particularly by Volkmann[7] and amongst the recent by Körösy and Julia Bell.[8] Volkmann's data are given in two tables, the more valuable one of which is here in part reproduced (table 291). According to these observations, which show a lower pulse rate for every group of the "taller" series, stature would seem to bear a slight correlation

[7] Körösy (Kornel)—D. Arch. Klin. Med., December, 1910, 267–282.

[8] On Pulse and Breathing Rates and Their Relation to Stature. Biometrika, 1911–12, VIII, 232–6.

of an inverse nature to pulse rate, *i.e.*, the taller the stature for a given age the slower, within very moderate limits, the pulse.

From Mackenzie (1902)[9]: "as a general rule it can be said that the larger the frame the slower the pulse. The pulse of tall men is slower than the average—in some instances markedly so."

Dr. Körösy, in careful observations on the pulse and breathing of 255 military recruits from 20 to 24 years of age found that there was no definite change in his averages as the stature increased, from which he deduced that there is no relation between pulse and stature or breathing and stature. Miss Julia Bell, who further analyzed these data, failed also to find any relationship between respiration and stature, but "there appears to be a

TABLE 291

Pulse and stature (Volkmann)*

Influence of stature at same age

MALES	SHORTER		TALLER	
	Stature	Pulse	Stature	Pulse
years				
20–25	149.5–167.4	74.4	169.5–195.5	71.3
25–30	138.3–164.5	71.6	164.8–183.5	70.3
30–35	146.6–168.9	68.7		
35–40	140.0–164.6	72.3	164.7–182.2	68.0
40–45	152.0–166.0	72.4	166.5–176.5	66.5
45–50	140.0–170.0	74.0	170.2–193.0	72.0
50–55	148.1–161.6	73.1		
55–60	144.4–162.0	76.3	162.3–180.8	75.4
60–65	150.1–163.0	78.0	163.0–180.0	75.4

* Volkmann (A. W.)—Die Haemodynamic nach Versuchen. 1850, 429.

After Vierordt, 154, abbreviated, children and adolescents left out—the taller show throughout a slower pulse, even as early as the first year.

slight tendency to a slower pulse with increasing stature"; though not much importance can be attached to the slight relationship based upon a given number of observations.

In the Old American adults the effects of stature on the frequency of pulse beat are fairly apparent. And they show that the pulse rate tends to increase with stature. The tallest men as well as the tallest women have more rapid pulse than the shortest; and if the pulse is given by regular subdivisions of stature, it is seen on the whole to rise with the latter. (See tables 292 and 293.)

[9] Mackenzie (James)—Study of the Pulse. 8°, Edinburgh and London.

RESPIRATION

Frequency in general

The action of the lungs is closely but not absolutely correlated with the action of the heart and under normal conditions, in the sitting posture, approximately four pulse beats correspond to one inspiration and expiration, giving about 18 respirations per minute as the general average for white males and 19 for white females. The range of normal variation is usually regarded as 16 to 24.

TABLE 292

Old Americans: Pulse and stature extremes

Laboratory series

	MALES			FEMALES		
		Stature	Pulse		Stature	Pulse
Shortest........	(17)	163.85	69.82	(16)	151.4	73.44
Tallest........	(20)	184.5	71.90	(18)	172.2	75.94

TABLE 293

Old Americans: Pulse vs. stature

MALES			FEMALES		
Mean stature			Mean stature		
160.01–170.0	170.01–180.0	180.01–190.0	150.01–160.0	160.01–170.0	170.01–180.0
(47)	(107)	(28)	(54)	(78)	(17)
70.2	70.1	71.7	74.7	75.0	76.0

Posture and respiration

Like that of the pulse, the frequency of respiration is materially affected by the position of the body, facts often forgotten in medicine. Guy, to whom we owe what are probably the best of the earlier observations on pulse and respiration, found the latter to average, with the subject lying, 13; sitting, 19; and standing, 22 per minute. Upon purely biological grounds, tests of both pulse and respiration in the standing position, which may be regarded as the true posture of man, would seem most proper. But man, and especially civilized man is habitually at least as much, and frequently (sedentary occupations) much more of a sitter than a stander which, with the added greater convenience, makes observations in the sitting position preferable.

Old Americans

The records on the Old Americans, Laboratory subjects, in normal health, sitting position, at rest and not knowing that the respiration was being observed, are shown in table 294.

The averages are not exceptional. The female exceeds the male by 1.1 respiration (pulse 4.9) per minute, and her respiration rate compares with that of the male as 106.4 (pulse 106.9) to 100; all of which is evidently quite normal.

TABLE 294

Old Americans: Frequency of respiration

MALES				FEMALES			
Laboratory series	Average per minute	Range	Pulse beats for 1 respiration	Laboratory series	Average per minute	Range	Pulse beats for 1 respiration
(192)	17.1	11–24	*4.13*	(158)	18.2	12–24	*4.15*

TABLE 295

Old Americans, males: Respiration (per minute)

Number of observations: 192

General average: 17.1

1st series of 48—17.1	4th series of 35—17.1
2nd series of 44—17.3	5th series of 33—17.2
3rd series of 32—16.9	

Minimum: 11.0   Maximum: 24.0

	TABLE OF FREQUENCIES						
	11	12–13	14–15	16–17	18–19	20–21	22–23	24
Number of cases....	2	4	34	68	49	28	6	1
Per cent............	*1.0*	*2.1*	*17.6*	*35.3*	*25.5*	*14.5*	*3.1*	*0.5*

The range of individual variation is larger than given ordinarily, though the upper limit is the same. The showing may be partly due to the conditions of examination, the subject being entirely at rest, sitting and unconscious that the movements of the chest were being counted. But the very slow rate in each case where met with was persistently slow and where the subject was aware of it was invariably declared to be habitual. It would seem therefore that the lower limit of normal variation of the respiration rate, as commonly taught in medicine, is too high. There are individuals in both sexes who at rest and sitting breathe normally no more than eleven or twelve times a minute.

TABLE 296

Old Americans, females: Respiration (per minute)

Number of observations: 158

Average: 18.2 (1st series of 49: 18.6; 2d series of 48: 18.4; 3d series of 36: 18.3; 4th series of 25: 17.2)

Minimum: 10.0.   Maximum: 24.0

	TABLE OF FREQUENCIES							
	10–11	12–13	14–15	16–17	18–19	20–21	22–23	24
Number of cases....	2	2	13	45	36	41	16	3
Per cent..........	*1.2*	*1.2*	*8.2*	*28.4*	*22.7*	*25.9*	*10.1*	*1.9*

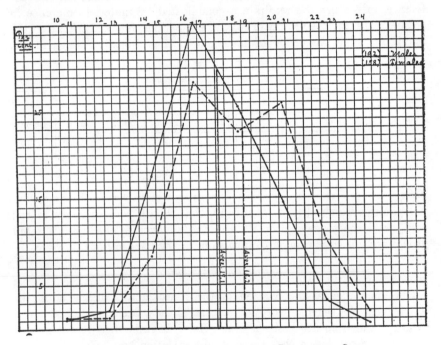

FIG. 46. OLD AMERICANS: RESPIRATION—LABORATORY SERIES

A respiration above 24 was found invariably connected with some derangement, and not infrequently this was also the case with that above 21.

The dispersion of the records is almost ideal in the males, but shows the same irregularity and bi-modal character as that of the pulse in the females. The cause of this peculiarity is for the present not clear. (See tables 295 and 296, and fig. 46).

Respiration and age

Respiration, like pulse, is known to be most frequent at birth, to diminish rapidly during infancy and more gradually during the later years of growth, to reach its minimum during early adult life, and again to increase slightly with advancing years. These facts are well shown by Quetelet's old series of observations[10] (table 297).

As to the effects of age on respiration within the adult period, satisfactory records are wanting. The data on the Old Americans are given in tables 298 and 299. They are largely negative and in the remainder not decisive.

As to the youngest and oldest, in the males there is practically no difference, in females the results are complicated by material difference in stature. Taking the records of regular age periods, it would seem that the maximum adult frequency of breathing during the adult stage in the

TABLE 297

Respiration vs. age (Quetelet)

	YEARS						
	0	5	10–15	15–20	20–25	25–30	30–50
Respirations per minute:							
Males.........	44	26	26	20	18.7	16	18.1
Females........	44			19	17	17	19

Americans occurs between 40 and 49; that it falls somewhat thereafter; and that it rises again after 59 with the advance of senility. But our groups are not large enough to furnish more than suggestions.

Respiration and stature

Our knowledge of the relation of these two factors during adult life is still very restricted. Körösy,[11] as has already been mentioned under "Pulse," and from his data also Julia Bell,[12] have in their recent studies come to the conclusion that there is no correlation between the two; but their observations have only extended to a series of recruits 20 to 24 years of age, hence mostly subadults.

The data on the Old Americans indicate that stature does have an effect on respiration.

[10] Physique sociale, 1869, II, 123–4.

For references to further more partial data see Vierordt's Daten und Tabellen.

[11] D. Arch. Klin. Med., December, 1910, 267–282.

[12] Biometrika, 1911–12, VIII, 232–6.

TABLE 298

Old Americans: Respiration in the young and old

Laboratory series

		MALES				FEMALES		
		Stature	Respira-tion	Number of respira-tions per 100 cm. of stature		Stature	Respira-tion	Number of respira-tions per 100 cm. of stature
Youngest*.....	(25)	175.1	17.16	*9.80*	(20)	163.5	18.40	*11.25*
All............	(184)	174.4	17.10	*9.80*	(158)	161.8	18.20	*11.25*
Oldest*........	(27)	174.7	17.12	*9.80*	(20)	160.1	18.50	*11.55*

* In which normal conditions existed.

TABLE 299

Old Americans: Frequency of respiration and age

Laboratory series

	YEARS				
	22–29	30–39	40–49	50–59	Above 59
Males.........	(70) 17 2	(44) 16.7	(37) 17.6	(23) 16.2	(10) 18.3
Females........	(48) 19.0	(55) 18 45	(26) 18.6	(24) 18.4	(2) 18.0

TABLE 300

Old Americans: Respiration and extremes of stature

Laboratory series

		MALES				FEMALES		
		Stature	Respiration	Respiration per 100 cm. of stature		Stature	Respiration	Respiration per 100 cm. of stature
Shortest........................	(25)	165.2	17.24	*10.44*	(20)	152.0	18.70	*12.30*
General Average.................	(184)	174.4	17.10	*9.80*	(153)	161.8	18 20	*11.25*
Tallest.........................	(25)	183.8	16.76	*9.12*	(20)	172.0	17.40	*10.12*
Difference between shortest and tallest (%) in favor of shortest...				*12.7*				*17.7*

This fact appears clearly from table 300 in which the frequency of respiration is given both for the mean and extremes of stature. In both sexes, but particularly in the females, the frequency of respiration is greatest in the short and lowest by quite an appreciable difference in the tall, while the averages are intermediary.

Much the same condition is also shown in table 301 where respiration is taken by stature groups of 10 cm. Respiration diminishes slightly as stature rises.

TABLE 301

Old Americans: Respiration vs. stature

Laboratory series

MALES			FEMALES		
Stature			Stature		
160.01–170.0	170.01–180.0	180.01–190.0	150.01–160.0	160.01–170.0	170.01–180.0
(47)	(107)	(28)	(56)	(85)	(17)
17.64	17.0	16.75	18.49	18.41	17.24

Respiration, and size and form of chest

An interesting inquiry made possible by our in many respects rather homogeneous series, is that into the effects, if any, upon respiration of the size and form of the chest. The results are shown in table 302.

TABLE 302

Old Americans: Respiration vs. size and shape of chest

Laboratory series

Size

		MALES			FEMALES	
		Mean chest diameter	Respiration per minute		Mean chest diameter	Respiration per minute
Smallest chests.....................	(20)	23.09	17.05	(20)	21.10	18.10
Largest chests.........................	(20)	29.18	17.15	(20)	26.97	17.85

Shape

		MALES			FEMALES	
		Mean chest index	Respiration per minute		Mean chest index	Respiration per minute
Relatively flattest chests................	(25)	64.43	16.84	(20)	67.67	17.90
Relatively deepest chests................	(20)	82.83	16.76	(20)	84.46	17.70

So far as the size of the chest is concerned there is found practically no difference in the males, but in the females with the smaller chests the respiration is a trace more rapid than in those of the largest thoracic cavities. In order really to decide the point, however, we should have observations on a much larger series of subjects so as to minimize the possible influence of collateral factors, such as stature, age, occupation and time at which examined.

So far as the relatively flat and deep chests are concerned, the flat in both sexes show respiration a trace more rapid than the deep, but the difference is too slight to be of any moment.

TEMPERATURE

The normal temperature in white people, under the tongue, is generally understood to be close to 98.7°F. (37.1°C.). The "norms" given by va-

TABLE 303

Old Americans: Mean temperature (sub lingua)

Laboratory series

	MALES				FEMALES		
	Mean temperature				Mean temperature		
	°F.	°C.	Extremes		°F.	°C.	Extremes
(184)	98.57	36.98	96.7–99.5	(154)	98.82	37.12	97.5–100.1

rious observers and in the text-books of physiology[13] range from 97.7° to 98.9°F. (36.49° to 37.19°C.), but in some of these cases the records refer to temperature in the axilla or in the rectum, which are not strictly equivalent to that under the tongue. The Old Americans, where more than usual care was taken to ascertain the normal conditions, show the record given in table 303.

[13] Landois and Stirling—Text Book of Human Physiology. 4th ed., Philadelphia, 1892, 126, 197–8, 409. In closed axilla the temperature is slightly lower—36.49 (mean of 505 individuals, J. Davy), 36.5–37.25 (Wunderlich), 36.89 (Liebermeister), in the rectum slightly higher—38.01—than that under the tongue.

Schäfer (E. A.)—Textbook of Physiology. 1900, I, 747, 788; V, 101–2. 100 men 27 years old; average of 1897 adult males.

Mackenzie (James)—The Study of the Pulse, 8°, 1902, Men 25 to 30 years of age.

Greene (Chas. Wilson)—Kirke's Handbook of Physiology, 1917, 206–7, 284, 479.

Paton (D. Noël)—Essentials of Human Physiology. 8°, 1920, 400–1, 538–9, 287.

See also Davy (J.)—Physiological Researches, 1863; Jürgensen—Die Körperwärme des gesunden Menschen, 1873; and Vierordt (H.)—Daten and Tabellen, 1893, 238 *et seq.*

These results are substantially identical with those of various European whites, and even more strikingly than so many others—for in this case we are dealing with the gage of the most complex internal processes covered by the term metabolism—show the inherent unity of the whole race, as well as the great stability of the involved functions.

What appeared to be the normal range of variation ranged in the males from 96.7 to 97.5; in the females from 97.5 to approximately 100. When however, the records are charted it appears that a strictly normal limit

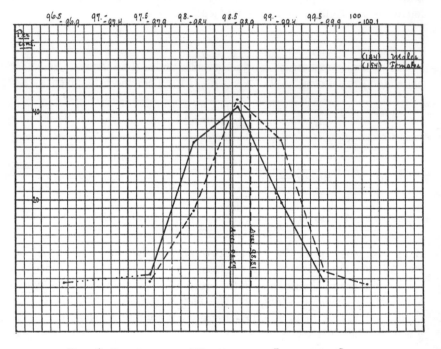

FIG. 47. OLD AMERICANS: TEMPERATURE—LABORATORY SERIES

should be placed with both sexes close to 97.5, while the maximum in the females is probably 99.8 or 99.9. The two lower records in the males are probably due to a temporarily lowered metabolism such as may take place before meals; while in the one female where the temperature was a trace above 100 there was probably some undetected small disturbance. (See tables 304 and 305.)

The curves showing the dispersion of individual variations in temperature are steep and quite regular though of a somewhat peculiar summit;

the female curve however, is almost an exact reverse of the male. The significance of this could only be established with much larger series of observations.

TABLE 304

Old Americans, males: Temperature

Number of observations: 184
General average: 98.57°

1st series of 44—98.53°   4th series of 35—98.88°
2nd series of 42—98.36°   5th series of 32—98.51°
3rd series of 31—98.64°

Minimum: 96.7° Maximum: 99.5°

	TABLE OF FREQUENCIES						
	96.7°–96.9°	97.0°–97.4°	97.5°–97.9°	98.0°–98.4°	98.5°–98.9°	99.0°–99.4°	99.5°–99.9°
Number of cases.....	2	0	6	61	76	36	3
Per cent...........	1.1		3.2	33.1	41.2	19.5	1.6

TABLE 305

Old Americans, females: Temperature

Number of observations: 154

Average: 98.81° (1st series of 47—98.8°; 2nd series of 46—98.6°; 3rd series of 37—98.7°; 4th series of 24—99.2°)

Minimum: 97.5°. Maximum: 100.1°

	TABLE OF FREQUENCIES					
	97.5°–97.9°	98.0°–98.4°	98.5°–98.9°	99.0°–99.4°	99.5°–99.9°	100.0°–100.1°
Number of cases............	2	27	66	52	6	1
Per cent....................	1.3	17.5	42.8	33.7	3.9	0.6

Temperature and sex

In the opinion of Vierordt, who based himself on his own observations as well as extensive older literature,[14] "sex in the adults has no perceptible influence on the body temperature;" and there is little definite on the point in more recent authors. The fact is, however, that critical studies

[14] Daten und Tabellen, 2nd ed., 1893, 240.

on the same subject, studies made by one observer, under regulated conditions and taking due account of the factors of class, health, age, occupation and stature, are still wanting or are insufficient.

The observations on the Old Americans show plainly that there is a
sex difference in temperature. The two sexes in the Laboratory series are
represented by fair and nearly alike numbers of persons; these were in
normal health at the time of the examination, they are of practically one
social class and of not much differing occupations, and the records were
all taken by the author in the same way, at the same place, by the same
instrument and under conditions which could hardly be better. The
results show the mean temperature of the females to be one-quarter of a
degree higher than that of the males, and the curves of the records demonstrate conclusively that the temperature of the females is in general slightly
higher.

Temperature and age

The question of the influence of age upon the temperature of the body
within the span of life before senility sets in, is equally one on which there
is still no little uncertainty. There is very little on the point in literature
so far as the ordinary tests of temperature are concerned; Landois and
Stirling[15] give the data shown in table 306, which, while not taken uniformly would seem to indicate that there is little if any change in body
temperature between the ages of twenty-five and sixty.

On the other hand Harris and Benedict[16] in their painstaking experimental studies on metabolism, have obtained results which show that
"throughout the whole range of what we commonly designate as adult
life the heat production of the individual decreases;" the correlation between age and heat production is negative in sign, "lower daily heat production being associated with greater age."

Our ordinary thermometer tests on the Old Americans gave results
which are grossly as shown in tables 307 and 308.

These figures show that a slight excess of temperature in the females
over the males is present at all ages. As to changes in body temperature
with age, the male series shows exceedingly little of such difference, but
in the females the difference in favor of the young is more perceptible
though not exceeding one-quarter of a degree. From the clinical point
of view it is permissible therefore to say that during their adult life from

15 Physiology, 1892, 414.
16 Biom. Study of Basal Metabolism in Man. Carnegie Institute of Washington, 1919,
125.

24 to 60 the males show almost none, the females (22 to 60) a slight diminution in body temperature.

TABLE 306

Temperature and age (Landois and Stirling)

AGE	TEMPERA-TURE		AGE	TEMPERA-TURE	
years			*years*		
New-born	37.45	Rectum	25–30	36.91	Axilla
5–9	37.72	Rectum and mouth	31–40	37.10	Axilla
15–20	37.37	Axilla	41–50	36.87	Axilla
21–30	37.22	Axilla	51–60	36.83	Axilla
			80	37.46	Mouth

TABLE 307

Old Americans: Temperature and extremes of age

Laboratory series

	MALES			FEMALES	
		Stature	Tempera-ture		Stature	Tempera-ture
Youngest..................	(25)	175.3	98.57	(20)	163.7	98.95
General average..............	(184)	174.4	98.57	(154)	161.8	98.82
Oldest......................	(25)	174.8	98.55	(20)	159.6	98.70

TABLE 308

Old Americans: Temperature and age

Laboratory series

MALES					FEMALES				
24–29 years	30–39 years	40–49 years	50–59 years	Above 59 years	22–29 years	30–39 years	40–49 years	50–59 years	Above 59 years
(70)	(45)	(37)	(22)	(10)	(46)	(56)	(27)	(25)	(2)
98.56	98.60	98.62	98.49	98.65	98.93	98.77	98.92	98.72	98.75

Temperature and stature

The problem of a possible influence upon body temperature of stature
within adult life, is equally as unsettled as those of the effects of age and
sex. In general it seems to be taken for granted that there is no such
effect. Our observations on the Old Americans show differently (tables
309 and 310).

The differences are small, amounting to less than one-half of a degree; but small as they are their regularity is too marked to be without significance. In their studies on heat production and stature Harris and Benedict[17] found that "the constants for adults are positive throughout, indicating greater total heat-production by taller individuals;" and our results appear to agree with this conclusion.

TABLE 309

Old Americans: Temperature and extremes of stature

Laboratory series

		MALES			FEMALES	
		Stature	Temperature		Stature	Temperature
Shortest......................	(25)	165 2	98 45	(20)	152.0	98.59
General average.............	(184)	174.4	98.57	(154)	161.8	98.82
Tallest......................	(25)	183.9	98.74	(20)	172.0	98.93

TABLE 310

Old Americans: Temperature vs. stature

Laboratory series

MALES			FEMALES		
Stature			Stature		
160.01–170.0	170.01–180.0	180.01–190.0	150.01–160.0	160.01–170.0	170.01–180.0
(49)	(104)	(29)	(57)	(80)	(17)
98.52	98.55	98.75	98.78	98.83	99.02

TEMPERATURE, PULSE AND RESPIRATION VS. CORPULENCE

There remain a few words to be said about a possible effect on the body temperature and the related functions of pulse and respiration of the weight of the body as shown by the Old Americans. Taking the lightest and the heaviest of the low medium and tall stature groups among our subjects, we obtain the simple ratios in table 311.

The results of these comparisons are rather disconcerting. Functional differences in the lighest and heavies individuals exist, and they appear to be of the same type for all the statures, but they are of opposite values

[17] Biometric Study of Basal Metabolism of Man. Carnegie Institute of Washington, 1919, 96; also 105–106.

in the two sexes. The lightest among the males show throughout a perceptibly lower pulse with a trace lower temperature, but a trace more rapid respiration, than the heaviest of the same groups. This seems to imply a weaker metabolism with possibly a shallower respiration (less intake of air) in the lightest as compared to the heaviest males. It may be remarked that none of the heavy males were obese, that is abnormally

TABLE 311

	WEIGET	TEMPER-ATURE	PULSE	RESPIRATION
Males				
Short: Statures below 169.5 cm.:				
10 lightest..........................	119.65	98.37	68.22	17.30
10 heaviest..........................	167.75	98.54	70.55	16.70
Medium height: Statures 169.6–179.9 cm.:				
10 lightest.........................	124.7	98.23	70.80	17.90
10 heaviest..........................	200.3	98.56	74.10	17.80
Tall: Statures 180 cm. and above				
10 lightest..........................	141.5	98.59	68.70	17.40
10 heaviest..........................	189.6	98.97	71.40	17.10
Females				
Short: Below 156.9 cm.:				
10 lightest..........................	98.6	98.75	75.25	17.89
10 heaviest..........................	145.7	98.49	74.40	18.80
Medium height: 157–166.9 cm.:				
10 lightest..........................	104.45	98.75	76.78	17.50
10 heaviest..........................	177.35	98.79	75.90	17.90
Tall: 167 cm. and above:				
10 lightest..........................	119.8	98.92	77.78	17.20
10 heaviest..........................	170.7	98.97	72.44	17.60

fat. But there were also no truly obese women, yet the conditions in this sex are in all the groups and throughout, the reverse of those in the men. The lightest women, as compared to the heaviest, have slightly more rapid pulse, practically the same temperature, and a trace less frequent respiration. These conditions are particularly marked in the shortest group. Here, apparently, and in the female sex as a whole, it is the stout in whom there is slower metabolism with possibly shallower and hence more frequent respiration. The whole subject is evidently a complex one and may well repay a further, special, investigation.

Under strict regulations as to normality of subjects and rest in a sitting posture during examination, observations on the Old Americans show conditions which ordinarily are more or less obscured.

Pulse

The averages obtained are 70.6 for the males; 75.5 for the females.

The individual variation is larger than generally appreciated.

Dispersion differs in the two sexes, being remarkably regular in the males, bimodal in the females.

The bimodal condition in the females corresponds to a similar condition in respiration. Its cause is not apparent.

Influence of sex. The pulse in the females is more rapid at all ages and with all statures than that of the males.

The difference is physiological (metabolic) and not physical factors.

Effects of age. The influence of age between 24 and 60 on pulse frequency is small.

During the sixth decade there are traces of slight slowing followed by increased frequency as senility sets in.

Effects of stature. The pulse rate tends to *increase* with stature in both sexes.

Respiration

The average respiration was found to be 17.1 in men, 18.2 in women.

The individual variation is large.

The dispersion is almost ideal in the males, bimodal (as with pulse) in the females.

Effect of age. The results are largely negative or not decisive. Age then, between 24 and 60 has no regular effect on respiration.

Effect of stature. Respiration diminishes slightly in both sexes as stature rises.

Size and form of chest. The small- and large-chested show practically no difference in rate of respiration in the males; in the females with the smaller chests respiration is a trace more rapid than in those of large thoraxes.

The flat chested in both sexes show slightly more rapid respiration than those of deep chest.

Temperature

Averages: Males, 98.57; females, 98.82.

The range of variation is moderate in the males, slightly larger (upwards) in the females.

The dispersion is somewhat peculiar but quite regular.

Sex. The observations plainly show a sex difference at all ages and statures, the mean temperature of the females ranging one-fourth of a degree higher than that of the males.

Age. Within the age limits of this series the males show very little effect of age; in the females a progressive slight diminution in temperature takes place as age advances.

Stature. The effects of stature, though slight, are regular; in both sexes temperature rises slightly with rise in stature.

Temperature, pulse and respiration vs. corpulence

The results are not harmonious in the two sexes.

The lightest males show lower pulse and slightly lower temperature with a slightly more rapid respiration than the heaviest. The lightest females have a slightly more rapid pulse, the same temperature and a trace slower respiration.

These points call for a special inquiry.

MUSCULAR STRENGTH

The most convenient and perhaps satisfactory tests of muscular strength are those of maximum pressure in each hand, which may be supplemented by traction; and for these tests the most convenient instrument is the classic Mathieu's or Collin's dynamometer.[18] It was this instrument which was used by the writer, the method being briefly as follows: "The object of the observer is to secure the maximum effort in each hand and he

---

[18] These instruments, it is well known, are not entirely accurate; when tested mechanically they show errors, but these errors appear to be much the same in the different instruments of French make (there are German imitations); and as the instrument is by far the most handy dynamometer in existence, its use appears permissible and the results may be safely compared, though they should not be taken for perfect values and should not be contrasted with records obtained by instruments of different makes.

must stimulate the subject to a maximum exertion. As a rule at least two tests are to be made with each hand, after which fatigue ensues" (A. H., Anthropometry, pp. 87–88).

Pressure; traction

The results of these dynamometric tests when they are properly made, are remarkably dependable. Repeated with the same subject the record steadily keeps the same value as long as the health and tone of the person remain the same; but let these change even slightly and the records grow

TABLE 312

Old Americans: Muscular strength

PRESSURE		LEFT *vs.* RIGHT HAND (R = 100)	TRACTION	TRACTION *vs.* MEAN PRESSURE
Right hand	Left hand			
Males				
41.8	36.1	*86.4*	22.3	*57.2*
Females				
23.2	19.4	*83.6*	10.5	*49.1*

Felmale vs. male strength (M. = 100)

STATURE	SIZE OF HAND (MEAN DIAMETER)	SIZE OF CHEST (MEAN DIAMETER)	PRESSURE		TRACTION
			Right hand	Left hand	
92.8	*86.8*	*90.6*	*55.5*	*53.7*	*47.1*

less. The value of the tests is in fact such, that were they better known they would be of much use in medicine, particularly in hospitals.

Due to injuries of hand or arm or other causes, the pressure test could only be secured on 235 men and 190 women of the Laboratory series, while those of traction were possible on 232 men and 180 women. The results, in kilograms, are given in table 312.

Seriation. The range of variation of the individual records of muscular strength varies very considerably in the males as well as the females; and the dispersion of the records is very irregular in the males. (See tables 313 to 316, and figures 48 and 49.)

TABLE 313
Old Americans, males: Pressure force in hands

Number of observations in right hand—219; in left hand—216

General average in right hand—41.8; in left hand—36.1

Right hand	Left hand
1st series of 47—41.5	1st series of 47—36.9
2nd series of 50—41.2	2nd series of 50—35.3
3rd series of 45—41.1	3rd series of 44—35.6
4th series of 46—41.7	4th series of 46—35.9
5th series of 31—43.7	5th series of 30—36.9

Minimum: Right hand—22.6. Maximum: Right hand—60.0

Minimum: Left hand—18.0. Maximum: Left hand—52.5

TABLE OF FREQUENCIES

NUMBER OF CASES	18-20	20.1-22.5	22.6-25.0	25.1-27.5	27.6-30.0	30.1-32.5	32.6-35.0	35.1-37.5	37.6-40.0	40.1-42.5	42.6-45.0	45.1-47.5	47.6-50.0	50.1-52.5	52.6-55.0	55.1-57.5	57.6-60.0
Right hand..			2	1	14	5	22	9	28	29	39	23	18	12	11	2	4
Per cent.....			*0.9*	*0.5*	*6.4*	*2.3*	*10.0*	*4.1*	*12.8*	*13.2*	*17.8*	*10.5*	*8.2*	*5.5*	*5.0*	*0.9*	*1.8*
Left hand...	4	5	5	4	21	26	39	23	35	19	18	8	8	1			
Per cent....	*1.8*	*2.3*	*2.3*	*1.8*	*9.7*	*12.0*	*18.0*	*10.6*	*16.2*	*8.8*	*8.3*	*3.7*	*3.7*	*0.5*			

TABLE 314
Old Americans, females: Pressure force in the hands

Number of observations in right hand—184; in left hand—185

General average in right hand—23.3; in left hand—19 4

Right hand	Left hand
1st series of 45—24.6	1st series of 45—20.5
2nd series of 50—22.05	2nd series of 50—17 7
3rd series of 45—23 3	3rd series of 45—19 4
4th series of 44—20 0	4th series of 45—20.0

Minimum: Right hand—12.6. Maximum: Right hand—40.0

Minimum: Left hand— 8.0. Maximum: Left hand—35.0

TABLE OF FREQUENCIES

NUMBER OF CASES	8-10	10.1-12.5	12.6-15.0	15.1-17.5	17.6-20.0	20.1-22.5	22.6-25.0	25.1-27.5	27.6-30.0	30.1-32.5	32.6-35.0	35.1-37.5	37.6-40.0
Right hand..........			8	14	29	28	49	18	24	4	8		2
Per cent............			*4.3*	*7.6*	*15.8*	*15.2*	*26.6*	*9.8*	*13.0*	*2.2*	*4.3*		*1.1*
Left hand..........	3	10	23	30	51	23	23	13	6	2	1		
Per cent............	*1.6*	*5.4*	*12.4*	*16.2*	*27.6*	*12.4*	*12.4*	*7.0*	*3.2*	*1.1*	*0.5*		

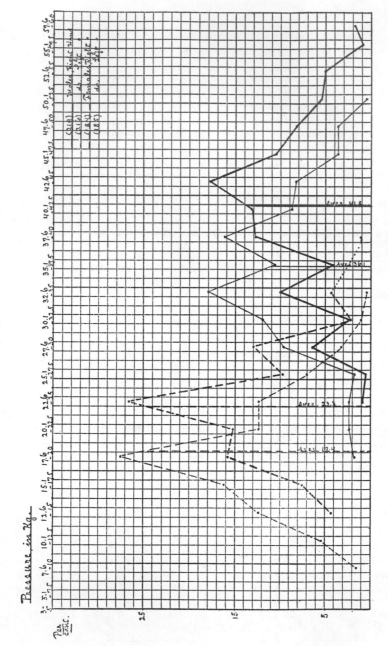

FIG. 48. OLD AMERICANS: MUSCULAR STRENGTH—LABORATORY SERIES

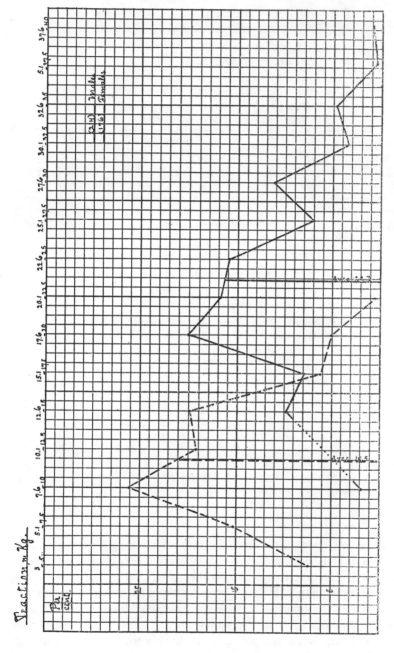

FIG. 49. OLD AMERICANS: MUSCULAR STRENGTH—LABORATORY SERIES

TABLE 315

Old Americans, males: Traction

Number of observations: 214

General average: 22.3

1st series of 45—20.2   4th series of 46—24.1
2nd series of 50—22.2   5th series of 30—24.9
3rd series of 43—20.0

Minimum: 8.0.   Maximum: 40.0

		TABLE OF FREQUENCIES											
		8.0–10.0	10.1–12.5	12.6–15.0	15.1–17.5	17.6–20.0	20.1–22.5	22.6–25.0	25.1–27.5	27.6–30.0	30.1–32.5	32.6–35.0	35.1–37.5	37.6–40.0
Number of cases	4		21	17	43	36	34	15	24	7	10	1	2
Per cent	1.9		9.8	7.9	20.1	16.8	15.9	7.0	11.2	3.3	4.7	0.5	0.9

TABLE 316

Old Americans, females: Traction

Number of obsevations: 176

General average: 10.5

1st series of 46—10.38   3rd series of 45— 9.8
2nd series of 50— 9.83   4th series of 35—13.5

Minimum: 3.0.   Maximum: 22.0

	TABLE OF FREQUENCIES							
	3–5 kgm.	5.1–7.5 kgm.	7.6–10.0 kgm.	10.1–12.5 kgm.	12.6–15.0 kgm.	15.1–17.5 kgm.	17.6–20.0 kgm.	20.1–22.0 kgm.
Number of cases	13	27	46	34	35	11	9	1
Per cent	7.4	15.3	26.1	19.3	19.9	6.2	5.1	0.6

Sex

The sex comparisons show that the muscular strength of the females in this class of Old Americans (the females were either clerical or more or less at leisure) does not compare favorably with that of the males, being but slightly more than half that of the latter in pressure, and even less than half in traction (muscles of the arms and shoulders). The left hand compares less favorably with the corresponding hand in the males than the right, and the comparison is even considerably worse in that direction.

Regrettably, data on females of other nationalities or occupational groups are not available; but judging from the relative proportions in the two sexes of the stature, hand, chest, etc., the rather poor muscular showing of the Old American females does not seem to be an entirely sound one. Yet as will be seen from table 317 (by Quetelet) the proportion in hand strength between the two sexes is much the same in the Old Americans as it was in the Belgians that Quetelet examined; and very similar data were obtained on another series of subjects reported by Pagliani,[19] though relating to another muscular test. Nevertheless it was very perceptible during the examinations that women who were accustomed to physical exercise or who were doing their housework, showed decidedly better results.

Strength and age

That muscular strength in general diminishes as age advances is well known empirically as well as that there are various exceptions to the rule; but exact data in this respect are hard to find. The most comprehensive records are once more those of Quetelet[20] which in abstract give the values shown in table 317.

These records show quite conclusively that there is a direct correlation between muscular strength and age not only during development but also during later years. In the Belgian series, the maximum in the males is not reached until about the thirtieth year and a gradual decline begins soon afterwards. In the females, data from thirty to forty years are missing, but the indications are that the strength behaves similarly. The relation of the strength in the left hand to that of the right shows interesting variations.

The records of the Old Americans given in table 318 differ in a number of respects from those of the Belgians.

In Quetelet's Belgian series a gradual decline in strength began in both sexes from the thirtieth year; in the Americans a similar condition is manifest in the women, but in the men the maximum strength is not reached and surpassed until about the middle of the fourth decennium. In the Belgians, the decline of strength after it has set in was in both sexes more marked and reached, especially in the males, lower levels than in the

---

[19] Untersuchungen zur Naturlehre des Menschen und der Thiere. 1881, XII, 91.

[20] Anthropométrie, 364; La Physique sociale, II, 115. Also in Vierordt (H.)—Anatomische Daten und Tabellen, 1893, 292. Measured with Regnier's dynamometer. The means of Quetelet's first series only are given as more complete and evidently more reliable.

TABLE 317

Muscular force in Belgians

AGE	MALES				FEMALES				FEMALES vs. MALES† (MALES = 100)
	Hand pressure		Left vs. right hand* (R = 100)		Hand pressure		Left vs. right hand* (R = 100)		
	Right	Left			Right	Ieft			
years									
6	4.0	2.0	50.0						
8	7.7	4.6	60.0		3.6	2.8	77.8		52.0
10	9.8	8.4	85.7		5.6	4.8	85.7		57.1
12	13.9	11.7	84.2		10.1	7.0	69.3		62.9
15	27.8	22.6	81.3		15.0	14.1	94.0		57.7
20	39.3	37.2	94.6		22.0	19.4	88.2		54.1
25	44.1	40.0	90.7		24.5	21.6	88.2		54.8
30	44.7	41.3	92.4						
35	43.0	39.8	92.6						
40	41.2	38.3	93.0						
50	36.4	33.0	90.7		23.2	20.0	86.2		62.3
60	30.5	26.0	85.2						

* Calculated from Quetelet's data.

† Calculated from Quetelet's data.   Means of the two hands $\frac{(R+L)}{2}$ compared.

TABLE 318

Old Americans: Muscular strength and age

Laboratory series

	MALES					FEMALES			
	24–29 years	30–39 years	40–49 years	50–59 years	Above 59 years	22–29 years	30–39 years	40–49 years	50–59 years
Pressure:	(86)	(61)	(45)	(33)	(11)	(70)	(68)	(32)	(26)
Right hand....................	42.3	43.2	40.9	40.3	39.3	25.2	24.0	23.0	18.3
Left hand.....................	37.2	37.0	35.7	34.0	31.8	21.1	20.0	19.4	15.1
Traction:.....................	(84)	(61)	(45)	(32)	(10)	(69)	(61)	(30)	(26)
	23.5	22.7	20.9	21.6	20.7	12.1	10.2	10.6	9.3
Pressure of left vs. right hand (R = 100) ...	87.9	85.6	87.3	84.4	80.9	83.7	83.3	84.3	82.5

Old Americans. Finally the relation between the strength of the left and the right hand is more favorable in the Belgians of the Quetelet series, due probably to a class and hence functional difference between that series and the Old Americans.

An interesting difference is found in both sexes in the behavior with age of pressure and traction. The traction strength reaches its maximum in both sexes about a decade later than does pressure and while pressure has already begun its decline which progresses steadily towards the end of life.

Strength and stature

A further study of our data shows that muscular strength is not only affected by age, but that it stands also in a marked correlation with stature. On the average, the taller the stature within a fairly homogeneous group functionally such as the Old Americans, the greater the muscular strength. The rise in mean pressure averages in the males 10.4 per cent for each 10 per cent increase in body height, in the females 9.75 per cent; and it is even greater, especially in the females, in traction. The short males and the short females appear to a disadvantage. (See table 319.)

Further light on the subject will be obtained by comparing the mean pressure (of the two hands) with the mean stature of the several stature subdivisions. The resulting ratio or index rises very appreciably with each stature group, which proves that as stature rises the strength increases not merely absolutely but also relatively. On the average therefore, the taller the individual the better endowed he or she is with muscular strength. The tall on the whole are also the strong, the short on the whole the weak.

Comparative data

The same tests as on the Old Americans have also been taken on the immigrants, with some odd but very interesting results.

In the first place it was observed that among the immigrants who were in general of the hand working classes (laborers and artisans) the difference in pressure between the two hands, outside of the left-handed, was considerably less than it was among the Laboratory (mostly clerical-professional) class of the Old Americans. In numerous instances, especially among such people as the Poles and Russian Jews, the two hands were very nearly of equal strength and at times, though the subject was admittedly right-handed, the left hand showed a slight excess of strength over the right.

The results of the observations on the immigrants are given in table 321. The mean pressure strength of the Old Americans when compared with these newcomers is seen to be rather high notwithstanding the fact that on the average they have a somewhat smaller (narrower) and less muscular hand than most of the immigrants. The only group that slightly

TABLE 319

Old Americans: Strength vs. stature

Laboratory series

	MALES				FEMALES			
	150.01–160.0	160.01–170.0	170.01–180.0	180.01–190.0	145.0–150.0	150.01–160.0	160.01–170.0	170.01–180.0
Pressure:	(2)	(58)	(141)	(36)	(3)	(65)	(112)	(18)
Right hand........................	31.5	37.9	42.3	46.9	17.7	22.4	23.6	27.3
Left hand........................	25.0	32.4	36.7	40.7	15.3	18.3	20.0	22.7
Traction.............................. ⎰⎱	(2) 17.5	(56) 19.3	(138) 22.4	(36) 27.3	(3) 9.5	(63) 9.8	(106) 11.05	(16) 14.1
Left *vs.* right hand (R = 100).............	79.4	85.4	86.7	86.7	86.8	81.7	84.7	83.1
Increase in mean pressure (*per cent*)........		11.0	9.8				6.7	12.8
Increase in traction......................		13.8	18.0				14.0	21.6

TABLE 320

Old Americans: Mean hand pressure-stature index

	MALES				FEMALES			
	150.1–160.0	160.1–170.0	170.1–180.0	180.1–190.0	145.0–150.0	150.1–160.0	160.1–170.0	170.1–180.0
Index.....	18.1	21.0	22.5	23.9	11.2	13.0	13.3	14.5

exceeds the Americans in this respect is the Irish, the poorest showing being that of the Rumanians, Armenians and Russian Jews. The favorable showing of the Americans is however limited to the right hand—the left hand is both absolutely and relatively slightly below that of most of the other groups and is essentially connected with their tall stature. Taking subjects of approximately the same stature, most of the immi-

TABLE 321

Muscular strength: Old Americans and immigrants

Arranged in order of mean hand pressure $\dfrac{(R+L)}{2}$

	OLD AMERICANS (LABOR SERIES)	IRISH*	CROATIANS	RUSSIANS	POLES	ENGLISH	NORTH ITALIANS	GREEKS	HUNGARIANS	SOUTH ITALIANS	RUMANIANS	ARMENIANS	RUSSIAN JEWS
Stature...............	174.44	171.6	171.8	169.8	170.4	170.2	169.6	168.3	166.5	163.4	168.7	167.4	164.6
Mean pressure.......	38.95	39.35	38.0	37.95	37.75	37.40	36.95	36.80	36.60	36.0	35.15	35.10	34.50
Pressure:													
Right hand........	41.8	39.9	38.6	38.8	38.1	38.0	37.8	37.3	37.3	36.7	35.6	36.4	34.7
Left hand.........	36.1	38.8	37.4	37.1	37.4	36.8	36.1	36.3	35.9	35.3	34.7	33.8	34.3
Traction..........	22.3	25.8	25.3	25.8	25.9	25.8	25.6	25.3	25.1	24.2	24.0	21.9	23.2
Mean pressure-Stature index†	22.3	22.9	22.1	22.35	22.3	22.0	21.8	21.9	22.0	22.0	20.8	21.0	20.96
Traction *vs.* stature.	12.8	15.0	14.7	15.2	15.2	15.2	15.1	15.0	15.1	14.8	14.2	13.1	14.1
Left *vs.* right hand...	86.4	97.2	96.9	95.6	98.2	96.8	95.5	97.3	96.2	96.2	97.5	92.9	98.8

* The frequency of cases where the strength in the left hand was nearly equal, equal or even greater than that of the right is in all these groups, especially the Poles, greater than in the Old Americans.

† Mean pressure $\dfrac{(R+L)}{2} \times 100$

Stature

grants are, even in the right hand slightly stronger than most of the Old Americans. The cause of this is undoubtedly occupational.

In connection with the pressure tests it has been repeatedly observed by the writer that the hard and broad hand of the workingman will not give a very high pressure record. The highest records are made by large, sinewy or muscular but pliable hands, especially when backed by an above-average nervous strength.

TABLE 322

Old Americans: Strength test in left-handed

MALES			FEMALES		
Pressure		Traction	Pressure		Traction
Right hand	Left hand		Right hand	Left hand	
28.5	34.5	20.0	17.0	17.0	8.5
30.5	30.0	20.0	18.0	19.0	
33.0	37.0	20.0	20.0	19.0	8.0
33.5	34.5	24.0	20.0	21.0	14.5
36 0	36.0	16.0	20.0	24.0	11.5
37.0	40.0	22.5	23.0	22 0	7 0
38.5	38.5	23.0	23 0	22.0	11.0
41.0	43.0	23.0	23.0	26.0	9.0
42.0	45.0	20.0	23.5	24.0	15.0
43.5	43.5	28.0	24.0	24.5	12.0
43.5	46.5	27.0	25.0	24.5	18 0
45.0	48.0	25.0			
46.0	47.0	23.0			
(Aver)..38.3	40.3	22.4	21.5	22.1	11.4

Contrasted with the good showing of the Old Americans' hand in pressure is that of traction which calls upon the strength of the muscles of the arm, shoulders and chest. In this respect the Old Americans, both absolutely and relatively to stature, are very perceptibly weaker than any of the immigrants, being approached only by the Armenians. This result in people who do on the average but little muscular work, might have been expected, but in view of the good hand pressure, particularly in the right hand, it could hardly have been anticipated that it would be so pronounced.

The left-handed

Left-handedness is known to occur among whites in from 2 to 3 per cent of cases. Among the 247 Old American males (Laboratory series) the condition was acknowledged by the subject to exist in 13 cases or 5.3 per cent; among the 210 females in 11 or 5.2 per cent of cases; but some of these individuals used the right hand nearly (though not quite) as much as the left. The matter is difficult to gage. There are subjectively different grades of left- as well as right-handedness, not a few of which are near the border line; and objectively, *i.e.*, by tests of muscular strength, matters are even more uncertain, particularly among the laboring classes where the strength in the left hand frequently approaches or even equals that in the right without left-handedness being present. There are actually cases of left-handed in which the right hand is the stronger and *vice versa*. The detailed strength tests in our left-handed are shown in table 322.

SUMMARY

The tests comprised are hand pressure and bi-manual traction with Collin's dynamometer.

The averages obtained are: Pressure: Males, right hand 41.8; left hand, 36.1 kgm.; females, right hand, 23.2; left hand 19.4 kgm. Traction: Males, 22.3; females, 10.5.

The individual variation is large in both sexes. Dispersion is irregular in the males, less so in the females.

Influence of sex. The females compare unfavorably with the males. They show but slightly above one-half of the strength of the males in pressure, less than one-half in traction.

Influence of age. The maximum strength in Old American males is reached during the fourth, in the females during the third decade of age. In traction the maximum of both sexes is reached somewhat later. Pressure begins to decline after 50 in the males, after 40 in the females, with traction following some years later.

Influence of stature. As stature rises both pressure and traction strength increase, and that not only absolutely but also relatively to the height of the body.

In general, the taller the individual the better endowed he or she is with muscular strength and *vice versa*.

Comparative. In absolute measurements the Old Americans compare favorably with various groups of European immigrants in right hand pressure, somewhat less favorably in left hand pressure, and are perceptibly weaker in traction.

Relatively to stature most of the immigrants show slight to moderate advantage in muscular power.

Left-handedness. Acknowledged in 5.3 per cent of the males; in 5.2 per cent of the females.

There are different grades of left-handedness as well as right-handedness and dynamometric tests do not differentiate these conditions clearly, except where one or the other condition is well marked.

CHAPTER VI

ABSTRACTS

I. NORTH AND SOUTH

In the chapter on Pigmentation it has been shown that while some differences in those respects between the northern and southern contingents of the Old Americans exist, on the whole they are much less than the general notions on the subject would have led us to anticipate; and so far as measurements are concerned the case, it will be seen from the next abstract, is quite similar.

Taking account of the differences in age of our two main groups of males, one of which (Laboratory) includes a large majority of people from the northern and the other (southern "Engineers") a large majority of those from southern states, it will be observed that the essential measurements are identical or nearly so. The mean stature is practically the same, the size of the head identical. In form the head of the southerners is a trace narrower and a trace higher.

The only difference of account is in the height of the face which is greater in the southerners, but this, it has been pointed out, is doubtless a difference of an occupational nature.

An interesting feature is that the nose in the southerners, who are also derived from parents and grandparents who lived in the south, is not broader than that of the northerners. The fact is that many parts of the southern states, especially at higher elevation, differ but little from the more northern states in the temperature of summer and that both heat and cold are mitigated artificially, so that actually the mean degree of heat to which the more southern and the more northern Old American families have been subjected in the course of their existence is probably not much different. It must however also be borne in mind that we are not comparing the people of the most northern with those of the most southern parts of the country, but in the main those who proceed from the more central and southern regions of the north with those of the more northern states of the south.

On the whole it may be said that while there are minor differences between the older American stock of the north and the south, in all essentials the two are exceedingly similar.

387

Southern vs. other Old Americans

	LABORATORY (ALL STATES BUT MOSTLY EAST AND NORTH-EAST	SOUTHERN STATES (SOUTH OF MARY-LAND AND DISTRICT OF COLUMBIA)
Mean age (years)...............................	42.5	24.5
Stature...	174.4	174.1
Weight...	151.2	148.0
Height sitting..................................	92.3	91.3
Height sitting *vs.* stature......................	52.9	52.2
Head:		
Length......................................	19.8	19.8
Breadth.....................................	15.5	15.4
Height......................................	13.9	14.0
Cephalic module................................	16.40	16.40
Cephalic module *vs.* stature....................	94.0	94.2
Cephalic index.................................	78.3	77.8
Face:		
Height to nasion............................	11.9	12.3
Height to crinion	18.45	18.9
Breadth diameter bizygomotic maximum	13.9	13.9
Facial module, physiognomic.....................	16.15	16.40
Facial module, morphologic......................	12.94	13.10
Facial Index:		
Physiognomic...............................	75.1	73.6
Morphologic................................	86.1	88.7
Nose:		
Length......................................	5.35	5.4
Breadth.....................................	3.6	3.5
Index.......................................	67.7	65.0

II. VARIABILITY

Every organic trait, even under most normal conditions and in the purest stock, shows a certain range of variation or oscillation about the mean. This range is known to be itself variable, larger or smaller under different conditions; and it differs under all conditions for most, if not all the traits. It is a phenomenon of the greatest biological importance for it is probably intimately connected with and underlies the higher grades of variation, namely those of groups, races, species and genera. In view of all this the variability of the Old Americans should be studied more comprehensively and attentively than was possible in the detailed reports on special characters.

But a thorough study of individual variability in all the traits examined in the Old Americans would be an undertaking calling for such a number of subjects and so much of higher mathematical work as to be almost beyond the possibilities of one worker. It is a task to be undertaken only by endowed centres of research with sufficient help and other facilities. All that is possible in the present instance is to abstract the data and present them as simply and intelligibly as the material may allow. Even then however, the result will be found to be of much interest. The following table gives, first, an abstract of the means, second, that of the sex values, and third, that of the range of variability in each sex of each character.

Old Americans: Relation of proportions in the two sexes

Laboratory series

Males 247, females 210

	AVERAGE IN MALES	AVERAGE IN FEMALES	AVERAGE FEMALE *vs.* MALE PROPORTION* (M. =100)	RANGE OF VARIATION† Male	Female
				per cent	*per cent*
Age (years).............................	42.5	41.0			
Stature cm.	174.44	161.84	*92.8*	*20.69*	*19.65*
Arm spread	179.2	161.2	*90.0*	*24.48*	*23.34*
Height of trunk (height sitting)............	92.33	87.27	*94.5*	*16.89*	*18.90*
Length of lower limbs below the ischia	82.11	74.57	*90.8*	*15.38*	*17.84*
Height sitting-stature index................	*52.94*	*53.92*	*101.9*	*13.68*	*14.59*
Weight‡ (nude) { pounds................	150.3	127.3	*84.7*	*72.2*	*94.3*
{ kgm....................	68.176	57.742			
Weight (nude): Grams per centimeter.......	390.7	356.8	*91.3*		
Head:					
Length.............................	19.78	18.62	*94.1*	*17.18*	*15.04*
Breadth.............................	15.48	14.80	*95.6*	*20.03*	*17.57*
Height.............................	13.93	13.33	*95.7*	*18.66*	*18.02*
Module (mean diameter)...................	16.39	15.57	*95.0*	*15.24*	*12.84*
Module *vs.* stature (mm. of mean head diameter per 1 meter of stature)...............	94.02	96.30	*102.4*	*19.95*	*20.05*
Cephalic index..........................	*78.28*	*79.40*	*101.4*	*25.77*	*17.27*
Mean height index.......................	*79.0*	*79.72*	*100.9*	*20.50*	*21.20*
Face:					
Height to nasion......................	11.93	11.09	*93.0*	*25.16*	*21.64*
Height to crinion......................	18.45	17.53	*95.0*	*24.93*	*22.81*
Height to forehead....................	6.58	6.45	*98.0*	*48.63*	*40.31*
Diameter bizygomotic maximum........	13.86	12.99	*93.7*	*18.04*	*20.02*
Facial module (mean diameter):					
Physiognomic........................	12.94	12.04	*93.0*	*19.25*	*17.76*
Morphologic.........................	16.15	15.26	*94.5*	*17.83*	*17.50*
Facial index:					
Physiognomic........................	*75.10*	*74.08*	*98.6*	*24.10*	*25.51*
Morphologic.........................	*86.08*	*85.39*	*99.2*	*29.28*	*29.39*

Old Americans: Relation of proportions in the two sexes—Continued

	AVERAGE IN MALES	AVERAGE IN FEMALES	AVERAGE FEMALE vs. MALE PROPOR-TION* (M. = 100)	RANGE OF VARIA-TION†	
				Male	Female
				per cent	*per cent*
Diameter frontal minimum..................	10.59	10.12	*95.6*	*24.55*	*21.74*
Diameter bigonial.........................	10.63	9.84	*92.6*	*33.87*	*28.46*
Gonio-frontal index........................	*99.87*	*102.9*	*103.0*	*34.34*	*24.96*
Nose:					
Length...............................	5.35	4.94	*92.5*	*37.38*	*38.38*
Breadth..............................	3.61	3.25	*90.0*	*36.01*	*30.77*
Index................................	*67.45*	*65.98*	*97.8*	*55.72*	*36.81*
Mouth: Width..	5.37	4.95	*92.2*	*39.11*	*40.40*
Left ear:					
Length...............................	6.69	6.10	*91.2*	*58.30*	*30.45*
Breadth..............................	3.79	3.47	*91.6*	*40.90*	*28.83*
Index................................	*56.70*	*56.85*	*100.3*	*71.96*	*29.78*
Chest:					
Breadth..............................	29.76	26.62	*89.4*	*46.37*	*47.35*
Depth................................	21.70	20.03	*92.3*	*64.52*	*57.41*
Module (mean diameter)...............	25.73	23.32	*90.6*	48.25	46.78
Chest module *vs.* stature (= mm. per deci-meter of stature)	*14.75*	*14.41*	*97.7*		
Chest index...............................	*72.93*	*75.30*	*103.3*	44.95	44.74
Left hand:					
Length...............................	19.28	17.34	*90.0*	*26.45*	*26.51*
Breadth..............................	9.18	7.87	*85.7*	*35.95*	*21.60*
Index................................	*47.64*	*45.39*	*95.3*	*24.14*	*20.94*
Left Foot:					
Length...............................	26.12	23.32	*89.3*	*26.80*	*24.86*
Breadth..............................	9.49	8.35	*88.1*	*30.56*	*31.10*
Index................................	*36.33*	*35.84*	*98.6*	*28.63*	*25.69*
Left leg: Circumference....................	36.1	35.5	*98.3*	*42.65*	*34.37*
Physiological:					
Pulse................................	70.6	75.5	*106.9*	*45.30*	*60.94*
Respiration...........................	17.1	18.2	*106.3*	*75.80*	*65.93*
Temperature..........................	98.57	98.8	*100.3*	*28.41*	*26.31*
Strength:					
Pressure { Right hand (kgm.)...........	41.8	23.3	*55.5*	*88.52*	*116.4*
Left hand (kgm.).............	36.1	19.4	*53.7*	*90.03*	*128.9*
Traction.............................	22.3	10.5	*47.1*	*143.5*	*181.0*

* Calculations generally made from totals.

† $\left(\dfrac{\text{Range of Variation x 100}}{\text{Average}} \right)$

‡ About 4 pounds (1.814 kgm.) to be deducted for nude weight; subjects were weighed with shoes and indoor clothes on (less hat, coat and vest in men, less hat and coat in women).

Before commenting on the just given data it will facilitate matters if the sex relations as well as the ranges of variation in the two sexes are given in a consecutive arrangement:

Old Americans; Average female vs. male proportions

	FEMALES (MALES = 100)
Muscular strength: Traction	47.1
Pressure, left hand	53.7
Pressure, right hand	56.5
Weight	84.7
Hand breadth	85.7
Foot breadth	88.1
Foot length	89.3
Chest breadth	89.4
Hand length	90.0
Arm spread	90.0
Nose breadth	90.0
Chest, mean diameter	90.6
Lower limbs, length	90.8
Ear. length	91.2
Ear breadth	91.6
Weight, gram-cm. ratios	91.3
Mouth	92.2
Chest, depth	92.3
Nose, length	92.5
Face, diameter bigonial	92.6
Stature	*92.8*
Face:	
Height to nasion	93.0
Physiognomic module	93.0
Diameter bizygomotic maximum	93.7
Morphologic module	94.5
Head:	
Length	94.1
Module	95.0
Breadth	95.6
Diameter frontal minimum	95.6
Height	95.7
Trunk height	94.5
Hand index	95.3
Chest module *vs.* stature	97.7
Nasal index	97.8
Forehead, height	98.0
Leg, girth of	98.3
Foot index	98.6

Old Americans: Average female vs. male proportions—Continued

	FEMALES (MALES = 100)
Facial index, physiognomic	98.6
Facial index, morphologic	99.2
Ear index	100.3
Body temperature	100.3
Head, mean height index	100.9
Head, cephalic index	101.4
Height sitting-stature index	101.9
Head module-stature index	102.4
Gonio-frontal index	103.0
Chest index	103.3
Respiration	106.3
Pulse	106.9

The above data show plainly:

That the Old American female differs from the male mainly in all those dimensions and measurements which relate to muscular development and strength;

That relatively to stature she shows similar development as the male most plainly in the facial and external head dimensions;

That relatively to stature she shows better development in the height of the forehead and adiposity of the leg; and

That both absolutely and relatively to stature she exceeds the male in pulse, respiration and temperature.

As to ratios and indices, she shows lower weight-stature, hand, nose, foot and both facial indices; but she has a higher ear index, mean height index of head, cephalic index, height sitting-stature index, head module-stature index, and especially the gonio-frontal and chest indices.

The outstanding favorable feature is her good development of the head.

With her tall stature and good head development, if the Old American female were brought up with more attention to her muscular development, which is quite feasible, she would appear in a decidedly favorable anthropological light.

Range of variability

The preceding tables give also the ranges of variation of the various measurements and indices in the two sexes.

In order that these data may be perused with greater facility, the ranges are given herewith in the order of their magnitude:

Old Americans: Abstract of variability

MALES		FEMALES	
Least variable			
Height sitting-stature index	13.7	Mean head diameter	12.85
Mean head diameter	15.2	Height sitting-stature index	14.6
Length of lower limbs	15.4	Head length	15.0
Trunk length	16.9	Cephalic index	17.3
Head length	17.2	Facial module, morphologic	17.5
Facial module morphologic	17.8	Head breadth	17.6
Facial breadth (diameter bizygomotic maximum)	18.0	Facial module, physiognomic	17.75
		Length of lower limbs	17.8
Head height	18.7	Head height	18.0
Facial module, physiognomic	19.25	Trunk length	18.9
Cephalic module-stature index	19.95	*Stature*	*19.65*
Moderately variable			
Head breadth	20.0	Facial breadth, (diameter bizygomotic maximum)	20.0
Mean height index of head	20.5	Cephalic module-stature index	20.05
Stature	*20.7*	Hand index	20.9
Facial index, physiognomic	24.1	Head, mean height index	21.2
Hand index	24.1	Hand breadth	21.6
Arm spread	24.5	Facial height, lower (M-N)	21.6
Diameter frontal minimum	24.6	Diameter frontal minimum	21.7
Facial height, total (M-C)	24.9	Facial height, total (M-C)	22.8
Facial height, lower (M-N)	25.2	Arm spread	23.3
Cephalic index	25.8	Foot length	24.9
Hand length	26.4	Gonio-frontal index	25.0
Foot length	26.8	Facial index, physiognomic	25.5
Temperature	28.4	Foot index	25.7
Foot index	28.6	Temperature	26.3
Facial index, morphologic	29.3	Hand length	26.5
		Diameter bigonial	28.5
		Ear breadth	28.8
		Facial index, morphologic	29.4
		Ear index	29.8
Variable in a higher degree			
Foot breadth	30.6	Ear length	30.5
Diameter bigonial	33.9	Nose breadth	30.8
Gonio-frontal index	34.3	Foot breadth	31.1
Hand breadth	35.9	Leg, girth	34.4
Nose breadth	36.0	Nasal index	36.8
Nose length	37.4	Nasal length	38.4

Variable in a higher degree—*Continued*

Mouth width....................	39.1	Forehead, height.................	40.3
Ear breadth.....................	40.9	Mouth, width...................	40.4
Leg, girth......................	42.6	Chest index....................	44.7
Chest index.....................	44.9	Chest module..................	46.8
Pulse...........................	45.3	Chest breadth.................	47.4
Chest breadth...................	46.4		
Chest module...................	48.2		
Forehead, height................	48.6		

Most variable

Nasal index.....................	55.7	Chest, depth..................	57.4
Ear length......................	58.3	Pulse........................	60.9
Chest, depth....................	64.5	Respiration...................	65.9
Ear index......................	72.0	Weight*......................	94.3
Weight*........................	72.2	Strength: pressure { right hand..... 116.0 / left hand...... 128.9	
Respiration.....................	75.8		
Strength:		Traction......................	181.0
Pressure { right hand........... 88.5 / left hand............ 90.0			
Traction....................	143.5		

* Normal boundaries less definite than with other measurements.

Notes on variation

An analysis of the preceding data shows a number of highly suggestive conditions.

The variability of the different measurements and ratios is very uneven. About the most stable character is the mean diameter of the head or cephalic module, particularly in the females. Another character that shows small variation is the trunk-stature relation (height sitting-stature index). The length of the lower limbs varies less than the length of the trunk and both are amongst the less variable features. Head length varies slightly less than head breadth or head height, the variability of the latter two being about similar.

A remarkable showing is the relatively moderate variability of the cephalic index in the females; in the males this variability is very perceptibly greater.

The breadth of the hands and feet, the dimensions of the nose, mouth and ear, the forehead and the dimensions of the chest vary considerably.

The length of the nose, length of the ear and depth of the chest vary more than the breadth of these parts, while in the hands (males) and feet (both sexes) the breadth varies more than the length.

The depth of the chest, the weight of the body, the rate of respiration, the nasal and ear index (males) and above all the muscular strength, especially in the females, vary greatly. The variability in traction is enormous.

There are further important sex differences.

The number of measurements and characters recorded is 48. Of these the males show a greater variability in 28; the variability is very nearly equal in the two sexes in 11; and it is greater in the females in 9, three of which relate to the tests of strength. In a large majority of dimensions the male Old Americans, therefore, are the more variable.

More in detail it will be noted that the males vary more than the females especially in:

> Breadth of head
> Cephalic index
> Height of forehead
> Gonio-frontal index
> Nasal breadth and especially index
> Ear dimensions and especially index
> Hand breadth

The variability is about equal in the two sexes in:

> Head height
> Height sitting-stature index
> Cephalic module-stature index
> Mean head height index
> Morphologic facial index
> Nasal length
> Width of mouth
> Breadth of chest
> Chest index
> Hand length
> Foot breadth

The females vary more than the males in:

> Height of trunk
> Length of lower limbs
> Weight
> Breadth of face
> Physiognomic facial index
> Muscular strength, especially traction

Much of this constitutes an incentive to further research and will be of value in future comparisons.

Variability according to group.

It remains to show the variability in the three regional groups of the Old American males. There are, it will be seen, important differences.

Old Americans, males; Percental values of variation in the three groups

$$\left(\frac{\text{Range of variation} \times 100}{\text{Average}} \right)$$

	LABORATORY SERIES (247)	"ENGINEERS" (SOUTHERN AND MIXED STATES) (347)	TENNESSEE HIGHLANDERS (133)
Mean age (years)..............................	42.5	23.6	25.1
Stature...	20.7	21.3	15.6
Weight...	74.4	81.8	63.8
Height of trunk (height sitting)...................	16.9	28.8	15.4
Height of trunk *vs.* stature......................	13.7	25.8	9.3
Head:			
Length.....................................	17.2	17.7	15.9
Breadth....................................	20.0	18.8	16.6
Height.....................................	18.7	23.6	16.2
Cephalic module (mean diameter).................	15.24	15.27	11.8
Module-stature index...........................	20.0	24.4	19.1
Cephalic index................................	25.8	22.9	20.1
Mean height index.............................	14.7	20.5	15.4
Face:			
Height to nasion............................	25.2	30.7	24.1
Height to crinion...........................	24.9	25.4	21.6
Breadth (diameter bizygomatic maximum)....	18.0	22.1	16.85
Facial module (mean diameter):			
Physiognomic..............................	19.25	18.3	17.5
Morphologic...............................	17.9	19.1	18.0
Facial index:			
Physiognomic..............................	24.1	30.1	27.2
Morphologic...............................	29.3	28.3	27.1
Nose:			
Length......	37.4	38.9	24.9
Breadth....................................	36.0	31.7	34.5
Index......................................	55.7	70.7	42.0

On looking over the preceding figures it will be readily seen that two of the groups, the Laboratory and southern "Engineers," while differing somewhat, are nevertheless closely alike and that both differ substantially from the Tennessee highlanders.

Taking the the two main groups, the Laboratory and "Engineers," it is seen that the latter show somewhat greater variability. Among the 22 items compared the "Engineers" show slightly to moderately greater variability in 12, are about equal in 4 and vary slightly to moderately less than the Laboratory group in 5 items. The reason for these conditions lies probably in the main in the greater occupational heterogeneity of the "Engineers."

The most interesting condition is however shown by the highlanders. They vary slightly to moderately less than the men of the Laboratory group in every item but two, and they also vary somewhat to markedly less than the southern "Engineers" in every item but one. This is clear evidence of their greater physical homogeneity, which is due in all probability partly to their lesser admixture with other racial elements and partly to prolonged inbreeding.

III. OLD AMERICANS: INFLUENCE OF AGE

OBSERVATION MEASUREMENT	MALES	FEMALES
Pigmentation:		
Hair................	Mostly more or less perceptible gradual darkening, up to time greyness sets in	Same
Eyes................	In general very gradual dulling, fading and lightening	Same
Stature..................	Facts not sufficiently clear owing to rising stature (due to other factors) in youngest generation	Same
Weight...................	Increase in general with age to middle life, then decrease	Same
Length of arms............	Young adults show longer arms than the old; but other factors than age probably involved	Same, but difference less marked
Height of trunk, neck and head (height sitting)....	Relatively higher in the old than in the young adults	Same
Length of lower limbs......	Relatively somewhat longer in the young than in the old; cause probably functional	Same
Head:		
Length................	Slight increase absolute as well as relative (to stature) in length of head through larger part of adult period	Same
Breadth.............	Increases during adult period to fifth or sixth decade of life; but increase slighter and less regular than in length	Same

OBSERVATION MEASUREMENT	MALES	FEMALES
Height..............	No appreciable age effect	Slight but fairly regular absolute and relative growth to sixth decade
Cephalic index...........	Influence of age negligible	Same
Mean height index........	But little influenced by age during adult period	Same
Size of head..............	Slight progressive increase absolutely as well as relatively to stature to sixth decade	Same
Face: Height; breadth.....	Breadth increases with age; height augments very moderately to middle life	Slight growth with age in both facial dimensions to middle life
Forehead:		
Height..............	Increases slightly with age during adult life in conformity with rest of head	Same
Breadth (lower)	Slight increase during adult life to middle age.	Same
Nose...................	Both length and breadth increase during adult life, increase in length somewhat exceeds that in breadth; nasal index rises moderately as age advances	Same
Subnasal portion..........	Age shows no influence so long as teeth are not worn or lost	Same
Mouth...................	Width increases with age	Same
Lower facial breadth.......	No appreciable effect	Slight increase with age
Ears....................	Growth with age in both dimensions, though more in length; ear index decreases with age	Same
Chest...................	Grows perceptibly during adult life both in breadth and depth; but more in depth; chest index increases with age until senility begins	Same, but less difference than in males
Hands...................	Keep on growing slowly during adult life, growth is symmetrical; slight if any change in hand index	Same
Feet....................	Continue to grow slowly during adult life. Growth harmonious; no appreciable change in index	Same
Leg.....................	Augments till after thirty	Same, till after forty
	Mostly diminishes gradually after senility sets in	Same

OBSERVATION MEASUREMENT	MALES	FEMALES
Physiological observations:		
Pulse.................	Between 24 and 60 influence of age small; during sixth decade traces of slight slowing, followed by increased frequency as senility sets in	Same
Respiration..........	Between 24 and 60 age has no regular effect	Same
Temperature.........	Very little effect between 24 and 60	Progressive slight diminutions as age advances
Muscular strength....	Maximum in hand pressure reached during fourth decade; in traction somewhat later	Maximum pressure reached during third decade; in traction somewhat later
	Pressure begins to decline after 50; traction some years later	Same, after forty; traction some years later

Résumé

The following is the effect of ages between 24 and 60:

GRADUAL AUGMENTATION	LITTLE IF ANY EFFECT OR NOT SUFFICIENTLY CLEAR	GRADUAL DECREASE
Weight	Stature	Ear index
Head length and breadth	Length of arms	
Size of head as a whole	Length of trunk and lower limbs	
Height and breadth of face	Height of head	
Height of forehead	Cephalic index	
Length and breadth of nose	Mean height index of head	
Nasal index	Subnasal height of face	
Width of mouth	Lower facial breadth	
Length and breadth of ears	Hand index	
Depth and breadth of chest	Foot index	
Chest index	Pulse	
Length and breadth of hands	Respiration	
Length and breadth of feet	Temperatures	
Girth of leg		
Muscular strength		

The following are the effects of advancing senility:

GRADUAL AUGMENTATION	LITTLE IF ANY EFFECT OR NOT SUFFICIENTLY CLEAR	GRADUAL DECREASE
Length (particularly dorsal) and breadth of nose		Stature
Width of mouth		Weight
Length and (slightly) breadth of ears		Facial height
Frequency of pulse		Chest
		Girth of leg
		Temperature
		Strength

Remarks

From all the preceding it is evident that age is a factor of very real importance in anthropology, and that in the future it should invariably receive close attention.

The surprising fact is the number of dimensions, including, at least in such a class of subjects as the Laboratory series of the Old Americans, all the head diameters, that keep on growing appreciably up and into the fourth or fifth decade of life. This justifies the conclusion that a full development of the individual is not accomplished in such a category of persons as here dealt with, until about middle life. Then ensues a period of stability to be followed sooner or later, according to the part, by a gradual involution or senility.

Senility in general is marked by a loss of substance, but there is a marked exception—the integumental structures of the face and head (the nose, mouth, ears, also face hairiness) mostly keep on increasing slowly up to very old age.

IV. OLD AMERICANS: INFLUENCE OF STATURE

OBSERVATION MEASUREMENT	MALES	FEMALES
Pigmentation...........	Stature, as such, has no effect, but light eyes and hair due to racial causes are more often met with in the tall, dark eyes in the medium or shorter	Same
Weight.................	Increases materially with stature	Same
Length of arms..........	Arms are still longer in the short than in the tall	Same
Height of the trunk, neck and head (height sitting)	Relatively long in those of short stature, and *vice versa*	Same
Length of lower limbs.......	Long in the tall, short in the short	Same
Head		
Length.............	Direct positive correlation; steady increase as stature rises	Same
Breadth.............	A similar but decidedly lesser increase than with head length	Same
Height..............	Increases in general as stature rises	Same
Cephalic index...........	In general tall stature goes with a lower cephalic index, but the differences are not large	Same
Mean height index.........	The index grows as stature advances	Same
Size of head..............	The higher the stature the larger in general is the head and vice versa; the progression however proceeds at a diminishing rate as stature rises, so that the ratio of the size of head to stature decreases plainly as stature advances	Same

400

OBSERVATION MEASUREMENT	MALES	FEMALES
Face: Height; breadth.....	Both facial height and breadth augment with rising stature	Same, less so than in the males
	Morphologic index is higher, physiognomic lower, in tallest than in shortest individuals	Same
Forehead;		
Height.............	Increases with size of head, which augments with stature	Same
Breadth (lower)......	Increases with stature due to increase in size of head	Same
Nose..................	Affects both nasal dimensions and index, through its effects on size of head and face; but breadth increases only where there is substantial increase in breadth of face; nasal height increasse more than breadth: nasal index decreases with rise in stature	Same
Subnasal portion..........	Influence positive though probably indirect	Same
Mouth..................	Close though indirect correlation (through size of face)	Same
Lower facial breadth.......	Correlates naturally with size of face, which in turn correlates with size of head, which correlated with stature	Same
Ears..................	Direct effect on size of ears both in height and breadth; but increase lags behind that in stature; ear index diminishes slightly with rising stature, due to relatively slightly lesser increase in ear breadth than length	Same
Chest..................	Both dimensions correlate directly with, but increase at a lesser rate than, stature; rate of increase in the two diameters is much the same, the chest index being but little affected	Same
Hands..................	Direct and positive correlation with stature, particularly in hand length	Less marked than in males
	Hand index diminishes slightly as stature rises	Less marked than in the males
Feet..................	Influence direct and pronounced; affects both measurements alike	Same
Leg..................	Increases with rise in stature, though not proportionately	Same
Physiological observations		
Pulse..............	Rate tends to increase with stature	Same
Respiration.........	Diminishes slightly as stature rises	Same
Temperature........	Rises slightly with rise in stature	Same
Muscular strength	Both pressure and traction strength increase in general with rising stature, absolutely as well as relatively	Same

Résumé

The following is the effect of rise in stature:

AUGMENTATION	NO EFFECT	DECREASE
Weight	Chest index	Relative length of arms
Length of lower limbs	Foot index	Relative length of trunk
Length, breadth and height of head		Cephalic index
Mean height index of head		Nasal index
Height and breadth of forehead		Ear index
Height and breadth of face		Breadth and depth of chest
Length of nose		Hand index
Width of mouth		Frequency of respiration
Lower facial breadth		
Size of ears		
Size of nose		
Size of foot		
Girth of leg		
Frequency of pulse		
Temperature		
Muscular strength		

Remarks

Of all the factors which through direct or indirect correlation affect the bodily dimensions, stature is plainly the most important. It is of so much consequence that no anthropological work in which this factor has not received due attention can be of much value.

It is however evident that an increase in stature is more properly to be regarded as general increase in dimensions. In other words, stature alone is not a unit, being merely part of the greater unit of size, which embraces most if not all parts and organs.

Attention to the effects of stature is particularly indicated in the studies relating to the size of the head and its changes through educational or other factors.

The close correlation of the dimensions of the various parts of the body with stature does not mean, however, that these parts are not capable of individual and varied development outside of the influences of stature. That they are capable of such development is best shown by the further growth of many of them during adult life, after stature has become stabilized; and by the environmental and individual peculiarities in the development of different parts of the body regardless of stature.

OBSERVATION MEASUREMENT	MALES	FEMALES
Pigmentation............	No perceptible correlation, though light hair and eyes are for racial reasons (northern type) more commonly associated with dolichocephaly; dark eyes and hair occur in both head forms	Same
Stature..................	Moderately higher in dolichocephaly	Slightly higher in dolichocephaly
Weight..................	No influence discernible	Same
Length of arms..........	Nothing definite	Same
Height of trunk, neck and head (height sitting)....	No influence discernible	Same
Length of lower limbs......	No influence discernible	Same
Head:		
Length..............	The greater the dolichocephaly, the greater the length and *vice versa*, both absolutely and relatively to stature; head length-stature ratio, though somewhat irregular, shows a gradual decrease as the cephalic index grows higher	Same
Breadth.............	Proceeding from dolicho- to brachycephaly, head breadth increases even more than its length decreases; breadth-stature ratio tends towards an increase as the cephalic index increases	Same
Height..............	Shows progressive slight augmentation in progress from dolicho- to brachycephaly; head-stature ratio remains constant for all cephalic indices	Same
Mean height index........	Tends to be slightly higher in brachycephals, than in dolichocephals, outside of the influence of stature	Same
Size of head..............	Effects slight; in favor of brachycephaly	Same
Face; height; breadth.....	Marked but uneven influence affect'g breadth most, morphologic height least; proceeding from dolicho- to brachycephaly the morphologic index grows higher	Same
Nose...................	Slight and indirect, if any, effect on nose height; but little, if any, effect on breadth; no appreciable effect on nasal index	Same

403

OBSERVATION MEASUREMENT	MALES	FEMALES
Subnasal portion..........	Influence slight if any	Same
Mouth...................	No influence apparent	Same
Lower facial breadth.......	Influence indirect through breadth of face	Same
Ears....................	Effects slight	Same
	In dolichocephals, ears relatively slightly higher and broader	Ears slightly broader in dolichocephals
	Index trace higher in dolichocephals	Index appreciably higher in dolichocephals
Chest....................	No appreciable influence	Same
Hands...................	No material effect	Same
Feet....................	Tend slightly to excess of breadth in brachycephals; to excess of length in dolichocephals	Same
Leg.....................	No influence apparent	Same
Physiological observations		
Pulse................	Nothing definite	Same
Respiration..........	Nothing definite	Same
Temperature.........	Nothing definite	Same

Résumé

INCREASE WITH DOLICHOCEPHALY	INCREASE WITH BRACHYCEPHALY	NO APPRECIABLE EFFECT
Stature	Head breadth and height	Weight
Head length	Mean height index	Length of arms, trunk and lower limbs
Size and index of ears (slightly)	Breadth of face	Nose
Length of feet	Morphologic facial index	Nasal dimensions and index
	Lower facial breadth	Subnasal portion of face
	Breadth of feet	Mouth
	Foot index	Chest
		Girth of leg
		Pulse
		Respiration
		Temperature

Remarks

The conditions shown in the preceding abstract are very instructive and important.

They afford no proof that either dolichocephaly or brachycephaly is connected, except to a slight degree, with characteristic conditions in the rest of the body. This means that, excepting the head and a few dependent measurements, the rest of the body, whatever the head form, remains the same.

It appears therefore to be a valid conclusion that dolichocephaly and brachycephaly merely mean morphological variations in the head of the same body, group, stock or race of people. There is no evidence that the two types of head represent distinct old strains or races of man. For if they represented such different strains there would doubtless be also some differences in the rest of the body, and these differences would in some way manifest themselves in mixtures of the two strains, such as is apparently represented by the Old Americans.

If these indications are sustained by further studies the influence upon anthropology of the new light they show can hardly be estimated.

VI. OLD AMERICANS: COMPARATIVE

OBSERVATION MEASUREMENT	MALES	FEMALES
Pigmentation.............	Much like general average of Great Britain	Same
	Scarcity of pronounced blonds and brunets; large majority of intermediates	Somewhat more blondes and especially brunets: still majority intermediate
Stature..................	Tallest of all larger groups of whites	Same
Weight..................	About the same as Americans at large of same age and stature; close to that of Englishmen (Beddoe's series)	Slightly lighter for same age and stature than American women at large
	Relatively to stature about the same as Europeans in general	Slightly heavier than European groups available for comparison
Length of arms...........	Are relatively shorter (in the clerical, professional and well to do classes) than those of most other groups of whites available for comparison; cause probably functional (occupational)	Same
Height of trunk, neck and head (height sitting).....	No substantial difference from whites in general; stand closest to English and Scotch	Same
Length of lower limbs......	No substantial difference from whites in general; stand closest to English and Scotch	Same

OBSERVATION MEASUREMENT	MALES	FEMALES
Head, cephalic index......	Close to that of the present people of the British Isles	Same
Mean height index.........	Occupies about a medium position contrasted with that of other groups of whites	Same
Size of head...............	Shows superiority, both absolutely and relatively to stature over all groups of recent white immigrants available for comparison; the Tennessee Highlanders, however, stand, on a level with the immigrants	Same
Face, height; breadth......	Is smaller (Laboratory series) relatively to stature, particularly in breadth, than in Europeans of the artisan and laboring classes	Same
Forehead:		
Height...............	Little difference from other groups of whites	Same
Breadth (lower)......	No substantial difference from other whites	Same
Nose...................	Is absolutely rather high with moderate breadth as contrasted with other whites; relatively to stature, facial dimensions and age nasal height is near the medium, nasal breadth slightly submedium as compared to whites; as a result nasal index slightly below average of whites in general	Same
Mouth	Decidedly moderate in width as compared with other whites	Same
Lower facial breadth.......	In general more moderate than in ordinary whites of other groups	Same
Ears...................	Relatively to stature are very near the average of other whites	Same
Chest...................	About equal in breadth, not quite so deep as in the European immigrants available for comparison; index below that of any of the immigrant groups	Same
Hands...................	Are shorter and especially narrower (Laboratory series) than those of other whites, resulting in lower index: the cause in all probability functional	Same
Feet...................	Are shorter and especially narrower (Laboratory series) than those of other whites, resulting in lower index: the cause in all probability functional	Same

OBSERVATION MEASUREMENT	MALES	FEMALES
Leg....................	Is but moderately developed (Laboratory series) compared with immigrants; relatively to stature is less stout than in any group available for comparison; cause is probably functional (occupational).	Same
Physiological observations:		
Temperature.........	Nothing decisive, due to lack of equivalent data for comparison	Same
Muscular strength....	Right hand pressure (Laboratory series) compares favorably with European immigrants; left hand pressure less favorably and traction least Relatively to stature most of the immigrants show slight to moderate advantage in muscular power; causes are plainly occupational	Same, but available records on other groups of whites inadequate

Résumé

Compared with other larger groups of whites the Old Americans of the clerical, professional and leisure classes (Laboratory series) are characterized by:

> Intermediate pigmentation
> Tallest stature
> Relative shortness of arms
> Good size of the head
> Large range of cephalic index
> Relatively narrow face
> Rather long and narrow nose with lower nasal index
> Moderate width of mouth
> Moderate height of subnasal portion of face
> Moderate lower facial breadth
> Somewhat narrow hands and feet with lower hand and foot index

They differ little if at all from comparable whites in:

> Relative weight
> Relative height of trunk and lower limbs
> Height and breadth of forehead
> Dimensions of ears

They show at a disadvantage in:

> Muscular strength in left hand, arms and shoulders

In general they approach most closely, though differing more or less in many points, the people of Great Britain.

Taking the three groups of the Old Americans (Laboratory, southern "Engineers" and Tennessee highlanders) among themselves, they differ slightly to moderately in:

> Variability
> Pigmentation (slightly)
> Cephalic index (slightly)
> Mean height index of the head
> Size of head
> Size of face
> Facial indices; and
> Somewhat in the nasal proportions and index

The group that shows most differences are the Appalachian highlanders.

Most of the differences, however, are due to environmental and functional causes, and are not set racial characters.

Remarks

The Old Americans are seen to represent on the one hand a group of still considerable variability, but on the other hand a group that already comes closely to deserving the characterization of an anthropological unit. In other words, the "melting pot," while its work of unifying the many component elements is evidently not yet completely finished, has nevertheless advanced so much in that direction that the stock possesses already a moderately distinctive character.

The Old American stock, as it may now be called, stands in general nearer than any other branch of whites to the stock of Great Britain. But it is not, or no more, identical with the same; it is American. There is some justification therefore in speaking of the "American type" of white people. This is near the English, Irish and Scotch types, but is at least as different from any of these as these are different from each other.

From a purely morphological standpoint all the more important characteristics shown by this Old American stock are favorable, showing in some respects perceptible improvement and in none a degeneration. With rational guidance the improvement may well be extended.

Geographically the stock differs remarkably little. The north and south show much smaller regional differences than generally believed. The only section of the stock that does differ perceptibly and in some important points disadvantageously from the rest, is that of the isolated Appalachian highlanders. The reasons appear to be inbreeding and lack of cultural development, both of which can be remedied.

CHAPTER VII

The Future American Type

The observations reported in this volume show that the unmixed descendants of the older stock of Americans do present already an approach towards a physical type which may be called "American." With this type there still occur fairly numerous individuals of both sexes who through persistence or reversion show distinctly one or the other of the older types which have entered into the composition of the nationalistic groups that have built up the American. But in a good majority of the Old Americans these older types are more or less obscured and a new and somewhat differing type, an American type, is apparent.

The future of this type depends on conditions. If the Old American families could remain without further admixture for several more centuries the type would undoubtedly be further crystallized and fixed; but there is not much hope that this may be accomplished.

The Old Americans, or those whose ancestors for at least three generations on both sides have all been born American, are in a decided minority in the population at large. Except in a few limited localities they are surrounded and are being more and more permeated by newer elements which are partly of immigrant and partly of immigrant-native derivation. The close contact leads to more and more frequent intermarriage and as a result the old stock is gradually dissolving into the new, which process is further helped by the reduced fertility of the old stock in the cities. The prospects are, therefore, that in future generations the older type will gradually give place to a newer American type, which will be the result of a blend of the older population with the immigrants of the XIX and the earlier part of the XX centuries. Should immigration from now on remain as regulated and as restricted as it is at present the prospect of a further modification of the now forming type through these immigrants is restricted.

The interesting problem is, how may the immigration of the XIX and the earlier part of this century be expected to affect the older type; in other words, how will the newer type differ from the older.

In trying to solve this problem the student is confronted again with the lack of data as to exactly what in the anthropological or true racial sense the country did receive between 1820 and 1920. There are, however, from this period ample statistics as to the national affiliations of the new-comers.

From the Census and other data it is known that since 1820 the composition of the immigration tide to this country has been changing. The changes will be readily seen from table 323, though these have serious imperfections.

TABLE 323

	POPULATION 1790*	XIX CENTURY†	IMMIGRANTS	
			1820–1923‡	1899–1924§
English (and Welsh).................	83.5 ⎱ 90.2	15.8	⎱ 24.59	⎱ 9.08
Scotch..............................	6.7 ⎰			
Irish..............................	1.6	20.2	⎰	4.73
Canada and Newfoundland........		5.5	6.44	Not given
German............................	5.6	26.2	16.24	7.70
Austria-Hungary.................		5.4	12.25	2.88
Dutch..............................	2.0	Not given	0.67	1.20
Norway, Sweden and Denmark.....		7.5	6.47	5.59
French.............................	0.5	Not given	1.61	2.43
Italy..........................		5.45	13.14	22.36
Jews..............................	0.1	Not given	Not given	10.75
Russia and Poland (Slavs)........		4.8	10.89	19.93
All others..........................	0.1	9.0		

* Approximates from A Century of Population Growth in the United States. Publ. of U. S. Census, 4to, Wash., 1909, 116–117.

† Immigration and Census records.

‡ From a table in Appendix 1 of the Report of the Secretary of Labor for the year ending June 30, 1923 (printed opposite p.125 of the Secy's report), data on the Century of Migration are brought up to date. The total migration from September 30, 1820 to June 30, 1923 is reported to be 35,292,394. Hearings before Committee on Immigration and Naturalization, House of Repr., March 8, 1924, Serial 5-A, p. 1380. Wash., 1924.

§ U. S. Dept. of Labor: Ann. Rep. Commr. Gen. of Immigr., 1924, 114.

What these data show is that during the last 100 years this country has received proportionately to its earlier components many more Germans, Irish, Scandinavians, Italians, Slavs and Jews, with a considerably smaller percentage of the Scotch, Welsh and English and also less of the Dutch and French. Adding the new to the older blood, which, meanwhile, pure and admixed, has probably more than quintupled through excess of births over deaths, it may be said that the results will be a population with blood somewhat more German and Irish, with also a tinge more of Scandinavian, and especially Italian, Slav and Jewish. The great bulk of the population remains however, in origin or descent, British or more properly, Western European.

The problem, however, is more complex than this. It involves uneven distribution of the immigrants in different areas of the country, and uneven intermarriage. Moreover, it also involves the physical changes due to the American environment that, it has been seen, has had marked effects hitherto and that doubtless is still active.

There are numerous smaller or larger areas in the United States, particularly in the central and western states, which have been settled predominantly or even exclusively by groups of immigrants belonging not merely to one nationality, but in some instances even to a particular part of that nationality. There are many examples of this nature from the Pennsylvania "Dutch," to the Minnesota, etc., Scandinavians and Finns, and to the Southwestern Mexicans. In many of these localities these groups have for longer or shorter periods kept and still keep very largely to themselves, due to language and religious, occupational and perhaps educational conditions. Intermarriage with other parts of the population has in these instances been more or less slow. Such spots or areas will doubtless for still a long time to come perpetuate the type that the inhabitants have brought into this country, though according to indications there may be some environmental changes, more particularly in regard to stature.

In other areas, more especially in the agricultural states, even though intermarriage has become frequent and the immigrant stocks merge more rapidly into the surrounding population, nevertheless the newer comers from this or that part of Europe have occupied these regions in such numbers that the effect of their types will long remain perceptible in these localities. The country in general will probably retain, therefore, for some generations yet, a somewhat speckled character as to the type of its population.

From the remainder, doubtless a large majority, particularly in the cities, there is forming and will result a conglomerate which through ever-increasing intermixture may doubtless in the course of a few generations be expected to approach a newer blend—the American type of the not far distant future. This type, we may surmise from all the available data, will not be far from the Old American type of the present, and yet will be somewhat different, particularly in the physiognomy and in behavior.

This Neo-American type will in all probability be, in the average, tall, more sanguine, and perhaps less spare than the old. It will remain an intermediary white type in pigmentation, head form and other respects. It will show for a long time a wide range of individual variation in all respects. And it may well be expected to be a wholesome and effective type, for mixtures such as those from which it shall have resulted are, so far as scientific research shows, not harmful but rather beneficial, and conditions of life as well as environment in this country are still propitious.

The future of the Old American stock, therefore, need cause no concern. All available anthropological evidence points to the fact that just as the older population so the later comers to this country have been undergoing a gradual physical improvement, leading in stature and other respects in the direction of the type of the Old Americans. None of these newcomers are physically so different from the older stock that the admixture with them could be regarded as of possible biological danger. It is more likely that the newer admixture into the American stock, which is everywhere proceeding, will on the whole prove a wholesome stimulus and a leaven that will result in a substantial benefit for the future. The newer admixtures will retard the completion of a definite American physical type, but there is no indication that they constitute any real danger.

Just what the new Americans will be in world affairs will depend in the main upon the soundness of their organization and training and upon circumstances. So far as physique is concerned, the indications seem decidedly hopeful.

INDEX

413